THE CITY AS A WORK OF ART

The Quadrant from Piccadilly Circus, early twentieth century.

THE CITY AS A WORK OF ART
· LONDON · PARIS · VIENNA ·

Donald J. Olsen

Yale University Press
New Haven and London

Designed by Nancy Ovedovitz and set in ITC Garamond
type by The Composing Room of Michigan, Inc. Printed in
the United States of America by Halliday Lithograph,
West Hanover, Massachusetts.

Library of Congress Cataloging-in-Publication Data

Olsen, Donald J.
    The city as a work of art.

    Bibliography: p.
    Includes index.
    1. Architecture—England—London.   2. London
(England)—Buildings, structures, etc.   3. Architecture—
France—Paris.   4. Paris (France)—Buildings, structures,
etc.   5. Architecture—Austria—Vienna.   6. Vienna
(Austria)—Buildings, structures, etc.   I. Title.
NA970.047   1986   720′.94   85–24639
ISBN 0–300–02870–9 (cloth)
        0–300–04212–4 (pbk.)

12   11   10   9   8   7   6   5   4   3

For Helen Lowenthal

CONTENTS

PREFACE

The title of this book is a deliberate reference to the opening chapter of Jacob Burckhardt's *Civilization of the Renaissance in Italy,* "The State as a Work of Art." However much subsequent scholarship has disproved or modified Burckhardt's specific interpretations, the assumption underlying his book—that the categories of the art historian are applicable to other areas of history, that there exist connections between artistic styles and political forms, social institutions, economic practices, and ideological convictions—stands as a permanently valid insight. Just as Burckhardt examined the political behavior of the Italians of the fourteenth and fifteenth centuries for clues to the essential nature of their civilization, so we can regard cities as complex but legible documents that can tell us something about the values and aspirations of their rulers, designers, builders, owners, and inhabitants.[1]

The following pages will examine three cities—London, Paris, and Vienna—during their period of most significant growth, the century preceding 1914. It was then that each of them acquired its present shape and aspect. Each underwent a crucial upheaval that both irrevocably altered its physical structure and established a pattern for future change: in London, the cutting through of Regent Street by George IV; in Paris, the radical surgery performed by Louis Napoleon; in Vienna, the laying-out of the Ringstrasse. Each pursued a characteristic method for housing its expanding population: in London, the single-family house; in Paris and Vienna, the block of flats adapted to the special requirements of the two societies. Each responded to the aspirations of its dominant classes with institutions and built environments intended to serve their interests and reinforce their values: in London, the gentleman's club and villa suburbia; in Paris, the boulevard with all its attendant pleasures; in Vienna, the creation of a vast stage set on which its more fortunate citizens could pursue their daily lives in a manner that partook of the quality of grand opera.

The direction that each city chose to take was in large measure determined by its experience in earlier centuries. The decision of the Catholic Habsburgs in the sixteenth century to make Vienna their principal residence shortly after its citizens had embraced Protestantism, and while a Turkish army threatened from the east, left the nineteenth century with the legacy of a city that combined the functions and forms of a palace, a mission, and a fortress. In England the transfer of monastic property to secular hands in the sixteenth century, the weakening of the monarchy in the seventeenth, and the absence throughout of the threat of military invasion made London totally unlike the Austrian capital. The voluntary departure of Louis

XIV for Versailles and the forced return of Louis XVI to the Tuileries reflected special historical circumstances that made Paris different from the other two.

If the nineteenth-century city built on the achievements of its past, the twentieth-century metropolis has often regarded its heritage with scorn and contempt. The gleeful destruction that took place during the era of "urban renewal" and the creation of an architecture and an arrangement of urban space that repudiated earlier practice derived implicit support from the main body of urban historical scholarship. For while popular books celebrating the delights of cities like London, Paris, and Vienna abound, historians and respectable scholars in general have usually concentrated on the pathological aspects of the modern city. Poets, novelists, and crusading reformers have since classical antiquity contrasted urban vice with rural virtue. Only now have we amassed sufficient wealth and acquired an adequate technology to arrange our lives in a non-urban or post-urban fashion. If traditional cities are no more than diseased excrescences, one may reasonably argue that the sooner they are removed and replaced by something more responsive to our needs the better.

Yet the alarmed response to the decay and depopulation of many once flourishing metropolises would suggest that we are unwilling to contemplate a world in which cities no longer exist, no longer serve as magnets for the talented and the ambitious, no longer provide the concentration of ideas, objects of beauty, and opportunities of sociability that they have throughout recorded history. The pleasures that cities, especially capital cities, provide justify their existence irrespective of the wealth they may produce, the vice they may encourage, and the misery they often contain. Buoyed by such a conviction, we are today searching for ways to restore life to dying cities, and turn to those cities that retain an earlier vitality for guidance and inspiration.

However attractive the scale and appearance of the medieval city, the civilization that it represented, the economy that it embodied, and the technology that it employed are too far removed from our own for it to be an acceptable model for urban revitalization today. The nineteenth-century city constituted a response to demographic, economic, and technological challenges more nearly akin to those of our own age and, for all its well-documented inadequacies, possessed virtues that we might well emulate. The eagerness with which we preserve and restore whatever architectural fragments, often of dubious aesthetic merit, that have survived from the nineteenth and early twentieth centuries suggests that if we are to achieve an urban renaissance, it will be the nineteenth-century city that will be reborn.

I have, therefore, approached my three cities as objects to be cherished and understood rather than as evils to be exposed, as works of art rather than as instances of social pathology. My emphasis will lie on the nature and structure of each city as a whole, on the typical rather than the exceptional, on speculative building more than isolated monuments, on high mediocrity instead of exceptional masterpieces.

My tendency to dismiss the structural and aesthetic history of the three cities since the First World War with an occasional remark reflects a wish to suspend judgment, not an unawareness of its significance. We are today no more in a position to embark on a balanced appraisal of twentieth-century urban and architectural developments than were Europeans in the 1830s able to appreciate the achievements of the builders of eighteenth-century cities. Neither the starry-eyed propaganda of the town planners and disciples of the new architecture nor the appalled rejection with which we contemplate what those planners and disciples have done provides a satisfactory basis for dispassionate history. Only when the battle to save our cities has been won or lost can such a history be written.

We are, though, sufficiently removed from the passions and controversies of the nineteenth century to see it for what it was: neither an eighteenth century gone bad nor a twentieth century struggling to be born, but a period with its own concerns, its own values and aspirations, its own moral and intellectual assumptions, which need to be taken seriously. The visual arts of the century after Waterloo, long despised by aesthetes and critics—who made exceptions only for movements, like impressionism and the products of civil engineers, that either rejected or ignored dominant aesthetic standards—now seem less incongruous with the musical and literary masterpieces of those years. The consequences of an unprecedentedly rapid urbanization, long viewed as objects of shame, now seem as worthy of admiration and serious study as the scientific and economic achievements of the century.

The process of writing this book has been a voyage of discovery, carrying me outward from areas of earlier concern. From an initial curiosity about the workings of leasehold estates in London's West End that ultimately resulted in *Town Planning in London: The Eighteenth and Nineteenth Centuries,* I turned to an examination of the nature of the Metropolis as a whole in *The Growth of Victorian London.* An attempt to learn something about ground landlords and speculative builders in provincial towns was in part reflected in "House upon House: Estate Development in London and Sheffield," in *The Victorian City* (edited by H. J. Dyos and Michael Wolff). But until the late 1970s my explorations were bounded by the pleasant shores of England; the dangerous crossing of the Channel brought me into worlds hitherto only dimly apprehended, and made me even more dependent than before on the kindness and generosity of fellow scholars as I tried to make up for the comfortable insularity of earlier investigations.

Only those friends and scholars know the extent of my initial ignorance and can realize how much they contributed to diminishing it. Their advice and encouragement eased my fumbling attempts to know and understand Paris and Vienna, and thereby to see London itself in a new way. The patience with which they listened to half-formulated hypotheses, corrected factual misapprehensions, and suggested fruitful modes of inquiry can only be described as heroic. My colleagues in the Vassar history department, most notably the London historian Anthony Wohl, but also David Schalk, Hsi-Huey Liang, Rhoda Rappaport, Mildred Campbell, and Evalyn Clark, have given valuable support and advice. Barbara Miller Lane at Bryn Mawr suggested many ways in which architectural evidence can both enrich and transform our understanding of recent European history. The students in my experimental seminar "The City as a Work of Art" responded intelligently to interpretations I had formed and contributed insights of their own: I would mention in particular Margaret Partridge, Renée Scurlock, Ben Whitney, Brian S. Schick, Robert Friedman, Victoria Hecht, and Martha Lewis. Anne Wagner and Richard Pommer of the Department of Art, and Nicholas DeMarco, curator of slides and prints, were helpful with interpretations and gave practical assistance.

Dennis Costanzo, of the State University of New York, Plattsburgh, let me read his Ph.D. dissertation, "Cityscape and the Transformation of Paris during the Second Empire"; and Robert Fishman, of Rutgers University, lent me a copy of the paper on suburbia in London and Paris that he had read at the meeting of the American Historical Association in San Francisco in 1983. I also wish to thank David Van Zanten, of Northwestern University, for allowing me to read the dissertation of the late Ann Lorenz Van Zanten, "César Daly and the *Revue Générale de l'Architecture*."

In England Francis Sheppard, late general editor of the Survey of London, and David Reeder, reader in social and economic history at the University of Leicester, read and criticized my earliest attempted formulations of a comparative approach to the three capitals. Reeder was one of many participants at the Dyos Memorial Conference held at the University of Leicester in August 1980 who helped me put my ideas into focus. Anthony Sutcliffe, professor of social and economic history at the University of Sheffield, again and again gave me just the advice, idea, or piece of information that I needed to extricate myself from a cul-de-sac or proceed along an unfamiliar road. David Cannadine, of St. John's College, Cambridge, provided invaluable stimulation through both his published scholarship and his conversation. Hermione Hobhouse, Sheppard's successor at the Survey of London, and her associates in that endeavor have checked my wilder speculations with their detailed knowledge of London and architectural history. F. M. L. Thompson, director of the Institute of Historical Research, and his seminar on nineteenth-century England have given valuable encouragement and salutary caution. Gillian Tindall, the knowledgeable historian of Kentish Town and Bombay, has offered a sympathetic and critical ear. Conversations with Michael Robbins and Jack Simmons suggested fruitful insights.

François Bédarida helped introduce me to the mysteries of Paris. In Vienna, Franz Krieschmayer and three of the contributors to Renate Wagner-Rieger's magisterial *Wiener Ringstrasse* series—Doz. Dr. Hannes Stekl of the Institut für Wirtschafts- und Sozialgeschichte, and Dr. Peter Haiko and Doz. Dr. Walter Krause of the Kunsthistorisches Institut, University of Vienna—have helped me enormously in dealing with the scholarly resources and interpretative problems of that city.

At Vassar William Hoffman and Susan Lachmann, both in the class of 1983, Deborah R. Kelley and Susan Altschuler, class of 1987, and Ronald Shapiro '86, proved resourceful research assistants. For assistance with proofreading, I am grateful to the following Vassar undergraduates: Lisa Brohinsky '88, Jeffrey Crouch '87, Jocelyn Cruz, '87, Ann Kwiatkowski '88, Anne Gibbins '89, Martha Conway, '86, and Mariah Fredericks '88. Again and again Norma Torney, administrative assistant to the department of history, smoothed the progress toward publication. Martin S. Stanford gave valuable assistance in helping me make efficient use of the libraries of New York City. Evelyn Benesch, doctoral candidate in the history of art at the University of Vienna, guided me through the intricacies of the libraries and picture collections of Paris and Vienna, and has herself taken many of the photographs of contemporary Paris and Vienna that illustrate the text. Will Faller provided many of the prints from *The Builder*.

John Nicoll of Yale University Press, London, and Judy Metro in New Haven read the manuscript at different stages and made many valuable suggestions. Barbara Hofmaier gave zest and stimulation to the process of copyediting, while Nancy Ovedovitz and Charlotte Dihoff skillfully transformed copy into book.

A fellowship for 1979–80 from the John Simon Guggenheim Memorial Foundation made possible preliminary research. Vassar College, through its generous and enlightened policy of academic leaves, facilitated the writing of the book in 1983–84.

I wish also to thank the professional staffs of the Vassar College Library, the New York Public Library, the Alliance Française, the Austrian Institute, and the Engineering Societies Library—all in New York—the Seattle Public Library, the British Library, the London Library, the Guildhall Library, the Museum of London, and the British Museum; the Bibliothèque Nationale, the Bibliothèque Historique de la Ville de Paris, and the Musée Carnavalet; and in Vienna the Bundesdenkmalamt, the Nationalbibliothek, the Historisches Museum der Stadt Wien, and the Albertina Collection for their patience, learning, and helpfulness.

Urban historians will recognize how many of the ideas and how much of my approach stem from the writings of three seminal thinkers: Steen Eiler Rasmussen, Sir John Summerson, and Jane Jacobs. They, along with the others named above, may well be dismayed by some of the specific conclusions that I reach, but I hope they will nonetheless accept my gratitude for the example of independent thinking they have set me.

I would like to express belated recognition of the dedication with which, in the 1930s and 1940s, the teachers in the Seattle public schools conveyed to their students a sense of the excitement of learning and the importance of thinking for oneself. Finally, the pages that follow attempt a small tribute to the memory of L. P. Curtis at Yale, who introduced me to London as a subject for historical research; of T. F. Reddaway at University College, London, who taught me how to be a London historian; and of H. J. Dyos of Leicester University, who single-handedly turned urban history from what seemed in the 1950s a private obsession into the flourishing field of scholarship it has since become.

THE CITY AS LUXURY

1

Urban Virtue and
Urban Beauty

he city as a work of art? Surely not. The city as wasteland, perhaps, or as battleground, or jungle. The city as manifestation of all that is rotten in society, festering wound in the body politic, foretaste of hell in which brute force tramples the weak underfoot, corruption feeds on innocence, gluttony mocks hunger, unprotected virtue submits to triumphant vice. From Juvenal to Cobbett, from Saint Augustine to Jefferson, poets and moralists, publicists and philosophers have subjected the city to righteous abuse. In more measured language, the modern scholar approaches urbanization as a pathologist tracing the course of a disease.

Defenders of the city usually justify their position on economic rather than aesthetic grounds. They see the city as infrastructure, to be judged by the efficiency with which it facilitates the creation and distribution of wealth. To both attackers and defenders, the city is the product of vast, anonymous forces, not an individual creation. Any beauty it might possess would be incidental to its real nature, any visible structure one imposed by historical necessity rather than artistic intent.

Yet with rare exceptions, such as Ireland before the Viking invasions, the civilizations of the past have regarded cities as neither shameful nor inevitable, but as deliberate creations, worth making sacrifices to build, maintain, and embellish. Until the nineteenth century they were the home for no more than a tiny proportion of mankind, a luxury made possible by the labors of the agricultural majority. Wealth had to be extracted from the land, the forests, the mines, and the sea to maintain an unproductive urban minority. Fleets of ships laden with Egyptian grain were needed to make possible the splendors of imperial Rome. At the remote outskirts of their empire the Romans erected, in defiance of economic rationality, hundreds of towns, each complete with amphitheater, temple, and public buildings, "for show, amusement, and futile glory," as Huizinga remarks.[1] Only with the breakdown of political authority in the West were cities abandoned as irrelevant extravagances.

Beginning with the rise of towns in the tenth and eleventh centuries, and enormously accelerated by the Industrial Revolution in the eighteenth and nineteenth, some urban agglomerations acquired practical economic justification and produced more wealth than they consumed. With such examples in mind, scholars have applied the term Industrial City to the modern metropolis in general. Yet some cities, including most of the largest, grew and developed in ways inexplicable in purely economic and technological terms. London, Paris, and Vienna, though all engaged in manufacture and affected by the Industrial Revolution, achieved their present outward appearance more in defiance of industrialization than as its consequence.

It was a commonplace of classical aesthetic theory that the function of art was to please and to instruct, or, more accurately, to please in order to instruct. The Romantics and their successors placed even greater stress on art as the servant of morality. They perceived the city, the largest work of art possible, as necessarily making a moral statement. In London the notion of the Metropolis as a conscious expression of national glory lasted only for a few heady years under the Prince Regent: for most of its history London served as an expression of private values rather than of public exhortation. But on the continent city-building seemed too important a matter to be left to the citizens.

As nation-states established themselves in the course of the nineteenth and early twentieth centuries, older cities—Berlin, Rome, Budapest, Helsinki, Prague— transformed themselves into national capitals and adopted an external dress appropriate to their new roles. But it was the established capitals Paris and Vienna that underwent the most remarkable alterations in outer garb and inner structure, and in so doing became models that would be widely imitated.

Vienna was even more strident than Paris in asserting its identity and proclaiming its importance. Serving, sometimes simultaneously, sometimes successively, as a bastion of Catholicism while the majority of its citizens were Protestant, as the bulwark of Christendom with the Turks at its gates, as the champion of Christian monarchy against the French Revolution, as the stronghold of absolutism in a liberal Europe, as the residence of the formal heads first of the Holy Roman Empire and then of the German Confederation, without being the *capital* of either, it ultimately, after 1866, had to share with Budapest the honor of governing the Dual Monarchy, which consisted of what now forms parts of Italy, Yugoslavia, Romania, Czechoslovakia, Poland, and the Soviet Union, as well as Austria and Hungary. It presided over an empire bewildering in its diversity, a society ranging from peasant culture to the most sophisticated, with radically shifting political boundaries. Yet despite its precarious position, whether challenged by the Turkish or the Prussian or the Napoleonic army, or by national and social discontent within the borders of its realm, Vienna adopted a pose of serenity, splendor, and permanence. Far from expressing the nature of the society that produced it, Vienna is a magnificent denial of objective historical reality: a product of the human will and imagination, a triumph of art over reality.

Imperial Paris and London, too, were deliberate artistic creations intended not merely to give pleasure but to contain ideas, inculcate values, and serve as tangible expressions of systems of thought and morality. Though they attained their present shape in the nineteenth century, they, like Vienna, reflect a far older heritage: each a significant medieval commercial center with an autonomous, self-governing citizenry; each becoming in due course a royal residence and capital of a far-reaching state; each a significant cultural center (Paris achieving European preeminence in the thirteenth century, London and Vienna much later); each a favored resort for the leisured classes, with the appropriate service industries and manufacture of luxury goods for their consumption. By the start of the nineteenth century they were the three largest cities of Europe, each the capital of an empire as well as the cultural focus of a nation (although Austria's leadership of the incipient Germany was being challenged). Each experienced unprecedented growth in the century following 1814, benefited from industrialization and the revolution in transport, and became a banking center of world importance. Each was physically transformed as well as enlarged in the course of the century. Each could claim world preeminence in the realms of politics and economics, the arts and sciences, London perhaps especially in the former, Paris and Vienna in the latter.

Each has lost its empire, and some of its former economic and cultural importance, with Vienna's fall the most sudden and dramatic. Yet each has adapted itself to its changed functions with eminent success: each remains in its capacity as *city* a treasure to be preserved, an achievement of and monument to Western civilization, economically flourishing, culturally active, a joy to visit and a privilege to inhabit. While in no way immune to the anti-urban forces of the late twentieth century, they nevertheless retain a vitality and exercise an attraction that are the envy of less fortunate cities. They have managed either to adapt to or to ignore the cultural, social, intellectual, and economic revolutions of the past two centuries, retaining throughout their essential identities. By right they ought—Vienna especially—to be anachronisms, embarrassing relics like Liverpool or St. Louis, or museums like Venice or Charleston. Yet they thrive in an environment far removed from that in which they were built. Each is, above all, a work of art, a collectively created complex of buildings, streets, phenomena, experiences, and activities existing in time as well as in space, that serves, to paraphrase Gibbon, to promote the happiness and exalt the dignity of mankind.

No one can fail to respond, in some degree, to the attractions of the three cities. But to enter fully into their qualities as works of art, it will be necessary to abandon a number of twentieth century assumptions about the nature and function of art and to adopt some nineteenth-century ones in their place. For example, to our grandparents art was not morally neutral, but worked in the service of virtue: if, rather than elevate, it depraved, it ceased to be art. Ornament was not crime, but the addition of beauty and instruction to the satisfaction of material needs. Art began precisely where utility broke off. Form was not to follow function, but to transcend it.

The criteria for inclusion in the following chapters reflect such assumptions. The merely useful, being beneath the dignity of art and incapable of providing either instruction or the higher pleasures, will give way to the ornamental and superfluous. Just as heavy industry was expelled to the outskirts of Paris and Vienna, where it need never be seen by people of quality, so the economic foundations of the prosperity of the three cities will remain largely unexamined. There will be nothing on markets, but much on restaurants. The sanitary works of Baron Haussmann will be viewed not in their impact on mortality rates, but as they made the streets of Paris more suitable for idle promenading. Architectural discussion will deal with decorative façades rather than with their structural underpinning.

The stress on the superficial and the luxurious does not arise from a spirit of frivolity, but from the conviction that societies better reveal themselves at play than at work. It is when art takes over from utility that the outward forms of cities become significant. A pure and abundant supply of water, street networks adequate to the traffic, housing that provided the minimum of shelter, public transport that met the needs of the local economy: *all* cities had to provide these. Industrial cities, strictly speaking, provided little more.

Sheffield, economically flourishing, with a well-paid work force enjoying some of the highest housing standards in Victorian England, did not indulge in extravagant follies. To satisfy the demands of the spirit for something beyond food and drink and shelter, the aspiring Sheffielder had either to turn to inner resources or to leave Sheffield—for the harsh sublimity of the surrounding moors, the cultural riches of York, the noisy delights of Mablethorpe or Skegness. Philanthropic urges and the stirrings of a civic conscience alleviated but did not fundamentally alter the situation: the Ruskin Museum gave the citizens a glimpse of the beauty otherwise absent from their environment; a university would insinuate the attractions of useless as well as useful knowledge. But what Horace Walpole had termed "one of the foulest towns in England" in 1760 still struck George Orwell in 1936 as "one of the most appalling places I have ever seen."[2] It is no denial of the very real virtues of Sheffield to insist that it would be inappropriate to treat it primarily, or even secondarily, as a work of art.

London, for all its incidental ugliness, is a different matter entirely. Here both individual and national extravagance were at worst forgivable, at best laudable. Whether such extravagance took the form of an afternoon spent purchasing frivolities in Bond Street or the erection of pinnacled monuments along the Embankment, London offered possibilities of conspicuous self-indulgence and significant display that would have been out of place in an industrial city. To grasp the meaning of such self-indulgence, such display, the techniques of the economic historian are useless, those of the social historian inadequate. The art historian and the intellectual historian are better qualified to illuminate our understanding of cities that, like London, transcend in both aspiration and achievement the merely practical and utilitarian.

While waiting for the results of the refined analysis such specialists may engage in, we can perhaps achieve cruder but still valuable insights by using our eyes and by finding out how people in the century before 1914 themselves perceived London, Paris, and Vienna. The actual resident, his perceptions dulled by familiarity, will have less to tell us than the foreign critic or visiting tourist. The latter will be on the alert for whatever makes the foreign city different from his own, the distinctive tone that gives it its special character, and he can make comparisons that would not occur to the person for whom the city is the background for daily life. For the working resident, the pleasing distractions of the capital will at most occupy the occasional Sunday and holiday; for the tourist, the pleasures will form his daily occupation.

The passage of time makes a tourist of even the modern Londoner, Parisian, or Viennese who examines his own city as it stood a century ago. Released from the necessity of surviving on inadequate wages, immune to the deadly bacteria of its water supply, oblivious to the stench of its drains, he can enjoy the artistic excellences without being distracted by the material deficiencies. Such a selective approach need not distort his historical understanding, so long as he remembers that his city was then, as it is now, a workshop, a market, an office, perhaps also an arena for the class struggle, as well as, however imperfectly realized, a work of art.

THE CITY AS MONUMENT

2

The Monumental Impulse

he nineteenth was the most historically minded of centuries, the one most aware of itself as participant in a continuing drama. It possessed, at the same time, unexampled means for giving material expression to that awareness, most notably in its great cities. London, Paris, and Vienna had long contained monuments. Only in the nineteenth century did they try to *become* monuments.

A monument is intended to call forth fear or wonder in the observer: to remind him of the antiquity of the dynasty, the power of the regime, the wealth of the community, the truth of its ideology, or of some event—a military victory or successful revolution—that demonstrated such wealth, power, or truth. To succeed in its aims, a monument needs to jolt the individual out of his mundane concerns—catching the 5:37, remembering to renew a driver's license, buying postage stamps—to remind him that life involves more than such concerns, and that he is fortunate to be a citizen of such a splendid metropolis, a subject of such a benevolent ruler, an adherent of the one true faith. Any evidence of restraint, understatement, or, worst of all, parsimony, will subvert its intention. It should aspire to the sublime and evoke sensations of awe, not of affectionate familiarity, and certainly not of amused condescension. To the Bloomsbury Group, the Albert Memorial failed in its monumental intentions; they, indeed, resisted the appeal of all monuments. But for most people at most times the question is not whether to have monuments, but what shall be monumentalized.

The answer has usually been Church and State. On the whole, monuments to the church predominated before the Reformation, monuments to the state afterward, although in countries affected by the Counter-Reformation both religious and secular powers demanded and got intensified architectural expression. While such monuments need not be urban—El Escorial, Blenheim, and Versailles had nothing to do with cities—both the Church Militant and the Monarchy Resurgent ordinarily placed visual manifestations of themselves where they would have the most impact: in cities.

The place Vendôme, the Karlskirche, Inigo Jones's Banqueting Hall reminded citizens of the power of the monarch, as well as conveying more complex ideological and aesthetic messages. But they and other monuments were dwarfed by the city as a whole. Each city said more about the numbers and activities of its citizens, past and present, than about the taste or benevolence of the monarch. Judged by the aesthetic standards of the eighteenth century, the three cities were rude reminders of a barbarous past, incoherent in structure and gross in appearance. Nothing short of total reconstruction would make them appropriate symbols for an enlightened monarchy in a cultivated age. Yet despite countless proposals, the actual efforts to turn the cities themselves into monuments came only with the nineteenth century, long after the age of absolutism and enlightenment.

Although the inner core of each city bore uncomfortable witness to its medieval origins, suburban extensions during the seventeenth and eighteenth centuries showed a degree of order and decency that occasionally rose to monumentality. The building of the place Royale (today's place des Vosges) under Henri IV and of the Piazza in Covent Garden under Charles I gave architectural distinction to new areas of residential fashion in Paris and London. The ending of the Turkish danger by the victory of 1683 opened the extramural suburbs of Vienna to extensive and sometimes elegant building development. The replacement of the fortifications of Paris by a line of boulevards, carried out between 1670 and 1685, gave further impetus to expansion, as had the migration from the City of London consequent on the plague and fire of 1665–66. Yet the outward shape of all three cities failed to correspond to the increased wealth and power of the regimes or to the aesthetic and intellectual requirements of the Enlightenment.

London was the most modern in appearance. The fire of 1666 had destroyed most of the original City, which had been replaced by streets of uniform brick houses as regular and practical as the age of Newton and Locke could have wished. The new streets and squares that linked the City to Westminster were symmetrical and rectilinear in design and spacious in layout, particularly on the larger leasehold estates. But the City remained the medieval tangle it had been before the fire, while the West End, if decent and coherent in its better parts, did not achieve an emotional intensity appropriate to the position of London as the world's first city or Britain as the world's first power.

Paris outshone London in the size and splendor of its public buildings—the Louvre, the Tuileries, the Invalides had no rivals across the Channel—and boasted a collection of *hôtels particuliers* of unmatched elegance and taste. But its streets were narrow, filthy, and dangerous; its housing outmoded and congested. The occasional areas whose layout and architecture were worthy of the wealthy and cultivated city lay at or near its fringes. The inner core remained untouched by the hand of improvement.

Vienna was less squalid than Paris, yet it displayed even greater incongruity between the grandiloquent public buildings and private palaces and the confined and irregular streets they faced. Although suburban development had reduced some of the pressure on the old City, the original walls kept court, bureaucracy, and aristocracy to an area smaller and more congested than that of the City of London. Massive new palaces and blocks of flats had replaced the original medieval structures, but the old street pattern remained.

That Paris and Vienna were even slower than London to adapt themselves to the requirements of the modern world suggests how less than absolute "absolute monarchies" were. The absence of awe-inspiring public buildings and triumphal ways in London could be accounted for by the enforced poverty of its rulers and the disinclination of Parliament to increase taxes or the national debt. But the failure of the Bourbons and the Habsburgs to indulge in radical surgery on their capitals is but another instance of their reluctance to interfere with private interests and individual rights. The abundance of projects for urban embellishment shows that the eighteenth century *conceived* of the city as a unified work of art, but the means for its achievement were lacking.

The works of art being produced were at once vaster in scale and more coherent than had before been possible. *Don Giovanni* is as complex as *L'Incoronazione di Poppea,* but more unified; *Tom Jones* is more unified than *The Canterbury Tales.* Buildings grew not just by adding more of the same units but by incorporating larger spaces into elaborately balanced and articulated schemes. Versailles provided the model whereby palace and gardens of unprecedented scale served as a single monument to the idea of monarchy. From the monumental palace to the monumental town was the next logical step. Versailles, Potsdam, and St. Petersburg were made to express in their structure and appearance the respective concepts of the state held by the French, Prussian, and Russian monarchies.[1] But those towns were created from scratch by their rulers. London, Paris, and Vienna were already there, both in a physical sense and in the sense of a tight network of inviolable property rights, sacred to both constitutional and absolute princes.[2] The French Revolution did away with such scruples. Nineteenth-century governments of whatever political complexion were more willing to challenge vested interests in the cause of municipal improvement. More important still, they had financial resources and technological devices that enabled them to embark on schemes of a magnitude that would have daunted their predecessors.

3

The Remaking of London

 t is not surprising that London, the largest and richest city in the world, should have been the first to embark on a comprehensive program of reconstruction and embellishment. That it began such a program when the outcome of the Napoleonic Wars was still in doubt is a measure of national self-confidence. What is surprising is the brevity of the mood of assertive national and civic pride that brought about the operations, and the failure of the still richer kingdom and empire of Victoria to continue and expand the works begun under the Prince Regent.[1]

In some respects the building of Regent Street and the formation of Regent's Park followed patterns set by landlords and builders in the eighteenth and even seventeenth centuries. The existence of large landed estates permitted the establishment and enforcement of coherent plans of development for extensive chunks of property. The Earl of Bedford had, in the Piazza in Covent Garden in the 1630s, given London its first residential square. A succession of building acts had imposed a degree of uniformity on all new streets, while classical taste encouraged the subordination of the individual house to the terrace that contained it. Bedford Square, laid out in 1776, established the fashion for the square designed as an architectural whole. The Bedford estate and others were laid out in wide, uniform streets, punctuated by frequent squares which, from about 1790, were adorned with landscaped central gardens. Such squares were reserved for use by the occupants of the surrounding houses, but the royal parks had long been open to the public and contributed to the leafy spaciousness of the metropolis. If scantily supplied with medieval antiquities—Westminster Abbey and Westminster Hall being the most conspicuous—London boasted a fine collection of churches by Wren and his successors. Stately private mansions and a respectable assortment of public buildings adorned both the City and Westminster. Yet the most impressive aspect of Georgian London was not the monuments to the vanity of the great and powerful but the extent and decency of the districts that housed the middle classes, and the splendor and variety of the shops dedicated to their wants.

Despite its size and prosperity, despite the orderly layout and tasteful architecture of its better districts, late Georgian London was more likely to please than to astonish the critical observer. It could not match the palaces of Vienna, the public buildings of Paris, the vistas and grand architectural compositions of Nancy or Turin. Parliament occupied a makeshift cluster of buildings. None of the royal residences approached continental standards of size or opulence or even met those of the future George IV. Inigo Jones's Banqueting Hall suggested what the Stuarts might have done to enrich the capital's architecture had Parliament lost the Civil War or had James II been as clever and unscrupulous as his elder brother (fig. 1). William Kent's Horse Guards gave a modicum of distinction to the other side of Whitehall, but No. 10 Downing Street gives a more representative idea of the kind of building in which most governmental activities were carried on. The really impressive aristocratic mansions, like Northumberland House at Charing Cross, were exceptional: vastly wealthy peers of the realm for the most part contented themselves with an anonymous house in Grosvenor or St. James's Square, reserving architectural display for their country seats. The wealth of the City, similarly, was but slightly indicated by the Lord Mayor's Mansion House or the halls of the various livery companies (fig. 2, colorplate 2). Banks and businesses of worldwide importance were housed in buildings that on the outside looked like old-fashioned and somewhat grubby dwelling houses.

An assortment of parochial and ad hoc bodies saw to the paving, lighting, and cleaning of the streets, while sewer commissioners tracing their origins back to the Middle Ages provided for the drainage and sanitary needs of the Metropolis. With respect to paving, lighting, and sanitation, and to the material conditions of life, Georgian London far surpassed contemporary Paris.[2] But for the most part its urbanistic virtues lay precisely in those areas that did not show. A system of public fountains adorned with allegorical sculpture is, perhaps unfairly, more impressive than a system that pipes water to individual houses and makes such fountains unnecessary.

The vicissitudes of architectural taste combined with the situation of the monarchy and the church kept London visually unobtrusive and understated. While Italy and southern Germany had been experimenting with the expressive capacities of the Baroque, England had chosen a refined Palladianism. While France reveled in the frivolities of the Rococo, England at most allowed herself the delicate incised decorations of the brothers Adam. The severe restrictions on external ornament and projections of the building acts of 1707, 1709, and especially of 1774 deprived London of even those adornments that contemporary taste might have allowed. The gray brick that constituted the nearly universal building material was ill suited to architectural extravagance. To the educated eye, a residential terrace from eighteenth-century London consists of much more than the "plain brick wall with holes in it" that was all the Victorians could see, but placed next to a street in contemporary Vienna its good breeding and self-effacement would be lost in the other's dazzle. French and Austrian taste were, to be sure, themselves moving in a direction of greater austerity under Louis XVI and Joseph II, but Vienna never achieved the self-denying plainness of the late eighteenth-century London street.

English architects were neither incapable of nor averse to magnificence and display. But such magnificence and display were considered unsuitable and unnecessary for a London residence. The English aristocracy were territorial magnates, and the territory on which their power depended lay in the country. Even those with large landholdings in London could not hope to use them to overawe the turbulent body of electors for Westminster or the independent voters of the City.

1. *Inigo Jones's Banqueting Hall suggested what the Stuarts might have done to enrich the capital's architecture.* Whitehall looking north, c. 1842, Banqueting Hall to right. T. Shotter Boys. (Guildhall Library. Photo Godfrey.)

14

The expense lavished on the building and rebuilding of their country houses left even the richest of them with little remaining for architectural adventure in London.

The Church of England lacked the money and the inclination to indulge in an ambitious program of building. Neither were its component bodies (the monasteries having long since been dissolved) in a position to invest in the construction of anything like the vast *Stiftshäuser* that religious foundations were erecting in Vienna. Bishops, deans, and colleges behaved like their worldly counterparts in their capacity as urban landlords, granting building leases and leaving the risks to their lessees.

The monarchy, dependent for its income on Parliament, had all it could do to maintain its existing palaces, of which the most pretentious—Hampton Court and Windsor—were some distance from London. Not until the future George IV became Prince Regent was a member of the royal family able to persuade Parliament to finance the rebuilding of Carlton House and Buckingham Palace. The consequence was that London looked less rich than it was.

The decision of the Crown to develop Marylebone Park as a building estate and

2. The wealth of the City was but slightly indicated by the Lord Mayor's Mansion House. Cheapside looking west, Mansion House to left. T. Shotter Boys. (Guildhall Library. Photo Godfrey.) See also colorplate 2.

to link it with St. James's Park by a street to be composed seemingly of palaces inaugurated a brief, exciting period of grandiose schemes to transform the image of London from one of sober respectability to one of gorgeous state. Much of what even today lends London a degree of magnificence dates either in execution or in conception from the time of the regency and reign of George IV. Long before Napoleon III and Baron Haussmann imposed their vision of order and splendor on Paris, the Prince Regent and John Nash gave London its only boulevard in the form of the original Regent Street. Intended to link two royal palaces, the existing Carlton House and a new pleasure pavilion in Regent's Park, it combined the functions of a triumphal way with that of a street devoted to the luxury retail trade, where the elegant frivolities of shopping and promenading could take place against a background of architectural grandeur unequaled, in London at any rate, before or since.

Regent's Park (as Marylebone Park was renamed) was to contain the new palace and what Sir John Summerson has called a "National Valhalla," described by Nash as "a public building to receive the statues and monuments of great and distinguished men."3 Nash planned Trafalgar Square, dominated by the National Gallery, as an integral part of the Regent Street improvements. He also prepared plans for a second grand artery to connect Trafalgar Square with the new British Museum, whose present buildings were begun in 1823.4

Private landowners great and small—notably Lord Grosvenor, later first marquess of Westminster, the bishop of London, and the duke of Bedford—vied with the Crown Commissioners of Woods and Forests in schemes of urban magnificence. Speculative builders, of whom Thomas Cubitt was the most ambitious and most successful, entered into contracts to build whole neighborhoods on spacious and palatial lines. The New Road and the eastern boundary of Hyde Park, which had hitherto formed the northern and western limits of London, were to be crossed and outflanked. Tyburnia north of the park and Belgravia to the south were laid out for the erection of garden squares and terraces forming a succession of grand architectural compositions. Farther east the marquess of Northampton and the New River Company were laying out in Islington districts of squares and terraces intended for families of more modest means. South of the New Road, the Bedford estate had entered into contracts with Thomas Cubitt to complete, after more than a century and a half, the development of Bloomsbury in a dignified and impressive fashion.

That Carlton House was almost immediately taken down and the royal *guinguette* in Regent's Park never built suggests the fragility of the mood that produced Regent Street, but such alterations did nothing to undercut the street's stately impressiveness. Conceived as an architectural whole, with varied but consistent designs, it presented the pedestrian with a succession of happy surprises as he made his way from Pall Mall to Portland Place (figs. 3 and 4). Unlike the slightly earlier rue de Rivoli, whose arcades were matched by the covered walkway along the Quadrant, it did not continually repeat an identical pattern, but offered a wonderfully varied assortment of the elements of the then-fashionable Roman style,

3. *(opposite, above) Regent Street presented the pedestrian with a succession of happy surprises as he made his way from Pall Mall to Portland Place.* Lower Regent Street, looking south from Piccadilly Circus. Thomas Sheppard. (Guildhall Library. Photo Godfrey.)
4. *(opposite, below)* The same, after demolition of Carlton House and erection of Duke of York's Column. T. Shotter Boys. (Guildhall Library. Photo Godfrey.)

17

so that each stretch of roadway brought a new picture into view (fig. 5). That the elements were hackneyed and their execution slipshod did little to lessen their effectiveness, particularly to one accustomed to the standard straight brick London street.

London already had, on its leasehold estates, streets designed as a whole, if of lesser length. It also had, in Bond Street and the extended thoroughfare formed by Cheapside, Ludgate Hill, Fleet Street, and the Strand, long streets devoted to retail trade. But the designed streets were not shopping streets, and the shopping streets were a motley assortment of former town houses converted into shops. The result could be picturesque and attractive, but to the late Georgian eye the equally varied but more coherent way in which the individual shopfront in Regent Street was subordinated to the overall design came as an aesthetic revelation.

Nash took full advantage of the plastic capabilities of stucco to provide abundance of ornament at a less than ruinous cost. Stucco, a "sham" or "pretense" insofar as it imitated stone, and hence anathema to Victorian critics, has not had a good press over the years. Yet for London, with no stone quarries in its vicinity, stucco provided an opportunity to combine economical brick construction with ornamental capacities exceeding those of stone. For a nominal expense the most ordinary dwelling could be given simulated rustication on its ground story, while

5. *Each stretch of roadway brought a new picture into view.* The Quadrant, curving toward the northwest. (Guildhall Library. Photo Godfrey.)

more ambitious buildings could be adorned with pilasters, pediments, pillared porticoes, figurative sculpture in low or high relief—anything that the vanity of the householder might require or the imagination of the architect could devise.

Regent Street served a multitude of purposes. It offered a handsome speculation for London builders and enhanced the income of the Crown estate. It provided a triumphal roadway to impress visiting royalty, and a north-south route for ordinary traffic to relieve the already notorious congestion of London's streets. It gave the idle and opulent a stage on which to display their clothes and equipages and at the same time incorporated a main line of underground sewer linking the suburban development at Regent's Park with the existing main sewer in St. James's Park. It stimulated retail trade, provided new housing, and swept away insanitary slum property. In this last respect it anticipated virtually every street improvement for the following century: "opening up" and "cleansing" congested and unwholesome districts, replacing "rookeries" and substandard dwellings with broad avenues, where breezes could dissipate the pestilential miasmas postulated by the airborne theory of disease.

A study made ten years after the completion of Regent Street discovered that not only had rentals in the street itself gone up by a third, but property values in nearby streets had been raised. Only Bond Street suffered from the competition of the new shops. Unlike most of its successors Regent Street quickly became and remained what it was intended to be: a corridor of high-class retail shops. John Tallis's guidebook described it in 1838 as a "noble street," with "palace-like shops, in whose broad showy windows are displayed articles of the most splendid description, such as the neighbouring world of wealth and fashion are daily in want of . . . it should be visited on a summer's day in the afternoon, when the splendid carriages, and elegantly attired pedestrians, evince the opulence and taste of our magnificent metropolis."[5] Although Regent Street no longer vies with Bond Street for elegance, its decline is as nothing compared with that of Oxford Street. And if the annual motor trip of suburban families to view its Christmas decorations is but a pale reflection of the line of carriages that traveled its length on early Victorian afternoons, it has maintained its appeal into the motor age better than the younger Westbourne Grove.

Regent's Park was originally intended to be a garden suburb for the very rich, with fifty private villas situated so as to give the illusion that each had the entire park to itself. Here were privacy and seclusion with a vengeance. Less ambitious but more successful was the adjacent Eyre estate in St. John's Wood, with moderately sized villas along conventional streets, the prototype of the middle-class suburban housing estate. In 1824 even Eton College—the most lethargic of landowners—was contemplating dividing its 230-acre estate east of St. John's Wood and north of Regent's Park into no more than seventy-five building plots, of which the smallest would be more than half an acre in size, in expectation of a scale of mansion and class of resident immensely more grand than would in fact ultimately appear on the estate.

The plans for the completion of the Bedford estate in Bloomsbury and the development of Grosvenor estate in Pimlico and the bishop of London's estate in Paddington similarly overestimated the demand for vast town mansions. Writing in 1851, Christopher Haedy, the steward of the duke of Bedford, recalled how Cubitt's operations in Bloomsbury had "proceeded rapidly at first, but very slowly afterwards, in consequence of the new buildings near Hyde Park Gardens and in the neighborhood of Belgrave Square coming into successful rivalry with them." The houses proved "rather too large and too expensive for the locality, and the difficulty he [Cubitt] found in procuring purchasers and tenants for them made him hesitate to proceed with the erection of houses of a similar kind."[6]

Tavistock and Gordon squares are in layout and appearance the obvious successors of Bedford and Russell squares. The terraces, squares, and "gardens" of Belgravia and Tyburnia, and the even more outrageous terraces surrounding Regent's Park occupy an altogether more intense emotional realm (fig. 6). In them stucco is employed not merely to add decorative features to a predominantly brick façade, but to impose a grand design on the entire range of houses. The scale of buildings and layout grew to give the whole a larger-than-life quality: Eaton Square was the biggest in London, and Belgravia the most grandiloquent neighborhood. The spectacular terraces along Bayswater Road visually incorporated Hyde Park itself into their domain, as Carlton House Terrace did St. James's Park. Here were

6. *The even more outrageous terraces surrounding Regent's Park occupy an altogether more intense emotional realm.* Cumberland Terrace, Regent's Park. (Museum of London.)

residences fit to house the victors of Trafalgar and Waterloo, the merchant princes of a global empire, proud citizens of the greatest city on earth.

Between 1825 and 1837 the mood of self-confidence, the devotion to urban values, and the pride in London all came to an end. London experienced a crisis of perception that affected the social, aesthetic, and economic values of those whose wishes and actions determined its subsequent growth. Moral scruples about the propriety of gaudy architectural display, an aesthetic revolution, economic depression, and the discovery of disconcerting facts about the sanitary and social conditions of the metropolis brought the period of self-satisfied urban pride and grandiose speculative projects to a premature end.

The impact of those changes was not immediately obvious. Not only was the London of George IV still unmistakably there in 1837, but it continued to stand, more or less intact, for the rest of the century, an object of shame in the eyes of aesthetes and sanitary reformers, and increasingly in the eyes of ordinary Londoners as well. Even the suburban extensions of London built in the decades following 1825 represented to a great degree not new projects but the delayed realization of the ambitious schemes set forth in the building agreements of that year. And the building industry with cautious conservatism kept putting up modified versions of late Georgian housing long after advanced architectural opinion had rejected Georgian standards of taste.

But the joy had gone. London's burst of self-confident reconstruction—which anticipated in many ways the transformation of Paris in the 1850s and 1860s and Vienna in the 1860s and 1870s—lasted hardly more than a decade. The Third Republic continued to put into effect the policies begun by Napoleon III; in Vienna the spirit informing the creation of the Ringstrasse persisted until 1914. Victorian London repudiated the principles and assumptions that had supported the complacency, optimism, and activity of the decade between Waterloo and 1825.

Disillusion and Disgust, 1825–1837

The physical transformation of Regency London into Victorian London was not finished until 1901; the psychological revolution came with remarkable suddenness. Four explanations for the changed perception—respectively economic, medical, political, and aesthetic—suggest themselves: the financial panic of 1825, the cholera epidemic of 1832, the Great Reform Bill, and the altered conception of the beautiful embodied in Pugin's *Contrasts,* published in 1836.

The consequences of the banking crisis of 1825 were at once immediate, far-reaching, and permanent.[7] The drying up of the sources of credit, crucial to a group as lacking in independent capital resources as London's speculative builders, brought to an abrupt end the mania of speculation that had built Regent Street and was proposing to create for London so many other monumental embellishments and additions.

With the fall in the cost of money and building materials at the close of the Napoleonic Wars, London had experienced a resurgence in speculative building, but it did not become an explosion until the 1820s. In the years just before 1825, and to a remarkable extent in 1825 itself, the building agreements for Belgravia, Pimlico, Tyburnia, and northern Bloomsbury were concluded, on a scale and to a degree of ambitiousness unprecedented in London building history and unmatched since. So vast were the plans, and so far had Thomas Cubitt and lesser promoters overestimated the demand for luxury town houses that as late as Cubitt's death in 1855 streets and squares he had contracted to build thirty years earlier were not yet entirely finished.

The collapse of the credit market late in 1825 brought such schemes to an end. It was then that Nash's plan for the royal pleasure dome and the fifty villas in Regent's Park were abandoned by the Commissioners of Woods and Forests. Eton College gave up its grandiose ideas about its estate; not until 1840 did development there, on a far more modest scale, begin in earnest. Bloomsbury, Tyburnia, and Belgravia were eventually completed to their original specifications, but only after agreements had been renegotiated extending the deadlines for completion and drastically lowering the ground rents. For one of the consequences of the collapse was a dramatic and permanent fall in the price of building land.

The cost of undeveloped building land on the outskirts of English towns had roughly tripled between 1740 and 1820.[8] In London it reached a peak in 1825, fell sharply at the end of that year—by more than a third—and remained at that new low level until at least 1939.[9] Undeveloped suburban land could be had throughout the last three-quarters of the nineteenth century at from £20 to £40 per acre per annum, or from a penny to twopence per square yard; in the case of freehold, calculating at twenty-five years' purchase, this worked out at between £500 and £1,000 per acre. These prices applied equally to land destined for working-class residential, middle-class residential, and industrial purposes, and to provincial towns as well as to London.[10] During the 1930s land for new suburban building estates could be had for as little as £200 per acre freehold. Once it had been laid out for building, and still more once it had been covered with buildings, the value of any particular plot of ground would tend to rise, and in favored locations to rise enormously. In 1871 the architect Edward I'Anson—who was in a position to know—estimated that the value of land in the City of London had doubled over the previous half-century, and in very important sites it had quadrupled.[11] But for more than a century after 1825, the cost of undeveloped land coming onto the market either remained stable or fell.

The abundant assertions in late Victorian and Edwardian periodical and political literature that a significant cause of high rents, overcrowding, and urban distress in general was the inflated cost of land—or the more sinister burden of "ground rents"—and that landowners were deliberately holding land off the market in order to force its price up to even more exorbitant levels can only be called willfully misinformed. Like the learned treatises on witchcraft published in the sixteenth and seventeenth centuries, they amount to no more than confirmation of popular delusions by people who ought to have known better.

The original cost of land ordinarily represented less than ten percent of the value of a house. Villas in Adelaide Road on the Eton College estate renting in 1856 for £60 to £80 per annum paid £4 ground rent; that is, the price of the land accounted for between one-fifteenth and one-twentieth of the cost of the house. On the duke of Norfolk's estate in Sheffield, perhaps a penny to threepence of the three shillings threepence weekly rent for a working man's cottage represented ground rent. If undeveloped land in England had been free, the effect on the supply and cost of housing would have been minimal. As it was, the abundance of cheap land on the outskirts of all English towns encouraged the low-density development that distinguished English urban growth from that prevailing nearly everywhere else in Europe.

The collapse of the speculative boom revealed something that every generation of builders had to learn afresh: the large risks involved in projects of urban improvement. A great many people lost a great deal of money in 1825. One economic explanation for the replacement of the linked terrace by the detached villa as the normal unit for middle-class housing is that it reduced the risk of a building scheme. The whole of a crescent or square would have to be completed before any part of it could be sold at its full value, whereas one or two villas in a semirural setting might, if anything, be more valuable before they became surrounded by similar dwellings. Slow, piecemeal development, disastrous in a neighborhood of squares and terraces, would be a prudent way of proceeding with a district of villas.

For many years after the collapse of 1825 no large-scale speculation that depended on an ever-expanding market for magnificent urban residences could hope to attract investors. Private capital grew more cautious about the time that the reformed House of Commons and the new, democratically elected vestries were showing greater interest in lower taxes and lower rates than in public splendor. And when building developers became reckless again—as they did by the 1840s—it was from overoptimism about the demand for suburban coziness, not urban luxury.[12]

An event that had an even greater effect on the way Londoners and others looked on the metropolis was the cholera epidemic of 1832. Although London had had fluctuations in its mortality rate and although that rate had been generally high, it had not experienced since 1665 any single, dramatic, killing epidemic that affected the public consciousness as strongly as the coming of the cholera in February 1832. Remarkable was not so much the number of deaths—5,300 in 1832 and 1,500 the following year—as the unexpectedness of the epidemic, its unpredictability, and the swiftness with which death came to the afflicted. It is usually regarded, quite correctly, as providing the impetus for the whole movement of sanitary reform that, for all its agonizing slowness of execution, proved ultimately one of the most admirable achievements of the Victorian period. But it was equally significant as the shock that contributed most to the changed perception of London. Late Georgian London was perceived as clean and healthy; early Victorian London was at the time—and still is—*perceived* as being dirty and deadly. That its mortality rates were lower and its sanitary standards higher than those of Continental cities did little to alter the image. Dickens reinforced the false image by imposing his brilliant but perverse vision of London on the consciousness both of his contemporaries and of posterity.

Leigh's New Picture of London had proclaimed in 1818 that "its healthfulness is equal to that of any other metropolis in existence." It attributed the salubrity of modern London to its wide streets, an abundant domestic water supply, and "its system of sewers and drains," all of which "wholly do away with the unhealthiness and liability to epidemic and other disorders which usually prevail among crowded populations."[13] Eight years later John Britton boasted that "since the complete extinction of the *Plague* by the great fire of 1666, this metropolis has fully deserved to be considered as one of the most healthy on earth; and . . . its increase to an almost indefinite extent is not likely to be attended with additional unwholesomeness."[14] In *Emma,* first published in 1816, Jane Austen expected her readers to take Mr. Woodhouse's assertion that "nobody is healthy in London, nobody can be" as simply one more instance of his valetudinarian imbecility. The coming of the cholera made such complacency impossible after 1832.

The passage of the First Reform Bill the same year by no means constituted the triumph of the middle classes that it is sometimes called, but it did produce a House of Commons more sensitive to middle-class opinion. The bill abolishing the select vestries in 1831[15] and establishing ratepayer control of the primary units of local government in London inaugurated a long period in which those responsible for the provision of municipal services were above all concerned with questions of economy. The small shopkeeper and property owner predominated both in the electorate and in the vestries. The Metropolitan Board of Works, established in 1855, was elected by the vestries and other local units, not directly by the population. The improvements those bodies initiated had to justify themselves on grounds of practical utility. Grand gestures in the service of beauty or visual expressions of municipal pride could be considered only if connected with projects remedying some undoubted evil or promoting obvious economic gain. A system of sewers, the removal of obstructions to traffic, new streets to replace insanitary areas, yes; triumphal ways, monumental edifices, promenades adorned with heroic statuary and commemorative fountains, no. The most notable contribution of the Metropolitan Board of Works to the embellishment of London—the Victoria Embankment—was built essentially as a lid to cover both the intercepting sewer that conveyed the wastes of the metropolis far down the Thames and the underground Metropolitan District Railway. The high-minded London County Council that took over and expanded the duties of metropolitan government in 1889 was less averse in theory to grand gestures, but in practice concentrated on education, housing, and electric tramways rather than schemes of artistic extravagance. London, having been given Waterloo Place and Trafalgar Square, had to content itself with such expressions of glory while its governors concentrated on drains and ventilation and keeping rates down.

The period between 1825 and the accession of Victoria did not merely see the growth in influence of a class that cared less about beauty than about economy and efficiency; it witnessed an abrupt change in the standards by which people decided what was beautiful and what was not. The names given to that revolution in taste—Romanticism, the Gothic Revival, the onset of Victorianism—and the interpretations put forth to account for it—industrialization, the substitution of bourgeois for aristocratic standards, a willful abandonment of classical values—are all unsatisfying. It can only be said that a profound change took place in the way cultivated Englishmen looked at cities and buildings. There was little agreement on how London ought to look, but near unanimity in condemning the way it actually did. A critic writing in 1866 contemptuously dismissed both the elegant simplicity of late eighteenth-century domestic architecture and the inventive splendor of the Regency:

> As it did in Rome, stucco appeared in London at a period when all kinds of architectural decoration had sunk to the lowest possible state of degradation, lower even than Roman art ever sank, even in its basest form. . . . in England . . . towards the close of the last century, all kinds of architectural decoration, domestic or monumental . . . utterly died out; for the trumpery little street porticoes of ordinary dwelling-houses, and even the mean attempts at ornamentation in the wretchedly meagre and starveling style . . . of the period, cannot be said to have constituted decoration.

The "sham stone, sham columns, sham capitals, and sham cornices" of Regent Street and Regent's Park may have made "a great impression on the not over-

7. *As late as 1896 H. H. Statham found it amusing that Regent Street had once been taken seriously as architecture.* The Quadrant, Regent Street, c. 1896. (Museum of London.)

fastidious taste of the multitude," but could only disgust the cultivated observer.[16] As late as 1896 H. H. Statham, editor of the *Builder,* found it amusing that Regent Street had once been taken seriously as architecture (fig. 7). "It is a curious evidence of the importance which was then attached to this effort in street design," he told the Architectural Association, "that there exist, in the Crace collection [at the British Museum], two complete drawings to scale of the two sides of the street, on long sheets of paper giving successive segments of the design. We laugh at this now."[17]

To the modern reader such passages are very nearly inexplicable, worthy of filing away with treatises commenting on Chaucer's ignorance of the elementary rules of prosody or Shakespeare's failure to maintain the unities of time and place. But it would be unwise to attribute the Victorian rejection of the genius of Adam, Chambers, Soane, and Nash to stupidity and insensitivity. For unless we understand why they detested Palladianism and neoclassicism alike we shall never see the works of their own age as contemporaries did. The blindness of the Victorians to the self-evident (to us) beauties of Georgian and Regency London may seem more comprehensible if we compare the aesthetic revolution of the 1830s with the one we are experiencing today. Both then and now there has been an overreaction to the toppled orthodoxy of the previous generation. The orthodoxy of classicism, with its orders, its unvarying proportions, its claim to determine the rule of beauty

25

in all times, places, and circumstances must have seemed to the intelligent layman of the 1830s as absurd and stultifying as the orthodoxy of the Bauhaus seems today. For decades we dutifully refrained from admiring, or even seriously looking at, all but a select handful of Victorian buildings—and those mostly because they contained exposed ironwork or excessive quantities of glazing or were designed by engineers or discontented prophets. The rest we dismissed as ugly or at best amusing. The Beaux Arts constructions of the twentieth century were too unimportant to merit either hatred or laughter.

How different everything looks today. Just as the contemporaries of Pugin and Ruskin were rediscovering medieval architecture, we are finding once-unregarded masterpieces in our midst. The revelation, when its façade had been cleaned, of the transcendent beauty of Waterhouse's Natural History Museum, of the dazzling invention of Scott's Midland Grand Hotel, of the once-despised glories of Riverside Drive has made it all too easy to lose patience with the quieter, occasional beauties of the style that has transformed our cities since the Second World War. If in rediscovering James Burnham and Stanford White we unjustly denigrate Walter Gropius and Mies van der Rohe, it stems from the zeal of the convert. But it is also because, in their innumerable and well-established disciples and imitators, Mies and Gropius represent an enemy to be fought, a clear and present danger to whatever integrity our cities yet possess.

So did the older neoclassical architects and builders appear to the critics of the 1830s. Just as today's aesthetic revolution has had but the slightest effect on the kind of buildings that are actually going up—the half-hearted references to traditional building forms and historical ornaments by which the Post-Modernists pretend to be revolutionaries reflect confusion and unease in the profession, not an awareness of what has to be done—so the speculative builders of London long continued to produce degraded versions of Regency terraces as if the critical revolution had never occurred. Even worse than the aesthetic shortcomings of the new London streets were the extent and solidity of the old. For all the complaints about the supposed flimsiness of houses erected under ninety-nine-year leases, the bulk of Georgian London was going to outlive its Victorian critics.

The Victorian Alternative

Despite the stubborn persistence of the Georgian fabric and Georgian forms, London as early as 1837 was starting to adopt a Victorian dress, both in new buildings and, through reconstruction and refacing, in old. The new seriousness of the Gothic Revival, as expressed by Pugin and Ruskin and the Ecclesiologists, was less portentous than what was happening within classicism itself: the move from Roman or Greek to Italianate forms, and what to later eyes appeared as a willful coarsening of detail. Architecture grew more emphatic and assertive, with window dressings, porticoes, and other features more deeply incised, more protruding, bigger, everywhere more visible, more unmistakably themselves. Such a rise in intensity enabled architecture better to fulfill its role as the embodiment of a system of ethics and a teacher of truth and morality.

By the 1850s the impulse to monumentality was being expressed in private buildings rather than in public improvements, most notably in commercial structures in the City. The transformation of the City into today's specialized business center produced a dramatic rise in the cost of land, making it uneconomic either to reside there or to continue to use converted dwelling houses for commercial purposes. The new buildings that rose in their place displayed an assertive originality absent elsewhere in Victorian London (figs. 8 and 9).

"Purpose-built" office blocks were going up in Moorgate as early as the 1840s, but the most extensive rebuilding took place in the late 1850s and 1860s. Not only did banks and insurance companies require more space for their own purposes, but they could always count on being able to let extra space as offices. The new structures were not of dingy brick or mendacious stucco but of elaborately ornamented stone. Display was both feasible and desirable. "Though the cost of such decoration as is now indulged in is considerable, the great cost of ground makes the per-centage come out but small," explained the *Builder* in 1864. "Some sort of architectural effect may be advantageous commercially, by attracting attention; and in the case of a bank, a particular sort can help the impression of stability of the concern"[18] (fig. 10).

"There were in the City of London, in my recollection, some thirty years ago," recalled Edward I'Anson in 1864, "certain houses let out in separate floors, and used as offices—but these were few . . . merchants dwelt in the city over their counting-houses, and next to their warehouses, going to their country houses at Edmonton, Tottenham, and Hackney." Not until the 1840s did the purpose-built office block become common. By the time he spoke, "almost all the eligible sites in the City have been converted to this purpose, and . . . there is scarcely a private house left in the City: all are pulled down or converted into offices."[19]

The new office blocks gave the City a monumentality elsewhere lacking in London (fig. 11). "The Roman Corso, the Neapolitan Toledo, or even the glories of the Rue de Rivoli, or the Boulevard Sebastopol, will be overtopped and out-vied by the continuous line of merchant palaces in Cornhill, and Lombard-street, and Bishopsgate-street, and Cheapside," exclaimed one critic in 1866, "all of which are now destined to become more monumental in their materials and proportions, and even more picturesque in their architecture, than the once-deemed matchless streets of the grandest old German towns, or even the glorious canal-ways of Venice herself"[20] (figs. 12 and 13).

No one could have said the same about the new residential developments of the 1860s. The size and pretensions of the houses going up in the terraces, squares, and crescents of South Kensington and Bayswater were fully equal to those of Belgravia, Tyburnia, and Regent's Park, but the effect was less that of monumentality than of a bloated domesticity (fig. 14, colorplate 1). Ground landlords, builders, and tenants looked for respectability, repose, and reassurance rather than personal expression and artistic adventure. The dullness of English speculative architecture was a byword among critics both domestic and foreign. The *Allgemeine Bauzeitung,* published in Vienna, found it insipid and lacking in the kind of aesthetic sense that animates and gives character to a building surface. Streets produced by London's speculative builders lacked any appearance of virtuosity or taste and consisted merely of uniform rows of houses, each as like as one egg to another.[21]

What few critics would grant the speculative builder was that if he built monotonously, he built abundantly; if flimsily, cheaply. London's greatest flaw in the eyes of the aesthete—her interminable stretches of mass-produced houses, each with its walled garden in the rear, each displaying the lowest common denominator of contemporary taste in its street facade—was in fact its greatest glory. No continental city, not even Bremen or Amsterdam, gave as large a proportion of its families the

8. *(left) The new buildings displayed an assertive originality absent elsewhere in Victorian London.* Royal Insurance Company, Lombard Street. From *The Builder* 15 (1857): 319.
9. *(right)* Nos. 48 and 49, Cheapside. From *The Builder* 32 (1874): 809.

blessing of a house of its own, however small and ugly, with its own patch of ground, to cultivate or not as it would. Not until the great council estates of the 1920s and 1930s was such a blessing possible for the poorest of the population, and the still inadequate supply of council houses means to this day that those most in need are least likely to have it. But even in the 1860s many a London artisan enjoyed a degree of separateness, spaciousness, and privacy in his dwelling that a middle-class Parisian or Viennese might have envied.

What produced such rows of residential banality had not changed in essentials since the late eighteenth century. The building agreement whereby the speculator contracted to put up a certain number of houses of a specified value, often according to plans and elevations prescribed by the estate; the building lease granted as the houses approached completion; the restrictive covenants as to repair and occupation; the requirement that at the end of the lease the building revert to the ground landlord in a proper and substantial state: all followed patterns fixed by the great landed proprietors of the Georgian metropolis. The structure of the building industry itself, in which small and undercapitalized craftsmen were able to survive and prosper alongside giant firms like Cubitt's, remained in its main outlines what it had been under Charles II. The operation of the leasehold system, the general approach to estate management by which the ground landlords strove to insure that on their ground the most valuable houses possible be built, and the methods by

10. *"Architectural effect . . . in the case of a bank can . . . help the impression of stability of the concern."* National Provincial Bank, Threadneedle Street. From *The Builder* 23 (1865): 909.

which builders raised their capital and put up their houses all reflected continuity rather than change.[22]

Although the mood of optimistic excitement and complacency that accompanied the making of Regent Street had evaporated, new streets continued to be cut through the older built-up areas, in the name of slum clearance and the relief of traffic congestion. Sanitary improvements, particularly after the formation of the Metropolitan Board of Works in 1855, were pursued with vigor. Up to the middle of the century London remained preeminent in Europe not only in size and wealth, but in its devotion to civic improvements. Such preeminence would shortly be challenged, but in 1850 London remained for continental cities the standard against which their own shortcomings had to be measured.

From the perspective of the *Allgemeine Bauzeitung* of that year—before either Paris or Vienna had embarked on its program of physical regeneration—London represented the model to be admired and imitated, both for its past achievements and for its present policies: "In no city of Europe in recent years has more been done for internal improvement, both with respect to the beautification of streets and in sanitary respects, than in London." It applauded the demolition of the slums of St. Giles's and the related formation of New Oxford Street, which it described as among the most beautiful erected in London in recent times, far surpassing Regent Street architecturally.

It found most to praise in London's sewer system and water supply. The sanitary

30

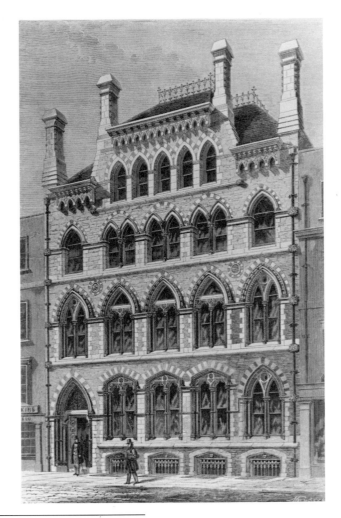

11. *(opposite) The new office blocks gave the City a monumentality elsewhere lacking in London.* Crosby House, Bishopsgate. Lithograph by Robert Dudley. (Museum of London.)
12. *(left) "The continuous line of merchant palaces in Cornhill, and Lombard-street, and Bishopsgate-street, and Cheapside."* National Discount Company, Cornhill. From *The Builder* 16 (1858): 11.
13. *(right)* Another view of Bishopsgate Street. From *The Builder* 19 (1861): 125.

crisis that was to call into existence the Metropolitan Board of Works did not require the establishment of a sewer system where none had existed, but the rehabilitation and extension of one that surpassed in magnitude the aqueducts of antiquity and was being continually enlarged and improved. However inadequate and overtaxed, London's sewer system was unique in the modern world. The water system, "which serves every single house up to the third story, will be extended even to the poorest houses and lodgings, whereby everybody will share this true luxury and comfort of life."[23] The provision of running water to a significant proportion of London's dwellings seemed unimaginable luxury in contemporary Vienna and Paris. "Every English house has a cistern on its top floor, which serves all its rooms and water closets [*cabinets d'aisance*]," reported César Daly in 1855. "The privy [*fosse d'aisance*] does not exist. Waste matters pass through a drain into the public sewer, with all the waste water [*eaux ménagères*] of the town, and from there everything is transported to the river." We have heard much of sewer lines with outlets at a higher level than their intake; it is reassuring to learn that sometimes, at least, they per-

14. *The size and pretensions of the houses going up in Bayswater were fully equal to those of Belgravia, Tyburnia, and Regent's Park, but the effect was less that of monumentality than of*

a bloated domesticity. Westbourne Terrace, Hyde Park. Lithograph by G. Hawkins after J. Johnston, c. 1850–1855. (Museum of London.) See also colorplate 1.

formed as they were intended. "I have traveled about a distance of four miles in these sewers," Daly reported, "and I have been able to observe that the quantity of water discharged into them . . . has so diluted everything that one only notices dirty water; I was surprised to find that the odor was much less offensive than I would have imagined."[24]

But it was not just in sanitary engineering that London seemed outstanding. Théophile Gautier, certainly no anglophile, granted it in 1852 a quality of over-powering grandeur. "The general aspect of London has something which astonishes, and causes a sort of stupor—it is in truth a capital in the sense of civilisation," he wrote in his *Caprices et zigzags;* "all is great, splendid, disposed according to the last improvements. . . . Paris, in this respect is at least a hundred years behindhand, and, to a certain extent, must always be inferior to London."[25]

A decade later he need not have made such a concession. For by then Paris had at least equaled and was striving to surpass London in outward splendor. Vienna had embarked on the creation of the Ringstrasse and would soon outshine London in magnificence. London, to be sure, could look forward to a succession of improvements: the Victoria Embankment, Queen Victoria Street, Northumberland Avenue, Charing Cross Road, Shaftesbury Avenue, and the less visible but more significant reformation of its sewerage and water system. By the 1890s it was beginning a series of projects of civic embellishment that revived, in another guise, the spirit that had informed the age of Nash: Admiralty Arch and the Mall, the new government buildings in Whitehall, Kingsway and the Aldwych, and a County Hall to confront the Palace of Westminster from across the Thames. Yet in the eyes of the world, and in its own as well, London's supremacy, in all save size, wealth, and population, had long since passed to continental rivals. First Paris, then Vienna came to stand for the city of the future.

4

The New Paris

n Paris the ancien régime lasted until 1852. Neither the Revolution of 1789 nor the actions of the first Napoleon fundamentally altered the appearance or nature of the French capital. Already an anachronism under Louis XVI, its "dense, dark, intricate streets . . . where lanes still followed the ramparts of Louis the Stout and Philip Augustus"[1] were even less suited to the needs of the still more populous and vastly richer metropolis of Louis-Philippe. No great conflagration had, as in London, swept away the medieval city, and schemes for massive reconstruction remained just that.

Apart from the razing of the Bastille and the changed use of many buildings, the Revolution had left Paris physically intact.[2] On the other hand, it did bring to an end many of the earlier legal obstacles to improvement and redevelopment. Property belonging to emigrés and the church, amounting to one-eighth of the city's total area, changed hands. Much of this land—in particular outside the line of boulevards consisted of pleasure grounds, and was divided into small parcels and turned into building sites.[3] But the main body of the densely built city of more than half a million residents remained untouched.

Napoleon I intended major structural alterations yet put few into effect. Edward I'Anson, speaking in the late 1850s, described Paris during the reign of Charles X as belonging to another age. The place de la Concorde was then "a vast plain of mud in Winter, and of shifting sand in Summer." The site of the western extension of the Louvre toward the Tuileries was occupied by a cluster of "closely-packed houses, booths, and mean shops." Except for a few new monuments like the Arc de Triomphe and a few new streets like the rue de Rivoli, Paris still looked much as it had under Louis XIV[4] (fig. 15).

Nor did fundamental changes take place under Louis-Philippe. "The inner streets were narrow, crooked, crowded, ill built, and very unsavoury," recalled a correspondent of the *Morning Post,* writing in 1862: there were "huge, tall houses overshadowing the way, from whose *gouttières* the foot-passenger shrank in awe, and down whose streets the water flowed unheeded, or stagnated undisturbed" (fig. 16). Few streets were wide enough for one vehicle to pass another, and most seemed "purposely laid out to perplex and bewilder the traveller."[5] Practically all of Paris was crowded into the area confined by the line of the *grands boulevards*

15. *With the exception of a few new streets like the rue de Rivoli, Paris had not "materially changed in aspect since the time of Louis the XIVth."* Rue de Rivoli looking westward, Tuileries Gardens to the left. (Musée Carnavalet.)

north of the Seine, and pushing toward but not reaching the boulevard Montparnasse on the south. The boulevards themselves occupied the line of fortifications, dating from the time of Charles V and Philip Augustus, that Louis XIV had had demolished. They remained a semirural promenade through most of the eighteenth century. Within the built-up area, streets were no wider than fifteen to twenty-five feet, and usually much narrower. The closest to being thoroughfares were the parallel rues Saint-Denis and Saint-Martin on the right bank and the connecting rues de la Harpe and Saint-Jacques on the left, which pierced the city from north to south (fig. 17). No practical route existed from east to west, except that provided by the Seine and its quais.[6]

Much of the Paris of the ancien régime, both the streets of today's first seven *arrondissements* and the high, narrow, backward-sloping houses that line them, is still intact. Today such back passages contrast delightfully with the standardized regularity of the rest of the city and are eagerly sought by the affluent looking for desirable flats and the tourist looking for the picturesque. But down to the 1850s such streets and such houses *were* Paris, except for the new, more regular and spacious suburban developments to the west and northwest. They were then being deserted by the rich and moderately well-to-do as quickly as the new districts had space for them, and avoided by all but the most intrepid tourist. For however carefully preserved such streets have been, the loathsome odors that then pervaded them are mercifully no more.

"To stand close to a defective sewer today is to recapture the essence of early- and mid-Victorian towns," writes Anthony Wohl in his study of English urban sanitation.[7] Paris lacked the luxury even of defective sewers. It is a measure of the foulness of its streets and dwellings that English visitors, their expectations lowered and their sensibilities coarsened by the sanitary conditions of their own towns, were invariably horrified by the stench and filth of Paris. "In a city where everything intended to meet the eye is converted into graceful ornament," wrote Mrs. Trollope in 1835, "where the shops and coffee-houses have the air of fairy palaces . . . where the women look too delicate to belong wholly to earth . . . you are shocked and disgusted at every step you take . . . by sights and smells that may not be described."[8]

The French had long admitted, and deplored, the sanitary inferiority of Paris to London. The stairs and public passages of its houses stank of urine, wrote Louis-Sebastien Mercier in the 1780s; the conveniences on the landings emitted a pestiferous stench; the backs of houses were disgusting, washed only by the rain. In London, by contrast, people did not relieve themselves against the walls of houses in the street, but retired to uninhabited back passages or used the well-maintained privies in the yards behind the houses.[9]

Domestic piped water came late to Paris. Before the great improvements of the 1850s and 1860s water carriers had sold from the streets, but "the poor, who cannot afford to pay a penny for a pailful," would crowd "round the standcock with domestic utensils . . . to lay in a day's supply, and even scooping water out from the gutters." The system of waste disposal, if ingenious, left much to be desired. "Faecal matters are stored in cesspools below the houses, or they are received into casks, which, when full, are carted away." The liquid contents of the cesspools were emptied into the gutters.[10] Mortality statistics reflect the consequences. The same cholera epidemic that in 1832 killed 5,500 of London's 1,778,000 inhabitants, killed 20,000 of Paris's 861,400.[11]

Paris had yet to become the city of light. As late as 1850, many streets were lighted by oil lamps suspended by wires from houses on opposite sides.[12] One moved from the brilliantly lighted boulevards "into outer darkness," observed Mrs. Trollope, "and there is not a little country town in England which is not incomparably better lighted."[13]

Nor was the architecture of the typical street calculated to compensate for the dirt, the darkness, and the danger. To the eye of a contemporary of Ruskin, trained to perceive beauty above all else in surface ornament, such a street had no architecture at all (fig. 18). Neither did it possess the regularity and subtle proportions that the building acts had imposed on eighteenth-century London streets or that the owners of leasehold estates there required of their builders. In Paris, houses varied in size, stories varied in height, windows failed to align with their neighbors, buildings jutted forward to create bottlenecks: no organizing principle unified the street. There was only the uniform plainness of the plastered walls. The streets managed to be at once disorderly and monotonous, neither coherent nor picturesque (figs. 19 and 20). The varied fan lights, the porticoed doorways, the decorative ironwork separating area from street, the lamp standards, the details of

16. *"The inner streets were narrow, crooked, crowded, ill-built, and very unsavoury . . . the water flowed unheeded or stagnated undisturbed."* Marville, rue de la Colombe. (Musée Carnavalet. Photo Lauros-Giraudon.)

brickwork that gave aesthetic distinction to Georgian London had no counterparts in Paris. Only where a classical *porte cochère* announced the unseen presence of an *hôtel particulier,* or town mansion, did the domestic streets offer specifically architectural delight.

17. *The closest to being thoroughfares were the parallel rues Saint-Denis and Saint-Martin and the rues de la Harpe and Saint-Jacques.* Marville, rue Saint-Denis. (Musée Carnavalet. Photo Lauros-Giraudon.)

Yet for all its congestion and disorder, for all its sanitary inadequacies, the Paris of Balzac and Dumas *fils* was a rich and cultivated metropolis with pleasures and satisfactions no other city in the world could match. Nor were such pleasures invariably hidden behind *portes cochères*. Long before Haussmann, the line of

18. *(above) To the eye of a contemporary of Ruskin such a street had no architecture at all.* Rue du Faubourg Saint-Martin, looking south in 1984. (Evelyn Benesch.)

19. *(below) The streets managed to be at once disorderly and monotonous, neither coherent nor picturesque.* Marville, rue Boucher, first arrondissement. (Musée Carnavalet. Photo Lauros-Giraudon.)

20. *(opposite)* Marville, rue de la Grande Truanderie. (Musée Carnavalet. Photo Lauros-Giraudon.)

boulevards extending from the place de la Bastille to the Madeleine prefigured in their shape and contents the pleasures he would lavish on the rest of the metropolis.

The interior boulevards "have become through the expansion of Paris agreeable promenades lined with fine houses, shops, restaurants, theaters and cafés," observed a guidebook of 1828.[14] In attempting to visualize the scene along the *grands boulevards* at any period between the reign of Charles X (1824–30) and the early years of the Third Republic, we must forget what we know about that congested and rather shoddy stretch of roadway today. Instead we should try to extract everything that is most appealing about the boulevards Saint-Germain and Montparnasse and the streets that intersect them, the Champs-Elysées and the Sixteenth, the Centre Pompidou and the gentrifying Marais, and arrange it, jostling for space, from the boulevard du Temple to the boulevard de la Madeleine.

To live either on or as close as possible to the boulevards was the goal of those Parisians able to choose their place of residence. Accordingly the principal building speculations of the 1820s, 1830s, and 1840s hugged the northwestern borders of the *grands boulevards,* with the district of the rue de la Chaussée d'Antin the most desirable of all (fig. 21). Paris had been expanding, particularly toward the north and the west, throughout the eighteenth century. Apart from the aristocratic faubourg Saint-Germain on the left bank, the most extensive building took place on the right. By the 1770s and 1780s new streets were being opened north of the western boulevards and in the vicinity of the rue du Faubourg Saint-Honoré, north of the Champs-Elysées.[15] But the great boom came after the Restoration, with the most rapid expansion, as in London, in the years 1820–26. During those years the districts of Saint Georges, north of the western boulevards; François Ier, between the avenue des Champs-Elysées and the Seine; and Passy, in the present sixteenth arrondissement, became areas of feverish speculation.[16] Mrs. Trollope was struck by "the rapid increase of handsome dwellings . . . as white and bright as newborn mushrooms, in the northwestern division of Paris." She was reminded of "the early days of Russell Square, and all the region about it. The Church of the Madeleine, instead of being . . . nearly at the extremity of Paris, has now a new city behind it." She predicted that Paris would be "seen running out of town with the same active pace that London has done before her; and twenty years hence the Bois de Boulogne may very likely be as thickly peopled as the Regent's Park is now."[17]

A report from the chamber of commerce in 1847 supports the comparison with the activities of Burton, Cubitt, and others in the development of Bloomsbury. Formerly, it remarked, property owners built houses either for their own use or as a permanent capital investment; but the recent growth in population, the cutting up of large urban estates, and the opening of new neighborhoods had turned building into an "industrial enterprise" in which the production and sale of houses was carried on as with any other manufactured product. The resulting speculations had resulted in periodic overproduction and, during the previous three decades, periodic crises.[18]

The demolition and reconstruction associated with the Second Empire had already begun under Louis-Philippe. "Here are whole quarters rising above the ground . . . new streets are cutting here and there, houses demolishing to widen others, and paving and gas-lighting . . . introduced into the dullest and apparently most impassable localities," the *Builder* reported in 1847. "The gay capital of fashion, taste, and elegance seems to be rebuilding,—to be rising anew out of the

21. *The district of the rue de la Chausée d'Antin[is] the most desirable of all.* Marville, rue de la Chaussée d'Antin. (Musée Carnavalet. Photo Lauros-Giraudon.)

ashes of that old Paris, whose dark, dirty, narrow streets,—whose quaint, crazy-looking houses . . . formed so striking a contrast with the splendour and magnificence of some of its public buildings."[19]

Not just the quantity of new building, but the luxury of the erections, "indicative of a taste for ornament and decoration, which, in the richer quarters of the town, are lavished with a profuse hand on the exterior of the houses inhabited by the middling classes,"[20] excited the wonder of contemporaries. For César Daly in 1840, "the need for luxury and magnificence has overrun all classes of society; one is no longer content with what is necessary." Public places also responded to the demand: cafés, theaters, concert halls vied with each other's paintings and gilt; their decorators searched for inspiration in "all the ages of the past and all the countries of the world." A revolution had taken place in the domestic architecture of Paris during the 1830s:

> Stone has banished plaster, and marble, formerly reserved for the basements of very refined shops, now displays its thousand colours on the façade of the upper stories, where one sees it surrounded by rich sculpture. The interiors follow the same path. Fireplaces, all in choice marble, are everywhere surmounted by mirrors of a sort found rarely in the houses of the English aristocracy.[21]

But however impressed contemporaries were by the improvements to old Paris and the creation of a new Paris beyond the boulevards, the magnitude of the operations of the Second Empire would dwarf them in retrospect. Begun with the aim of making Paris as clean and spacious and modern as London, they ended by making her the embodiment of nineteenth-century urban civilization, a realized ideal toward which cities throughout the world would aspire.

Paris Remade, 1852–1870

"The second of December 1851 had two great victims: the Republic and Old Paris," wrote Raymond Escholier shortly before the outbreak of the First World War. "We know today that the Republic was only wounded, but the old Paris, struck in the heart by Baron Haussmann, never rose again. . . . Of the old picturesque city . . . hardly anything remains save a few *hôtels* dishonored by advertising placards, a few blocks of stinking houses, a few notorious alleys." Physically, more remained (and remains) of the earlier Paris than Escholier suggests, but the fundamental character of the city was utterly transformed. "In eighteen years, the city had to change in form, even in its way of life and activities," Jeanne Gaillard has concluded; everything was affected: "employment, lodging, the family."[22] No one questions that Haussmann made Paris totally different from what it had been in 1852. There is less agreement on why he did so. What lay behind the decision of Napoleon III to devote so much of the energies and resources of his regime to the rebuilding and embellishment of his capital?

One answer frequent at the time and still widely accepted is that the whole operation was intended to prevent popular insurrection: cutting great swaths, too broad to be blocked by barricades, through working-class districts would break up the proletariat into *quartiers* geographically isolated one from another.[23] The long, straight avenues would permit the rapid deployment of troops from one part of the city to another in case of an outbreak and at the same time provide artillery with unbroken lines of fire. Amédée de Cesena explicitly proposed this interpretation in his guidebook to Paris in 1864.[24] It has since become a historical commonplace, particularly satisfying because it seems hard-headed and unsentimental in its denial of aesthetic, sanitary, and philanthropic motives.

The difficulty with the interpretation is that it uses a local and temporary explanation to account for an approach to urban design that had dominated theoretical writings on the subject since the sixteenth century and was being put into practice in cities that did not fear revolution as well as in those that did. Long avenues radiating at equal intervals from concentric open spaces can be found in the plans of

Wren for London and L'Enfant for Washington as well as in the Rome of Sixtus V, the Versailles of Louis XIV, and the Karlsruhe of Karl Wilhelm. Descartes's preference for straight streets and the geometrically regular was shared in principle by nearly everyone in the seventeenth century and by the vast majority in the nineteenth.

By the time of the Second Empire such aesthetic preferences had been reinforced by the newer concerns of sanitary reformers, convinced of the healthfulness of open spaces. The objection to rebuilding existing cities along Cartesian lines was less theoretical than practical: it would simply cost too much money. This was why no one, least of all Wren, seriously expected his scheme for London to be put into effect after 1666. Newly founded cities—Philadelphia, St. Petersburg, Washington—or newly laid out quarters of older cities—Bloomsbury, the New Town of Edinburgh, the Amalienborg quarter of Copenhagen—could indulge in the luxury of spacious, geometrical layout; but high property values in existing built-up areas made any basic alteration in the street pattern prohibitively expensive.

The criticism Haussmann faced while prefect of the Seine, the kind that ultimately resulted in his resignation, was not that his program would inhibit popular insurrection but that it was too costly. To defend on purely aesthetic and sanitary grounds the expense and disruption that the works of demolition and reconstruction involved was not enough. Every possible argument had to be brought to justify the upheaval of life in the capital. A very persuasive argument was that it would stimulate the economy both of Paris and of France, at once providing immediate employment for labor and capital and creating an infrastructure for future growth. The military and counterrevolutionary argument provided further justification, but there is no reason to think it the sole motive of the regime, and little reason to think it the primary motive. If it had been, the whole operation would have proved an exercise in futility, for it neither saved the emperor from downfall nor prevented the establishment of the Commune in 1870. That the Third Republic, while reversing so many of the policies of the Empire, continued Haussmann's projects for Paris virtually unchanged suggests a general consensus on the desirability of his approach to urbanism. There are no grounds for questioning the sincerity of Haussmann's statement in his memoirs that, although his improvements did in fact serve military purposes, such were not the original cause of their being undertaken.[25]

No military reason dictates that the boulevard Malesherbes take off from the place de la Madeleine toward the northwest at precisely the angle that the boulevard de la Madeleine takes to the northeast. If the eastward extension of the rue de Rivoli and the line of the boulevard de Sébastopol cut up the politically dangerous faubourg Saint-Antoine into manageably isolated segments,[26] they also satisfied a crying need for north-south and east-west thoroughfares through the congested metropolis. Boulevards cut through working-class quarters could be said to perform counterrevolutionary functions, but what equivalent justification could be given for the wide avenues that converged on the place de l'Etoile? The likelihood of the bourgeois residents of the eighth and the sixteenth arrondissements throwing up barricades and needing to be mown down by the imperial artillery was slight. The argument that the boulevards, depending on their location, were intended either to give pleasure to the middle classes or to oppress the working classes is like James Thurber's cook's explanation of night as being made partly for rest, partly as a punishment for the wicked.

Had there been no uprising in 1848 and had considerations of public order not been central to the regime, the program of *percées* and reconstruction might have proceeded with less speed and determination; but the nature of the program would not have differed fundamentally from what it was. From the point of view of sanitation, broad avenues were essential to ventilate unhealthy neighborhoods, to clear away disease-ridden blocks, and to provide lines along which main sewers could be constructed. From the point of view of communications, the flow of traffic through Paris could have been aided only by the cutting of streets through its heart: either a few extremely wide ones such as were in fact built, or many more of moderate width. From the aesthetic point of view, straight lines, symmetrical layouts, the termination of vistas by monumental objects, and architectural uniformity seemed, given France's long commitment to classicism, self-evidently desirable. From the economic point of view, the interests of property owners and businesses alike in the older quarters demanded streets that would be at least as broad and handsome as those which had already been built in the competing newer quarters to the north and the west. As the writer of Haussmann's obituary wrote, "it is hardly fair to quarrel with the memory of Haussmann for having accomplished, a little too soon for some of us, what some one else must inevitably have carried out not long after."[27]

Whatever their ultimate justification, the initial impact of the works of the fifties and sixties was one of shock and disorientation, as age-old landmarks and seemingly permanent street patterns vanished overnight (fig. 22). "Those parts of the city which are in a state of demolition," wrote the American journalist Henry T. Tuckerman, "present enormous high walls with the irregular smoke-stains of the dismantled chimneys, moving zig-zag higher and higher, and looking ready to topple

22. *The initial impact of the works of the fifties and sixties was one of shock and disorientation.* Demolition in rue de la Harpe, in preparation for the boulevard Saint-Michel, 1857. (Musée Carnavalet.)

over as you slowly pass through a crush of vehicles and debris of mortar and stones." Yet renewal proceeded as fast as destruction. He was equally struck by "the fresh tint of nearly every structure along the principal thoroughfares—the effect of whitewash, paint, or the mason's hammer renewing the face of the stone-work, and giving a singular lightness to the streets; sidewalks, too, have multiplied, and the whole aspect of Paris made new, commodious, and progressive."[28]

The first two major operations involved the southward extension of the boulevard de Strasbourg, begun under the Second Republic, by the boulevard de Sébastopol, which in turn would become, as it crossed the Ile de la Cité, the boulevard du Palais, and, on the left bank, the boulevard Saint-Michel; and the eastward extension of the rue de Rivoli to join the rue Saint-Antoine. Together the two lines would form the *grande croisée,* providing long-needed north-south and east-west thoroughfares, crossing at the place du Châtelet.

The rue de Rivoli as created by Napoleon I had gone no farther east than the Louvre, but by 1855 it had been extended as far east as the place Saint-Jean. "All the houses that are going up so quickly between the Louvre and the Hôtel de Ville are constructed with great luxury of decoration, too much perhaps, since the expense that it requires raises the rent to a considerable level, even for the upper stories," observed the *Revue générale de l'architecture.* Meanwhile the boulevard de Strasbourg, open for eighteen months, and "completely furnished with wide pavements and lamp standards," remained entirely unbuilt. Apart from its northern extremity, close to the Gare de l'Est, speculative builders had yet to be attracted to the new line. Even at the junction with the boulevard Saint-Denis, houses that had long been built up to the first-floor level were only then gradually being brought to completion. The left bank was in more desperate need of the stimulus promised by Haussmann's programs of demolition and reconstruction than the right, yet it responded even more slowly to the improvements it did receive. There demolition for the rue des Ecoles had taken place two years earlier, but no construction had followed, either of the new roadway or along its route: it presented the appearance of a town in ruins, "a vast and sad desert . . . and in bad weather a pile of mud."[29]

The boulevard de Sébastopol was opened as far as the Seine on 5 April 1858. "Venetian masts were erected on each side at regular distances, from which waved national banners, bearing figures or inscriptions . . . with the initial and crown of Napoleon III. . . . The different regiments garrisoned in Paris marched to the sounds of the music of different bands."[30] By 1861 "magnificent edifices" bordered the boulevard, according to *L'Illustration,* which heralded its opening as "the rejuvenation of this quarter, formerly one of narrow and unhealthy streets, and worm-eaten houses."[31] A correspondent of the *Morning Post* the following year praised both the architecture and the businesses of the boulevard. "The shops are as fine as any in Paris; but there is this peculiarity . . . : the upper floors are almost exclusively devoted to business. It is here the merchants who trade with Manchester and our great towns have their counting-houses."[32] Paris, though, was never to create a specialized business district like the City of London: wholesale and retail trade, manufacture, and residence coexisted in the new Paris as they had in the old.

The rebuilding of the Ile de la Cité deprived that quarter of virtually all its housing and made it instead a concentrated mass of administrative buildings. The process required the demolition of the tightly packed slum that crowded around Notre Dame and Sainte Chapelle, which had vied with the area between the Louvre and the Hôtel de Ville in squalor and misery. Across the Seine the left bank extension of the boulevard de Sébastopol, today's boulevard Saint-Michel, was opened as far as the Cluny Museum by 1859 (fig. 23). "In all directions ancient streets are widened out, and put in proper alignments; new boulevarts break out; the restoring and embellishment of religious edifices continue; and many squares will shortly, by the verdure of the lawns and beauty of flowers, delight the inhabitants of the most populous quarters of Paris."[33] The preliminary works for the boulevard Saint-Germain, which would ultimately provide a link on the left bank between the eastern and western extremities of the *grands boulevards,* also began in 1859.

Meanwhile the Champs-Elysées were being replanted, rearranged, and brought to something like their present appearance. By 1860 the whole area between the place de la Concorde, the Rond-Point, and the Cours-la-Reine had been covered with lawns, clusters of trees, walks and benches; "the metamorphosis was complete and the result charming."[34]

The formal opening on 13 August 1861 of the boulevard Malesherbes, jutting off to the northwest from the place de la Madeleine, was the great event of the year (fig. 24). "All the Parisians still in Paris have, since last week, made the pilgrimage to the boulevard Malesherbes," according to X. Feyrnet in *L'Illustration;*

---

23. *Across the Seine the left bank extension of the boulevard de Sébastopol, today's boulevard Saint-Michel, was opened as far as the Cluny Museum by 1859.* Boulevard Sébastopol, rive gauche, from *L'Illustration.* (Musée Carnavalet.)

Vue du boulevard Sébastopol (rive gauche), prise des Thermes.

24. *The formal opening on 13 August 1861 of the boulevard Malesherbes was the great event of the year.* Boulevard Malesherbes with decorations, from the place de la Madeleine. (Musée Carnavalet.)

"all of us, rich and poor, workers and idlers, the old and the young, on foot, by horse, or by carriage, have tried out the great new road . . . and we have all found it very fine and very worthy of ourselves."[35] Although executed under the Second Empire, the boulevard had been planned in the time of Napoleon I. It turned slightly to the west at the crossing of the rue de la Pépinière, thereby enabling the new church of Saint-Augustin to terminate the vista. From there it proceeded to the neighborhood of the parc Monceau and the lively suburban development growing up around it.[36]

Here there was no concern to break up a potentially insurgent proletarian quarter or to ventilate an overcrowded and disease-ridden district, as in the boulevard de Sébastopol and the extended rue de Rivoli. The streets that the new boulevard intersected and the houses sacrificed in its path were new and costly. What this improvement did was to combine the aesthetic purpose of rendering the place de la Madeleine symmetrical—providing a western exit precisely balancing that of the boulevard de la Madeleine to the east—with the economic one of encouraging the building development of the seventeenth by giving it a convenient and splendid link with the fashionable center. Yet on the surface the construction of the boulevard Malesherbes precisely paralleled that of the *grande croisée*: expropriation, demolition, creation of an infrastructure of sewerage, water, and gas supply; provision of broad, tree-lined pedestrian walks, and the erection by building speculators of lines of ornamental blocks of flats, with shop facilities at street level. That the boulevard Malesherbes is today what it was from the beginning, the more elegant street from the standpoint both of residents and commercial establishments, and that the façades of the boulevard de Sébastopol have fallen into disrepair ought not to obscure their formal and structural identity.

Like the earlier boulevard, the new one was opened with "tall masts with banners; and . . . numerous garlands and shields, and at night stars of gas; the yet unoccupied ground . . . and the faces of earth and rock, actual cliffs, left by the excavation of the road, were screened by tiers of festoons of leaves, suspended from poles."[37] To create the roadway, no fewer than 84 houses had been sacrificed. Already 114 new buildings bordered the boulevard, and, said Baron Haussmann at the ceremonial opening, "it is impossible to foresee how many will arise on the immense plots of ground that border the streets that cross it and which have been unused up to now, for want of outlets."[38]

The speed with which the whole was completed astonished Parisians and foreigners alike. At the start of 1861 the bulk of the work of demolition and excavation had not even begun.[39] By August 300,000 cubic meters of earth had been removed in order to prepare a level, macadamized roadway. Elegant cast-iron lamp standards and lines of trees ornamented the boulevard. All that in six months of frenzied and purposeful activity. "Yes, six months to pull down so many houses, to bring this immense road through gigantic cuttings, to raise these stately *hôtels*, it is the realization of the impossible. . . . Soon we shall not be content unless we construct a palace between lunch and dinner."[40]

The new boulevard promised to raise property values on the streets that it intersected. "This boulevard is full of surprises," Feyrnet informed his readers. "At every moment one comes across some familiar street that one didn't expect to find there, and that is itself very surprised to be seen. They cut a poor figure, these old and modest streets, beside their proud younger sister, and, if their walls have ears, they hear mortifying exclamations: Oh! how narrow she is! how badly dressed [*mal tournée*]! how miserably built! Isn't she ashamed to show herself with her dirty façades, her queer windows, her worm-eaten doors?" He cited as an example the rue de la Pépinière, which "formerly passed for having a very respectable width, and enjoyed, in the neighborhood, a certain consideration; some even granted it majesty and pardoned its want of foot pavements and the excessive liberty it took with alignments. . . . Today, what a fall from grace! A myopic provincial asked me the name of that *lane*."

Yet however it might suffer from comparison, a street intersected by a boulevard was sure to participate in its prosperity.

> The most fortunate people in Paris are, for the moment, the tenants in the ex–rue de Rumfort. . . . They lived in a corner cut off from the world, practically lost; no noise, no movement, no distractions; they could . . . watch the grass grow between the paving stones; the air they breathed was charged with boredom. . . . One bright day, without changing residence and without rise in rent, they found themselves in the middle of Paris . . . they went to sleep in the rue de Rumfort, they woke up on the boulevard Malesherbes.[41]

For all the forced brightness and exaggeration of the article, the underlying assumption was and remains characteristically Parisian: that civilization and happiness are to be found only in Paris, and especially in those parts blessed with the greatest concentration of life, the highest intensity of activity. Movement and noise are virtues, quiet and retirement foreshadow the tomb.

The impact of the boulevard Malesherbes extended to the plaine de Monceau. Of that still mostly empty district, Haussmann exclaimed, "it is not a new district, it is an entire city that is being founded there, and no one can calculate its future development!"[42] The location, at a comparatively high elevation adjacent to the growing northwestern outskirts, was as important as the amenities of the parc Monceau itself. At the top of the heights separating the quartier de l'Europe from Asnières and Neuilly, it enjoyed the clean and healthy air so prized by contemporaries. Now connected with the most fashionable and prosperous portions of the New Paris by the fine new boulevard, its future seemed assured. The continuing prestige of London as a model of fashion and elegance was reflected in the attempt to name the area around the parc Monceau *le West End*. If you are asked where the boulevard Malesherbes leads, advised Feyrnet, "answer boldly: to *West End*. . . . One could give it a French name, but that would have been vulgar; an English name was far more fashionable."[43]

Underneath the impressive new streets and boulevards was going forward a mammoth program of sewer construction designed once and for all to end the reputation of Paris as externally dazzling but rotten within. By 1862 César Daly, while admitting that Paris still lacked a collection of broad streets comparable to those of London, thought that in all other respects it now surpassed the British capital.[44] The *Morning Post* agreed that London fared poorly in comparison with the new boulevards of Paris:

> Suppose the line of the Strand, Fleet-street, Cheapside, and Cornhill pulled down and rebuilt in the most stately manner—the like with Holborn and Oxford-street; let them imagine wide streets from the Great Eastern, Great Northern, and Euston-square stations to the Bank, and thence to London Bridge; similar great arteries running directly and traversing London from north to south, and crossing each of our bridges—our friends may then form some little idea of what has been done, and shortly will be completed, at Paris.[45]

Despite the predictions of Haussmann and the hopes of the Pereire brothers, it was not the boulevard Malesherbes that was to lead directly to the most fashionable new quarter of Paris, but the Champs-Elysées. In the 1860s the Arc de Triomphe still stood at the western entrance to Paris, with scattered villa settlements to the west and south. At the Etoile itself houses were accumulating, and streets were being laid out, "lined with elegant residences, where not long ago could be seen nothing but waste-lands," according to *L'Illustration*. "In Paris, it only needs a few years to transform a swamp into a magnificent quarter."[46] Great public works were shortly to commence in the neighborhood. "Vast works of excavation have been carried out to take the crest off the butte de l'Etoile and to isolate the Arc de Triomphe, which, in a few years, will find itself surrounded by a circle of palaces, separated by broad boulevards and fine avenues," reported the *Revue générale de l'architecture* in 1863. To the east, that part of the avenue des Champs-Elysées between the Rond-Point and the Etoile was seeing fine houses and costly *hôtels* replacing old and mean dwellings "that disgraced the most magnificent entrance to the great city."[47]

Accompanying the annexation of the present outer arrondissements and the expansion of the city to the outer fortifications in 1860 was the removal of the customs wall, dating from 1786–88; the exterior boulevards that ran along its length were incorporated into the main street system. By 1863 the transformation of the outer boulevards was far advanced on the right bank and had begun on the left. The result would be "a vast promenade, the finest and most extensive in the world," that might become within twenty years, César Daly predicted, "the rendez-vous of elegant Paris," then confined within the existing boulevards des Italiens and de la Madeleine.[48] The exterior boulevards have never achieved such a role, but the assumption of the transience of fashion and the inevitability of changes in social geography is revealing. Far from fearing change, the nineteenth century had domesticated it and found in it cause for exhilaration and pride. Daly could contemplate an ever-expanding Paris, with newly favored districts replacing older ones as they faded into somnolence and decay. The health of Paris depended not on what happened in any particular quarter but on its growth and vitality as a total organism.

The 1860s saw the attempted rejuvenation of existing quarters as well as the development of new. The covering over of the southern reaches of the canal Saint-Martin to form the boulevard Richard Lenoir, begun in 1861, was an example. Other works included the replanting of the place du Trône (today's place de la Nation), and the improvement of the old interior boulevards. New trees were planted, new street lamps installed, together with structures for the use of cab drivers and for the omnibus service, newspaper kiosks, and others for the sale of bonbons and oranges. "If Rome has its monuments, its ruins and its memories, London its rustic parks, its squares, its wide streets, its vast docks and its lively river, no city today can be compared with Paris for its gardens, its elegant parks, its rich foliage and its ravishing flowers," exclaimed Daly in 1863.[49]

"In reality, Paris today . . . is already so different from Paris yesterday that one would call it almost a new city," wrote Amédée de Cesena in 1864. He scoffed at those who regretted the destruction of the familiar and the picturesque, preferring narrow and tortuous streets to broad and regular avenues, decrepit and unhealthy lodgings to elegant and salubrious dwellings. "If the hammer of the demolishers has annihilated some vestiges of the past that one would have liked to preserve . . . it destroys even more haunts of thieves and places of debauchery." He predicted the rapid growth of new towns around the boulevard du Prince Eugène (now the boulevard Voltaire), in the plaine de Monceau, and south of the Champs-Elysées. He exulted in the spaciousness of the streets being pushed through the older parts of Paris. "Streets that were once famous for their breadth and extent are today no more than of the second, or even of the third rank."[50]

The Exhibition of 1867 provided a particular impetus, not only for works in and around the Trocadéro and the champ de Mars, but throughout a Paris that was preparing itself for the critical inspection of visitors from all over the world. "Go where you will, the mason and carpenter, the painter and the whitewasher . . . are at work," reported the *Builder*. Complaints about foul odors were becoming a thing of the past. "Not even in the old quarter have I . . . been offended by a noisome smell." By the end of 1866 the rue de Turbigo had been completed, and the new Halles Centrales and related street improvements were far advanced. South of the Seine the Luxembourg Gardens were being refurbished and new streets being made along its borders.[51]

Balancing the splendid residential suburbs to the west were new industrial and working-class quarters to the north and east. La Villette, la Chapelle, and Batignolles presented "a close network of streets, leaving between them only a few open spaces, whose number was diminishing day by day; new towns, commercial and industrial towns *par excellence,* have sprung up there . . . at the gates of the old city," J.-G. Legrand informed the readers of *L'Illustration* in 1867, "there where open countryside lay until recently; and in these streets what movement, what life, what intensity of traffic!" He found far less development in the outer arrondissements of the left bank. Vaugirard, Grenelle, la Maison-Blanche, la Glacière remained somnolent. Except for concentration around the stations at Ivry and Montparnasse, and at Montrouge, there was nothing: "scattered dwellings, a few narrow streets, vast extensions of wasteland."[52]

In February 1868 active demolition in preparation for extending the rue de Rennes toward the river had begun, and the Gare Montparnasse was visible from the place Saint-Germain-des-Prés. By July "the clearance for the new Place de l'Opéra and the new street from the Palais Royal to lead to it has been undertaken on a scale which is truly appalling," wrote the *Builder.* The new street promised to be "the most magnificent in Europe."[53] But time was running out both for Haussmann and his master. The opera house would not be completed until the early years of the Third Republic, and the intended avenue Napoléon that would lead to it became instead the avenue de l'Opéra. The empire that the new Paris was to monumentalize collapsed, but the city that it had transformed remained to delight successive ages.

The Paris of the future, however brilliant and prosperous one may suppose it, will never resemble the Paris of 1870. In contemplating its present ruins or the monuments which will later rise on their sites, one will examine with a growing interest the drawings or the descriptions that represent it at a time when the Prussians, the Jacobins, and the Internationale had not yet tried to destroy it.[54]

Paris after Haussmann, 1870–1914

So did the author of a guidebook whose publication had been interrupted by the events of 1870–71 justify issuing it unchanged. The physical destruction wrought by the Prussian bombardment and the Commune in its last hours had turned a contemporary description into a historical document. Surely the Paris of the new Republic would be very different indeed.

One would not have expected any regime, whether republican, Bourbon, or Orleanist, to view with favor the Paris that had so deliberately been made the expression of the values of the discredited empire. The fall of Haussmann in 1869 could be said to prefigure the fall of his master and to signify a rejection of the principles of urbanism which he had imposed on Paris. Just as the Revolution of 1848 in Austria had led to an architectural revolution, the establishment of the Third Republic might reasonably be expected to bring about a sharp break in the aesthetic and structural history of Paris.

Writing in 1872, the architect Daniel Ramée suggested the need for such a break. "During the eighteen years from 1852 to 1870," he wrote, "Paris and many other towns in France have completely changed their aspect. The venerable monuments which recall the national traditions and memories and glories of the past have been gravely marred and mutilated, cut down . . . to make way for edifices of no intrinsic artistic merit." A bad regime had given France bad architecture. "Under the Second Empire everything was sacrificed to the consolidation of the throne of Napoleon, and in pandering to the depraved tastes of those who helped to establish it. . . .

Architecture itself was without unity, without knowledge of its lofty purpose, without sincerity, without healthful fancy, and last of all without . . . elegance."[55]

Yet in fact very little changed. The Third Republic devoted its first years to repairing the damage effected by the Commune, after which it set about completing the interrupted street improvements and building plans of Baron Haussmann. The further schemes on which it embarked either had been contemplated by Haussmann or were consistent with his plans. Architectural styles changed, but only gradually.[56] The Republic consolidated and fixed, seemingly for all time, the imperial vision of a transformed Paris. By the 1920s there arose demands for a genuine break with the Haussmannian tradition, for policies that would bring Paris from 1870 into the twentieth century. Depression and war prevented such a course until the late 1950s, and even then the works of Haussmann, along with what of the older Paris he himself chose to spare, were mostly left as they were. It is therefore to the policies of the Third Republic, both deliberate and inadvertent, that we owe the preservation of the Paris of Napoleon III. What was intended as the epitome of modernity has become, over time, a treasured anachronism.

Anthony Sutcliffe has described the persistence of both the physical fabric and the economic activities of the first four arrondissements as "an astonishing survival from the past that is unique among the centres of the cities of northern Europe."[57] To be sure, the same cannot be said of the rest of Paris. Most of the area of the outer ring of arrondissements had not yet been built upon in 1870, and the helpful practice of inscribing the date of construction on building façades makes obvious what a large proportion of today's Paris dates from the late nineteenth century and the years before 1914. The last thirty years have wrought vast changes. Clusters of towers looming on the southwestern and southeastern horizons suggest that much of Paris is of very recent construction indeed, and today the majority of the population of the metropolitan region no longer lives in Paris itself but in one of the older suburbs or newer satellite towns.

The additions made to Haussmann's Paris by the Third Republic were Haussmannian in spirit. Those made by the Fifth Republic, while at odds with Haussmann's theory and practice in all respects save in self-confidence and ruthlessness, are mostly relegated to the outlying parts that neither the tourist nor the careful resident need ever visit. The Maine-Montparnasse Tower, the Centre Pompidou, and the Right Bank Expressway are harder to avoid, but on the whole Paris is either as Haussmann left it or as he intended it to be.

Once the task of rebuilding or replacing the 238 buildings left in ruins by the Commune—notably the Tuileries, the Palais Royal, and the Hôtel de Ville—was accomplished, the demand was to complete the interrupted street improvements. Maxime du Camp in 1875 looked forward to the northward extension of the rue de Rennes to the Seine, and the extension of the avenue de Maine through the faubourg Saint-Germain and across the Tuileries gardens to join the rue Castiglione. Neither of those acts of vandalism ever took place, and in the pleasure given by the boulevard Saint-Germain we can perhaps forgive the destruction of the eighteenth-century *hôtels* and gardens necessary to complete that fine thoroughfare. For du Camp there would be nothing to regret: "The boulevard Saint-Germain is uncompleted; one of its outlets loses itself in the rue Haute-feuille . . . the other expires on the threshold of the rue de Bellechasse; between these two points, there is an ugly labyrinth, badly paved, demanding sun, air, and some facility of circulation."[58]

With the Exhibition of 1878 drawing near, Paris rushed to complete this and other improvements, so as to show the world that it had not merely recovered from the war and the siege, but was abounding in wealth and strength. The avenue de l'Opéra was finished in time to receive visitors to the exhibition. The city of Paris had not been authorized to issue the loan for making the street until June of 1876, but by November 1877 the roadway had been completed, and sculptors were "chiselling the heads of windows and the foliage of scrolls" on the buildings that were going up. The project required the leveling of the old butte de Moulins and the demolition of houses going back to the seventeenth century (fig. 25). "As we passed, one side of the Church of St. Roch stood on a cliff," reported one observer; "not far off, the Italian Opera-house stared grimly from its still more uninviting square. . . . Any one who may have lost himself a few years ago in some of the narrow alleys, with a sole gutter running down the middle, now disappeared, may well marvel at the true magnificence to which they have suc-

---

25. *The leveling of the old butte de Moulins and the demolition of houses going back to the seventeenth century.* Marville, demolition in preparation for the avenue de l'Opera. (Musée Carnavalet. Photo Lauros-Giraudon.)

cumbed."[59] The resulting avenue came to represent to the French their resurgence after humiliating military defeat: "la rue des grandes consolations," as one Parisian described it.[60]

Even after the exhibition closed, building continued at full speed. "From the humblest mortar-mixer to the upholsterer putting the last finishing touches to the completed home, there reigns at present . . . an activity resembling strikingly that noticeable in England," the *Builder* reported in 1879. "Even under the Empire, when the whole of Paris seemed enveloped in scaffolding," the activity was "scarcely equal to that at present reigning." South of the Champs-Elysées the quartier Marboeuf was "a forest of scaffold-poles—a wilderness of blocks of stone and cement and iron joists; the Boulevard St. Germain is still encumbered by the contractors' wagons."[61] A recent study of building in Paris from 1820 to 1940 shows it reaching a peak in 1880.[62]

Activity had scarcely abated in 1882: "Wagon after wagon laden with huge blocks of half-dressed stone, ton after ton of cement, pass daily through the gates of the city. . . . Palaces of stone, designed to last practically for eternity . . . are rising in every neighbourhood, to accommodate a population which is yearly becoming more able to house itself comfortably." Building was particularly active in yet another district calling itself the "West End," this one lying between the Champs-Elysées and the Trocadéro.[63] The architectural critic Emile Rivoalen was aghast at the spectacle of "entire cities built in haste, as one would do after a fire having destroyed a third of Paris." What would become of the new quarters being built north and south of the Arc de Triomphe, as yet deserted? What was the point of demolishing flats renting at ten thousand francs in order to offer their displaced tenants new ones at twelve and fifteen thousand? "The six-story buildings, with stairways in marble and mosaic, with solemn and icy vestibules, where, silently, the lift rises and descends at the least pressure on a marvelous device, these houses are empty."[64]

Whatever the temporary setbacks in building speculation, Paris in 1883 seemed rapidly growing toward perfection "in its lively and carefully studied architecture, in its well-paved streets and well-kept roadways, in its rapidly-growing area of cleanliness . . . and above all . . . in the love of art."[65] Philip Gilbert Hamerton was struck by its utter modernity. The changes it had undergone in the past generation made it seem "as new as Boston or New York—I had almost written, as Chicago."[66]

Robert Kerr, writing in 1891 of "the style of Paris in our day," was as much impressed by its consistency as by its excellence: "In England we have now taken to Flemish Rococo; France continues wholly French. The English cities have passed through a course of counterfeit Gothic. . . . We know not what we shall be next . . . [but] France knows perfectly well that she will remain French."[67] That architecture was to take some surprising steps before the century was over, and in the new century experiment with odd forms of ornament, offering possibilities of sinuous grace, freer and more expressive uses of classical forms. But Paris by 1900 had ceased to lead the world in urban design.[68] Its spurt of confident self-transformation lasted longer and was more far-reaching than London's had been, but like London's eventually slowed to a halt.

The faults of the no longer New Paris are notorious.[69] It solved the problem of housing the working classes mainly by driving them outside its boundaries. It contributed nothing to the planning or layout of the suburb. It is, for all its splen-

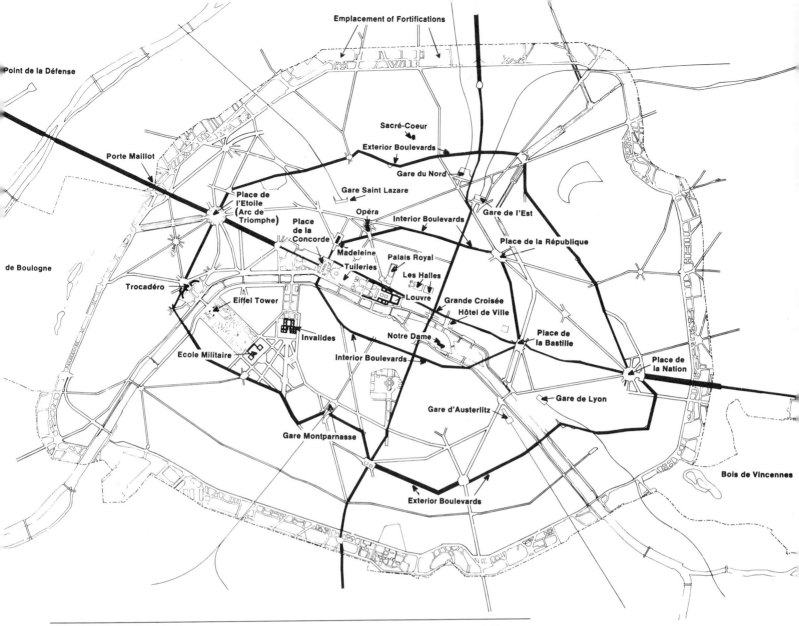

Major elements of the Parisian street system. Norma Evenson, *Paris: A Century of Change,* 1979, page 17.

did effects and fineness of detail, ultimately boring. Yet now that the initial enthusiasm for the twentieth-century science of town planning, with garden cities and superblocks and streets in the sky and pedestrian zones and satellite towns, has cooled, the Paris bequeathed us by the Second Empire and early Third Republic does not look all that bad. If the Parisians can be persuaded to stop taking their nineteenth-century heritage for granted, and give it a fraction of the attention less fortunate cities lavish on "historic districts" that are both newer and of lower quality than the most ordinary of Haussmann's boulevards, the results could be dazzling. Perhaps, though, we ought to be grateful for their lack of self-consciousness in dealing today with what was when new a program of deliberate self-glorification.

5

The Vienna of Franz Joseph

Vienna in 1857 n Christmas Eve 1857, Emperor Franz Joseph issued his famous memorandum ordering the demolition of the fortifications enclosing the old City of Vienna and their replacement by an ambitious town-expansion plan (fig. 26). The area of the walls and the surrounding glacis would be used to link the ancient City with the suburbs that had grown up around it in the 170 years since the repulse of the Turks in 1683 had made extramural residence safe. From a baroque *Residenzstadt* awkwardly fitting into the physical structure of a medieval *Bürgerstadt,* Vienna was about to transform itself into a metropolitan *Weltstadt.* Utilizing the technology and incorporating the values of the nineteenth century, it strove to rival London in wealth and the New Paris in splendor, while preserving all that was best of the older Vienna.

Like Londinium and Lutetia, Vindobona had been a Roman settlement. Like London and Paris, its geographical location enabled it to become an important trading center in the centuries that followed the departure of the Roman legions. Like the other two, Vienna became a royal residence and political capital, although not quite a national capital. As the seat of the Holy Roman Emperor it gave disunited Germany whatever political capital it could be said to have. Yet the fact that the greater part of the emperor's subjects in his other capacities were non-Germans kept Vienna from being, like Paris and London, a focus for national—as distinct from dynastic—loyalties. Conversely, the multinational Habsburg dominions contributed to the cosmopolitanism that made Vienna a cultural center of world importance.

Geography provided aesthetic as well as economic benefits. "In regard to latitude and altitude, Vienna does not differ very materially from London," Thomas Blashill told the Royal Institute of British Architects in 1888, "but its situation, far inland, and in the vicinity of snow mountains, makes a very material difference in its climate. Its summer glows with a heat of which we may judge from a few days that sometimes occur in an exceptionally hot English season." Winters were cold, but changeable. All seasons had clear, brilliant sunshine. "Vienna is first of all *bright.*"[1] Generations of Viennese architects had taken advantage of its natural brightness by providing sharply etched contrasts between light and shadow (fig. 27). Both in old Vienna and new, the sculptural qualities of street façades enhance the effect of the city's dazzling sunshine.

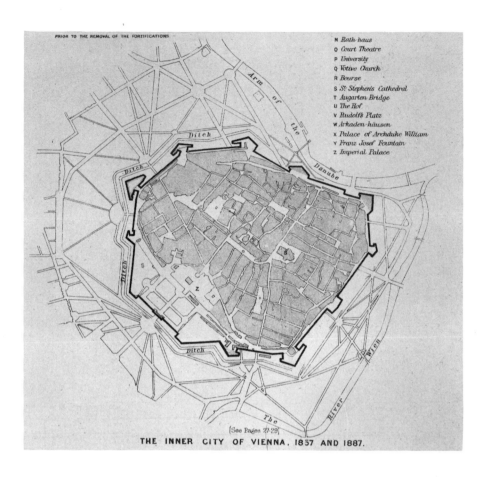

PRIOR TO THE REMOVAL OF THE FORTIFICATIONS

N *Rath-haus*
O *Court Theatre*
P *University*
Q *Votive Church*
R *Bourse*
S *St. Stephen's Cathedral*
T *Augarten Bridge*
U *The Hof*
V *Rudolf's Platz*
W *Arkaden-häusen*
X *Palace of Archduke William*
Y *Franz Josef Fountain*
Z *Imperial Palace*

[See Pages 27-29]

THE INNER CITY OF VIENNA, 1857 AND 1887.

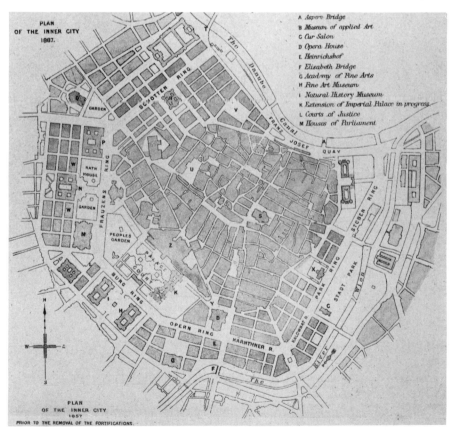

PLAN
OF THE INNER CITY
1887.

A *Aspern Bridge*
B *Museum of applied Art*
C *Cur Salon*
D *Opera House*
E *Heinrichshof*
F *Elisabeth Bridge*
G *Academy of Fine Arts*
H *Fine Art Museum*
I *Natural History Museum*
K *Extension of Imperial Palace in progress*
L *Courts of Justice*
M *Houses of Parliament*

PLAN
OF THE INNER CITY
1857
PRIOR TO THE REMOVAL OF THE FORTIFICATIONS.

26. Plans of Vienna, 1857 and 1887.
Royal Institute of British Architects,
Transactions, n.s. 4 (1888), following
page 28.

27. *Generations of Viennese architects had taken advantage of its natural brightness by providing sharply etched contrasts between light and shadows.* Portal of Palais Brauner, Singerstrasse 16. (Bildarchiv der Österreichischen Nationalbibliothek.)

The encircling walls and glacis, "like an emerald ribbon around the City . . . with its flourishing avenues of trees, with the clear refreshing air, drifting across from the neighboring mountains and vine-covered hills," bestowed "an advantage that Vienna shares with no other large European city"[2] (figs. 28 and 29). Much had been done to transform the fortified zone into a parklike amenity since the decision of Joseph II in the 1780s to lay out lawns on the glacis and plant linden trees and erect benches along the paths.[3] Mrs. Trollope in 1836 found the walk along the fortifications "varied by many bastions, several plantations of ornamental trees, and in one or two points by public gardens. . . . Some of the pleasantest mansions in the town have their principal windows looking upon the Bastey." The fosse, or ditch surrounding the wall, had been "converted into drives and walks of great beauty" (fig. 30).

Within the narrow confines of the walls, which could "be walked round by a party of ladies, chattering all the time, within the hour,"[4] lay the City, occupying the same space that it had since the thirteenth century. Eighty-five percent of the ground had, by the middle of the nineteenth century, been covered by buildings.[5] "The City of Vienna, confined by walls and trenches, cannot enlarge its building land, yet the demand for flats, shops, and workshops within the City, the center of all political and economic intercourse [*dem Vereinigungspunkte alles Staats- und bürgerlichen Verkehrs*], is rapidly increasing," explained the *Allgemeine Bauzeitung* in 1836. Such needs were being met by the construction of taller buildings that contributed to further congestion.[6]

The Vienna of Metternich, despite its cramped layout and old-fashioned appearance, was the seat of a great European power, preeminent as a cultural center, and surpassed in population only by London and Paris. The outward manifestations of its economic and political importance and its cultural supremacy were concentrated along the twisting streets of the original City. "One is startled in the narrow roughly-paved streets to find palatial residences of size and grandeur; decorated within, too, at great cost," reported an English visitor in 1863[7] (fig. 31).

Density of population and building ought here to conjure up images not of

28. *The encircling* glacis, *"like an emerald ribbon around the City."* Glacis, from Karlskirche, 1850. Lithograph. (Museen der Stadt Wien.)

29. *(above)* View of Imperial Palace and the terrace of the empress. (Grafische Sammlung Albertina.)

30. *(below) The fosse, or ditch surrounding the wall, has been "converted into drives and walks of great beauty."* View across glacis from Augustiner Bastei toward Karlskirche and inner suburbs. (Grafische Sammlung Albertina.)

31. *(opposite) "One is startled in the narrow roughly paved streets to find palatial residences of size and grandeur."* Palais Fürstenberg (Rakoczyhaus), Himmelpfortgasse 13, 1899. (Bildarchiv der Österreichischen Nationalbibliothek.)

poverty and squalor, but of opulence and display. Poverty and squalor were to be found in abundance, but in the suburbs, beyond the walls. The City had, since the seventeenth century, served to house primarily court and aristocracy, and the luxury trades that catered to their needs, and secondarily members of the bourgeoisie rich enough to afford its high rents. Medieval Vienna had been an important center of commerce, bourgeois in character. Yet as early as the fifteenth century the volume of its long-distance trade was declining, and by the time of the first Turkish siege of 1529 it had become a town of shopkeepers and small craftsmen. Four years earlier Emperor Ferdinand I had deprived it of its political independence and its medieval liberties. From 1533 the Habsburgs made it their favored residence, while the landed nobility built themselves palaces within its walls. Ecclesiastical bodies were encouraged to settle there to help combat the widespread Protestantism among the commerical classes. Lesser nobility bought bourgeois houses or rented lodgings. By the time of the last Turkish siege in 1683, the character of the City had become fixed: until the collapse of empire, court, and aristocracy alike in 1918, it would remain a center of power, wealth, and pleasure, supported by bourgeois and proletarian suburbs.[8]

For Vienna, the "rise of the middle classes" had been a medieval phenomenon, with the modern age characterized by the triumph of crown, church, and aristocracy. The Counter-Reformation succeeded ultimately in turning what had in the sixteenth century been a mostly Protestant city into a wholly Catholic one, the baroque splendors of whose churches and monastic foundations gave physical expression to that triumph. The efforts of Joseph II to bring the secular values of the Enlightenment to his empire were undone by his successors. The defeat of Napoleon and the ascendancy of Metternich seemed to mark the end, once and for all, of the threats posed by liberalism, nationalism, and the ideologies produced and disseminated by the French Revolution. Mrs. Trollope was enchanted: Vienna was everything that Cincinnati was not.

Meanwhile Vienna flourished economically, more from the production and consumption of luxury goods than from long-distance trade or manufacture for export. Its population doubled, from 80,000 to more than 160,000 between 1683 and 1770. The greater part of the increase occurred in the suburbs, which by 1779 contained 3,832 houses, three times the number to be found in the *Altstadt*.[9]

Austria industrialized rapidly in the course of the nineteenth century, and by the last third of the century the outer suburbs of Vienna were being covered with textile mills, engineering plants, and chemical works. Yet as late as 1888, Thomas Blashill correctly pointed out to his English audience that Vienna was "not what we should call a manufacturing or commercial city."[10] Its impressive rise in population and wealth came more from its position as the imperial capital than from heavy industry.[11] The growth of the bureaucracy, the desire of the expanding nobility to reside near the court, and the development of luxury trades and services largely accounted for the increase in population. While there were by 1850, particularly in the southeastern outskirts, some relatively large manufacturing establishments, most of the roughly 20,000 workshops and so-called factories of the period were small operations of skilled craftsmen, inconspicuously housed in buildings of mixed residential, commerical, and manufacturing purposes.[12] Even in the early twentieth century, more than half of Vienna's 375,000 industrial workers were in firms employing twenty or fewer. Only eight factories, all of them in the metallurgical field, had more than a thousand workers each.[13]

The metropolis housed its new residents and functions in three ways: more intensive utilization of the existing built-up area, outward movement at the periphery, and, after 1857, the exploitation for very special purposes of the land between City and suburbs. The first two processes had long been at work. Gardens were built over, stories added to existing buildings, and older structures replaced with new and taller ones. The suburbs still had the spacious eighteenth-century summer retreats as potential building sites. The one- and two-story village structures still found along thoroughfares and trading streets could be replaced by taller, more urban buildings. Such low structures had long disappeared in the City, along with any vestige of garden ground, but there it made economic sense to pull down a building and replace it by another in order to add as little as a single floor of rentable space.

By 1840 urban Vienna had expanded toward the west by up to a mile and a half. From Meidling to Währing the boundaries had reached the Linienwall, the customs barrier, while to the southwest there was building as far as Schönbrunn. At Favoriten to the southeast the erections of the Südbahn and Ostbahn railway companies stood as a barrier to expansion, and in Leopoldstadt the Prater together with the Nordbahn and Nordwestbahn were comparable obstacles. But within such boundaries there remained much room for development. Between 1840 and 1914 three-quarters of the buildings within the built-up area had been replaced by newer ones. In the inner suburbs new streets were inserted into the existing pattern, while in both City and suburbs narrow building parcels were consolidated to permit the erection of larger structures.[14]

Changes in physical structure did little to alter the social character of the different parts. In London and Paris, all classes of the population had participated in the migration from older to newer districts, with the aristocracy as early as the seventeenth century abandoning its older dwellings for more spacious and modern ones in Covent Garden and the Marais, St. James's and Saint-Germain-des-Prés. In Paris the commerical classes remained at or near their place of business until the nineteenth century, but in London the more prosperous merchants were already in the eighteenth century moving from the City, both to the terraces and squares of the West End and to nearby villages like Hackney and Hampstead.

The Viennese upper classes saw no reason to abandon their palaces or lodgings in the crowded City in the seventeenth or eighteenth century, and very little reason to do so even after the provision in the Ringstrasse of attractive building sites and luxury housing in the mid-nineteenth. They did, to be sure, erect summer palaces in the inner suburbs, but these were never intended to do more than supplement their main residences in the City. Prince Eugene, once the summer season was over, moved from the Belvedere back to his town palace in Himmelpfortgasse, less than a mile away. By their persistent loyalty to the original City the aristocracy gave Vienna the quality that most distinguishes it from London and Paris: a stable socioeconomic geography, concentrating in the center everything that is fashionable, beautiful, and expensive.

Fashion, beauty, and money abounded in the City, but it would be wrong to think of the adjacent suburbs (*Vorstädte*) as repositories of crime, poverty, and disorder, like Southwark and the areas east of the City of London. In addition to aristocratic summer retreats, they contained the residences of prosperous burghers and independent craftsmen, along with churches, public buildings, monastic foundations, inns and taverns serving travelers bound for the outer reaches of the empire, and the nuclei of agricultural villages that had been engulfed by the metropolis. What remained of dairy farms, market gardens, and vineyards gave the suburbs the pleasantly semirural quality that still prevails farther out in Grinzing and Döbling.

The Linienwall surrounding the inner suburbs was not demolished until 1890 to form the present *Gürtel,* or belt parkway. Beyond it lay further settlements, overwhelmingly agricultural until, late in the nineteenth century, they became the industrial and working-class *Vororte,* incorporated into the municipality in 1890 and 1904.[15] Even within the inner suburbs, as recently as 1848 market gardens occupied the area between the Augarten and the Prater in Leopoldstadt, together with much of Alsergrund and Margareten. A large proportion of the vegetables consumed in the capital were grown inside the Linienwall.[16]

The description of the inner city by Victor Tissot in 1878 would have been equally accurate before the walls were taken down and the Ringstrasse developed:

> The "City," like a dark island, lost in the middle of the white sea of the suburbs, has remained the center of commercial, political, and social life; the pickaxe of the demolishers has respected these winding streets, these narrow squares, all full of old relics, and where the heart of the ancient monarchy still beats. The six-story houses, with great arched doorways, massive caryatids, are found at every step in this labyrinth of dark and picturesque streets, that meander, that intersect each other . . . that transport you mentally many centuries into the past.[17] [Fig. 32]

Picturesque and evocative it surely was, but in no sense a city of the nineteenth century, not if we think of it as the century of the steam engine, free trade, and material progress. "If we come to know," wrote an English visitor in 1850, "that there are no omnibuses in Vienna, not even cabs, but merely some very expensive *fiacres,*—that with the exception of the city, no gas is yet in use, and this but in a few shops,—Vienna can hardly range but in the second class of the metropolises of Europe."[18] Only, in fact, on the first of July 1845 had gas lights been extended from the major squares to the principal streets of the City, something that had been commonplace in London for nearly three decades. "Metropolitan Improvements" in the *Kaiserstadt* were confined to such operations as the removal of gateways obstructing traffic from the City to the suburbs, and to proposals for new bridges over the Danube Canal and the river Wien. New streets were being constructed in the inner suburbs, and efforts made for the better alignment of streets in the City as new buildings replaced old. In May 1847 the *Allgemeine Bauzeitung* could report that the whole of the Inner City was now lighted by gas, along with the major suburban streets.[19] Anything like a comprehensive system of sewerage, not to speak of the domestic supply of piped water, was still decades away, although the Kaiser Ferdinand system had from 1841 been bringing to the City water from the Danube in cast-iron pipes.[20]

In one respect Vienna had long been in the forefront of urban developments: in the erection of massive blocks of flats. The conversion of single-family houses for multiple occupation was already a common phenomenon in the sixteenth century.[21] By the late eighteenth century purpose-built blocks of flats, of impressive dimensions, were going up in the City. With the abolition of many monastic founda-

---

32. *(opposite) "The pickaxe of the demolishers has respected these winding streets . . . that transport you mentally many centuries into the past."* Baroque houses in Kurrentgasse. (Bildarchiv der Österreichischen Nationalbibliothek.)

tions, their City properties were converted in the 1780s into vast multiple dwellings.[22] Such houses, and their later successors, excited the moral disapproval of an English critic in 1850:

> These houses, or rather fortresses, bear no analogy to any structure existing in London. Imagine a building four or five stories high, with a frontage of ten or fifteen, nay, twenty and forty windows. . . . How is it . . . when it will happen that twenty families and their visitors will have to pass the same staircase? Where is then the privacy, I would fain say the sanctity, of a respectable English household? Such a house resembles, day and night, a beehive, and as the houses are quite open, none can boast of a home, but rather consider himself lodged in a market-place.[23]

The Viennese themselves were having qualms about the moral and social consequences of flat-living, but an increasing population and high land values impelled them to build still more flats, taller if not wider, in City and suburbs alike. The *Allgemeine Bauzeitung* reported in 1847 the completion or partial erection of no fewer than 95 private housing blocks, and the granting of official permission for the expanding and modernization of 400 older buildings.[24] The years before and after the Revolution of 1848 also saw the erection of numerous public buildings, notably a mint, a customs house, and several railway termini.

The regime was, however, a notably frugal one, limiting new buildings to those deemed essential, and making them as plain and inexpensive as possible. Mrs. Trollope complained of the accommodations at the "Bourg theatre," "formerly a tennis-court, for which it is much better fitted by its shape and proportions than for its present service. But the erection of a new Bourg theatre would be an expense wholly belonging to the government . . . and I am told that it is much more in the spirit of the dynasty of Austria to build hospitals than playhouses."[25] Official aesthetic taste favored an austere neoclassicism, in contrast both to the florid baroque that had dominated Viennese building until the late eighteenth century and to the splendors of the Ringstrasse style that was to follow.

Vienna responded to the imperial memorandum with alacrity and an outpouring of creative energy; growing in size and wealth, it was eager to exploit the possibilities offered by the new technology and to commemorate in stone and plaster both itself and its age. The demolition of the walls gave it an opportunity to prove itself worthy of the nineteenth century. The granting of the constitution that inaugurated the so-called Liberal Era in 1860 provided the political counterpart. By the time Victor Tissot wrote, Vienna, physically unconfined, politically and aesthetically liberated, had leapt into splendid modernity: "There, where yesterday menacing bastions still loomed over broad moats, ravishing gardens spread themselves out, there extend fine boulevards, and there rise buildings with marble staircases and façades sparkling with frescoes in gold"[26] (fig. 33).

Yet if the Ringstrasse reflected the spirit of a newly dominant and self-confident liberalism, much of the nature and structure of the metropolis remained the same. If it constituted a revolution in urban design, it was, as Macaulay described the English revolution of 1688, a preserving rather than a destroying revolution. Just as much of what remains healthy about the British Constitution depends on the pragmatic decisions and creative compromises of the Glorious Revolution, so the ability of Vienna to survive the disasters of the twentieth century, to become the economically viable, aesthetically satisfying, and psychologically exhilarating place that it is today, depends in large measure on the men who planned and built the Ringstrasse.

The imperial memorandum of 1857 called for a new war office, a city marshall's office, an opera house, a building to house the imperial archives, a library, a town hall, and appropriate museums and galleries.[27] The *Notizblatt der Allgemeinen Bauzeitung* for January 1858 praised the comprehensive nature of the order, pointing out that all earlier proposals for extension of the Inner City had limited themselves to building on certain stretches of the glacis between the Schottentor and the Danube Canal and at the Kärntnertor. It predicted an end to the housing shortage and a Vienna appropriate to the vastness and worth of the emperor's domains. It looked forward to the time when the Austrian capital, plentifully supplied with flats for all classes of the population, would take second place to no other European capital in size and majesty.[28] The prediction of the effect on Vienna's beauty and splendor proved more accurate than that regarding its housing shortage, which continued unabated until the 1920s.

As in Paris, memories of 1848 kept considerations of public order in the forefront of plans for urban betterment. There was even a proposal for building a wall to protect the bourgeois quarters from the proletarian districts. In the end such discussions led to no more than the erection of barracks, the Rossauer Kaserne and the Franz Josephs-Kaserne, at the extremities of the Ring where it joined the Danube Canal.[29]

On the first of September 1859 the emperor approved a plan providing two thoroughfares, one the Ringstrasse, strictly speaking, and a parallel *Lastenstrasse* for necessary but less than noble traffic. It did little to facilitate through-traffic between City and suburbs, so that although the Ringstrasse proved less of a barrier than the walls it replaced, it serves to this day as both a practical and psychological expression of the distinction between *Stadt* and *Vorstadt.*[30]

Despite contemporary descriptions of the wall and glacis as a belt strangling the capital, they had not seriously interfered with the growth of Vienna insofar as its utilitarian functions were concerned. For a century and a half, housing, industry, and trade had found ample room in the suburbs within the Linienwall. Beyond lay the zone of outer suburbs, still mostly market gardens, vineyards, and village settlements. Nor was the area involved in the urbanized and potentially urbanized sector impossibly vast: it lay mostly within walking distance of the Inner City and would shortly be served by an efficient network of horse tramways. Six separate railway stations served as termini for lines capable of providing commuter services to any number of dormitory settlements that might be built. The *town expansion* that the demolition of the walls permitted was, therefore, of a very specialized kind.

What Vienna lacked in 1857 was not room for essential and useful functions, but room for the pomp and spectacle of its court, the time-wasting rituals of its leisure classes. For those no amount of space in Favoriten or Ottakring would do: only land

The Creation of the Ringstrasse, 1857–1914

33. *(overleaf) "There, where yesterday menacing bastions still loomed over broad moats, wide trenches, ravishing gardens spread themselves out, there extend fine boulevards, and there rise buildings with marble staircases and façades sparkling with frescos of gold."* Aerial view of Inner City and the surrounding Ringstrasse Zone, 1962. Danube Canal and Leopoldstadt to the north. (Landesbildstelle, Vienna-Burgenland.)

34. *In Vienna as in Paris the new opera house fixed the center of the rebuilt metropolis.*

that was easily accessible from the Hofburg and the Herrengasse, the Graben and the Stephansplatz could meet the need for space in which to perform worthily the ceremonies of a Residenzstadt.

An opera house that could accommodate the grandiose productions demanded by Meyerbeer and his successors, and at the same time provide the noble and opulent audience with a spacious and dignified setting for self-display, was an urgent need of the musical capital of Europe. Accordingly Siccardsburg and van der Nüll's Opera was the first of the major public buildings in the Ringstrasse and located at its most strategic point: where the Kärntner Strasse, busiest and most fashionable of City streets, emerged into the town expansion zone. In Vienna as in Paris the new opera house fixed the center of the rebuilt metropolis (fig. 34), but the Vienna Opera stood immediately adjacent to the traditional center, as if the Paris Opéra had been placed on the right bank just north of Notre Dame.

The opera house was only the most important of a succession of linked institutions, open spaces, and residences intended to provide a total environment for those who lived nobly (figs. 35 and 36). "The connection of residential blocks with great public buildings, representative squares, parks and avenues . . . had no prototype in Vienna," Elisabeth Lichtenberger has written.[31] Yet in a very real sense the Inner City itself both before and after 1857 provided just such a model, if a less coherently organized one. What the Ringstrasse did was to create, by intention, the kind of arena for the mixture of activities appropriate to a leisure class that had hitherto been confined to the City.

It would be more true to say that no other European capital had anything like either City or Ringstrasse. The juxtaposition of cultural and educational institutions with upper-middle-class housing found a contemporary parallel in South Kensington, but while London's museum zone lay in what were then the outskirts of town, the Ringstrasse immediately adjoined the center of wealth, power, and prestige. Nothing in Paris, either before or after the transformations of Baron Haussmann, remotely approached the degree of concentration achieved by the Ringstrasse. Had the Louvre, the Sorbonne, the Opéra, the Bourse, the Théatre Français, the Chamber of Deputies, and the Hôtel de Ville been placed along the Champs-Elysées, something comparable might have emerged.

Opernring, city side. (Museen der Stadt Wien.)

The Ringstrasse, far from dispersing the attractions of the City, enabled it to expand just enough so that its major institutions could occupy prominent sites along its borders. The adjacent apartment blocks were arranged to maximize the number of rooms looking directly onto the street, thereby rendering residence as "representational" as art and scholarship, administration and finance, and the rest of the activities monumentalized along the great street.[32] The Ringstrasse offered what no suburban site possibly could: conspicuousness. To lure the aristocrat or wealthy burgher from his palace or flat in the Altstadt, more than a spacious, lavishly decorated dwelling was needed: it had to occupy a site where it could awe his social inferiors and satisfy the requirements of his social equals, as well as enable him to emerge directly into the arena of social, political, and economic power.

Carl Schorske has contrasted the "spatial conception" governing the layout of the Ringstrasse with baroque planning, in which "space served as a magnifying setting to the buildings which encompassed or dominated it." No long vistas led the eye to a single monument; no radial avenues linked City with suburbs. The buildings along the Ringstrasse were "rarely . . . oriented to each other under some principle of subordination or primacy." The individual structures "float unorganized in a spatial medium whose only stabilizing element is an artery of men in motion."[33]

The shape of the town-expansion site, determined by the curving walls it replaced, made any really extensive vistas impractical. "A strong radial system . . . to link the outer parts and the city center" with "vast vistas oriented toward the central, monumental features"[34] would have required massive destruction in both *Stadt* and *Vorstadt,* wanton, unthinkable extravagance, particularly when so much new building land lay available in the expansion zone itself.[35] The vistas that Haussmann gave Paris depended on the scale of his demolitions. To the extent that his *percées* cut through slum areas, he kept compensation charges within reasonable limits. No comparable areas of depressed land values existed either in Vienna's City or in the portions of the suburbs that abutted on the Ringstrasse zone. Any street that opened a City monument to distant view would have destroyed other baroque and classical buildings in its path that were even then regarded with admiration and respect.

35. *A succession of linked institutions, open spaces, and residences intended to provide a total environment for those who lived nobly.* Schottenring looking north, c. 1920. University in left foreground. (Bildarchiv der Österreichischen Nationalbibliothek.)

Within the limits set by the size and shape of the building land at their disposal, the makers of the Ringstrasse were able to introduce some short vistas that were quite effective. The view of the Votivkirche from the Schottentor (fig. 37), that from the Burgtheater across the Rathaus Park to the Town Hall, and, grandest of all, from the Burgtor to Fischer von Erlach's royal stables, flanked by the two museums and dominated by Maria Theresa, greater than life-size, render the short stroll from the University to the Hofburg an intensely emotional experience.

The absence of terminating vistas and the architectural assertiveness of the public buildings along the Ringstrasse make that boulevard less of an aesthetic whole than Haussmann's boulevards, where the eye is drawn to the monument at the end undistracted by any marked individuality in the flanking structures. Yet the failure to isolate selected monuments for emphasis, such as the Paris Opéra or the buildings set in the gardens of the Champs-Elysées, did emphasize that the Ring-strasse was, for all the high pretensions of its buildings, still a *street*—along which one could ride, stroll, and shop as well as contemplate heroic statuary and architectural representations of the spirit of commerce, learning, drama, political wisdom, and all the rest.

A word about "baroque planning." The age of the baroque—stretching from sixteenth-century Italy to eighteenth-century Germany and Austria—saw very little baroque planning in its cities. Whatever the possibilities offered by a palace in open countryside or a new town being laid out from scratch, the magnificent squares, radiating avenues, and open vistas proposed for existing cities remained for the most part in architectural sketchbooks until the latter half of the nineteenth and early twentieth centuries. Christopher Wren's famous scheme for London was recognized by everyone as posing insuperable practical economic and political difficulties, even when the City lay empty after the Great Fire. Still greater objections prevented any severe cutting into the dense, substantial, and valuable building stock of seventeenth-century Paris or Vienna. The splendid façades of Fischer von Erlach and Lucas von Hildebrandt within the City of Vienna can be seen only obliquely from the narrow streets and passages on which they front. Here as in most European towns baroque buildings face medieval streets; "baroque" streets and squares are occupied by modern buildings.

If, arguably, the designers of the Ringstrasse failed to take full advantage of the space vacated by the fortifications to isolate public buildings and relate one to another through symmetrical positioning and contrived vistas, they did make it

36. Opernkreuzung, 1887. Watercolor by Rudolf von Alt. (Museen der Stadt Wien.)

possible for them all to be viewed satisfactorily and in comfort, if only from across the wide boulevard itself. By placing them along a continuous street, one that changed direction at irregular intervals, they offered the pedestrian a kind of aesthetic pleasure similar to that which the old City does provide: that of surprise, as first one and then another startling object comes into view.

The speed with which the whole expansion area was filled astonished both Viennese and foreigners. The Franz Josefs-Kai, running along the side of the City facing the Danube Canal, was opened in 1858, with the rest of the Ring roadway completed for a formal opening on May Day 1865 (fig. 38). "Already a whole town has arisen," reported the *Builder;* "and, though many plots have yet to be filled, this part of Vienna bids fair to become the fashionable quarter for the future. . . . From the bridge of Aspern, along the Horticultural Gardens as far as the Kärntner Thor, many handsome mansions have been constructed, partly by archdukes and the old Austrian aristocracy, partly by merchant princes and wealthy manufacturers"[36] (fig. 39).

Apart from the Opera House, the early buildings were mostly residential. The most active period of building began in 1868 and came to a sudden end with the stock market crash of 1873. In those five years no less than 40 percent of the total dwelling space in the Ringstrasse had been completed.[37] Recovery soon followed and building resumed. Trade followed the affluent residents to the new blocks of flats, and at the street level "shop follows upon shop, and *cafés* and *restaurants*

37. *The view of the Votivkirche from the Schottentor.* Portion of city wall and new Palais Ephrussi to left, c. 1880. (Bildarchiv der Österreichischen Nationalbibliothek.)

38. *The Franz Josefs-Kai was opened in 1858.* Franz Josefs-Kai, Hotel Metropole to left. (Museen der Stadt Wien.)

alternate . . . [yet] the brilliant Ring street (unlike the Paris boulevard) is not a favorable site for business," an English visitor reported in 1877. "The best houses and firms who have moved their businesses to the Ring are mostly sorry for it."[38] The statement is a little extreme, given the number and extent of luxury establishments in the Ringstrasse. Still, by and large, the very best shops continued to occupy the sites in the Graben, Kärntner Strasse, Kohlmarkt, and the other fashionable streets in the Altstadt, just as most of their aristocratic customers remained in their City palaces (figs. 40 and 41, colorplate 3).

39. *"From the bridge of Aspern, along the Horticultural Gardens as far as the Kärntner Thor, many handsome mansions have been constructed."* Parkring and Kolowratring (today's Schubertring), 1873. (Museen der Stadt Wien.)

40. *The very best shops continued to occupy the sites in the Graben, Kärntner Strasse, Kohlmarkt, and the other fashionable streets in the* Altstadt. The Graben, c. 1890. (Bildarchiv der Österreichischen Nationalbibliothek.)

The first decade and a half of the formation of the Ringstrasse were notable for residential development; most of the public buildings, however, date from the 1880s. The residential blocks were similar architecturally and recalled the palaces of the eighteenth-century City. The public buildings embodied greater stylistic variety. The Votivkirche, by Heinrich von Ferstel, begun in 1856 and completed in 1879, was the first archeologically correct Gothic Revival building in Vienna.[39] Notable also as the only ecclesiastical structure in the whole of the Ringstrasse zone, it is set back in today's Rooseveltplatz from the main boulevard in the suburban direction. Adjacent to it, but facing directly onto the Franzenring (today the Dr. Karl Lueger Ring) is the University (1885), also by Ferstel, in the style of the Italian Renaissance. Next, facing one another across the Rathaus Park, are the northern Gothic Town Hall (1884), by Friedrich von Schmidt, and the early baroque Hofburgtheater, by Gottfried Semper and Karl von Hasenauer. Then come the German Renaissance Courts of Justice by A. von Wielemans (1881) and the

Greek Houses of Parliament by Theophil Hansen (1883). The Art History and Natural History museums lie just across the Ring from the New Hofburg, the half-completed extension of the imperial palace. Both museums were designed by Semper and completed in 1881 by Hasenauer. Originally they were intended to be linked to the palace by a triumphal arcade crossing over the roadway itself.

The annexation of the outer ring of suburbs in 1890 occasioned a reexamination of the policies to be pursued in rendering Vienna—now approaching two million in population—worthy of its political, cultural, and economic importance. By then the Ringstrasse had nearly achieved its modern appearance, making the suburbs

41. Kohlmarkt, 1900. Watercolor by Richard Moser. (Museen der Stadt Wien.) See also colorplate 3.

beyond look drab and commonplace by comparison. The municipality announced an international competition for the best plan to improve and expand the metropolis. The plan would include provision for a city railway, or *Stadtbahn,* and proposals "for building better dwelling-houses with social and sanitary improvements; and for the unlimited building of factories, by arranging separate districts for dwellings and factories." The segregation by function which Vienna had hitherto neglected was proposed as a principle of its replanning. Specifically, the announcement cited the outer suburbs that adjoined the Wienerwald from Kahlenberg to Hetzendorf as "specially suitable for dwellings and family houses," while relegating to Favoriten, Simmering, Brigittenau, and the banks of the Danube "the factories, which with the noise of machinery, the smoke, and smell are unpleasant." Proposed residential districts were to consist of "semi-detached villas or blocks of houses with a definite number of stories, and with or without front gardens." Industrial districts were to have streets suitable for "large public workshops," as well as dwelling houses "with proportionally large gardens or courts." The inclusion of plans for blocks of dwellings in the industrial districts reveals that the intention was less to segregate manufacture from residence than to segregate the middle-class villas "from Kahlenberg to Hetzendorf" from the noise and smoke and smell. The principle of segregation was to be, as before, more social than functional.

Another stipulation does suggest a departure from the principle that had hitherto governed the planning of Vienna, in indicating that new streets might be pushed through built-up areas. "The old street system is to be modernized . . . to promote the sanitary and convenient arrangement of the city, by improving the present principal streets . . . as well as by proposing new thoroughfares." *Dégagement,* on Parisian lines, was also envisaged. "Where historical monuments . . . form welcome landmarks, the laying out of squares and street openings or widenings is to be considered, so that the present buildings and monuments are seen to better advantage."[40]

The First World War, the collapse of the Habsburg empire, and subsequent impoverishment postponed the realization of any such plans until a time when saner views of traffic control and architectural preservation rendered them unthinkable. The one sensible scheme contemplated by the competition, the *Stadtbahn,* was carried out, with stations and engineering works designed by Otto Wagner, giving that system an architectural prestige unique among the world's rapid transit systems. Wagner's general plan for urban expansion, providing for a city immensely more vast than Vienna was ever to become, with broad avenues and monumental squares uniting efficiently laid out residential quarters, was never put into effect.[41]

Vienna's need for physical growth was rendered less urgent by the dramatic fall in population and the contraction of its economic and administrative functions after 1918. Its lapse into poverty and weakness saved both the historic center and the surrounding countryside from devastation. The expansion that has taken place since the Second World War, across the Danube, into UNO-City and beyond, if of questionable urbanistic merit, has at least helped save the beauties of the Wienerwald to the west from suburban desecration.

The additions that were made to Vienna in the years after 1890 were more utilitarian than monumental, particularly under the influence of the new Christian

Socialist municipal administration of Karl Lueger. Most new building was residential and industrial and located at the expanding fringe of the metropolis.[42] Public buildings, except for social institutions such as schools and hospitals, played a lesser role than earlier. The main exception came at the Stubenring end of the Ringstrasse. The demolition of the Franz Josephs-Kaserne left space to be filled, notably by Otto Wagner's headquarters building for the Postal Savings Bank and the new War Ministry. Visually the two buildings represented the two dominant trends of the prewar years: the one Sezessionism and the other "stripped-down classicism." Yet both, as they face each other on opposite sides of the Ring, maintain the conspicuous monumentality inherent in the Ringstrasse tradition. Attempts to assimilate Otto Wagner into the subsequent so-called modern movement require ignoring or playing down the aspects of his genius that belong to an earlier, less restricted view of the representative function of civic architecture. Just as his Stadtbahn stations raised the daily journey from home to work to the level of heroic art, so the Postsparkasse gave to the saving efforts of the ordinary man or woman a fittingly dignified setting.

Both examples prefigured the fate of Vienna after 1918 and still more in our own days: a city designed to meet the needs and contain the pleasures of a powerful court and self-indulgent aristocracy has been inherited by the people at large. From one of the most rigidly hierarchical societies in Europe to one of the least class-ridden, Austria has changed immensely since the Ringstrasse was built. Its vast *Grosswohnungen* have been cut up into apartments suitable for today's smaller families with more restricted views as to what is necessary for an evening party. Coachloads of overseas tourists dine in hotel suites designed for aristocratic receptions. The Palais Schwarzenberg itself incorporates a hotel. The Graben contains something called the Chattanooga Snackbar. An underground station faces St. Stephen's Cathedral. The Kärntner Strasse has become a pedestrian zone. High-rise workers' flats dominate the trans-Danubian horizon. A network of motorways conveys those workers to their holidays in Italy and Yugoslavia or to performances of *Kiss Me Kate* at the Bregenz Festival. There are far fewer cafés than in 1914, and most of those close early, since their customers are at home watching *Dynasty: der Denver Clan* on TV. UNO-City and the adjacent international conference center give Vienna a new, if unheroic, role in world affairs.

Vienna today is not the carefully preserved capital of Ruritania but a prosperous and efficient part of the 1980s. What makes it particularly relevant to the eighties—in a way that would have escaped us in the sixties—is its living demonstration of the infinite adaptability of good architecture and good urban design of any period before 1914 to whatever demands we make on it, and the needlessness of the "purpose-built." The purposes for which Vienna was built have long since ceased to matter, but Vienna itself matters as much as ever.

6

The Process of
Urban Embellishment

irst London, then Paris, and finally Vienna attempted to turn themselves into monuments in the course of the nineteenth century. London, between 1811 and 1837, remade itself along the line connecting Regent's Park with St. James's Park and Trafalgar Square; Paris, between 1852 and 1870, cut great swaths across itself, north to south, east to west, and diagonally, planting trees and flowers wherever it could; Vienna, beginning in 1857, turned a fortified zone into a ring of pleasure. The three programs shared a number of characteristics: they resulted from the initiative of the central government; depended for their success on the attraction of private investment by speculative builders and developers; were intended to make royal or imperial residences more prominent; created public parks; mixed public and private buildings, ecclesiastical and secular purposes, residential and commercial uses; used architecture mainly in the classical tradition (broadly defined); put up monuments of national, imperial, dynastic, or cultural significance; built wide streets both to facilitate traffic and to serve as fashionable promenades; and combined aesthetic with social and sanitary motives. London and Paris incorporated slum clearance in the preliminary demolitions; in Vienna no destruction of residential or commercial property, slum or otherwise, was necessary.

One peculiarity, indeed, of Vienna is that it has never indulged either in the cutting through of *percées* or in systematic slum clearance as these operations were carried out in London and Paris. Vienna has had problems coping with vehicular traffic, it lacks open spaces in much of its area, and it has had more than its share of overcrowded, insanitary dwellings, but neither *slum* nor *îlot insalubre* expresses the shape that poverty, congestion, and squalor have taken there. Schemes for improving the living conditions of the poor, raising standards of public health, and facilitating the circulation of traffic have taken less heroic, less brutal, but not less effective forms than those employed in London and Paris. Such differences in approach account for much of the distinctive charm of Vienna today: it has responded to changed demographic, social, economic, and technological conditions by adaptation and addition rather than by destruction and replacement. It was preservationist in practice long before it became so in theory.[1]

Each of the three cities aspired to transcend utility and achieve monumental expression. The form that such expression took in each instance ultimately went out of fashion. Each was enthusiastically received as it was going up, but sooner or later came to seem old-fashioned, misguided in its principles, an object at best of amused indifference, at worst of vehement hatred; each ultimately came to bask in popular affection and critical admiration. The last stage happened to Regent Street in the 1920s, to the Ringstrasse in the 1960s, even later to Haussmann's Paris.

As for the stage of critical rejection, the plaster ornamentation of Regent Street and the Regent's Park terraces was hardly dry, figuratively speaking, when attacks opened on its formal solecisms, its duplicity, and its inappropriateness as street architecture. Yet stucco facing dominated the new and rebuilt streets of London for several decades after the 1820s, and Regent Street enjoyed great success as a fashionable promenade and location for luxury shops. Unaccountably to modern eyes, the Regent's Park terraces proved less successful in attracting residents than Regent Street did in attracting shoppers. But neither, after the very first years, received more than qualified, condescending praise from architectural critics.

The Ringstrasse was subjected to detailed, often captious criticism from the start, and the suicides of Siccardsburg and van der Null as a result of the attacks made on their design for the opera house suggest how cruel and effective that criticism sometimes was. But for the most part, as the Ringstrasse took shape it became the focus of civic, national, and imperial pride that it was intended to be. Not until the 1890s, when Camillo Sitte attacked the principles of urban planning that underlay it, and when Otto Wagner and the Sezessionists repudiated the aesthetic principles informing its architecture, did it begin to sink in general esteem. But it is inconceivable that at any stage in its popularity anyone would have considered rebuilding it as a whole, as Regent Street was. The lamentable intrusions of modern structures today fill gaps created by military action in 1945, not by the kind of willful destruction by developers and planners that has disfigured London.

Architectural fashions changed in France, too, but more slowly. By the 1890s, a taste for a more sculptural treatment of façades had made the buildings of the Haussmann era seem flat and monotonous in their form, timid and insipid in their decoration; but the value of the boulevard and the desirability of still more *percées* to ventilate and embellish Paris seemed as self-evident as they had in the fifties. Le Corbusier's proposal to flatten the whole of central Paris and replace the eighteenth-century streets and nineteenth-century boulevards with tower blocks might have astonished the bourgeoisie, but it was not pursued as a practical possibility. The massive demolitions and redevelopments of our own day have, with the notable exception of the district of Les Halles, been confined to the outer arrondissements, leaving the Paris that the tourist sees essentially that of the mid-to-late nineteenth century. With minor cosmetic exceptions, Haussmann's boulevards are intact, as is the earlier maze of streets through which they cut. They are often in a state of shocking disrepair, recalling the nonchalance with which Roman and Byzantine remains are treated in Istanbul. The boulevard de Sébastopol, opened with such pomp and pride in 1858, is all there, and had it existed in any British or American city would long since have been filled with specialty shops and theme restaurants on the street level and converted to expensive condominiums above. No such thing has happened in Paris, or is likely to happen very soon, for the boulevard de Sébastopol is endlessly duplicated wherever one goes. If Parisians are only just now rediscovering and gentrifying the Marais, they will have decades to go before they set to work turning the boulevard de Sébastopol into a Covent Garden or a Pioneer Square or a SoHo. It is a tribute to the richness of the Parisian cultural heritage that they can ignore the legacy from the Second Empire and Third Republic on the grounds that there is so much of it, and that it is all they can do to keep track of the eighteenth century and earlier. One hopes, though, that they will not lose their more recent heritage through inadvertence, as the English have with so much of Victorian London.

To a great extent what survives of the Paris of Louis XVI, Napoleon III, and the Belle Epoque is more physical than spiritual. The crumbling façades of the boulevard de Sébastopol would shock the Parisian of the 1860s much less than the state of degradation into which even the western portions of the *grands boulevards* have fallen: today they embody all the elegance and sophistication of Market Street in San Francisco, Canal Street in New Orleans, and Broadway in New York. Which is no more than to say that the streets and neighborhoods of Paris, like those of New York, London, and San Francisco, have their vicissitudes, with the fashionable promenade of one period becoming the combat zone of the next. Parisians of the 1860s spoke with wonder of the decline of the Palais Royal as a center of evening entertainment, of the boulevard du Temple as a street of popular theaters, and of the Chaussée d'Antin as a wealthy residential district. Macaulay in the 1840s could smile at the subjects of William III taking foreign visitors to admire Soho Square, just as he could imagine future New Zealanders inspecting the ruins of London Bridge. The fickleness of fashion, the transience of prosperity are commonplaces of urban life: how briefly Carnaby Street blazed! who remembers Biba's? where are the coffee bars now? Surely the one constant of urban geography is change.

Other places, perhaps, but not in Vienna. A subject of Franz Joseph, even a subject of Maria Theresa, would, if he could return to the Vienna of the 1980s, discover that the layout of things is pretty much as he remembered it. The best shops are still in the Graben, noblemen's palaces (admittedly no longer containing noblemen) still line the Herrengasse, and people still try to live as close to St. Stephen's Cathedral as their resources will allow. It would take the subject of Maria Theresa longer to discover that the Ringstrasse separates suburbs from City much as the wall and glacis of his age did, and to lament the appropriation by the middle classes of the sites of aristocratic summer retreats of his day; but by and large the social decline radiating visibly from an aristocratic City to a bourgeois inner suburbia and a proletarian outer suburbia interspersed with vineyards and country villages that he remembered would help orient him as he walked from the Schottentor through Josefstadt toward Hernals and the Wienerwald beyond. The subject of Franz Joseph, once he learned that his familiar Stadtbahn had become the U-Bahn and why the Hofburgtheater was now simply the Burgtheater, would have no difficulty at all in finding his way about and would usually see the kinds of people doing the kinds of things in the kinds of places he would expect.

I exaggerate, of course. Recent scholarship documenting and quantifying the physical and socioeconomic changes that have taken place over the centuries, and particularly since 1857, demonstrates how illusory and superficial is much of the seeming stability of Vienna's fabric and structure. Yet given the impact of the French Revolution and the Napoleonic Wars, the Revolution of 1848, the Industrial Revolution; its sudden demotion from capital of a multinational empire of fifty million to overgrown head of a tiny central European republic; the end of its days as a cosmopolitan center of Western culture—at periods the musical, scientific, medical, and scholarly center of the world; depression, inflation, the massacre of its Jewish population, invasion, occupation, partition; and finally the age of the common man, the Economic Miracle, socialism, and the egalitarian consumer society— and the list is far from exhaustive—that Vienna has survived at all, much less in a recognizable form, would seem enough of an achievement.

For all their aspirations toward monumentality, the three cities were more than public buildings, grand avenues, and expressive façades. Even the grandest of their inhabitants had finally to go home to wife and children, to dinner, and to bed. What did he find when he got there? What lay behind the stuccoed front of a Nash terrace, the neo-Grec scrollwork of a *maison à loyer* on a fashionable boulevard, the caryatides and atlantes supporting a Ringstrasse façade? Each of the three cities had its ideas and suspicions about the sort of domestic life that was led in the other two. How accurate were they? What were the nature and comparative importance of the private life and the public life of the three capitals?

THE CITY AS HOME

7

The Building and
the Dwelling

he two dominant institutions of the nineteenth century, the two focuses of loyalty, were the family and the nation-state. For nations that had not yet achieved statehood and for states whose very existence depended on the denial of nationality, the second posed a problem, as it certainly did for Vienna. But the family was something everybody could agree to praise: it posed no threat to church or state; nor was it incompatible with ideas of individual liberty. Domesticity represented uncontroversial good. Under such circumstances the nature, size, external appearance, internal arrangement, and location of the family dwelling occupied a central place in urban theory and practice. Opponents of the city questioned the compatibility of domestic values with urban life and doubted that the family could flourish in the midst of metropolitan distractions as it was supposed to in rural surroundings. Defenders of the city admitted the danger but thought that means could be found to strengthen the relations between husbands and wives, parents and children within the urban structure.

Between the late Middle Ages and the end of the eighteenth century there had developed, throughout western and northern Europe, a belief in the values of individualism, privacy, and domesticity. Domesticity "sealed off the family . . . [from] the surrounding world. . . . People begin spending greater proportions of their time at home," writes Edward Shorter.[1] Richard Sennett regards the emphasis on privacy as particularly characteristic of the nineteenth-century family, which stressed the distinction between "private reality" and "the public world outside the home." The family provided both "a refuge from the terrors of society" and "a moral yardstick . . . to measure the public realm of the capital city"; public life was perceived as "morally inferior."[2]

Huizinga saw in the architectural history of the preceding centuries growing concern for the individual and his family at the expense, perhaps, of the community:

> [A] shift from the social to the individual took place when the Renaissance saw the main task of the architect no longer in the building of churches and palaces but of dwelling-houses; not in splendid galleries but in drawing-rooms and bed-rooms. Art became more intimate, but also more isolated; it became an affair of the individual and his taste. In the same way chamber music and songs expressly designed for the

**The Family and the
Individual**

satisfaction of personal aestheticisms began to surpass the more public forms of art both in importance and often in intensity of expression.[3]

Stress on the identity of the individual can be seen in the encouragement of private confession in the thirteenth century and in the development of mysticism in the later Middle Ages. The Puritan diary as a device for systematic introspection, the use of the letter not merely to convey information but to express personal feelings, and the invention of the novel, the art form best able to analyze the individual personality and portray relations between individuals, suggest fundamental alterations in the way men and women perceived themselves and their place in the broader world. Such developments accompanied what Lawrence Stone has called the rise of "affective individualism," whereby the values of love, intimacy, and affection strengthened family units, encouraging the notion that self-realization could best be achieved within the family and a circle of close friends.

Domesticity, intimacy, privacy, and individuality do not necessarily or invariably support one another. Families can thwart the aspirations of their individual members, intimacy with outsiders can undermine the family unit. Nor ought architectural evidence be made to bear more interpretation than it can carry: what matters ultimately is how people *use* buildings and their internal spaces. No number of separate rooms will encourage withdrawal and introspection in winter if only one of them is heated.

Yet domestic architecture has value as a historical source. Richard Weiss has compared a house with a suit of clothes, outwardly expressing the person within. Like costume, "the house is an outer garment, a legible expression, filled with meanings, of the man in his family and friendship, with his animals and possessions, in his country and his landscape."[4] The dwellings of London, Paris, and Vienna illuminate the respective attitudes of the three societies toward domesticity, familial affection, privacy, and individuality.

London
The English were convinced that nowhere were domestic virtues better or more extensively cultivated than in England. Paris certainly, and Vienna so far as they knew about it, seemed on the whole more suitable for extramarital adventure than for sober family life. "A Frenchman cares less for comfort at home than for amusement abroad," wrote the *Building News* in 1857; "his idea of a house scarcely extends beyond a *salon* and a *salle à manger,* and, provided they be showily fitted up, he himself puts up with much that to an Englishman would be intolerably annoying."[5] The pleasure-loving Frenchman and the domesticated Englishman persist as stereotypes into our own day:

> Paris, the French agree, is a place to drink and eat in, and to walk and talk. It is the setting for a life of consumption, not of accumulation. Unlike London it is not, by and large, a place in which to have babies . . . or to save up for a new carpet, and there are no gardens in which to grow things. . . . [Even] well-off, professional families frequently live round echoing courtyards in apartments so cramped that anything resembling what educated Anglo-Saxons regard as family-life is impossible in them.[6]

So wrote, not entirely tongue-in-cheek, a perceptive English francophile in 1969. With how much greater horrified fascination did insular Georgians and Victorians look on the dubious spectacle of family life in Paris.

The English prided themselves on the intensity of their love for home. "It is one of our noblest characteristics to feel the charms of home, and in this word is included every blessing of domestic life," exclaimed the pseudonymous Sir Charles Darnley in 1823. "The great store that the English still set by owning their home is part of this powerful sense of the individual personality," wrote Hermann Muthesius in 1904. "The Englishman sees the whole of life embodied in his house."[7]

It was again and again asserted that English family life was possible only in a separate house, never in a flat. "*Indoor comfort* is essentially a Northern idea, as contrasted with a sort of outdoor enjoyment which is equally a Southern idea, and Oriental," wrote Robert Kerr in 1864. "Hence the difference between the French habits . . . and the English."[8] The separate house offered not only a more comfortable but a more moral life. The lax morals of the French, and probably other Europeans as well, resulted from their propensity for flat living. For Hermann Muthesius, "to live in a private house is in every way a higher form of life. . . . One cannot expect the present-day urban flat to replace all the moral and ethical values that are inherent in the private house." Life in a flat led to "instability, dissipation and shallowness in human society," while the Englishman's house gave him "closer contact with nature and the greater bodily and spiritual health which it brings"[9] (fig. 42).

Whatever its moral significance, the most obvious difference between most English and most continental cities was and is that the former are made up of small

42. *The Englishman's house gave him "closer contact with nature and the greater bodily and spiritual health which it brings."* Back gardens, Muswell Hill Place. (Museum of London.)

dwelling houses, the latter of large blocks of dwellings. In England, typically, the unit of dwelling and the unit of building are the same; on the continent the former is but a portion of the latter. Recent years have, to be sure, seen the widespread adoption of the single-family house in northern and western European cities and of the block of flats throughout England. In the nineteenth century, the Low Countries and individual cities elsewhere, such as Bremen, followed the English pattern, while Newcastle and its surrounding towns lived in flats on the continental model. Even in London, which *looked* as if it consisted overwhelmingly of single-family houses, two-fifths of all families had to share a house with others in 1911.[10] Beyond that the nature of both "house" and "block of flats" might vary tremendously: a back-to-back cottage in Leeds was a very different thing from a mansion in Queen's Gate; a Ringstrasse *Zinspalast* from a *Mietkaserne* in Hernals. Yet the contrast between the house-proud Englishman and the flat-living Continental held broadly true.

The difference had not always been so marked. The fundamental unit of the three cities in the medieval and early modern period had been the individual house, as often as not incorporating both workrooms and a shop facing the street. The nobleman's palace, coaching inn, church, monastery, or hospital were no more than occasional exceptions in any town devoted to manufacture and trade. It was when Vienna changed its character from that of *Bürgerstadt* to one of *Haupt- und Residenzstadt* in the seventeenth century that the traditional house began to be replaced by something much larger: aristocratic *Palais*, monastic *Stifthaus*, or—by the mid-eighteenth century—the first of the monster blocks of flats. Paris during the same period saw the building of a great many *hôtels particuliers* by nobility and bourgeoisie alike, but unlike the *Palais* of Vienna, as additions to rather than replacements of the traditional narrow house. The purpose-built *maison à loyer,* or block of flats, dates in its present form from the 1830s, although there were eighteenth-century predecessors. Only in London did the medieval house, as transformed and standardized after 1666, become and remain the normal and ubiquitous dwelling.

As late as 1911 no more than 3 percent of dwellings in England and Wales took the form of flats; the rest were separate houses, mostly arranged in long terraces.[11] Foreign visitors looked on the phenomenon with admiration, but the English themselves were often less pleased. The small size of the individual unit had contributed to "the London of stupid stucco, of dull, respectable 'brick boxes with slate lids' . . . acre upon acre of poor, dingy streets."[12] Frederic Harrison argued in 1887 that "the old, poisonous, crumbling houses of older London are doomed. And we must boldly face the necessity of rebuilding London some day for the masses in blocks."[13]

Londoners long resisted being rehoused in blocks, whether model dwellings for the poor, economical lodgings for the middle classes, or luxury flats for the rich. The houses they did occupy were remarkably standardized in form. Apart from the rare mansion that took the shape of a country house—Southampton House, Bloomsbury Square, for instance—the aristocratic town dwelling differed hardly at all in structure and not at all in outward decoration from that of a City tradesman. The ubiquity of the arrangement—two rooms per floor with staircase and hall to one side—astonished foreigners. "The structure is so uniform," wrote the Vienna *Gemeindezeitung* in 1862, "that only in larger houses, that have three and more rooms on each floor, can one doubt for an instant where each door must lead."[14]

The similarity of plan and uniformity of appearance of the standard London house contributed to ease of construction, in large or small quantities. It was adaptable to a variety of uses. No structural alterations whatever were required to turn it into a lodging house or private hotel, and only comparatively few (this mostly in the twentieth century) to convert each floor into a self-contained flat or any two into a "maisonette." Knocking holes into party walls could join two or more adjacent houses to create a larger hotel or larger flats. Conversion into a bank, or solicitors' offices, or a doctor's surgery was equally simple. The front parlor on the ground floor could become a shop, with a show window added for displaying goods.

Before the middle years of the nineteenth century, which saw the development of the purpose-built structure, practically any London building that was not a private dwelling had originally been one. This is true still of most of London between the City and Hyde Park, apart from the major thoroughfares, and of most suburban shopping streets as well. It had been true of the City itself until changing business needs replaced converted seventeenth- and eighteenth-century dwelling houses with specialized office blocks in the 1850s and 1860s (fig. 43).

The narrow terrace house, "built in long, uniform rows," produced an effect "dreary in the extreme," according to Hermann Muthesius. The architecture "does not usually vary between one house and the next, their façades run on with the same features to the point at which the developer has staked the limit of his plot."[15] Such terraces were rarely given to architects to design, and the profession looked with interest and favor at the aesthetic and social advantages that the block of flats seemed to offer. English architectural journals from the 1850s onward are filled with articles on blocks of flats in continental cities, on proposals for flats in English towns, and on the very occasional ones that actually got built in London. The Victorian public took to the idea with less enthusiasm. The first important blocks of flats went up in the early 1850s in Victoria Street—a Parisian-like *percée* which, connecting Parliament Square with Belgravia, would have seemed the ideal site for the experiment. Yet, as E. T. Hall recalled in 1901, some of "those stuccoed buildings in Victoria-street . . . remained for years unfinished, so little or so slowly did the idea take on."[16] A later development in Grosvenor Gardens (1865–68) was more successful. There followed the notorious eleven-story Queen Anne's Mansions, begun in 1874, and Richard Norman Shaw's Albert Hall Mansions of 1879.

By the early twentieth century new blocks of luxury "mansion flats" were going up all over London, although they were not yet regarded as providing proper homes for families, but rather as meeting a number of special circumstances. "Many people of the well-to-do classes who formerly only hired a house for the season now take a flat by the year . . . to which they can come when they please." Bachelor suites were to be found "in the side streets of clubland."[17] Hermann Muthesius feared that the demand for flats among the rich indicated a weakening of traditional values. "The more desultory, hastier life of today is beginning to loosen the ties . . . of English home-life . . . foreign influences have found their way into England. . . . Instead of the patriarchal family life of earlier times, many English families nowadays favour variety, freedom from encumbrances, liberty of movement, social distractions. It is for this section of modern England that flats exist." Solid English society resisted such temptations. "There is a firm belief all round that it is out of the question for a family with children to live in a flat."[18]

The many mansion flats in the West End of clearly Edwardian architecture sug-

43. *Practically any London building that was not a private dwelling had originally been one. This was true of the City itself until changing business needs replaced converted seventeenth- and eighteenth-century dwelling houses with specialized office blocks in the 1850s and 1860s.* Shops and offices in converted houses, Cornhill, c. 1830. G. Scharf. (British Museum.)

gest that a considerable section of London society was coming to prefer flat-living. The vast extent of "semi-detached London," mostly of twentieth-century origin, suggests that an immensely larger section continued to prefer "dull, respectable 'brick boxes with slate lids.'"

Paris   If for more than a century the English have regarded the flat with mingled fascination and suspicion, uncertain whether it could be an acceptable substitute for the private house, the Parisian middle classes greeted it from the outset as a boon.

The block of flats, in the sense of a building designed from the outset for multiple occupation, with separate suites of rooms each on a single floor, had made its appearance in Paris by the late seventeenth century, but did not become the dominant dwelling type until after the Revolution. Some were converted from noblemen's mansions; in other instances the street frontage of an *hôtel particulier* would be let as flats while the owner occupied the main building *entre cour et jardin*. Many were erected in the new streets north of the western boulevards during the eighteenth century.[19] Yet contemporary architectural theorists were little interested in the subject and tended to dismiss it with a few generalities.[20]

The Revolution made available a great many noble and ecclesiastical dwellings for conversion into flats, but only with the Restoration did new blocks of apartments start to go up in substantial numbers. The luxury and convenience they afforded made a great impression on contemporaries. "Though I am by no means prepared to say that I should like to exchange my long-confirmed habit of living in a house of my own for the Parisian mode of inhabiting apartments," wrote Mrs. Trollope in 1836, "I cannot but allow that by this and sundry other arrangements a French income is made to contribute infinitely more to the enjoyment of its possessor than an English one."[21]

César Daly linked the rise of the bourgeois flat to the decline, since the Revolution, of the aristocratic *hôtel*. The new multiple dwellings brought to the many some of the comforts enjoyed by the fortunate few of the ancien régime:

> There are today many small fortunes and many small *rentiers*. These small fortunes demand analogous apartments, and each apartment must necessarily be composed of a minimum number of rooms of a fixed nature, since this results inevitably from the needs of the households which are always the same. . . . Speculation has tried to respond to these needs, and architecture has lent itself with its customary versatility: ceilings are lowered, houses are made higher, rooms are diminished in width and length, and in the same space can be found eight to ten times more lodging than before.[22]

The *Allgemeine Bauzeitung* of 1843 commented on the multiplication of such dwellings in Paris:

> So there rises on the site of the splendid *hôtel* and its large garden . . . a dozen towering houses and, where once hardly a single family lived, ways are now found of quartering half a regiment of tenants. And for each household there is a complete flat with all the little comforts that are required in Paris—of course with rooms far less lofty and airy than those of the demolished *hôtel;* for all dimensions are reduced to a minimum, so that the rooms only contain as much air as is strictly necessary for breathing. And indeed they are more like the interior of a posting carriage than a comfortable flat.[23]

William H. White described the plan of a typical Parisian block of flats as it had developed by 1873. A carriage entrance led into a courtyard, from which a grand staircase and a smaller set of service stairs led upward. The ground floor was devoted to shops facing the boulevard and coachhouse and stabling behind. Each flat had "two cellars allotted to it in the *sous-sol,* and two bedrooms in the roof for a male and a female servant." Physical comforts were better taken care of in the seventies than they had been earlier, with running water in the newer houses even on the upper floors. Central heating warmed the public corridors, although not the flats themselves.[24]

"The magnificence of the great Parisian streets results from the habit of living in flats, as by this system a single house produces a large rental, which enables the builder to give it a magnificent front," wrote Philip Gilbert Hamerton in 1883. Flat-living was "the only practical way of reconciling wide streets with a dense population. Parisians look upon it as simply rational, and they can point to their own city as evident of the apparent spaciousness which results."25 Yet there was a tradition of criticizing the *maison à loyer* as a building type, and exalting the individual private house as morally, sanitarily, and aesthetically superior.26 Through most of the nineteenth century a larger proportion of Parisians occupied single-family houses than Londoners lived in flats, but the dominance of the multifamily dwelling was never seriously threatened.

Hôtels particuliers continued to be built, particularly in newly developing quarters, such as that to the west of the Invalides on the left bank, and beyond the Etoile on the right. They were not necessarily of the size and pretension of those in the avenue Foch, but included many of more modest proportions. Even so, as each district grew in population, building density, and property value, such dwellings gradually gave way to tall blocks of flats. Raymond Escholier wrote of their fate in 1913:

> Who has not come across such a private house of the Second Empire, generally set back from the street, crushed between two blocks thirty metres high [fig. 44]? Its two stories make a sad show next to the seven or eight stories of its insolent neighbors, with their bold projections and monumental heights. Deprived of air and light, the owner of the house . . . observes with dismay the dust of the road coming into it. In the end, he will have to resign himself, most often, to giving up his house—at a good price—to some building firm and go live in one of the *upper* stories of one of these vast blocks, that he had so long decried.

Escholier thought the triumph of the big apartment block and the decline of the private house a consequence of the demand for such modern devices as the telephone, the electric light, and the lift, and the new requirements of hygiene.27

An examination of the outer reaches of metropolitan Paris today will show that the private house did not die away after 1914, but the *hôtel particulier* as a specifically urban architectural type has become a thing of the past. Within Paris proper, the triumph of the flat is complete.

Vienna

Ludwig von Förster, writing in 1847, pointed to a significant piece of negative architectural evidence—the failure of a single medieval dwelling house, or indeed any earlier than the late seventeenth century, to survive into the mid-nineteenth century—for the victory of court, church, and aristocracy over bourgeoisie for mastery of Vienna.28 No physical catastrophe, like the fire of London, accounted for the fact; it was rather that the new owners of the City were rich enough to rebuild their dwellings.

The narrow, gabled medieval house, combining street-level shop with workrooms and living quarters for family, servants, and workmen, was in every way unsuitable for the nobleman, royal official, or bureaucrat. Vienna, a city devoted rather to consumption than to production, required architectural forms that would make that consumption both agreeable and conspicuous. For the fortunate few the palace did just that; by enabling the maximum number to live in immediate proximity to splendor, power, and pleasure, the block of flats (*Miethaus*) did the same for the moderately fortunate.

44. *"Who has not come across such a private house of the Second Empire, generally set back from the street, crushed between two blocks thirty metres high?"* Villa, 74 avenue Mozart, sixteenth arrondissement. (Evelyn Benesch.)

A palace being beyond the means even of most of the well-born and affluent, the multifamily dwelling became the norm for the upper as well as the middle classes by the seventeenth century. Many proprietors of palaces let out one or two stories as lodgings.[29] Since the values and aspirations of the occupants of flats were the same as those with palaces of their own, the architectural forms of the *Miethaus* came to imitate those of the *Adelspalast*. By throwing together the sites of several adjacent plots, room for more spacious flats as well as a more impressive external façade was achieved. By 1770 the baroque block of flats with a wide frontage had replaced the majority of narrow-fronted blocks of medieval origin.[30]

Really large blocks, containing more than one hundred flats each, were to be found by the late eighteenth century. The great monastic foundations led the way with the Melkerhof, Schottenhof, and Klosterneuburgerhof; secular landowners and investors followed. A frequent practice was for the building owner to occupy the entire first floor as a *Herrschaftswohnung*.[31] With symmetrically arranged façades, large inner courtyards, and impressive staircases, such blocks enabled their occupants to participate in a spaciousness and dignity greater than their individual means would have allowed.[32]

Mrs. Trollope found even more remarkable "than any outward splendour in the numerous and closely-wedged mansions of the noblesse . . . the incredible multitude of handsome residences that are to be found under one roof in Vienna." Among these she cited the Bürgerspital, near the Kärntner Tor. A hospital converted "into a most astonishing collection of handsome dwellings," it comprised "ten distinct internal courts, and twenty staircases; is fitted up in many parts with great elegance, contains two hundred inhabitants, and produces an annual rent of . . . about eight thousand five hundred pounds sterling"[33] (fig. 45).

In 1847 Ludwig von Förster boasted of the "much altered and imposing appearance" that Vienna had achieved during the previous thirty years in particular through the erection of bourgeois blocks of flats. An Englishman visiting Vienna three years later agreed that a great change had taken place: "Over the whole town, but especially in the inner city, numbers of the houses of the *smaller burgesses* have disappeared, and huge piles are erected in their stead."[34]

The Viennese *Zinspalast* (literally "Rent-Palace") gave the nineteenth-century burgher the *representation* of the eighteenth-century palace. What had been the privilege of the noble family in the past now became available for the occupant of the new multifamily blocks. Yet one could by no means take for granted that splendid apartments lay behind a splendid façade. The entrance, vestibule, and staircase might be disproportionately grand with respect to the cramped, dark,

---

45. *The Bürgerspital comprised "ten distinct internal courts, and twenty staircases; is fitted up in many parts with great elegance, [and] contains two hundred inhabitants."* Bürgerspital before its demolition in 1875. (Museen der Stadt Wien.)

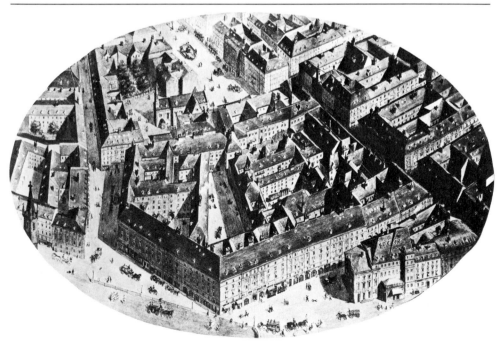

46. *The entrance, vestibule, and staircase might be disproportionately grand.* Elisabethstrasse 5, ground floor vestibule. Ludwig zon Zettl, architect, 1870. (Kunsthistorisches Institut der Universität Wien. Photo Johanna Fiegl.)

and ill-ventilated flats to which they led[35] (fig. 46). Mere comfort was willingly sacrificed to the appearance of aristocratic grandeur.

With the development of the Ringstrasse zone after 1857 came a resurgence of palace-building proper, as well as palatial imitations. Other members of the royal family built themselves little Hofburgs, combining ceremonial with domestic functions.[36] At the moment of triumph for the liberal bourgeoisie, the period in which the Industrial Revolution came to Austria, the palace not only served as the dominant architectural model, but itself enjoyed an upsurge in building activity, suggesting that the old ruling class still ruled, not just in the sense of having captured the popular imagination, but in reality.

Writing of the period 1848–1914, Arno Mayer has pointed out that "the economically radical bourgeoisie was as obsequious [to the old aristocracy] in cultural life as it was in social relations and political behaviour."[37] Nowhere was this more evident than along the Ringstrasse, where they went out of their way to build and occupy residential blocks whose form and structure glorified aristocratic values and posited a life-style contemptuous of thrift, sobriety, diligence, the single-minded pursuit of gain, and every other conceivable bourgeois virtue.[38] As Carl Schorske has observed, "the new Viennese middle-class man aspired to be not so much a patrician as a nobleman, in his outward appearance even if not in his inner values."[39]

In 1860, just as the block of flats was about to achieve its most splendid manifestation in the early Ringstrasse development, the art historian Rudolf von Eitelberger and the architect Heinrich von Ferstel published a pamphlet calling for the revival of the private house for the Viennese middle classes. They proposed not the modern English type of dwelling, but an adaptation of the medieval house, with ground-level shop, owner's flat above, and workrooms on the upper floors. Their explicit aim was to strengthen the bourgeois family and through it the bourgeoisie as the bulwark of the state. "The solidity of the state and the guarantee of its existence lie in the hands of the propertied class. . . . The citizen of a town who can own a house supports the state in a wholly different way from one who does not."[40]

By rendering it unnecessary for the householder to leave home to pursue his business activities, the combination of domesticity and work under the same roof would have equally happy moral and social consequences. The greater privacy and separateness of the dwelling unit would strengthen family ties, while the proximity of the workrooms, storerooms, and shop would instill in the sons an interest and pride in the work of the father. Above all, the proposal sought to combat what the authors saw as the corruption by luxury of traditional bourgeois values. The modern bourgeois flat appealed to the unworthy aspirations of the class to an inappropriate style of living, symbolized by folding doors (*Flügelthüren*) and ornamental shutters (*Spalettläden*). They called instead for a dwelling that would "meet the needs of bourgeois life" and be "comfortable, livable, and cheap."[41]

The failure of the Viennese bourgeoisie to build so much as a single house on the lines suggested by Eitelberger and Ferstel indicates how deeply rooted these "unworthy aspirations" were and how corrupted by luxury traditional bourgeois values had already become. A dwelling that was comfortable, livable, and cheap would no longer do: only one that was splendid, luxurious, and expensive could satisfy demands for an aristocratic style of life. To live frugally in a low dwelling over one's own shop might have seemed appropriate in the medieval town, but centuries of exposure to a court and aristocracy engaged in self-indulgence and competitve display had convinced the Viennese middle class that happiness was to be found more readily in a palace.

The architect Ferdinand Fellner responded to Ferstel and Eitelberger with another pamphlet, *Wie soll Wien bauen?* While accepting their assumptions about the moral function of architecture and the desirability of using it to strengthen both family ties and the integrity of the individual, he argued that the modern flat could best achieve such purposes, promoting privacy through its single-purpose rooms. The *Allgemeine Bauzeitung* argued that the Viennese *Zinshaus* combined elegance with comfort and seclusion (*Abgeschlossenheit*). Neither Berlin, where flats were inadequately separated from one another, nor Paris, where flimsy construction subjected the flat-dweller to the noise from neighboring households, provided the solid satisfactions of the Viennese dwelling. Nor were the stereotyped houses of England and America appropriate models for imitation.[42] Ferstel himself went on to design some of the most splendid blocks of flats in the Ringstrasse zone.[43] The flat remains to this day the nearly universal Viennese dwelling.

8

Inside the Dwelling

t is customary to treat the history of the dwelling from the Middle Ages onward as one of gradually enhanced provisions for personal comfort and privacy. The course from the promiscuity of the multipurpose great hall to Virginia Woolf's room of one's own has been presented either as the progressive triumph of refinement and recognition of the worth of the individual, or as the victory of egoism over the demands of human fellowship. All members of the medieval household were in the closest physical proximity, while eating, at work, at play, and even in sleeping arrangements. Lines of demarcation between public and private, domestic and civic, inner and outer, personal and collective were less distinct than they were to become by the nineteenth century, or even the eighteenth. The physical structure of the medieval house reflected and encouraged such a state of things. All-purpose rooms were the rule, in aristocratic, peasant, and artisan dwellings alike. Neither the structural arrangements nor the way the rooms were used made possible privacy, individuality, or intimacy in the modern sense.[1]

First in noble households and then, very gradually, lower in the social scale came structural provision for "withdrawal at will from the common life and the common interests of one's fellows. Privacy in sleep; privacy in eating; privacy in religious and social ritual; finally, privacy in thought."[2] It is by no means clear how the distinction between things public and things private emerged, nor when the desire to shut oneself off from the outside world came to seem other than the aberration of a hermit or an eccentric. The encouragement of introspection by late medieval devotional literature, the advantages of solitude for reading the new and more abundant printed books, the emphasis on the individual personality in Renaissance thought ought to have brought about some modification in the noisy confusion of domestic life among those classes able to afford the installation of a few partitions.

Late medieval houses did offer more rooms to which either the ladies or the whole of the noble family could withdraw from the activity of the great hall. But even the elaborate multiroom dwellings of the Renaissance and baroque lacked provisions for individual privacy. If they had more rooms, such rooms were little more intended for specific, limited purposes than the great hall had been, nor were they furnished with single-purpose fittings. Portable tables, to be set up for meals where and when needed, and even portable beds were common until the sixteenth century.[3]

The Public and the Private

The seventeenth century saw some evidence of a desire to establish greater distance between family and servants, through such devices as the bell rope, which enabled servants to be available when needed without being inconveniently there at other times. Such physical separation may, paradoxically, have stemmed from the breakdown of the older social hierarchy. When the reality was unmistakably there, symbolic representation was unnecessary; with the reality gone, formal expression came to seem essential. For Lewis Mumford the move toward domestic privacy had from the start "marked the beginning of that new alignment of classes which was to usher in the merciless class competition and individual self-assertion of a later day."[4]

With clearer boundaries separating family from servants and the outside world, earlier boundaries of formality and reserve between husband and wife, parents and children, could now be taken down.[5] Yet architecture responded with surprising slowness to the wish to be alone. "All those agreeable arrangements . . . now admired in our modern mansions," wrote Pierre Patte in 1769, "in which the apartments are separated with so much art—those back staircases which render domestic service so easy—have only been invented in our time."[6] Mercier in 1782 included among the recent wonders of Parisian architecture "secret and invisible staircases, little unsuspected cabinets, false entries that mask real exits . . . and those laybrinths where one hides to indulge in one's tastes, eluding the curious eyes of the servants."[7]

The tastes indulged in were not necessarily those that strengthened family bonds: architectural subdivisions permitting greater privacy did not always work to encourage domestic intimacy. A critical article in a German periodical in the early 1850s suggested that they had quite the opposite effect: "Our private town-houses of the sixteenth and seventeenth centuries opened to the comer at once large areas, halls, and courts. . . . Those large spaces . . . were for the use of *all* the members of the household. . . . In the *modern* residences of the wealthy citizen, however, all the spaces belonging to the *communality* of the family and household have been reduced to the least possible compass." Such a room plan isolated the members of the family not only from visitors and servants but from one another. The article noted that the family room, "the common abode of man and wife, children and domestics," was becoming smaller and smaller or even disappearing, while "the *separate* rooms of the members of the family become every day more numerous and distinct. Father, mother, and children claim now a whole set of different rooms. . . . Parents dwell separate from each other, and the cradle of the children stands no more close to the couch of the mother. The nursery, especially, cannot be distant enough from the abode of *polite* parents."[8]

But for the most part internal changes in European dwellings helped make possible closer and more affectionate relations within the family. The division between rooms and sections of the house was made on the basis of social, functional, and moral criteria. The last category may account for the growing tendency to ban visitors from bedrooms, or, to put it another way, to move beds out of rooms open to strangers. As late as the eighteenth century ostentatious beds were found in the reception rooms of the continental nobility, although the bourgeoisie shunned the practice as decadent. The bedroom itself became a forbidden zone, sharply differentiated from the domestic living rooms.[9]

In all such changes England led the way. As early as the sixteenth century even a yeoman's house might contain "the kitchen, the buttery, the best parlor, two or three separate bedrooms, the servants' chamber, besides the truncated medieval hall now shorn of many of its functions."[10] By the nineteenth century, subdivision into single-purpose rooms had in the greater country houses reached a peak of refinement, efficiency, and absurdity. Elaborate systems of back passages kept armies of servants invisible. Separate staircases for masters and servants, men and women, family and guests led to specialized rooms, each isolated from the others, each appropriate for one use only.[11] Rooms acquired names—breakfast room, smoking room, and the like—specifically indicating their purpose.[12] The proportion of bedrooms to reception rooms increased: private sleeping arrangements were coming to seem more important than impressing visitors.

"All sorts of influences", wrote Hermann Muthesius in 1904, "combine to make the English room essentially different from the continental. Perhaps the most striking difference is the lack in England of communicating doors between the rooms."[13] Robert Kerr had forty years earlier in *The Gentleman's House* wrestled at length with the problem of intercommunicating doors. Though he allowed them in special cases, they were always fraught with danger. One might, for instance, be permitted to link the drawing room with the boudoir, library, or morning room. "For a small room such a door is always to be discouraged; but that the ladies find it to be occasionally of service . . . cannot be disputed. Its general purposes . . . [are] for private exit."[14] In the eighteenth century connections between rooms had been as common in England as they continued to be on the Continent. Muthesius attributed their banishment in Victorian England to the "diminishing desire for sociability," which was gradually replaced by the "desire to live quietly, in self-sufficiency, secluded from the hubbub of the city."[15]

Even the rich could not indulge in the luxury of subdivision and segregation in their town houses to the extent that they could in the country, but all classes in London strove for a degree of personal privacy greater than that achieved by their counterparts in Paris or Vienna. To this end they sacrificed others, in particular the facilities for entertaining with maximum éclat. The result was an increasing complexity of floor plan, often at the expense of the size of individual rooms, made more difficult by the growing number of servants in the ordinary middle-class household: each new servant represented a further threat to privacy, which had to be offset by yet another separate corridor, yet another way to make the servant always accessible, but never inopportunely there.

Kerr hailed the improving provisions for domestic privacy, especially those that facilitated the "separation of the family from the servants, and the still further retirement of the female sex."[16] Even within the rooms occupied by the family there were degrees of publicity and privacy. "In a superior house, the dining-room, the drawing-room, the library, the billiard-room, and the hall and staircase, are of a public character," Kerr explained, "whereas the gentleman's room, sometimes the morning-room, and in all cases the boudoir . . . are strictly private." Bedrooms and the nursery had "a special privacy."[17]

Kerr thought London houses "generally very defective in respect of plan."[18] Yet the nature and shape of the standard London terrace house enabled it both to respond to the demand for segregated, single-purpose rooms and to provide visual

The London House

expression of the principles that lay behind that demand. Building plots being typically deep but narrow, houses could grow only by expanding to the rear and by adding extra stories. There was rarely space for more than two rooms, front and back, flanked by the staircase and corridor, with a possible third room in a narrower rear extension. Each floor was assigned a particular kind of room, and a distinction made between rooms facing the street and rooms at the back.[19]

From his study of houses built by Thomas Cubitt on the Grosvenor estate in Belgravia, César Daly concluded that the typical London house consisted of six levels, including the ground floor and basement. The basement was the "atelier" of the house; the ground floor was the realm of "l'hospitalité gastronomique" and belonged in particular to the master of the house, who had there his library and dressing room. The lady of the house ruled the first floor, devoted as it was to drawing rooms and a boudoir. Above were bedrooms, the nursery, and at the very top rooms for the female servants[20] (figs. 47 and 48).

The house thus provided sexual as well as social and functional segregation. The dining room had to show "a certain masculinity, gravity and sternness [*Ernst und*

47. *(below and opposite) The typical London house consisted of six levels.* Elevation and plans for third-class house, Lowndes Street. From *Revue générale de l'architecture* 13 (1855), pls. 20–21.

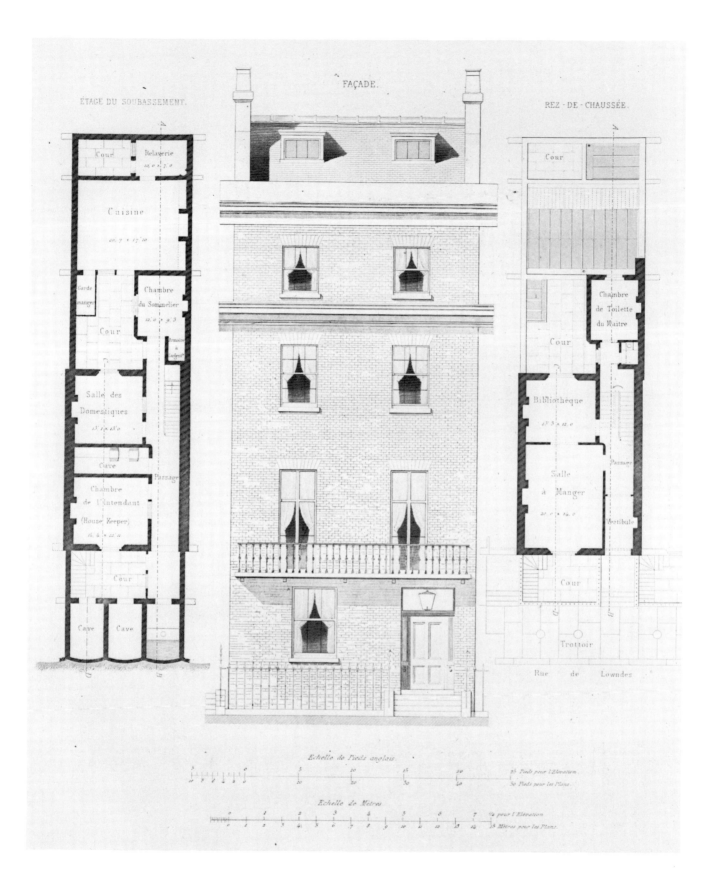

ÉTAGE DU SOUBASSEMENT.

FAÇADE.

REZ - DE - CHAUSSÉE.

Cour

Relayerie

Cuisine

Garde manger

Chambre du Sommelier

Cour

Armoire à l'argent

Salle des Domestiques

Cave

Passage

Chambre de l'Intendant (House Keeper)

Cour

Cave Cave

Cour

Chambre de Toilette du Maitre

Cour

Bibliothèque

Passage

Salle à Manger

Vestibule

Cour

Trottoir

Rue de Lowndes

Echelle de Pieds anglais.

25 Pieds pour l'Elévation.

50 Pieds pour les Plans.

Echelle de Mètres.

½ pour l'Elévation.

25 Mètres pour les Plans.

105

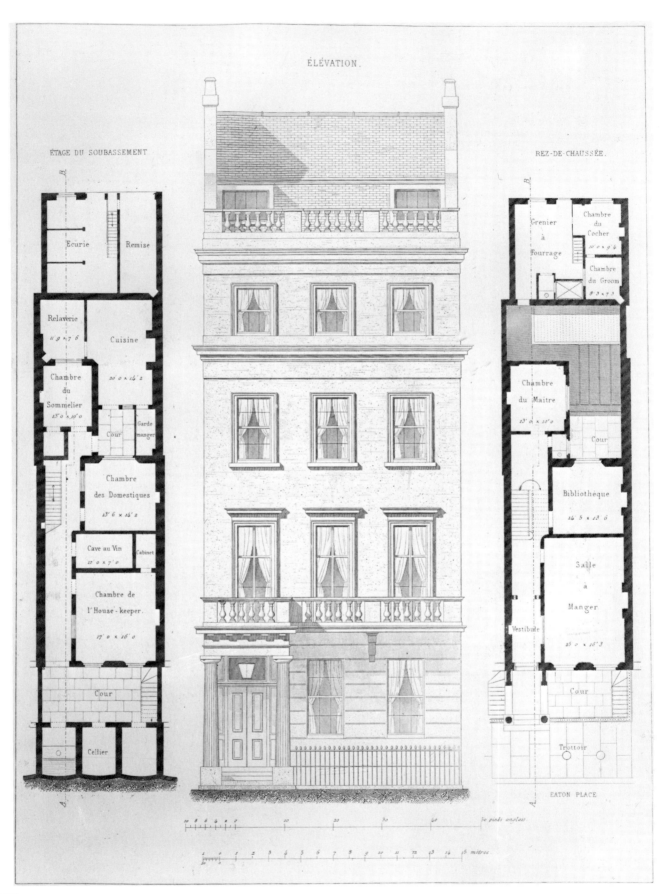

ÉLÉVATION.

ÉTAGE DU SOUBASSEMENT

Ecurie   Remise

Relaverie
11'9 × 7'6   Cuisine

Chambre   20'0 × 14'2
du
Sommelier
15'0 × 10'0
                    Cour   Garde
                            manger

Chambre
des Domestiques
13'6 × 14'2

Cave au Vin
12'0 × 7'0   Cabinet

Chambre de
l'House-keeper.
17'0 × 16'0

Cour

Cellier

REZ-DE-CHAUSSÉE.

Grenier   Chambre
à   du
Fourrage   Cocher
               10'0 × 9'6

               Chambre
               du Groom
               8'3 × 7'3

Chambre
du Maitre
13'0 × 10'0

                      Cour

Bibliothèque
14'5 × 13'6

Salle
à
Manger

Vestibule   25'0 × 16'3

               Cour

            Trottoir

EATON PLACE

50 pieds anglais

15 mètres

106

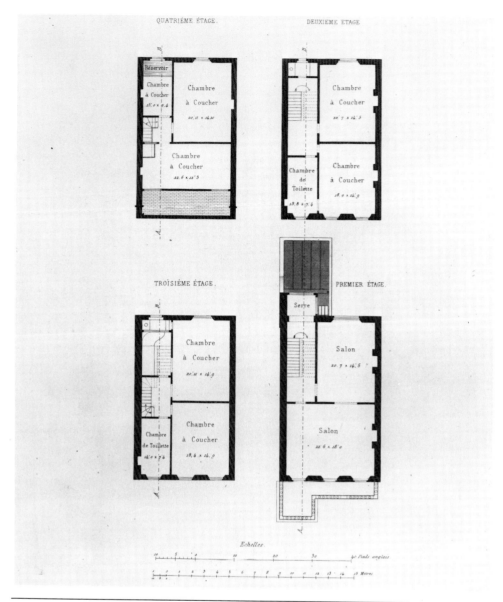

48. *(opposite and above)* Elevation and plans for second-class house in Eaton Place. Eaton Place was the residence of the Bellamys in *Upstairs, Downstairs*.

Strenge] in its character," while the drawing room was expected to show "feminine charm [*weibliche Anmuth*] and elegant daintiness [*elegante Zierlichkeit*]."[21] The former required furniture that was "somewhat massive and simple (what is called heavy)"; it needed not be "sombre and dull," but its whole aspect was to be one "of masculine importance." In more pretentious houses the dining room was used only at mealtimes. In smaller houses, "the Dining-room is used as a Family Sitting-room . . . sometimes for the evening alone, at least in winter, when Paterfamilias, having done his day's work and dined, refuses to move any more from his easy chair." A more private retreat for Paterfamilias was the adjacent library, "not a Library in the sole sense of a depository for books," but "rather a sort of Morning-room for gentlemen than anything else. Their correspondence is done here, their reading, and, in some measure, their lounging."[22]

One flight up was the drawing room, "the Lady's Apartment essentially, being the modern form of the Lady's Withdrawing-room or perfected Chamber of Mediaeval plan." Accordingly it needed to suggest "cheerfulness, refinement of elegance, and what is called lightness . . . the rule of everything is . . . to be entirely ladylike." For further privacy the lady could retreat to the boudoir, "the Lady's Bower of the olden time."[23] Middle-class women were in the nineteenth century encouraged to withdraw more and more from the public to the private sphere, and the planning of dwellings that would increase the possibilities and stress the appropriateness of modest female withdrawal was in keeping with the new ideology.[24]

That a house plan permitting a high degree of separation of husband from wife appealed to English instincts is suggested by a passage in George Gissing's *In the Year of Jubilee:*

> "The only married people," Tarrant pursued, "who can live together with impunity, are those who are rich enough, and sensible enough, to have two distinct establishments under the same roof. The ordinary eight or ten-roomed house, inhabited by decent middle-class folk, is a gruesome sight. What a huddlement of male and female! They are factories of quarrel and hate—those respectable, brass-curtain-rodded sties—they are full of things that won't bear mentioning."[25]

The lady in her drawing room or boudoir was separated not only from her husband on the ground floor but from the servants in the basement kitchen (fig. 49). "The lady of an English house never sets foot in the kitchen and the cook would not want her to do so," Hermann Muthesius explained to his German readers.[26] A German cook would have expected her employer to play an active role supervising something so important as the preparation of meals.[27] Describing the typical day in the household of a high court official in the Vienna of the 1770s, Karoline Pichler remarks that only when the hour for the main midday meal approached did his wife "leave the kitchen, in which she, ever since the gentlemen had left for their business, had been engaged with great practical knowledge [*Sachkenntnis*] with the preparation of the midday meal, in order to dress."[28]

Above the drawing-room floor came the bedroom floors, of decreasing state as one went upward. Each bedroom, Jacob von Falke explained, "requires only one single and independent entrance." This was in contrast to the frequent continental situation in which it was necessary to pass through one bedroom to reach the second, a state of affairs that confirmed the worst English suspicions about continental morals. The position of the bed also differed from continental practice: "In contrast to our manner of placing the bed lengthwise against the wall, in contrast to the French custom of concealing it in a gloomy alcove, the large, wide bed, with canopy and curtains, is placed with its head against the wall, so that it extends in a free and airy fashion into the room."[29] An English bedroom was seldom seen by other than its occupants. Balzac observed that in England the sanctity of the marriage chamber was such that even servants were forbidden entry, and other Frenchmen commented with wonder and amusement at its character of withdrawal and mystery.[30]

The nursery floor lay just above that containing the parents' bedroom. "Except when they are driven out or taken for a walk, the children spend the whole time in the nursery under the supervision of women engaged for the purpose and contact with their parents is far less frequent than in continental households," according to Hermann Muthesius. "Everything, including meals, is separate." The arrangement

49. *The lady in her drawing room was separated from the servants in the basement kitchen.* Kitchen, Torrington Square, October 1851. G. Scharf. (British Museum.)

certainly made life pleasanter for adults. The children remained "separate members of the household until adolescence," and so strictly were they segregated that "a stranger may visit the house without being in the least aware that there are children in it."[31] Kerr, to be sure, while upholding the principles of privacy and segregation in this connection, was aware of the equally important ones of domesticity and motherhood. "As against the principle of the withdrawal of the children for domestic convenience, there is the consideration that the mother will require to have a certain facility of access to them. . . . No English mother, even a duchess, will confide her children wholly to other hands than her own."[32]

Daly pointed out that the service stairs were, untypically, carpeted between the floor containing the parents' bedroom and the nursery floor, "in order that the thoughtless acts of childhood have fewer risks to run, and that the child who, happy to run and say good morning to his mother, rushes down the stairs, does not become the victim of his affectionate outburst [*tendre emportement*]."[33] The explanation sounds more applicable to a French family than an English, in which the nanny would surely have been able to exercise greater control over such thoughtless and impulsive behavior. My suspicion is that the carpet was there more for the mother's benefit than to encourage the children to pay unexpected visits to their parents' bedroom.

The complacency with which the middle-class Victorian regarded his pattern of domestic living is odd, considering how much effort was expended on isolating the different members of his family one from another. Children were relegated to the nursery and only brought before parents when carefully scrubbed and on their best behavior at tea, and they were sent away to school at an age that continues to horrify Europeans. Father would, to be sure, emerge from the library to join Mother, in her drawing room, if he was not spending the evening at his club, but the general design of the house seemed intended to separate both the sexes and the generations. On architectural evidence one would have to say that the Victorians valued the individual and cherished privacy more than they did domestic intimacy.

The main beneficiaries were the parents, the father in particular. Middle-class children, lumped together with brothers and sisters in day or night nursery under the watchful eye of nurse or governess, had precious little privacy. Nor were preparatory schools or even public schools, with their communal dormitories and elaborate provision for constant surveillance, designed to produce introspective, independent individuals. One gathers from *Tom Brown's Schooldays* that even the provision of separate beds at Rugby in the 1820s was a daring innovation, while Eton, with its separate sleeping cubicles and study rooms, was regarded with admiration for providing what in other contexts would seem the bare minimum for individual decency. Among the affluent classes, personal privacy was a privilege to be earned by a childhood and adolescence in which it was consistently denied.

Although the physical layout of the Victorian middle-class house made individual isolation technically feasible, it is far from clear how much advantage the members of the family actually took of the possibility. Bedrooms were intended to be used only for sleeping: the bed-sitting room, where it existed, was regarded as evidence of decadence and sloth. The practice of lighting fires in bedrooms only as a special privilege during periods of sickness suggests that for practical purposes they were in any event uninhabitable. Fanny Price, to be sure, braved the icy chill of her room—actually the disused school-room, not her bedroom—at Mansfield Park even before Sir Thomas ordered a fire to be lit there, but her disinclination for general society was regarded as eccentric, and even she seems to have spent most of the day attending Lady Bertram.

The basement, divided and subdivided into specialized work areas, gave, according to Daly, "the serious advantages of tranquility, privacy, cleanliness, and order."[34] From the elaborate nature of the kitchen facilities and subordinate offices deemed essential even in modest middle-class households, one would have expected Victorian England to be a gourmet's paradise. Kerr describes such facilities in a substantial domestic establishment as attaining "the character of a complicated laboratory . . . specially contrived . . . for the administration of the culinary art in all its professional details." The principle of maintaining separate rooms for each function was as rigorously adhered to in the basement as in the floors above. "In no circumstances (except they be very peculiar indeed)," warned Kerr, "ought a Kitchen to include the fittings proper to a Scullery,—for instance, the usual sink and plate-rack. Neither ought there to be any compromise of the independence of the Larder. . . . The use of a Kitchen as a Sitting-room for the servants can only be admissible in small houses."[35]

A wonderfully complex network of rooms and cupboards and passages lay behind the area of a London house. "The kitchen has a whole series of ancillary rooms, the larder is divided into storerooms for all the different provisions and there are various separate rooms for the various kinds of cleaning," wrote Muthesius in 1904. "Every size of house in England contains betweeen twice and four times as many domestic rooms as the continental house."[36]

Now that in the mostly servantless English households the kitchen has contracted to the manageable size that prevails elsewhere, we are as puzzled as Muthesius was by its former extent. Was Parkinson's Law at work, producing more and more separate departments to justify the employment of the size of staff deemed appropriate, necessitating in turn the hiring of even more kitchen and scullery maids to move food, pots, dishes, and other objects from room to room in order, with great expenditure of effort, to prepare something as simple as soft-boiled eggs and toast? The elaborate division of labor that Alexis Soyer introduced into the kitchens of the Reform Club may have encouraged unwise imitation in ordinary upper- and middle-class households (fig. 50). Certainly more servants as well as more elaborate equipment dispersed over more rooms were necessary to prepare simpler meals than those a German housewife and a single maid-of-all-work could between the two of them produce.[37] But it ill becomes a generation that is installing computers

50. *The elaborate division of labor that Alexis Soyer introduced into the kitchens of the Reform Club may have encouraged unwise imitation in ordinary upper- and middle-class households.* Reform Club, Kitchen. (Guildhall Library. Photo Godfrey.)

as a necessary part of every home to criticize an earlier one for making housekeeping needlessly complicated.

If a large and underworked kitchen staff producing boring meals gave the English householder the kind of satisfaction that a long perspective of reception rooms seen through folding doors gave his Viennese counterpart, one can only admire the skill and lunatic logic with which the whole operation was carried out. Less easy to understand are the subdivided kitchens in households that had neither the money nor the energy to squander on such foolishness: for the separate scullery came to be a nearly universal feature of English households of all sorts. By the middle of the century, the separation had taken place in medium-sized houses;[38] by the end of the century Muthesius found that "even in workmen's cottages the areas for cooking and washing-up are kept separate."[39] Under such circumstances the making of a pot of tea became a significant logistical operation. Fortunately for our view of working-class good sense, there is reason to think that between 1870 and 1914 working-class households were tending to relegate cooking from the kitchen to the scullery, particularly with the general introduction of gas cookers in the 1890s.[40]

There came in those years, even in middle-class households, a certain reaction against the overelaboration of mid-Victorian times. The Queen Anne style of the 1870s began a move away from the tall, formal, rationally subdivided house that Kerr had advocated, to something more like the standard middle-class dwelling of the twentieth century—with no basement, the kitchen and all the reception rooms on the ground floor, and bedrooms above. The English back garden that we know today, typically reached directly by french windows from the rear parlor, also dates from the late nineteenth century.[41]

"A remarkable change has come over the style of suburban villa building during the past twenty years," according to the *Builder* of 1909. "The scale on which the modern house is built is minute; the furniture of the Victorian period is always far too large for such interiors . . . the 'basement' style of house is quite discarded."[42] The change was most noticeable in the suburbs, but also affected new terrace housing in the towns themselves.[43]

What seemed to Hermann Muthesius most distinctive about the English house was the informality that reigned. "The habit of entertaining large numbers to great feasts which is so common in Germany . . . is virtually unknown in England," he reported. Dinner parties were kept small and simple. "The desire to impress his guests with special kinds of food and drink or to outdo . . . others is entirely alien to the Englishman and would be regarded as a mark of bad taste." Refreshments served at the middle-class "at home" are "of the simplest, even the most primitive kind, indeed, a German would pronounce them positively inadequate: they consist of coffee, tea, fruit-cup, cakes and sandwiches. But . . . no one would come on account of the food." The architectural dimension of such studied simplicity was the absence of what in Germany would be called the representational element, what the Victorians described with distaste as "showy." "One is struck," Muthesius noted, "by the slight importance that is attached to . . . purely ceremonial apartments. Houses designed for quite large households . . . contain, apart from a hall of variable size, no rooms that are not used for the purposes of every-day living."[44]

The dominance of the English Domestic style of architecture in late Victorian and

Edwardian times partly accounts for the appearance of informal ease. Already in the sixties, though, Kerr had stressed comfort, convenience, and "unassuming grace." Even if "the circumstances of the owner and his tastes are such that magnitude and refinement ought to expand into state, even grandeur must not be pretentious, or wealth ostentatious." Domestic considerations were always to be kept paramount: "The primary maxim in favor of family comfort in the Family-rooms must be understood to govern, without diminution, no matter what amount of state may reign elsewhere."[45]

Nowhere were considerations of comfort and practical utility more rigorously applied than in the bathrooms and lavatories. "Until recently the sanitary installations in the house represented an area over which England ruled supreme and all other countries were dependent upon her," wrote Muthesius in 1904.[46] The supply of piped water to houses in the more favored districts of London and the installation of storage cisterns in the individual dwellings permitted the widespread use of water closets far earlier than was the case in either Paris or Vienna. Fixed baths came somewhat later, but as early as 1840 César Daly could report that they were frequently to be found in newer houses in London. "The presence of a bathroom was taken for granted in England at a time when it was still an exception in the German house," wrote Muthesius sixty years later. "The smallest houses in England have bathrooms nowadays and . . . none of the new workmen's cottages lacks a bathroom."[47]

By the 1890s flats were becoming familiar features of many parts of London. To attract prospective tenants, architects strove to give them a degree of horizontal subdivision as great as the standard town house provided vertically. Space was squandered to give them an abundance of single-purpose rooms, separate corridors for the servants and the family, and a location for the kitchen far from the dining room. That the results even so failed to satisfy Victorian sensibilities is suggested by a passage from Gissing's *In the Year of Jubilee:*

> Another cab conveyed her to Brixton, and set her down before a block of recently built flats. She ascended to the second floor, pressed the button of a bell, and was speedily confronted by a girl of the natty parlour-maid species. This time she . . . had only a moment to wait before she was admitted to a small drawing-room, furnished with semblance of luxury. A glowing fire and the light of an amber-shaded lamp showed as much fashionable upholstery and bric-à-brac as could be squeezed into the narrow space. Something else was perceptible which might perhaps have been dispensed with; to wit, the odour of a very savoury meal, a meal in which fried onions had no insignificant part. But before the visitor could comment to herself upon this disadvantage attaching to flats, Beatrice joined her.[48]

Whatever the disadvantage, the next century would bring the kitchen and its odors more to the notice of visitor and Beatrice alike. In flat, terrace house, and detached villa, there would be fewer natty parlor maids to answer bells, and floor plans would lose their Byzantine complexity. Paterfamilias and the lady of the house might wish to retreat to library and boudoir, but in fact both are in the kitchen, respectively peeling onions and setting the table for themselves and their nannyless children. The middle-class household has become more domestic, if less private, than it ever was in Victorian days.

The Paris Flat

The Parisian flat was regarded with disapproval by Londoners, with complacency by the Parisians themselves, and with envy by the Viennese. Using criteria of degrees of spaciousness and privacy, and the availability of sanitary and other amenities, and leaving aside the very rich and the very poor, a family of equivalent economic status would be housed better in Paris than in Vienna, better in London than in Paris. The rich were of course housed splendidly in all three, the poor abominably.

Contemporary English and French accounts of the living arrangements of the Parisian middle classes in the middle years of the nineteenth century seem to be describing two entirely different things. Here is César Daly on the Paris flat as it was in 1840: "As to the layout of rooms and to those innumerable little arrangements that are so important in our homes today, we are incontestably more ingenious than our predecessors were, and families of moderate means, which are the hardest to lodge comfortably, have never been so well provided for as they are now." Yet the *Building News* found in Parisian flats nothing but "positive inconvenience of the most disagreeable kind."[49]

It is hard today to understand the delight which the subjects of Louis-Philippe took in their new, dark, oddly arranged flats, with none of the amenities subsequent generations would find indispensable: piped water, gas, central heating, water closets, bathrooms, to name a few. Their delight becomes less unaccountable if we compare them with the dwellings available to the ordinary Parisian of the ancien régime. The middle-class house of Victorian London was a recognizable version of the Georgian house. The new flats of the 1830s and 1840s in Paris—self-contained, on a single level, with rooms appointed for specific purposes—marked a revolutionary advance in comfort over what had existed before.

For all but the rich, the nastiness of life in ancien régime Paris did not end once the filth of the streets had been left behind. The lodgings to be had in the narrow, backward-sloping houses that lined them offered only the most basic of comforts. Too large for single-family occupation, too small to offer adequate accommodation for a family on any one floor, the standard Parisian house had all of the disadvantages of the London house with none of its advantages. The fortunate occupant of the ground floor would have a kitchen and a *salle;* other tenants would have to adapt for their purposes as many separate rooms on as many different floors as they could afford. Since the building was rarely more than two windows in width, and ordinarily offered no more than two rooms—often only one—on a floor, the possibilities of adaptation for a comfortably bourgeois style of living were limited.[50]

It was from such houses, which still abound in the narrow streets of the first four arrondissements, as well as in the fifth and sixth across the river, that those Parisians who could afford the higher rents flocked into the purpose-built flats of the quartiers Saint-Georges, Chaussée d'Antin, Saint Lazare, and de l'Europe during the Restoration and July monarchy. A.-L. Lusson, writing in 1847, accounted for the migration in large measure by the demand "for certain conveniences . . . notably this comfortable arrangement as a whole and in detail of our apartments, an arrangement which our architects strive to render ever more pleasant in their new constructions." In the new neighborhoods, every dwelling "offers the combination of varying rooms into a complete apartment, something very difficult to get in the houses of past ages."[51]

If César Daly perceived aesthetic deterioration from the days of the *hôtels par-*

ticuliers of the eighteenth century, he saw great improvement in the interior arrangements:

> That had to be: when an apartment is very small, and the antechamber, the kitchen, the privy [*les lieux*], the dining room, the bedrooms of the family and of the servants, are all reduced to tighter proportions and find themselves compressed one against the others, having only thin partitions to separate them, careful organization [*beaucoup d'ordre*] is necessary for everything to take place in a suitable manner [*pour que tout se passe convenablement*], so that everything is neat, salubrious, and well arranged. . . . Thus are our houses adapted to our manners and our new habits, and the plan of their distribution improved.[52]

Daly had earlier published the plan of a recently constructed block in the rue du Bac as an example of the skill with which they were now being designed. His comments suggest that even the best of the new flats left something to be desired. The light-well could, he suggested, be covered with a skylight and thereby become "a valuable annex to the kitchen." To do so would have deprived the *cabinet d'aisance* of the ventilation that it then possessed, and which he praised as an unusual refinement. In 1840, of course, neither kitchen nor privy would have had running water. The kitchen led directly to the servant's bedroom and, by another door, to an antechamber communicating with dining room, salon, and one of the family's bedrooms. He found it worthy of note that only one of the three bedrooms had to be reached through another.[53] The plan clearly represented an improvement over that in older buildings, but one can understand the snide remarks that the English made about the defective arrangements in Parisian flats.

Seen from Vienna, however, such flats seemed miracles of ingenuity, particularly in their ability to fit a variety of rooms into a tiny space (fig. 51). The *Allgemeine Bauzeitung* for 1843 observed that in what in the previous century would have been the area of a medium-sized room, an apartment providing all the necessities of modern life was now contrived, with everything in miniature. But the most striking quality of the new flats was the extravagance with which they were furnished. The marble chimney pieces, the velvet upholstery, the brocaded wallpaper, and above all the abundant mirrors dazzled contemporaries.

Depending on the observer, the Parisian flat represented unimaginable luxury or tawdry display, rational deployment of facilities for elegant living or a jumble of rooms subversive of both domestic comfort and true refinement (figs. 52–54). The *Allgemeine Bauzeitung* thought that German architects might profitably study the mode of distribution (*die Pariser Eintheilungsart*) for introduction into their own domestic buildings.[54] The *Building News* was convinced that the English had nothing to learn about domestic arrangements from the French. The publication in 1857 of the elevation and plans of a new Parisian block gave it an opportunity to fulminate against the architectural crudity and social indecorum of the French:

> What is dignified by the title of "ante-room" is no more than a dark passage! only nine feet by four—preceding the dining-room, which latter is, in fact, the actual and only entrance, it being impossible to reach any other room, even the kitchen, without passing through it. The door from the "ante-room" opens immediately against the fireplace in the dining-room, which is squeezed in between that door and another, so that sitting by "the fire side" is not to be thought of. And where does the second floor [door] lead to? why, plump into the kitchen. . . . On the opposite side of the dining-room is the drawing-room (about fourteen feet square), and beyond that

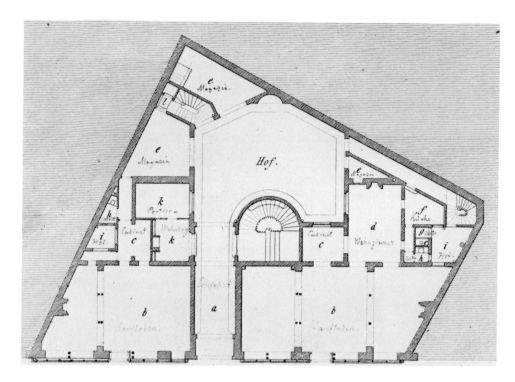

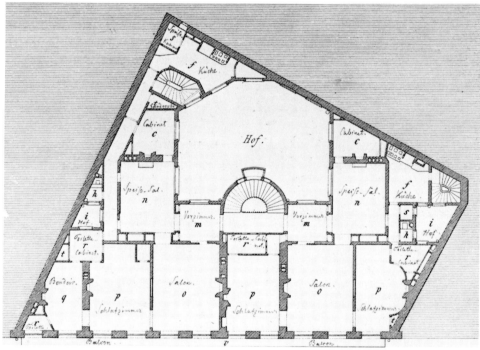

51. *(above) Seen from Vienna such flats seemed miracles of ingenuity.* Ground and first-floor plans, "Ein Miethaus in Paris" (A block of flats in Paris). From *Allgemeine Bauzeitung* 8 (1843), fig. 2.

52. *(opposite) Depending on the observer, the Parisian flat represented rational deployment of facilities for elegant living or a jumble of rooms subversive of both domestic comfort and true refinement.* Ground and first floor plans, *maison à loyer* at corner of rues Rumfort and Lavoisier. From *Revue générale de l'architecture* 10 (1852).

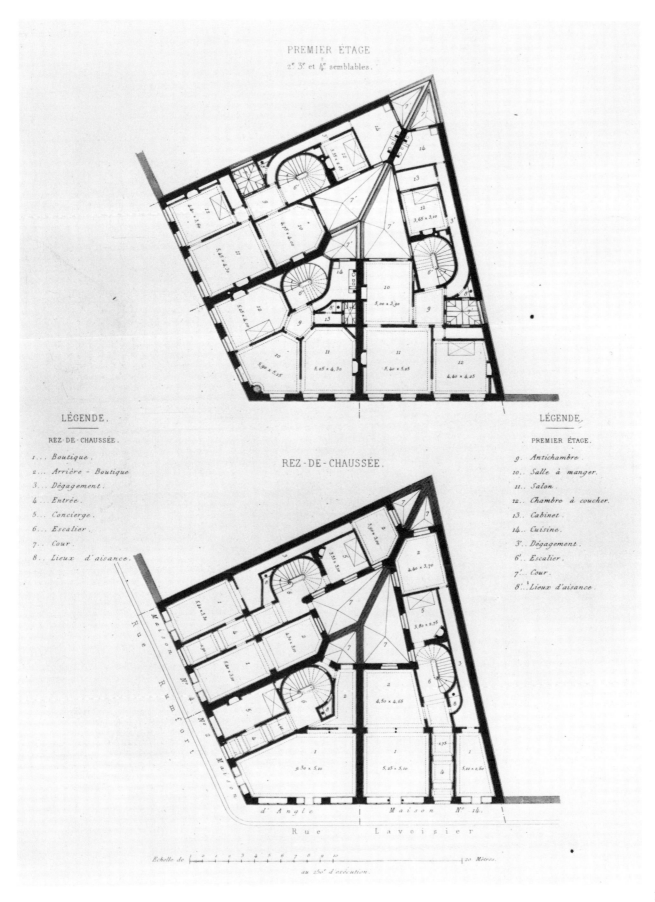

PREMIER ÉTAGE
2e 3e et 4e semblables.

LÉGENDE.

REZ-DE-CHAUSSÉE.

1... Boutique.
2... Arrière - Boutique.
3... Dégagement.
4... Entrée.
5... Concierge.
6... Escalier.
7... Cour.
8... Lieux d'aisance.

LÉGENDE.

PREMIER ÉTAGE.

9... Antichambre.
10... Salle à manger.
11... Salon.
12... Chambre à coucher.
13... Cabinet.
14... Cuisine.
3'... Dégagement.
6'... Escalier.
7'... Cour.
8'... Lieux d'aisance.

REZ-DE-CHAUSSÉE.

Échelle de 20 Mètres.
au 250e d'exécution.

117

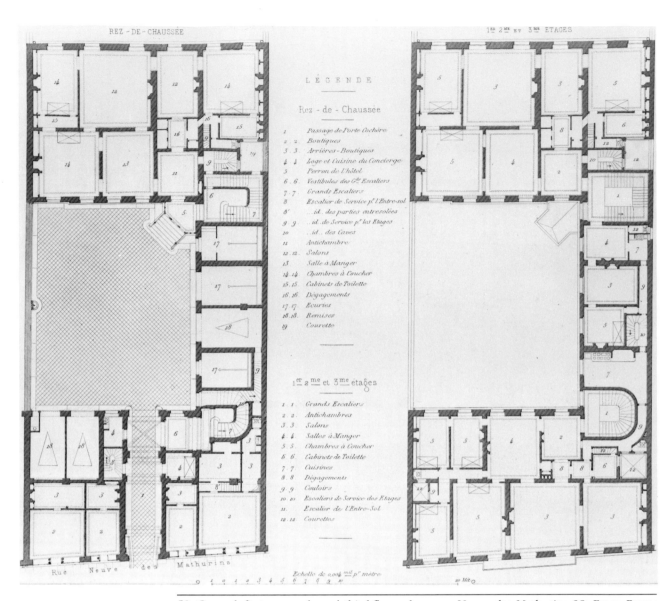

53. Ground, first-, second-, and third-floor plans, rue Neuve des Mathurins 39. From *Revue générale de l'architecture* 18 (1860), pl. 41.

two bed-chambers, one of which is the thoroughfare to the other, as the drawing-room is to both of them. How admirably, then, has decency, as well as comfort, been attended to.

The rooms looked onto a courtyard "so confined . . . that neither air nor sun can penetrate far into it." The whole spoke poorly for both the morals and the intelligence of the French:

A French family may not care at all for privacy—may see nothing objectionable in thoroughfare rooms—in having bed-chambers not only adjoining to and immediately communicating with sitting-rooms, but inaccessible except by passing through the latter. Of course, they do not feel incommoded, or they would not put up with such highly objectionable arrangement of plan. Put up with it, however, they do; and their doing so does not say much for their refinement.

Conceding that "in the fitting up of a boudoir they may be unrivalled," the journal found nothing else to admire in French domestic arrangements.[55] Yet from the

118

Viennese perspective the same arrangements were an object lesson in architectural ingenuity.

The *Allgemeine Bauzeitung* thought particularly noteworthy the self-contained independence of the Parisian flat. That it could be isolated by a single door from the staircase passage seemed an admirable innovation. Once inside that door, "its principal rooms are immediately accessible from the antechamber." From an Austrian perspective the Parisian flat was admirable for just the qualities that the *Building News* found lacking: convenience of arrangement and provision for the privacy of separate rooms. The writer especially praised the placing of an intervening passage between privy and kitchen on the one hand and the living rooms on the other to prevent the intrusion of unpleasant odors into them.

The Austrian critic was also struck by the assignment of specific purposes to the different rooms, which were not interchangeable according to the desires of the tenant. He was not referring to the extremes of contemporary English house-planning—with its breakfast rooms, morning rooms, business rooms, libraries, and the like—but to the fact that a bedroom remained always a bedroom and could not be converted at will into a drawing room or a dining room. A large proportion of the published floor plans of Viennese flats throughout the nineteenth century identify rooms only as *Zimmer, Vorzimmer,* and *Kabinett,* not as *Wohnzimmer, Schlafzimmer, Speisezimmer,* and so forth, suggesting that the Austrians maintained the older custom of undifferentiated—or at least variable—room designations longer than either the French or the English.

Rather than a small number of large rooms, the Parisian flat made use of the possibilities offered by a number of small, subordinate rooms (*kleine Nebenräume*), each performing a special function. Such specialized adjuncts compensated for the often "Lilliputian" scale of the flats: "one will not easily prefer a large bedroom without *Nebenräume* to a smaller bedroom, if the latter is connected to a dressing-room and a wardrobe."[56]

Both French and English literature on room planning stressed privacy and domesticity. César Daly advocated the separation of servants from family quite as consistently as did Robert Kerr. A separate set of service stairs in each block and the grouping of the domestic offices around it minimized unnecessary encounters between masters and servants. If intercommunicating doors were often included in plans, they ordinarily supplemented, rather than substituted for, the connection by way of the antechamber.[57]

Contrary to the English notion that the Parisian, submitting to the tyranny of the concierge, accepting the social promiscuity of the common staircase, and passing his hours of leisure at a table in a café, cared little about distinctions between public life and private, Daly was acutely aware of the necessity of keeping the two separate, even within the flat itself. "Our domestic and social existence . . . is divided into two very distinct parts," he argued: "the one is completely consecrated to intimacy, to family duties and affections, and it requires architectural arrangements that guarantee the freedom and discretion of private life; the other is mixed with the outer world by our relations, whether of business or of pleasure, and this second, so to speak public side of our life admits of more luxury and display than the first"[58] (fig. 55).

As the *Builder* observed in 1865, "it is not that the love of home-comfort is confined to this side the Channel; but the French plans . . . recognize that entertainments and receptions are of some importance to the cultivation of social and

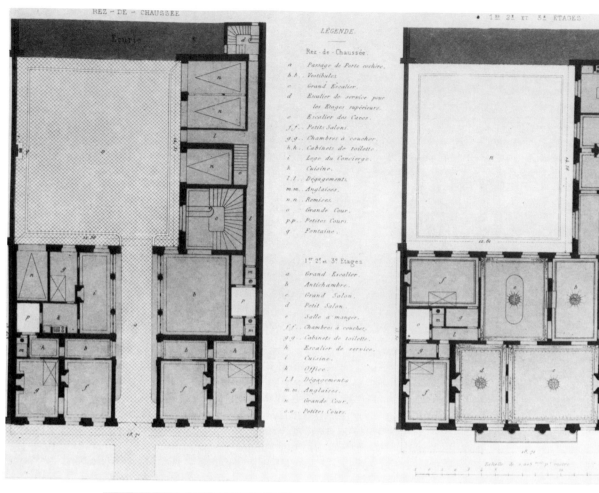

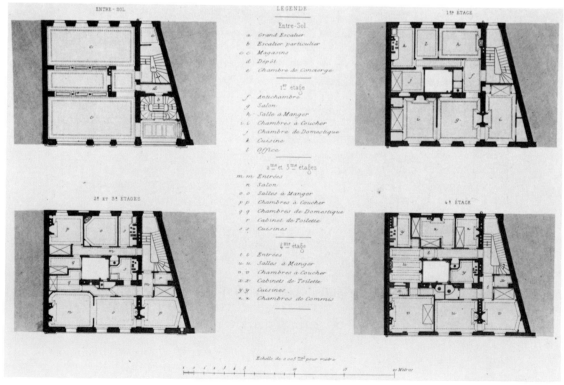

120

William H. White accounted for the small Parisian kitchen by the habit of the daily visit to the market: "hardly more than just sufficient for the day is brought home." He found no "intention or desire to increase the proportion of space allotted to kitchen accommodation," although "one room sufficed to contain what in London is divided into kitchen, scullery, servants' hall, housekeeper's room and butler's pantry!" Such a room, though, produced soups and stews "infinitely more palatable than any that usually issue from the wilderness under . . . the ordinary . . . houses of London." George Augustus Sala reflected the more usual English view. "The reason . . . why so many thousands of French people breakfast and dine at public eating-houses," he suggested, "is that their own small, pokey, and ill-ventilated kitchens are destitute of the appliances which are seldom lacking even in the kitchens of an English middle-class house of very moderate pretensions."[65]

Not just the size of the kitchen, but its location, sometimes "in immediate contact with the dining-room, separated from it by only a single door," shocked English critics.[66] But the practice of placing the principal bedroom next to the drawing room, from which it could be entered directly, seemed not merely a sacrifice in comfort but an affront to common decency. The French compounded the sin by actually using the bedroom as an extension to the drawing room. The *Allgemeine Bauzeitung* reported that company would congregate in the principal bedroom around a cozy fire even in the most elegant Parisian residences. The bed itself, sometimes hidden behind a curtain (*Coulissenthür*), was the only piece of furniture that suggested the room was a bedroom at all, everything else being relegated to the connecting dressing room. Daly included the principal bedroom of a flat in his category of areas open to visitors, "since, as a result of a certain case of manners, the absence of prudishness, and the intense love of company, the modesty of fortunes and the diminutiveness of lodgings in Paris, the bedroom of the mistress of the house often serves to supplement the drawing room."[67]

White sought to combat English suspicions that scenes of revelry and debauchery typically occurred in such flats, as people lurched through intercommunicating doors from *salle à manger* to *salon* to boudoir to bedroom, by describing a typical upper-middle-class Parisian household:

It is composed, say, of a gentleman and his wife, a daughter in her teens, a couple of children, a nurse or a lady's maid, a female cook, and a butler. . . . Husband and wife occupy the two bedrooms in the main building; their dressing rooms, and often a water-closet, adjoin, and the gentleman's bedroom is sometimes provided with bookcases and a writing table. The young lady has one of the two bedrooms behind, the two children the other; the nurse or lady's maid sleeps in a room, perhaps, on the opposite side of the kitchen. The two rooms in the roof are occupied respectively by the cook and the butler.

He described a typical day:

Before seven o'clock the porter has opened the great doors of the carriage entrance and admitted fresh air into the courtyard which undoubtedly requires it. There, a groom is rubbing down a horse, a coachman cleaning a carriage. In the different kitchens, tea or coffee is being prepared; this will be served before eight o'clock in the various bedrooms. Meanwhile the dust which is swept from the sitting rooms, the hall, the kitchen and the passages, is collected, carried down the servants' stairs, and deposited in the roadway. . . . To provide the two daily meals, the mistress attended by the cook, or the cook alone, goes to market. . . . Breakfast is taken between half-past 11 and half-past 12, dinner about half-past 6, in the dining room; nor is that room ever used by true Parisians for any other purpose than eating and drinking. It is never occupied as a family living room . . . as with us, visitors are received in the drawing room.

His point was to reassure his audience of the respectability and separateness of family life as actually lived in Paris. He explained that "though a great deal of traffic takes place upon the servants' stairs, very little time is spent by the members of the different families upon the principal stairs. Intimacy between superposed neighbours not only does not ripen, it does not grow."[68]

Few Parisians could afford the spaciousness he described. For all the luxury of the newest blocks, for all the ingenious contrivances that maximized the usefulness of every bit of space, the ordinary reaction of English visitors was one of concern at the degree of crowding the French seemed to take for granted. "We know what overcrowding is in London," wrote one Englishman in 1883; "it is a terrible evil, but it affects the poor only, whilst in Paris it affects the middle classes also." As one consequence, "the middle-class Parisian can very rarely invite a friend to stay with him. . . . Frequently the dining-room and kitchen are so small that it is found more convenient to dispense hospitality at a restaurant."[69]

"Behind the grandiloquent façades and the airy rooms fronting the boulevards," Gillian Tindall reminds us, "lie cramped, dark corridors, windowless bathrooms, cliff-steep servants' stairways, and always, at the top, a warren of small, brick-floored rooms initially without water or heat in which the most Parisian of Parisians live like resourceful mice in the crannies of a dwelling built for a mythical race of giants."[70]

The architect had to balance considerations of privacy and economy, rational segregation and making the best of the space at his disposal. On first examination, Second Empire room arrangements seem haphazard, with no very obvious grouping of reception rooms in one part, bedrooms in another, and service rooms in a third. The antechambers and *dégagements* do not in practice isolate individual rooms but at best supplement the intercommunicating doors. Nor do they serve all the rooms: to reach certain areas it is necessary to traverse dining room or *salon* or both. A contemporary Englishman might well conclude that either the French cared little for logic and order—an absurd supposition—or that they had no objection to sporadic interruptions of meals, conversation, sleep, or sexual activity, and placed a low value on both domestic intimacy and individual privacy—a supposition contradicted by other evidence.

How resolve the paradox? To begin with, it is harder to achieve physical separation on a single floor than in a house with five or six different levels. The attempts of late Victorian and Edwardian luxury flats in London to do so required an extravagant expenditure on long, dark corridors, often running side by side. The French chose to utilize the space available in a way that produced the maximum number of usable rooms, providing privacy through compact antechambers at strategic points rather than long, wasteful corridors.

Second, we shall beware assuming that French words mean the same as their customary English translations. *Chambre à coucher* is not the precise equivalent of *bedroom,* and *salle à manger* does not quite mean *dining room.* The principal bedroom employed as a somewhat more intimate extension of the *salon* was furnished with comfortable chairs and tables of the drawing-room sort. During the day and early evening hours it served as the private sitting room of the lady of the house, thereby doubling its use when not required for sleeping purposes. At an evening party it served to take the overflow from the main reception rooms. No one would be sleeping in it on such occasions, just as no one would use it as a sitting room while it was being slept in. The placement of the bed against the wall most distant from the door into the *salon,* and the banishment of dressing table, wardrobe, and washing facilities to a connecting *cabinet* obviated any sense of incongruity in its use as a sitting room. The Englishman, visualizing a bedroom as an icy chamber dominated by a large, centrally located bed and by a mirrored dressing table pushed against the window, found the idea of a lady receiving guests there at best peculiar, at worst shocking. To the French it was a way of obtaining two rooms for the price of one.

The use of the *salle à manger* to supplement or replace the antechamber has both historical and practical explanations. Down to the eighteenth century a specialized dining room was a luxury even in great houses: to remedy the lack, it became the practice to use an existing anteroom for eating purposes.[71] The English were accustomed to using the dining room as a sitting room between meal hours; and the meal hours themselves were more extended than was normal in France. After dinner the gentlemen remained there for prolonged drinking and conversation once the ladies had been banished to the drawing room. Any use of it as a thoroughfare would have markedly reduced its comfort and obviated its reason for being. By contrast the French never used the dining room except for dining. Since the entire family dined together, and since strangers did not pay formal calls during meal hours, no one would be passing through the dining room while it was being used as such. Outside mealtimes no one would be there to be disturbed: once again two rooms were achieved for the price of one. The English could afford to be more prodigal of space than the French, but they did not in practice necessarily achieve more privacy and separateness in their domestic lives.

The Viennese *Wohnung*

"We Viennese very seldom feel truly at home in our rented flats," admitted the *Allgemeine Bauzeitung* in 1860. "The *chez soi* of the French, the *at home* of the English express a comfort unknown to us."[72] Describing the splendid buildings of the Ringstrasse to the Congress of French Architects in 1884, Paul Sédille commented that "behind their rich decoration, there is very little. Plan hardly exists. There are none of those niceties of distribution which render life so easy and comfortable in our Parisian interiors." Jacob von Falke found Viennese flats, "in which kitchen, sitting room, and bedroom all lie in a row and one cannot reach the last room without passing through all the others: an unheard-of situation in England!" a matter for general reproach.[73]

The Viennese middle classes, Thomas Blashill told the Royal Institute of British Architects (RIBA) in 1888, "pay nearly twice as much in rent and other outgoings for very scanty accommodation on the upper floors of these grand houses, as would be paid here for a separate house and garden." Victor Tissot gave a French audience a similarly bleak picture. In the suburbs family accommodation was badly furnished and congested, with rents a third higher than in Paris. Subletting was commonly practiced, and in working-class areas houses generally resembled *hôtels garnis.*[74]

According to the census of 1910, 75 percent of the dwellings in Vienna consisted of *Kleinstwohnungen,* comprising a single living room (*Zimmer*) with in most cases a tiny kitchen annex, and in some a smaller sleeping chamber (*Kabinett*) attached.[75] Overcrowding affected a large proportion of the middle as well as the lower classes.

Under such circumstances analyses of the room arrangements of most Viennese flats tell us much about what they had to endure, but little about what they would have wished for themselves. If we can say with some confidence that Notting Hill and St. John's Wood and Highgate reflected the chosen styles of living and scale of values of their residents, we cannot do the same even for the relatively prosperous Mariahilf or Josefstadt. Here, all too often, the domestic environment imposed rather than reflected a life-style.

More revealing are the *Grosswohnungen* of the Ringstrasse and the substantial villas of Türkenschanze and Hohe Warte. Tissot believed that the well-off bourgeoisie lived at least as well as in Paris.[76] But their definition of comfort, the qualities they particularly prized in a flat, were different. A French critic, writing in 1873, thought the Viennese building owner cared more than his Parisian equivalent about an impressive façade, less about internal arrangements. "If he finds the rooms dark, the *dégagements* inconvenient, the smaller rooms badly ventilated, he is convinced that things couldn't have been otherwise and puts up with them, especially if his façade does him honor."[77] Actually the Viennese paid great attention to the details of internal distribution but approached them as they did the details of external decoration, seeking representation rather than comfort.

At one extreme petit bourgeois families sacrificed domestic comforts in order to maintain an appearance of gentility. Tissot described one such family in which the mother, the three daughters, and the two sons slept in the same room, with the beds pressed tightly one against the other. By such an expedient they were able to make one of their rooms a *salon*, containing a small set of shelves displaying busts of Schiller and Goethe and volumes of their poetry, and where they could receive guests.[78] In Vienna bourgeois families made the kind of sacrifice of space that working-class families in England made to have a Sunday-best parlor, "not to be used for relaxation," but "as a more controlled and formal social environment."[79]

At the other extreme were the *Herrschaftswohnungen*, occupying the entire first floor of buildings in the Ringstrasse and City. Here, too, space was devoted to public rooms at the expense of private family quarters. *Sacrifice* may not be quite the word, but the largest Ringstrasse flats were better suited for giving smashing evening parties than for a life of personal withdrawal or domestic intimacy.

The London suburban villa was trying to be a miniature country house, while the Parisian luxury flat aspired toward the condition of an *hôtel privé*. By contrast the Ringstrasse *Mietpalast* was just that: an imitation palace in which bourgeois householders could pretend to be old aristocracy. Among aristocracy and bourgeoisie alike, vestiges of an older way of living persisted well into the nineteenth century. As for the working classes, severe economic constraints kept them, until well into the twentieth century, from participating even in the moderate degree of separation and withdrawal possible for the English working classes.

Yet to Ferdinand Fellner in 1860 the contrast with eighteenth-century domestic habits was already great. Viennese burghers and manufacturers no longer ate in the kitchen at the same table with their workers, but withdrew to a private dining room. Their children would no longer share a bed under the roof with the apprentices.[80] Social distance was reshaping domestic life, but we are still a long way from Kerr's morning room, breakfast room, dining room, boudoir, and drawing room.

It was only gradually and hesitantly that even the grandest apartments in the City and Ringstrasse acquired corridors. Although Ludwig von Förster boasted that the principal rooms in the Renngasse flat he designed in 1847 for Adolph Freiherr von Pereira-Arnstein had facilities for "the greatest possible *dégagement*," many of its principal reception rooms were accessible only by passing through other rooms[81] (fig. 56). The banker and wholesale merchant Ludwig Ladenberg specified in 1863 that in the owner's flat in his building at Opernring 17 "one be able to go from the anteroom into the breakfast room and the bedroom, as well as from the kitchen, without having to go through the dining room in order to reach the living rooms."[82] Heinrich von Ferstel was careful to provide in his buildings a corridor paralleling the *enfilade* (or *Zimmerflucht*) of reception rooms.[83]

Corridors, however, were conspicuously absent from the plans of the house of the Count von Hoyos-Sprinzenstein in the Kärntner Ring, later part of the Hotel Bristol, and also designed by Förster (fig. 57). That this was not unusual is suggested by the comment of the *Allgemeine Bauzeitung* that "the inner arrangement of the building . . . is appropriate to the requirements and wishes of the noble family and the flats are set up according to the ordinary practice in Vienna."[84]

In the *Herrschaftswohnungen* of the 1870s there was a tendency to expand the anteroom by means of a corridor along the central wall, in contrast to the sixties when thoroughfare rooms were still the rule. Yet an extensive development of middle-class housing by Prince Schwarzenberg in Wieden in the 1880s was "based on the older system of Viennese planning, the rooms being without distinct cor-

56. *Ludwig von Förster boasted that the principal rooms in the Renngasse flat he designed in 1847 had facilities for "the greatest possible* degagement." *Plan of Renngasse 154.* Allgemeine Bauzeitung *12 (1847), pl. 127.*

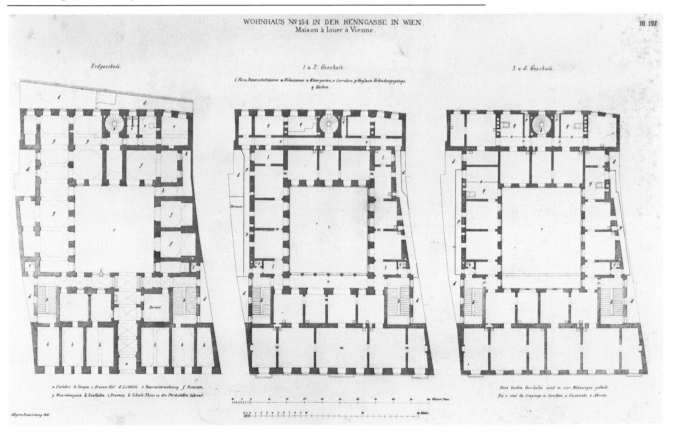

Kellergeschoss.

Erdgeschoss.

Mezzanin.

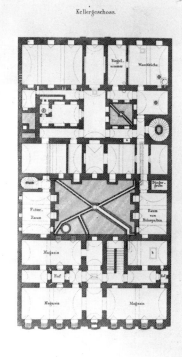
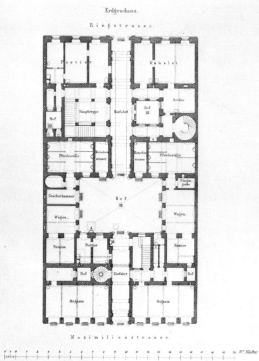
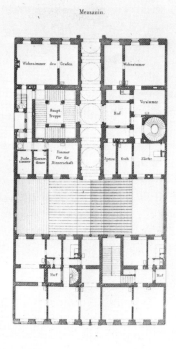

Erster Stock.

Zweiter Stock.

Dritter Stock.

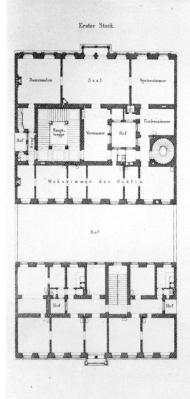
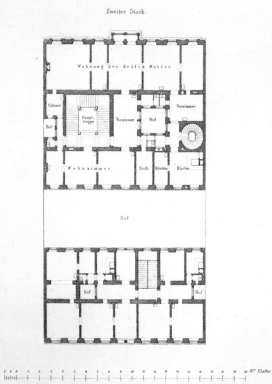
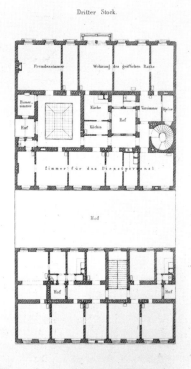

ridor communication." It was noteworthy that in the *Sühnhaus,* in the Schottenring, "there are only two principal rooms on the whole floor which are not entered directly from the vestibule or corridor."[85]

With or without corridors, all the flats of any social pretension strove to max-

---

57. *(opposite) Corridors . . . were conspicuously absent from the plans of the house of the Count von Hoyos-Sprinzenstein in the Kärntner Ring.* Two plates from *Allgemeine Bauzeitung* 29 (1864), pls. 615–16.
58. *(below) All the flats of any social pretension strove to maximize the size, number, and splendor of reception rooms.* "First floor, view through the suite of reception rooms." Dr. Karl Lueger-Platz 2. (Kunsthistorisches Institut der Universität Wien.)

imize the size, number, and splendor of reception rooms, arranged in a row along the main façade (fig. 58). Vast apartments, lavishly supplied with suites of public rooms, often offered no more than two bedrooms, one each for husband and wife. Where, one can only ask, were the children expected to sleep?[86] In smaller establishments, temporary beds might be set up in corridors, or revealed in curtained alcoves, but the seeming disregard for such practical needs as sleeping accommodation in flats of imposing size and splendor stands in striking contrast to the English obsession with separate bedrooms.

One's place in the social scale was indicated not by the number of bedrooms but by the splendor of reception rooms connected one to another by folding doors[87] (fig. 59). Their significance had once been appreciated in England as well. Jane Austen remarks in *Persuasion* on Sir Walter Eliot's house in Bath: "[Anne] must sigh, and smile, and wonder too, as Elizabeth threw open the folding-doors, and walked with exultation from one drawing-room into the other, boasting of their space: at the possibility of that woman, who had been mistress of Kellynch Hall, finding extent to be proud of between two walls, perhaps thirty feet asunder."

Middle- and upper-class flats became less splendid and more comfortable as 1914 approached. The formal antechamber became the convenient corridor, space that would once have been devoted to seldom used reception rooms was now given up to daily family purposes, bathrooms became standard fixtures in middle-sized as well as large flats.[88] Yet although running water, gas lighting, central heating, and fixed baths were introduced into favored buildings about as early as in Paris, they reached a small proportion of the residential buildings. As late as 1910, no more than seven percent of all dwellings had bathrooms, and only twenty-two percent private water closets. Kitchens in all but luxury flats rarely had their own water supply, but depended on a *Bassena* in the public corridor. Of a sample survey of twenty thousand dwellings made in 1919, sixty-one percent lacked both gas and electricity.[89]

Even so, F. Leonhard, after an extended examination of the blocks of flats erected, mostly in the City and Ringstrasse zone, over the previous forty years, concluded in 1905 that their tenants had every reason to be satisfied. Room dimensions were larger than in London, Paris, and Berlin, and the dark and narrow corridors of flats in other cities were absent in the best Viennese buildings. He praised the superior standards of building construction in Vienna, where thicker walls provided better protection against both sudden changes in temperature and outside noise. There was, admittedly, frequent incongruity between exterior display and interior reality: "The Viennese loves or at least used to love to adorn his house, often indeed more than is its due."[90] It is hard in retrospect to reproach the Viennese of past generations for such harmless vanity, considering the pleasure the exuberant domestic façades have given generations of pedestrians, unaware of the internal inadequacies they may conceal.

59. *One's place in the social scale was indicated by the splendor of reception rooms connected one to another by folding doors.* Dr. Karl Lueger-Platz 2. Interior. (Kunsthistorisches Institut der Universität Wien. Photo Johanna Fiegl.)

2

Social Geography

The Town as a Map of Society

f the domestic household is the microcosm of the city, so the city is the home writ large. If the medieval great hall housed together masters and servants, family and retainers, household and strangers, the medieval town contained rich and poor, gentle and simple, spiritual and secular, each in close physical proximity to the other. Just as the modern household strove to distinguish and isolate the service quarters from the family rooms, public areas from private, the modern city came to organize itself into districts devoted to manufacture, finance, wholesale and retail trade, and residence, with each in turn subdivided according to class, wealth, and function.

Would that it were so simple! Neither the idealized picture of the medieval household nor of the medieval town corresponds to untidy reality, and it would be rash to assume that nineteenth-century European families pursued their lives in quite the orderly fashion prescribed by Kerr and Daly. And although London, Paris, and Vienna arranged themselves physically into recognizable patterns, the logic underlying the structure of each was markedly different from that of the other two.

It is a commonplace that modern cities have become segregated on the basis of social, ethnic, or religious affinities into homogeneous neighborhoods, and by function into separate commercial, manufacturing, and residential zones. It is also customary to deplore both: the former as exacerbating social injustice, the latter as contributing to the boredom and artificiality of urban life. Jane Jacobs' Hudson Street, with its mixture of classes, uses, and activities, and Lewis Mumford's evocation of the organic society of the medieval town point up the shortcomings of cities divided into dormitory suburbs, business districts deserted on evenings and weekends, shopping malls, and once viable neighborhoods become "ghettos" for the dispossessed.

The division of classes and activities that characterizes most English-speaking cities is hard to defend. Yet the opposite extreme, in which each neighborhood would contain the same proportion of members of different classes, occupations, religious and ethnic groups, economic activities, and cultural institutions, is both unthinkable and unattractive. Hudson Street itself, for all its variety, is no microcosm of New York, but a very special mixture of some of its more colorful ingredients. Even the medieval city had streets devoted to particular trades, with goldsmiths in one, weavers in another. One likes to think of Lombard Street crowded with Italian moneylenders, the Fleischmarkt with butchers, and the rue des Mauvais Garçons with juvenile delinquents. There are sound economic and psychological reasons for certain groups to cluster together for business or residence or recreation. The larger a city becomes, the greater the possibilities for specialized subdivision. Given that certain locations will seem more desirable than others, those groups best supplied with money in a market economy, favor with the regime in nonmarket economies will have access to the most desirable areas.

Everybody could not have a room in the palace at Versailles, everybody cannot have a flat in Buda Castle or a house in the Boltons. What is historically significant are the different ways in which residents of different cities in different periods have perceived the relative desirability of particular streets and districts. That Oxford Street was once regarded as an especially favorable location for luxury specialty shops, that *West Side Story* was first called *East Side Story,* that much of Victorian Chelsea was a slum suggest the wonderful malleability of our conceptions of what is desirable and what is not. "Gentrification" itself is interesting not so much as indicating the wickedness of real estate speculators and the perversity of the professional classes but as posing the question Why does one generation shun Camden Town, the next go deeply into debt in order to acquire a laborer's cottage in N.W.1?

Socially mixed neighborhoods remained so because the middle classes required the services of their less affluent neighbors. To this day, I gather, the well-to-do residents of Henley-on-Thames approve of the council housing in their midst as providing an abundant supply of cleaning women. Historically a middle-class neighborhood would have a larger working-class population than a working-class district had middle-class residents. A middle-class household required a substantial number of working-class people, as domestic servants, repairmen, delivery boys, window washers, crossing-sweepers. By contrast a working-class district could do with a bare minimum of middle-class people—shopkeepers, clergymen, doctors, social workers—in their midst. Whitechapel and Stratford East early became more socially homogeneous than Belgravia or South Kensington ever could.

It is precisely because today's middle classes are less able to exploit the working classes that our cities have become more segregated than they were. It was only when the servantless, do-it-yourself household became the norm, with the large refrigerator, deep freeze, and the family car permitting once-a-week shopping at a distant supermarket, that the cluster of mews, back courts, and mean streets ceased to be the necessary adjunct to any middle-class neighborhood (fig. 60).

All this does not mean that medieval London and Paris were kept from being neatly divided into business districts, specialized shopping malls, and one-class housing estates only by their restricted population and the absence of commuter trains and convenience foods. The privileged classes in the Middle Ages did not feel the necessity for establishing a spatial distance between themselves and their inferiors. But it does, I think, help account for the limited nature of geographical segregation by class in eighteenth- and even nineteenth-century cities. By that time the will was there, but the means were not.

It is not surprising that London, larger, more technologically advanced, and earlier influenced by the new ideology of domesticity and privacy, should have achieved a more precocious degree of segregation than either Paris or Vienna. It

London

60. *It was only when the servantless, do-it-yourself household became the norm that the cluster of mews, back courts, and mean streets ceased to be the necessary adjunct to any middle-class neighborhood.* View from first-floor back window of 1 Torrington Square, showing backs of houses in Russell Square and intervening mews. G. Scharf. (British Museum.)

feared invasion neither by Turks nor Huguenots: its walls had, by the early seventeenth century, long ceased to perform a military function or to limit suburban expansion. The existence of court, parliament, and abbey in Westminster encouraged superior building development in that direction. The dissolution of the monasteries in the 1530s had much the same effect that the French expropriation of church lands two and a half centuries later was to have: making substantial plots of ground available for exploitation by private landowners and speculators. Finally, the plague and fire of 1665–66 gave both occasion and impetus to City residents to move to the more spacious and presumably healthier quarters being built to the west.

The ending, with the Restoration, of any serious royal attempt to prevent the outward expansion of London, and the eagerness of landlords to participate in the profits to be made by either selling their land or granting building leases, meant that it had ample space to sort itself out into socially and functionally differentiated neighborhoods. For a long time it took little advantage of the opportunity. Even on leasehold estates the tendency was to put together "little towns," with a principal square for what was hoped would be aristocratic occupation; wider and narrower streets for more and less genteel purposes; mews, courts, and passages for the poor. Church and market would provide for the spiritual and physical needs of the estate. Competition between estates and between builders gave London more squares and streets lined with houses intended for aristocratic families than there was aristocracy to fill them. The Piazza in Covent Garden and Lincoln's Inn Fields saw their early primacy threatened in the 1660s by the competing attractions of Bloomsbury and St. James's squares, and later by Hanover and Cavendish, Grosvenor and Portman squares. Covent Garden, laid out as London's Marais, with the Piazza its place des Vosges, enjoyed a briefer period of fashion than its Parisian counterpart. By the eighteenth century it had acquired another function, or rather two: as a fruit and vegetable market and as an entertainment district.

Bloomsbury, to the north, had one reasonably fashionable square and, in Great Russell Street, three great town mansions—Bedford, Montague, and Thanet houses—faced and rubbed elbows with less pretentious dwellings. To the south lay a cluster of modest streets and courts, and just beyond, what was to become the notorious rookery of St.Giles's. Only with the building development that began with Bedford Square in 1776 did the Bedford estate attempt to create a socially homogeneous residential suburb.

Bloomsbury failed to achieve, except partially and temporarily, a social character commensurate with its architectural excellence.[1] More successful was the Grosvenor estate in northern Mayfair. But however aristocratic many of its residents in the eighteenth century, not until the late nineteenth did it achieve a high degree of social homogeneity. Shops, taverns, and coffee houses abounded in the eighteenth century; many of the houses were subdivided for letting; and a large working-class population lived in the courts, passages, and mews leading off the principal streets. Tradespeople predominated away from Grosvenor Square and its adjacent streets, and the *Survey of London* has concluded that "the impression generally prevalent that this part of Mayfair was the almost exclusive province of the well-to-do and the well-connected is in some respects highly misleading."[2]

Yet Mayfair was probably the most socially homogeneous part of the West End. To the east the high ambitions of the owners and builders of Soho, Golden, and Leicester squares were at best temporarily met by their residents. Regent Street itself was in part a slum clearance project, and Nash was careful to restrict the number of openings onto it from the lower-class streets immediately to the east.[3]

If the notion of the Grosvenor estate as an exclusively aristocratic neighborhood is "highly misleading," that of a London divided between a fashionable and prosperous West End and a poverty-stricken East End is totally wrong. Hackney remained a commuting suburb for City businessmen well into the nineteenth century, while every other eastern suburb had pockets of gentility. Yet poverty characterized the East End more than affluence did the West. The worst slums of Victorian London were those branching off Drury Lane, and those swept away by the building of New Oxford Street in the 1840s and Victoria Street in the 1850s. Just as there weren't enough peers to fill the houses of would-be aristocratic squares, the middle class of Georgian London was neither big enough nor prosperous enough to fill the vast area between the City and Westminster. And upper and middle class alike attracted a far greater number of tradesmen, servants, artisans, beggars, prostitutes, criminals—all inevitable appendages to a genteel neighborhood.

The West End has never lacked a working-class population or a sizable body of the poor, but there were serious attempts to reduce their number beginning in the latter years of the eighteenth century. The stricter covenants that the Bedford estate imposed in Gower Street and Russell Square and that the Foundling Hospital included in its leases in the 1790s were designed to ensure social and occupational as well as architectural uniformity. Both hoped to exclude trade entirely, the Foundling Hospital reluctantly allowing conversions to shopfronts in two or three of its lesser streets. The Bedford estate was able to keep most of the area north of Great Russell Street free from shops. Although it failed to prevent conversions to lodging houses and private hotels, at least these were of the most discreet and respectable sort.[4]

To the west, the once permissive Grosvenor estate was, from the 1790s, inserting covenants in new leases to prohibit trade or manufacture in its major streets; by 1835 Upper Grosvenor and Upper Brook streets had become wholly residential.[5] It would successfully keep Belgravia both residential and fashionable. The landlords and builders of the new estates north and south of Hyde Park achieved a greater degree of social homogeneity than had the older estates.

The nineteenth century saw increased social and functional specialization, with the City of London the most dramatic example. In 1872 Edward I'Anson could observe that "the City, which teems with a daily traffic of millions of people . . . has scarcely any resident population." Its former residents had left it "because the rooms formerly used as living rooms are more valuable as offices, and a citizen may now live in a suburban villa or even in a Belgravian or Tyburnian mansion, upon the rent he obtains for the drawing-room floor of the house wherein his ancestors lived for generations."[6]

The suburbs to which the Citizens moved, and from which omnibus and train brought the City's vast daytime population, were mostly designed from the outset for a single class of tenant desiring a single size and type of house.[7] "For social reasons, dwelling houses in the same street . . . are generally designed for the same class of inhabitants," H. H. Statham told the Architectural Association in 1896. "A man who occupies a 200*l.* a year house does not want to have a fifty-pounder next door to him; there is an eternal fitness of things in these matters."[8]

The combination of homogeneity with modernity made such new communities—Notting Hill, West Kensington, Putney, Balham, and others still farther out—tempting alternatives to more central districts of late Georgian origin. The Bedford estate suffered particularly from such competition. "That estate was a century ago inhabited by families," recalled a writer in 1877; "and the gradations from the ducal mansion, or the large house in a large square occupied by some City magnate or prosperous merchant, to the small house in the bye-street, occupied by the small tradesman . . . were fairly provided for." But as St. John's Wood and Belsize Park and more distant regions were developed as single-class suburbs, the Bedford estate "was so hemmed in and built up that its original residential character was entirely changed" and with this came "a change in the class of inhabitants."[9] The coming of the respectable lodging-house keeper with her genteel tenants to Russell Square and the surrounding streets helped create a more standardized Bloomsbury than that in which the Sedleys and the Osbornes and the John Knightleys had lived at the start of the century.

The multiplication of competing suburban railways and the abundance of rental accommodation on the market gave the middle classes a freedom of movement and of choice that their equivalents today can only wonder at. In their selection of residence there was nothing that they shunned more—apart, of course, from lower-class neighbors—than any suggestion of a connection with trade. The London tradesman had long ceased to live over his shop.[10] And having fled his own shop, he had no intention of living in a street that had other shops in it.[11]

The Grosvenor estate in Mayfair was not immune from the competition of newer developments. Its population fell by thirteen percent between 1841 and 1871, principally among householders of independent means, who may well have moved to Belgravia, Kensington, and Tyburnia. Extensive rebuilding in the 1880s and 1890s halted and reversed the trend, and by the early twentieth century the neighborhood was devoted more exclusively to expensive private residences than ever before. Deliberate estate policy effectively expelled trade from many streets and saw to it that the poor were rehoused in model dwellings.[12]

Since the First World War and even more since the Second, the multistory town house designed with a corps of servants in mind has become impossible for even the wealthy to maintain. Converted into prestige offices or divided into flats, many have outwardly survived. By 1960 only about a third of the floor space on the Grosvenor estate was being used for residential purposes, and that mostly in new blocks of flats. Peers of the realm were still prominent among the reduced population, but business tenants contributed far more to the rent rolls.[13] More attractive to the well-to-do are districts of smaller town houses, and terraces of late Georgian or early Victorian workers' cottages, capable of conversion to meet current conceptions of comfort and luxury. The Bedford estate's long refusal of permission to convert houses into flats probably contributed to a loss of residential character in Bloomsbury greater than that in Kensington, where such conversions were early and commonplace.

It would be a mistake to exaggerate the degree of sociogeographical specialization and segregation in London. The number and popularity of districts like Islington, which has never quite achieved its long-predicted leap into fashion and elegance, not to speak of Camden and Kentish Towns, might indicate that under proper conditions social and functional mixture can persist indefinitely. Almost any district north of the Thames that retains a vestige of Georgian or Victorian character could be considered a plausible candidate for gentrification, if only because few of today's gentry can raise a mortgage on a house in an indisputably fashionable neighborhood. Much depends on the attitude of the local borough council, but more on the whims of fashion. By now, those people who wish to live in a genuinely segregated, socially homogeneous neighborhood have already moved to the appropriate outer suburb. Those who are willing to pay the price for a house or flat in or near central London are more likely to prize London for the variety and mixture of activities that it offers as a whole, than for the seclusion and uniformity of many of its parts.

Governmental policies since 1918, by encouraging the formation of council estates and, through tax relief on mortgage interest payments, the trend toward individual house ownership, have both strengthened the forces of social segregation and reduced the element of choice in the location of residence.[14] If poverty kept a large segment of Victorian London from exercising free choice as to place of residence, rational economic calculations today inhibit a great many house owners and council tenants alike from doing so.

Paris

It was a common conviction among the English that in their sense of class distinctions the French, here as in so many other areas, were lacking in delicacy and refinement. "It would be difficult to quote any custom of the French which English people might less readily fall in with," observed the *Architect* in 1873, "than that which assigns the tenancy of the half dozen successive storeys of the same house to just as many utterly dissociated and indeed discordant people, ranging from a jaunty viscount on the *premier étage*—not merely to a very small *rentier* on the *troisième,* but to a little nest of the humblest workpeople on the *cinquième,* all meeting on the common stair."[15] Edmond Texier's *Tableau de Paris* (1852–53) contains a much-reproduced caricature of a cutaway section of a Parisian block of flats that displays just such a situation, with the style of life changing from luxury to comfort to want to utter wretchedness as one moves upward. Any given *quartier,* if not perhaps any given street, would contain a rough cross-section of society as a whole.

Such a picture was never wholly accurate and became less so after the upheavals of the 1850s and 1860s. The most it would be prudent to venture is that at any given period the classes in London were probably more efficiently separated than they were in Paris. Whatever social mingling did exist in Paris—and it was less than the English thought—the French worried about such encounters less than the English did.

A degree of segregation had existed in Paris since the Middle Ages, at least with respect to the favored location of the residences of the upper classes. What made each district fashionable at any particular time was its proximity to the court and its associated pleasures. But Paris provided attractions of its own, for when the court moved to Versailles the rich and well-born continued to maintain and build *hôtels particuliers* in the former capital.

Whatever the causes, the eighteenth century saw an unmistakable westward movement of wealth and fashion, with the old aristocracy abandoning the Marais for spacious mansions along the rues de l'Université, Saint-Dominique, and de Grenelle in the faubourg Saint-Germain, and the new financial aristocracy building north of the river. Most of the new building took place on the right bank, on both sides of the line of *grands boulevards* west of the rue Saint-Denis.[16] The streets in the northwestern outskirts continued to develop after the Revolution, with houses designed to attract middle-class tenants from older and more congested districts. Many, although built solidly against the street frontage, boasted extensive gardens to the rear.[17]

The new building encouraged the separation of residence from business. Up to the early nineteenth century Paris had been characterized by concentration and mixture of both classes and functions. Production along with both wholesale and retail trade typically took place in the same street, frequently under the same roof. Workmen, employers, and merchants lived and did their business in close proximity. Even the separation between trades was not clear-cut, as all branches of manufacture and commerce tried to find room for themselves in the most desirable location: as close as possible to the rues Saint-Denis and Saint-Martin. With the coming of more sophisticated business methods in the early nineteenth century, those involved in trade began to move their offices westward toward the Bourse and the Banque de France[18] (fig. 61). The shift involved at most a move of a few hundred yards, remaining within the present second arrondissement. It would be like a move from Fenchurch Street to Lombard Street. What mattered was less the distance moved than the beginning of a functional and social separation within the same trade. The more advanced and prosperous merchants took the process one step further by establishing their residence in one of the new streets to the north of the line of boulevards, of which the rue de la Chaussée d'Antin was the most pretentious.

61. *Those involved in trade began to move their offices westward toward the Bourse and the Banque de France.* Marville, place de la Bourse, 1856. (Musée Carnavalet. Photo Lauros-Giraudon.)

Paris displayed a gradual falling off in social character from west to east. Both on the right and left banks the western arrondissements became predominantly residential and middle class. East of the rue Saint-Denis the population became more proletarian. Even the Marais had acquired a working-class character. "In the splendid hotels of the ancient aristocracy . . . industry at the present day has her throne," wrote an English observer in 1850. "Under the painted and gilded ceilings are displayed the wares of the tradesman. The boudoir is the counting-house of the honest merchant."[19] Yet it retained pockets of gentility. While each *quartier* had a dominant social character, none was completely homogeneous: patches of misery could be found in the midst of riches, while some quite well-to-do families lived close to the wretched slums of the Montagne Sainte-Geneviève.[20]

Residential developments invariably attracted commercial establishments into their midst. The rich in Paris did not share the Londoner's aversion to the physical proximity of trade. The western boulevards were at once the most desirable place to live and the center of trade and entertainment.[21] Although the development of the quartiers Chaussée d'Antin, Saint-Lazare, and their neighbors brought about a degree of social segregation, they also reflected the continuing wish of Parisians to live close to the center of both business and pleasure. If retail trade was linked less closely to manufacture than it had been in the eighteenth century, it became if anything more closely linked to its customers.

The property owners in the older streets of the right bank, and still more those of the long-stagnating left bank, viewed with alarm the development of the northwest, and the consequent departure of their more solvent tenants.[22] The journalist Perreymond, writing in 1841, noted that over the past centuries the commercial district had divided itself into subordinate centers; Paris had long since become several cities under a single name. The left bank had suffered the most. Building land in southeastern Paris was of low value, and built-up land either could not find tenants or could be let only at uneconomical rents. He corrected any notion we might have, if from nowhere else than *La Bohème,* of the Latin Quarter as an area of picturesque gaiety. Its youthful population sought its pleasures, along with the rest of Paris, in the western boulevards. "The students, forced to lodge close to their places of study, stay there as little as they can; and the establishment of public carriages enables them to seek far from the Latin Quarter the life and the activity that they themselves at one time produced in it."[23]

The then three arrondissements of the left bank submitted a memorial that predicted ruin for their part of Paris from loss of population to the northwest:

> The displacement of the Parisian population is easy to observe: taking the district of the Stock Exchange as a base, it is directed toward the Chaussée d'Antin, and follows in the direction of the quartier Saint-Lazare as far as the faubourg Saint-Honoré. . . . As a result of this movement, the left bank . . . finds itself threatened by an inevitable ruin . . . since all classes of the population always try to bring themselves close to the center . . . won't they try to establish themselves on the right bank, which puts within their reach commerce, entertainments, in a word all the pleasures intended to bring them the comforts and conveniences of life?[24] [Fig. 62]

The municipality took the threat of a decaying "central city" seriously enough to appoint a committee of inquiry into the problem of the displacement of population from the left bank. In 1845 Municipal Councillor Lanquetin proposed the abolition of tolls and the building of bridges, together with the creation of a network of new streets and the widening of the rues Saint-Denis and Montmartre.[25]

It was assumed that all classes would follow the more affluent in their move to the western right bank. The *Allgemeine Bauzeitung* predicted that the middle classes, having moved into the "new elegant houses," would attract those shopkeepers "that are dependent on the rich. But also all those whose business is not tied to a particular neighborhood seek to give up, as much as they can, the old, gloomy, and uncomfortable houses . . . and exchange them for healthier and more comfortable flats. The new *quartiers* gain thereby in importance, and the population is abandoning the center of Paris, to settle where elegance and wealth are to be found."[26] The problem was seen not as one of social segregation but of mass migration. Yet Councillor Lanquetin foresaw and deplored the former in 1841:

> The municipal interest, the general interest, the political interest demand equally, in the present state of our manners and customs, that all classes of the population live spread out and intermixed . . . in all *quartiers* of Paris. . . . The day when . . . these classes become separated, and we have aristocratic *quartiers,* proletarian *quartiers,*

62. *The displacement of the Parisian population follows in the direction of the quartier Saint-Lazare.* Marville, rue Saint-Lazare. (Musée Carnavalet. Photo Lauros-Giraudon.)

financial *quartiers,* and *quartiers* of poverty . . . will see destroyed the essential basis of public order and the way paved for fearful calamities for our country.[27]

The *Builder* in 1849, after such fearful calamities had in fact occurred, drew a similar moral:

> An evil is now growing around us of large districts entirely destitute of dwellings for the poor; the consequence is, they lose the advantage of the example of those of superior education; the rich, on the other hand, have not that control over their indulgences by the constant exhibition of poverty; these two classes, instead of growing up together on each other's sympathy and support, are so entirely estranged as to become dangerous to each other (this is clearly shown in the July riots in Paris, when faubourg fought against faubourg).[28]

Writing in 1847, A.-L. Lusson took for granted that it was *activity,* whether vehicular or intellectual or commercial, that made a neighborhood desirable.[29] Each group clustered around the appropriate center of activity: the nobility around the court, financiers around the stock exchange, and dealers in luxury goods around the boulevard Montmartre. "In all ages, industry attracts industry, commerce commerce, finance finance, luxury luxury." He was, to be sure, describing neither social segregation nor the separation of residential from other uses, but rather the tendency of people with like interests to congregate in the same place. He argued, though, that the middle classes were better able to regroup themselves within a city than the poor, whose place of residence tended not to change—an assertion that the next twenty years would disprove:

> The industrial population took little part in the displacement. The surroundings of the Temple, an ancient privileged site, remained the center of manufacture of objects of common use [*objets d'usage*]. The rues Saint-Martin and Saint-Denis continued to supply the city and the countryside with cloth, thread, ribbons intended for the needs of the middle classes, as the rues des Lombards, Saint-Avoye supplied them with drugs and spices, a state of things that has lasted into our own day.[30]

By 1870 Paris was certainly characterized by a degree of social and functional segregation greater than it had been twenty years earlier, but it is unclear how far the specific policies of the emperor and his prefect were responsible. "The real estate ideas of Baron Haussmann . . . were based on homogenization," Richard Sennett writes. New districts "were to be of a single class, and in the old central city rich and poor were to be isolated from each other. This was the beginning of 'single function' urban development. Each space in the city does a particular job."[31] The process required both radical surgery in the center and the encouragement of emigration to socially differentiated suburbs. The expansion of existing *beaux quartiers* to the west and the creation of new ones in the same direction were, according to Jeanne Gaillard, a matter of conscious imperial policy. The emperor, speculating along with his relatives in real estate in the developing west, had every motive to encourage its growth as a middle-class stronghold. Such a policy of decentralization contrasted with the earlier efforts of the July monarchy to revitalize central Paris by such schemes as the construction of the rue Rambuteau.[32]

Pierre Lavedan insists that the street improvements in the developing west grew out of calculations totally different from those that produced the *percées* through the center. "No more costly expropriations in overcrowded and commercial districts. . . . Napoleon III and Haussmann wished to raise the value of building ground that was as yet only partly urbanized, and create broad ways planted with trees, and arrange symmetrically radiating crossroads. They naturally foresaw that the rich would emigrate in that direction and erect luxurious mansions. It would be the equivalent of London's West End."[33]

Gaillard argues that imperial policy deprived the old center not only of fashion but of population and economic viability. Railways were forbidden to extend their lines into the dense network of streets in the old Paris. The Chemin de fer de Ceinture was built to encourage suburban development, notably where it passed by the bois de Boulogne. She blames Haussmann for separating and juxtaposing "two cities, that of the rich and that of the others."[34]

The argument may interject unnecessary complications into imperial policy while confusing consequences with intentions. It also fails to give sufficient weight to the need to counter contemporary charges of extravagance by doing everything possible to ensure the economic productivity of the public works. To do so, each new street would need to attract enough private capital to line it with substantial buildings, of a sort that would attract equally substantial tenants. Only by disproportionately increasing the assessed valuation of the areas traversed could the improvements justify themselves financially. The serious contemporary criticisms that Haussmann faced were not that his policies produced socially segregated neighborhoods, but that they were bankrupting the city and the state.

Private capital was more reluctant to invest along the *percées* through the decaying central quarters than in the expanding west. Eighteen months after the opening of the boulevard de Strasbourg, only the extreme northern portion had been built upon.[35] South of the river it took even longer for new streets to attract builders. "The tendency of the Parisian population to move to the northwestern region of the city has never been stronger than today," wrote the *Revue générale de l'architecture* in 1855. "On the one hand we see new streets pushing through and being covered with houses with a remarkable speed, while on the other, on the left bank of the Seine, *percées* opened for several years, the rue des Ecoles for example, still waiting for the first new houses to give them life."[36] Even by 1870 the new streets had failed to attract commerce to the left bank, which remained overwhelmingly residential.[37]

Haussmann was doing what every successful town planner must—cooperating with rather than ignoring market forces—when he built the broad avenues in today's sixteenth arrondissement, radiating from the Etoile, the Trocadéro, and the place de l'Alma. In his memorandum for 1857 he justified such projects by the necessity to prepare the ground for bourgeois habitation, promoting the westward exodus of the comfortable classes being pushed out of the center by commerce and industry.[38] Any other policy would have been economic folly.

Just as the ground landlord of a leasehold estate in London encouraged the building of residences that would provide the greatest reversionary value when the leases expired, it was in the interest of the Parisian municipality to maximize the assessed valuation of construction along the new streets and hence future tax receipts. Both ground landlord and municipality sometimes, for social reasons, encouraged the construction of workmen's dwellings, but they did so knowing that a financial sacrifice, both immediate and long-term, was involved.

It is not merely the encouragement of middle-class housing that Sennett, Lavedan, and Gaillard criticize, but its concentration at the western reaches of the right bank rather than its dispersal throughout the metropolis. In fact Haussmann attempted but failed to achieve just such a dispersal. To have succeeded would have meant changing the direction of a century and a half of building history.

Long before 1852, every indication was that the prospects for the middle-class development of the eighth, sixteenth, and seventeenth arrondissements were of the highest. The theoretical possibility of the eastern suburbs—between, say, the boulevard du Temple and the bois de Vincennes—attracting middle-class residents faced severe practical difficulties. Even so they did benefit from considerable public expenditure on new avenues, if fewer than those granted to the eighth and the sixteenth arrondissements.

The boulevard du Temple, until the 1850s preeminently the working-class entertainment district, was completely reconstructed, and the place du Château-d'eau (place de la République) totally rearranged and made the focus of a number of new radiating thoroughfares, including the boulevard Magenta, leading toward Montmartre; the boulevard du Prince Eugène (boulevard Voltaire), linking it with the place du Trône (place de la Nation), the eastern counterpart of the Etoile; and the broad and handsome avenue de la République (originally avenue des Amandiers), connecting the *grands boulevards* with Belleville and Ménilmontant. To these should be added the boulevard Richard Lenoir, built over the line of the canal Saint-Martin. As for parks, the improvements made in the bois de Vincennes were of a scale and nature comparable to those at the bois de Boulogne, while the new parc des Buttes Chaumont was both larger and more spectacular than the relandscaped parc Monceau in the eighth.

Nor was there any obvious difference in the scale, planning, landscaping, or architecture of new streets in central and eastern districts to distinguish them from those in the west. The universal complaint, on the contrary, was of standardized uniformity, regardless of district. "The same class of buildings, as like to each other as files of soldiers, are being erected everywhere—at the extremities as well as in the centre . . . everywhere new thoroughfares flanked with palatial buildings," reported the *Building News* in 1861. The *Builder* in 1882 was to express pleased surprise at the fact that "while, unquestionably, considerably larger sums are expended on the 'strangers' quarter' in Paris than . . . in more distant neighbourhoods, the system . . . is the same for all." It found everywhere "the same tall stone houses, the same pretty squares . . . the same green gardens . . . the same tree-planted streets and boulevards . . . there are not to be found, as with us, those differences so marked between one neighbourhood and another."[39]

Yet for all their abundance of physical attractions, the region east and northeast of the *grands boulevards* failed to attract the affluent or even the comfortable middle classes. It is fair to ask whether an even more generous provision of parks and boulevards and public institutions would materially have altered its social destiny. César Daly was convinced of the answer: "it is not enough to create fine roads to make them frequented, unless such roads lead more directly or more conveniently than others to the center of activity . . . of business or of pleasure."[40] No program of parks or boulevards would have made the eastern and northeastern outskirts easily accessible to the center of business and pleasure, by 1852 firmly attached to the western line of boulevards, and extending—with respect to pleasure—along the Champs-Elysées. The westward movement of fashion was already a century and a half old when Haussmann was appointed prefect. The line of the boulevard Malesherbes had been set by the first Napoleon, while the alignment of the Champs-Elysées gave the western outskirts further attractions. Farther west, Passy and Auteuil had long had a certain cachet as sites for rural retreats that Saint-Mandé and Charenton could not match. It is hard to conceive of policies that Haussmann might have pursued that could have done more than postpone the triumph of the west.

Writing in 1907, the American Edward R. Smith was more struck by the extent to which Haussmann resisted the forces pushing Paris westward than by his cooperation with them. "In 1853 the center had reached a point a little to the west of the present location of the Opéra," he pointed out. "In any American city a fact like this would have dominated every consideration. The civic center would have been placed as near as possible to the actual center of forces." But Haussmann rejected such a "cold-blooded commercial solution," and preserved the Ile de la Cité and its adjacent districts as the "monumental civic center." He saw the intersection of the *grande croisée* just north of the place du Châtelet as the victory of sentiment over economic reality. "An American student or architect, accustomed to the brutal civics of our land, finds it difficult to conceive a vast metropolis entering upon a period of transformation on historic lines, and in the face of conflicting commercial considerations; but that is precisely what happened in Paris."[41]

The interjection of an American dimension to the debate reminds us how stable Paris, London, and Vienna were compared to New York or Chicago or San Francisco, where the fashionable district of one generation becomes the slum of the next, leaving behind only the occasional façade as testimony to its former glory. Daly could write of the failure of the place des Vosges to prevent the social decline of the Marais, yet it was at least a century after that square was built before the westward exodus began. A century in New York saw residential fashion move all the way from lower Broadway to Fifty-ninth Street, leaving behind several complete neighborhoods in between, abandoned in turn by their restless occupants.

The street improvements of the Second Empire failed to lessen the contrasts between right and left banks. The southern extension of the boulevard de Sébastopol (today's boulevard Saint-Michel) was made on quite as grand a scale as the *percée* north of the Seine, while the boulevard Saint-Germain, not completed until the seventies, was an even more splendid left bank counterpart of the rue de Rivoli. The rue de Rennes, though never completed to the river, provided access to the Gare Montparnasse, and the Luxembourg quarter gained several new streets. Land values and rents climbed, but neither as fast or as far as on the right bank.[42]

The faubourg Saint-Germain, enriched by the compensation for the land needed for the boulevard of that name, retained its aristocratic character. South of the streets of eighteenth-century hôtels there persisted, on both sides of the rue de Sèvres, a large artisan population. To the east, in the fifth and sixth, the rise of rents brought about by the improvements and the simultaneous arrival from across the river of a working-class population displaced by the demolitions there led to a bourgeois move to the south, toward the Luxembourg. To the west, new streets of bourgeois *hôtels* beyond the Invalides were developed as a counterpart to similar constructions across the river.[43]

"For some Parisians . . . to go from the left bank to the right bank is almost an excursion into another city," wrote George Riat in 1904. The left bank was the realm of students, judges, priests, small tradesmen, of great public institutions. Life there was calm, devout, petit bourgeois, and a little boring, retaining both the streets and the atmosphere of an older time. By contrast the right bank was more cheerful, more active, more commercial, more eager for pleasure, strong emotions, and money. Above all it was continuing to push westward.[44]

Perhaps even more significant than differences between east and west, left and right, was that between city and suburbs. Haussmann, by demolishing slums and encouraging the erection of expensive blocks of flats along the new avenues, contributed to the sharp rise of rents in central Paris that brought about a working-class exodus, both to the newly annexed arrondissements of 1860 and beyond the municipal boundaries entirely. The consequence was a disproportionately middle-class Paris surrounded by a ring of industrial and working-class suburbs, surrounded in turn today by clusters of equally working-class *grands ensembles*. It may be unjust to deplore both cities in which the middle classes have fled to the suburbs, leaving a proletarian center, and those in which the working classes have fled, leaving a bourgeois center. Yet it is fair to ask whether Haussmann deliberately encouraged the working-class emigration, and what he might have done to prevent it.

Writing in 1852, the year of Haussmann's appointment, Daly found Paris already divided along class lines: "In Paris, as elsewhere, one lives according to where one's means permit; blocks of flats there form a series rising in importance, in convenience and in luxury, from working-class blocks and those for small craftsmen to the rich houses of the boulevards."[45]

The contrasts grew over the next decade. "Paris will soon be a network of boulevards lined with stone buildings, which will mask a group of narrow, dirty streets, and hide the objectionable dwellings of the poor," observed the *Building News* in 1861. "Where all the working classes will go to who are turned out of the demolished houses it is difficult to say. . . . They cannot occupy the new houses; they are far too . . . expensively rented."[46] The answer for more and more was to move to the suburbs. "Beyond the so-called external boulevards . . . [are] large areas which either are occupied by buildings of a very inferior description, or can hardly be considered as occupied at all," reported the *Builder* the same year:

> Except in the western part or suburb . . . the strangest contrasts may be noticed; and the impression which is left is often resembling that of an Irish village. . . . Occasionally, the main lines of streets, houses as lofty as those of central Paris, may be met with—many of them, judging from a certain character of elaboration in ornament, being recent erections,—but such structures are adjoined by buildings of very different character, sometimes of two stories, or in a bad state of repair, and sometimes by a mere shed or a store of materials.[47] [Figs. 63 and 64.]

Except for the sixteenth and seventeenth, the new districts annexed in 1860 were overwhelmingly working-class in character. Even small tradesmen hesitated to set up business there. Standards of construction resembled those of working-class quarters in provincial towns.[48]

The splendid blocks that came to line all of the new streets in favored districts, by concentrating the affluent under one roof, worked to destroy whatever social mixture had earlier existed within the same building. Yet Adeline Daumard doubts whether there was much mingling of classes even early in the century, when most houses in Paris were divided into lodgings of markedly varying importance and cost. In the rue Saint-Denis wholesale merchants and craftsmen in the same trade

63. *(above, opposite) "Beyond the so-called external boulevards . . . [are] large areas which either are occupied by buildings of a very inferior description, or can hardly be considered as occupied at all."* Marville, Haut de la rue Champlain, between 1856 and 1865. (Musée Carnavalet. Photo Lauros-Giraudon.)

typically lived in the same building, to their mutual advantage. But this practice was already dying out in the early years of the century, as the merchants moved to separate quarters farther west.

Although many buildings housed both workers and members of the petite bourgeoisie, there is little reason to believe that contact between the two was frequent. In working-class quarters and in the poor streets that lay behind more prosperous ones, a great many buildings, except for the shops on the ground floor, were entirely let to people of very limited means. At the other extreme, in fashionable streets, the upper stories were occupied by the servants and dependents of those who lived in the luxury flats underneath. Elsewhere, though there might ordinarily be social variation in residents as one moved upward in the building, the difference would not be vast. Even so, social segregation proceeded building by building or, more often, street by street, rather than *quartier* by *quartier*. Streets as elegant as the rue de la Chaussée d'Antin might contain some small dwellings occupied by poorer residents.[49]

With rare exceptions—as with the Ile de la Cité and the dense slums that stretched from the Louvre to the Hôtel de Ville—Haussmann's demolitions did not wipe out whole neighborhoods but rather worked to isolate them one from another. Behind every boulevard, with its elegant façades and middle-class residents, lay intact an older, working-class Paris. For all the extent and brutality of Haussmann's operations, Paris in the 1850s and 1860s was spared the enthusiastic

64. Marville, Chemin de fer de Ceinture, looking toward the buttes Elisa Borey. Both views in present twentieth arrondissement. (Musée Carnavalet. Photo Lauros-Giraudon.)

devastation which planners visited upon cities in the 1950s and 1960s. The sixteenth century is sometimes only a few steps away from the nineteenth. Classes were physically contiguous, if not necessarily intermingled in the same building or street. For Jeanne Gaillard, the most striking contrast between the housing policy of Second Empire Paris and that of cities in Alsace and the north is the comparative absence of social segregation in the former.[50]

Even within unquestionably bourgeois sections clear social and economic distinctions existed. Guidebooks written by Amédée de Cesena (1864) and Adolphe Joanne (1870) give valuable indication, in their advice on lodgings, of the comparative cost of particular neighborhoods. The former advised rich families in search of furnished apartments to confine themselves to the rue de Rivoli west of the Grand Hôtel du Louvre, the boulevards west of the rue de Richelieu, and the streets to the north as far as the rue Saint-Lazare. Beyond that they would find suitable accommodation near the Champs-Elysées, and along the boulevard Malesherbes. The latter two districts were particularly airy and spacious, "advantages particularly appreciated by the English, the Russians, and the Americans who are found here in such numbers that they seem to form three compact and distinct colonies."[51]

For families which, however rich, felt the need to moderate their expenditures, he suggested the faubourg Saint-Germain. More modern apartments at comparatively modest rents could be had between the rue Saint-Lazare and the exterior boulevards. Quiet and economical lodgings were available on the Ile Saint-Louis, in the Marais, and near the Luxembourg Gardens. For families of moderate income, who had to calculate their expenditures closely, sacrificing luxury and representation for comfort, he advised certain streets near the Madeleine, around the Palais Royal or the Grand Opera (then located in the rue le Peletier), and the quartiers de la Boule-Rouge and the Tuileries.[52]

Adolphe Joanne, writing just before the outbreak of the Franco-Prussian War, gave advice not only to the seeker after pleasure in the western boulevards, but to the merchant visiting Paris on business. His comments in the latter connection showed how far the division of the right bank center into streets specializing in particular trades had maintained itself. The visiting merchant would conduct most of his business in the area roughly between the rue Montmartre and the rue Vieille du Temple, between the boulevards and the Seine. More specifically, he advised traders in cotton prints, jewelery, and hardware to lodge themselves in or near the rues Saint-Denis, Saint-Martin, and the boulevard de Sébastopol; those dealing in the cloth trade and in lace to go to the rues de Cléry, de Mulhouse, du Sentier, Saint-Fiacre, and du Mail. Each other specialty likewise had its particular streets.[53]

As the century progressed the Chaussée d'Antin grew less residential, with luxury shops and businesses moving into its once opulent mansions. By the early years of the Third Republic the Champs-Elysées and the faubourg Saint-Honoré had become the fashionable district, even drawing residents from the declining faubourg Saint-Germain. The beginning of the urbanization of the sixteenth arrondissement began along the avenues radiating from the Etoile.[54]

If the earlier move to the periphery had been mostly working-class, the late nineteenth and early twentieth century saw a middle-class move away from the older central districts, at least by its more adventurous elements. The address book of the wife of a young banker living in the seventh near Sèvres-Babylone for the years 1893–1900, containing 215 addresses, shows a preponderance of entries from the fifth, sixth, and seventh arrondissements on the left bank and a substantial number from the eighth (Champs-Elysées). There was a tendency for her friends and acquaintances during the period to move from the left bank to the right, but only six had ventured as far west as the sixteenth. The eastern arrondissements were, understandably, sparsely represented if at all.[55] The still more daring middle classes were rediscovering the charms of the Ile Saint-Louis.[56]

With the early twentieth century the Champs-Elysées in turn lost their purely residential character. Luxury shops, theaters, and hotels took the place of private mansions.[57] "There are stylish hotels, automobile show-rooms, and the shops of furriers and dressmakers and *lingères*," wrote Sisley Huddleston in 1927. "Here is, perhaps, the most sumptuous road, with the finest perspective, formerly consecrated to princely habitations, and now invaded by merchants of *luxe*."[58]

Beyond the Arc de Triomphe, the avenue de l'Impératrice became first the avenue du Bois de Boulogne and then the avenue Foch without losing any of its original prestige. "It is a residential street for the very rich, with no hotels or shops or anything else suggestive of work or business in it," wrote Paul Cohen-Porthcim in 1930 (fig. 65). The avenue "does not belong to the Paris of the old Nobility, still less to that of the *nouveaux riches;* the nearest parallels to it are Park Lane in London, and the Tiergartenstrasse in Berlin before the War. . . . Most of the husbands of these smart women have an occupation—finance, the Stock Exchange, industry or politics." The whole of the sixteenth was by now busy and prosperous:

65. *"It is a residential street for the very rich, with no hotels or shops or anything else suggestive of work or business in it." Hôtel particulier,* avenue Foch, 1984. (Evelyn Benesch.)

"The Avenues Marceau, d'Jéna and Kléber take you through smart residential quarters; the Avenue Victor Hugo, now an exclusive shopping centre, leads to Passy and Auteuil which, though equally prosperous, do not rank as high socially; they are inhabited by a substantial *bourgeoisie* which belongs neither to the *monde* nor to high international society."[59]

Meanwhile, "the Faubourg Saint-Germain, shabbier than of yore, endeavours to keep up appearances . . . this is really decadence," wrote Huddleston in 1927. Cohen-Portheim reported that many of its mansions were "still occupied by the bearers of historic names; others are embassies or government offices. . . . Side by side with the great people live a sprinkling of old-fashioned little shopkeepers."[60]

Finally, in the 1960s, we come to the most socially segregated of all the units of the Paris metropolitan region, the newly erected *grands ensembles.* "This population is not, like that of a traditional *quartier,* the result of a slow stratification and the addition of isolated movements . . . extended over a long period," explains Jean Bastié. *"It arrived en bloc or in great waves."* The residents came not by choice but were selected on the basis of such criteria as former housing conditions, size of family, and occupation. The new satellite communities provided housing that was from every technical and quantifiable standpoint immensely superior to the slums from which their occupants came. But there was a price to be paid: "It is perhaps for leisure activities that the underequipment of the *grand ensemble* was most notable by comparison with the Parisian neighborhood of cinemas, theaters, sports grounds, and so on. . . . [In their new environment] remoteness, isolation, monotony could lead to a feeling of frustration and segregation."[61]

Meanwhile gentrification has been transforming the first four arrondissements. "The old Halles is a sad desert," complains Richard Cobb; "the Marais has become a museum, its original inhabitants dispersed to the *grande banlieue,* and replaced by middle-class intellectuals, their wives dressed like Gipsey-Rose-Lees in expensive rags, and armed with *le Nouvel-Observateur,* or by young technocratic couples, fresh from the *Grandes Ecoles*. . . . The Ile Saint-Louis is for millionaires, its central street for picture-galleries." Even the twentieth, "the most Parisian of any *arrondissement*," the "fortress-stronghold" of the skilled artisan and of "pretty well the whole cross section of the *petit peuple*," is threatened. "Traditional Belleville has not long to go; the property speculators, the high-rise blocks are closing in from two directions, from down below and from the top . . . and the blocks are soon occupied by middle-class professional people."[62]

What had once been a question of contrasting stories or buildings or streets or *quartiers* is fast becoming one that differentiates Paris from the rest of the metropolitan region, with Paris itself becoming increasingly middle-class and the surroundings—with exceptions like the villa suburbs to the west and southwest—overwhelmingly working-class. But the process still has some time to go, and the degree of social mixture remaining in central Paris is one of its greatest attractions.

Vienna

After the volatile sociogeographical histories of London and Paris, the comparative stability of the social map of Vienna becomes all the more remarkable. With a few exceptions, there is and has always been a marked decline in social prestige as one moves from the first *Bezirk* (City and Ringstrasse) to *Vorstadt,* and from *Vorstadt* to *Vorort.* The City housed court and aristocracy, the Ringstrasse was preeminently the home of the upper middle classes, the inner suburbs—which had begun as settlements of bourgeoisie and artisans alike—became gradually more middle-class, while the outer suburbs—except for the ones near Schönbrunn and the Wienerwald—were and are largely proletarian.

The process of social differentiation goes back to the seventeenth century, with the triumph of absolutism and the Counter-Reformation over the commercial and Protestant citizenry. As court officials and aristocracy acquired more of the property in the City, baroque palaces and blocks of flats replaced the older narrow gabled houses of the *Bürgertum.* Tradesmen and artisans moved into the suburbs, settling in existing village centers, along the major roads, or in wholly new developments.[63] In the century between 1750 and 1850 the "social distance" between the City and the ring of suburbs was the greatest it was ever to be.[64]

Such distance was reflected in the comparative level of rents, as Mrs. Trollope discovered. "We have met such various and unexpected difficulties in finding apartments, that I have repeatedly been upon the point of deciding that we must . . . content ourselves with a dwelling in the faubourgs," she wrote. In the suburbs "very excellent rooms may be found without difficulty, and greatly cheaper." Fortunately she found lodgings in the Hoher Markt and so was able to enjoy a City address.[65]

Neither City nor suburb was totally homogeneous. Within the City there were marked differences between streets and between quarters. The area along the Danube Canal was socially inferior, while the streets that lay close to the Hofburg, notably the Herrengasse, were the preferred sites for palaces of the high nobility (fig. 66). The luxury retail trade, then as now, concentrated itself in the Graben and Stephansplatz and along the Kärntner Strasse and Rotenturmstrasse[66] (fig. 67 and colorplate 4).

The suburbs were more heterogeneous than the City. From the late seventeenth century onward many nobility had purchased suburban vineyards on which they proceeded to erect summer palaces. In the western suburbs both ecclesiastical and secular landowners laid out settlements intended for small craftsmen forced to

66. *(opposite) The streets that lay close to the Hofburg, notably the Herrengasse, were the preferred sites for palaces of the high nobility.* Herrengasse, with Palais Liechtenstein, c. 1911. (Bildarchiv der Österreichischen Nationalbibliothek.)

67. *(above) The luxury retail trade concentrated itself in the Graben.* Graben. Aquatint by Rudolf von Alt. (Bundesdenkmalamt Wien.)

leave the City by rising rents. Similarly privileged quarters of foreign craftsmen were established in the late eighteenth century.[67]

By the early nineteenth century the different suburbs had acquired particular social characteristics. Josefstadt, for instance, was markedly bourgeois, while the complex of hospitals between Alserstrasse and Währingerstrasse had become surrounded by middle-class residences. Suburbs to the south and southeast contained a larger working-class component. Coaching inns lined the major long-distance roads, while the specific characters of long-established villages could still be felt. Between Mariahilferstrasse and Altlerchenfelderstrasse planned settlements of craftsmen persisted from their eighteenth-century foundations.[68]

The replacement of the fortifications by the Ringstrasse confirmed and strengthened older patterns. The Ringstrasse zone served less as a rival to the Altstadt than as an extension and complement, one that reinforced its social prestige and economic worth. The presence of the court between City and Ringstrasse assured the attractiveness of both until the fall of the monarchy in 1918. The prerepublican character of the two has maintained itself to this day, in a period that ought logically to have rendered the old social geography anachronistic and functionless.

"Up to the Hofburg . . . the town is commonplace," Ulysse Robert observed in 1899, approaching the City from the western suburbs.[69] With its grand and splendid buildings, the Ringstrasse accentuated the already disproportionate attractions of the central area. A Parisian moving to the eighth, sixteenth, and seventeenth arrondissements left behind the major cultural institutions and the centers of pleasure, but the Ringstrasse resident had everything at his immediate disposal: court, opera, theaters, the great museums, the most attractive parks, the best shops.

The old and new aristocracy and leaders of manufacture and finance eagerly took up building plots along the Ringstrasse. Frequently occupying the entire first floor of a building themselves, they had no difficulty finding tenants for the somewhat less grand flats in the upper stories, nor for the shops on the ground floor. The upper bourgeoisie and newer nobility that constituted the "Second Society" found the Ringstrasse the ideal location in which to pursue a style of living appropriate for their wealth and position.[70] Not only by their proximity to the existing aristocratic quarters but in their architectural appearance the new *Mietpaläste* asserted the attachment of their owners and occupiers to the symbols of aristocratic tradition.

The customary English way for a rich City man to insinuate himself, or rather his descendants, into the governing class was to purchase a country estate and set himself up as a landed gentleman. No London mansion, no taking of a house in Grosvenor Square, would serve to expunge the mercantile stain. In Vienna residence in the City, far from being incompatible with a noble manner of living, was essential to it. The Ringstrasse, though attached to the City, imitating it in its architectural forms, and surpassing it in physical magnificence, never succeeded in equaling it in fashion and prestige. The French aristocracy transferred itself to the Marais under Louis XIII, to Saint-Germain under Louis XV, and—if it could afford it—to the Champs-Elysées and beyond during the Third Republic; the Viennese aristocracy, once established in the Altstadt, stayed there.

Not all, even of the highest aristocracy, resisted the attractions of the Ringstrasse, and the area around the Schwarzenbergplatz saw a particularly strong concentration of their number.[71] Others, who had failed to adjust their investments to the changing economic patterns of the time, were not in a financial position to make the move. But a substantial proportion of those who were economically able to live wherever they wished—and who often invested their capital in Ringstrasse property—chose to remain in their inherited City palaces. The City continued to represent ancient tradition and aristocratic power; the Ringstrasse helped solve the problem of housing members of junior lines of good family or of finding newlyweds a suitable place to live, but it was still tainted by bourgeois associations. For those who had one, a City palace was not something to give up lightly.[72]

It would be wrong to exaggerate the social inferiority of the Ringstrasse. It served rather as the concrete expression of the admission to the ruling classes of both individuals and broader social groupings, who expanded and enriched the older governing class just as the Ringstrasse zone expanded and enriched the older City. The Ringstrasse united new aristocracy with old, money with birth, ability with rank, the arts and scholarship with politics and administration.[73] It represented what was healthiest about the last period of the Habsburg Empire: its openness to talent, new ideas, and new artistic forms, whatever their origin; its cosmopolitanism, its respect for learning and achievement, and its refusal to be shocked by the unconventional.

To be sure, different parts of the Ringstrasse attracted different segments of this wealthy, cultivated, and creative society. The high nobility preferred the Schwarzenbergplatz, the Opernring attracted the financial and official aristocracy (fig. 68), while the district near the Rathaus was favored by industrialists and financiers. The medical profession clustered around the Votivkirche because of the hospitals that lay behind it; lawyers and retail merchants were found near the Stock Exchange and in the Textile Quarter, which lay next to the Danube Canal.[74] But these were not distinct compartments, with nothing but old aristocracy in one quarter, nothing but bankers and industrialists in the other; rather, a larger than average proportion of certain groups lived in certain districts. And all groups met and mingled in the many cultural and political institutions of the great boulevard, and above all took part in the "Ringstrassenkorso" every afternoon between the Schwarzenbergplatz and the Kärntner Strasse. The Ringstrasse can better be understood as a meeting ground than as a device for sterile social segregation.

Austria, like Lady Catherine de Bourgh, liked to see the distinctions of rank preserved. The buildings along the Ringstrasse expressed such distinctions in both internal structure and external appearance. If in Paris the size of flats, along with their rents, diminished as one went upward within a given building, this was not reflected in the façade, which repeated the same decorative motifs up to the cornice line. The main staircase went all the way to the fifth floor; only the servants and the poor living under the roof had to use the back stairs. In the Ringstrasse the principal staircase might go no higher than the *Nobelstock,* or at most to the relatively pretentious quarters on the second floor; even if it did the house owner could exercise the option of excluding the tenant from it if he wished.[75] Embarrassing encounters on the stairs, which the English thought the inevitable consequence of flat-living, were thus avoided.

Such vertical differentiation went back to the eighteenth century and represented yet another way in which the block of flats imitated the baroque palace. Not until the end of the century did the coming of the mechanical lift render such distinctions unnecessary. Service rooms and family rooms were relegated to the rear in order that the major "representational" rooms could have a conspicuous outlook onto the street. If more than one flat occupied a floor, the one commanding the street also commanded the higher rent.[76]

The standard façade of the *Hochgründerzeit,* the period from 1865 to 1880, expressed a sharply differentiated hierarchy of uses for the different stories (fig. 69). When suburban buildings imitated Ringstrasse models, their architecture had

68. *The Opernring attracted the financial and official aristocracy.* Opernring, south side. Heinrichhof to left. (Museen der Stadt Wien.)

69. *The standard façade expressed a sharply differentiated hierarchy of uses for the different stories.* Schottenring 25. (Kunsthistorisches Institut der Universität Wien. Photo Johanna Fiegl.)

less connection with the socioeconomic realities behind the façades: there the grandly decorated first-floor windows rarely indicated the existence of a palatial flat for the building owner behind.[77] Buildings housing a relatively homogeneous population expressed in their outward appearance the structure of a highly differentiated and hierarchical society.

Since the Ringstrasse and City attracted to themselves all that was richest, most learned, most talented, and most beautiful, *Vorstadt* and *Vorort* had to make do with what was left over. This did not leave them a cultural desert, and in any event the treasures of the City were easily accessible to the whole Viennese population. Yet the social, economic, and aesthetic decline as one moved toward the outskirts of the metropolis was as marked in the so-called Liberal era as it had been under pre-1848 absolutism.

Ulysse Robert contrasted the splendor of the Ring with the sober plainness of the surrounding suburbs, composed of "straight streets, lined with houses of one to two stories, generally built on a uniform plan. . . . Instead of luxury, cleanliness reigns even in the poorest dwellings." Neither in picturesqueness nor in misery could they compare with streets like the rue Mouffetard in Paris. Yet the inner suburbs were being transformed, "as by enchantment, they were being covered by fine buildings replacing the primitive houses."[78] Such new, tall buildings were occupied more and more by the middle classes, as the older working-class population moved to the industrializing districts beyond the Linienwall.[79]

If a general rise in land values and rents had forced the middle classes into the inner suburbs, where they displaced the working classes into the outer, it would have been reasonable to predict that the upper classes would in turn be forced out of City and Ringstrasse by banks and insurance companies and corporate headquarters. If Vienna, for all its importance as a financial center, could not be expected to produce anything as intensely specialized as the City of London, something similar to the area around the Chaussée d'Antin would have seemed probable. And indeed in the years before 1914 the residential population of the City did fall, as flats were converted into offices and as commerce took over more of the building stock.[80] The Ringstrasse underwent much the same process. By 1914 a majority of the buildings in the area had three or more stories given up to commercial purposes or had less than 60 percent of their floor space used for residence. Only 8 percent were totally residential, and even these usually had shops on the ground floor. The Textile Quarter showed the greatest loss of residential function, while the Rathaus Quarter was the least affected by commercial intrusion.[81]

More remarkable than the shift toward commerce in the City and Ringstrasse was the strong and successful resistance of their prosperous residents to the pressure to leave. Despite the demands of finance and business for space in the Altstadt, despite the establishment by heavy industry of offices near the Opera and the Schwarzenbergplatz, the "noble residential character" remained as before in both. The old aristocracy could not have expressed its continuing power more effectively.[82]

After 1918 that power had vanished, but so had the forces of commercial expansion. As Vienna lost its importance as a financial and business center, demand for office space declined, and rooms earlier appropriated for such purposes were reconverted into residential flats. The deterioration in the economic position of the aristocracy and upper bourgeoisie led to the division of the larger luxury flats into smaller units. Thus, while the population of Vienna as a whole fell sharply after 1918, that of the Ringstrasse and City rose.[83]

Massive construction of public housing beginning in the 1920s and a revival of the private building industry after 1955 have raised the standards of housing for the mass of the population and narrowed the differences in space and comfort between the wealthy center and the outlying districts. Yet the social geography of Vienna remains today that of the metropolis of 1914, with a decline in the average size of flat from the inner to the outer districts, with the *Vororte* to the east and southeast still the poorest.[84]

After painting a horrific but all too accurate picture of the postwar American city, with its combination of urban decay and suburban sprawl, Elisabeth Lichtenberger contrasts the stability of Viennese geography since 1945:

> The metropolis is not expanding beyond the area it occupied during the *Gründerzeit* and interwar period. Its law of development demands, on the contrary, improvement and the filling up of the existing building stock. Its demographic stagnation means further that . . . compared to other fast-growing metropolises, all developments will take place relatively slowly. Restrictive measures of industrial and housing policies contribute, along with bad inner-city traffic conditions, to further delays.

The sharp division between Downtown and Suburbs with local Shopping Centers in North American cities stands in contrast to the spatial linking together of different economic activities with residence on Viennese soil.[85]

If City and suburbs are clearly differentiated from one another in a social sense, they share the functional mixture of residence, trade, and manufacture. Each has shops appropriate to the social and economic condition of the nearby residents: the Graben is Vienna's Bond Street, Mariahilferstrasse its Oxford Street; the principal thoroughfare of each outer suburb presents a lively picture of retail trade. Heavy industry is concentrated in the outer suburbs to the south and east and across the Danube, but workshops abound in the courtyards behind middle-class residential streets.[86] That such an integrated urban structure has persisted despite the astounding rise in living standards that Austria has experienced over the past generation is a matter for wonder and congratulation.

Anthony Sutcliffe has argued that insofar as the Haussmannite improvements in Paris were intended to revitalize the right bank center, they must be considered a failure. The continued move of residents and the more prosperous businesses away from the center, the failure of private capital to replace its outmoded building stock, and the loss of their former dominant place in the Parisian economy of the streets around the rues Saint-Denis and Saint-Martin support his interpretation. Whether the decay would have been more precipitate and the shift of population and activity to the west more complete without the demolitions and *percées* is another question. But Sutcliffe's argument points to one certain conclusion: judged by the same criteria, the Ringstrasse was an outstanding success.

If the first *Bezirk* can be regarded as roughly equivalent to the first four *arrondissements,* its history since 1860 has seen anything but decay. True, its resident population, though substantial, is less than it was 120 years ago, while in recent years the need for expanded office space has induced the larger corporations to move their headquarters away from the City, but the Altstadt and Ringstrasse zone combined *are* Vienna in a sense that the area bounded by the right bank boulevards no longer *is* Paris.

The situation of the two in 1850, before either of the great improvement programs began, was, to be sure, markedly different. The right bank center had lost most of its fashionable residents in the eighteenth century and had been losing its middle-class population to the newer western and northern districts for at least the twenty years preceding, while the Vienna Inner City, though severely congested, had neither slums to be eradicated nor a rebellious proletariat to be neutralized. Its congestion was upper-class and institutional, and was satisfactorily relieved by the splendid residences, spacious promenades, and massive public buildings that the Ringstrasse provided on its periphery. But it would be unfair to the excellence of the conception and execution of the City Expansion Program to assume that its success was a foregone conclusion. Town planning projects that achieve their intended ends are too rare for the success of the Ringstrasse to be taken for granted.

10

Villa Suburbia

he suburb, as it has developed in the English-speaking world, is the antithesis of the city. If the latter embodies diversity, concentration, excitement, movement, the clash of ideas, the former represents conformity, dispersal, boredom, serenity, loneliness. It also offers an even more appropriate environment for domestic withdrawal and personal seclusion than the single-class district of terraces and garden squares. More removed from centers of business and pleasure, it contains few attractions to compete with those of the separate household. The very dullness of the suburb, lacking in artificial amusements and social contrasts, throws its residents back onto their own resources. The physical separation of one house from another, made the greater in England by the high walls and hedges that surround front and back gardens, emphasizes the autonomy of each family unit and makes it easier to avoid speaking to neighbors. Although the social homogeneity of the typical suburb might seem to encourage cooperation in support of common class interests, the physical layout and implicit code of behavior serve to keep each family separate from the rest. Such physical and psychological fragmentation rarely promotes diversity of thought or behavior, but is consistent with conformity to unspoken but unquestioned rules. The most successful suburbs are everything that Jane Jacobs's Hudson Street is not.

The London dormitory suburb offered the ideal soil for nurturing domesticity: socially and functionally homogeneous, so as to exclude both competing styles of living and competing cultural values, it provided the reassuring sight of similar families in similar houses with similar gardens behaving in a similar fashion. With a journey to town a major expedition, temptations to stray from the path of respectability were minimized. The suburban home served as a comfortable prison for the wife in particular, to the extent that it was distant from London and poorly supplied with public transportation. The boredom endured by the proper English middle-class wife and mother, excluded from the kitchen and hence denied the creative satisfaction of planning and preparing meals, discouraged from interfering with the operation of a nursery controlled by nanny and governess, was made greater if her home was suburban. Nor would she be likely to offer much in the way of conversation to her husband on his return from town, cut off as she was from the stimulus of urban society.

London

Yet for all its evident disadvantages, most Londoners in a position to choose their style of residence have for the past century and a half chosen villa suburbia. London is unique among the great cities of Europe in the extent and ubiquity of its districts of detached and semidetached houses. From Ealing to Epping, from Golders Green to Croydon, and far into the Home Counties, greater London is made up of separate houses, rarely more than two stories tall, with front and back gardens absurdly lavish by continental standards. If not the London the tourist ordinarily sees, villa suburbia is where most of London lives.

Yet its suburbs dominate London only in terms of geographical extent. They have never achieved the status of fashion and have always been seen as either faintly improper, as in St. John's Wood, or more than faintly comic, as in Mr. Pooter's Holloway. The lush and spacious neighborhoods reached from Baker Street and Marylebone Stations, dubbed "Metroland" by an advertising campaign of the Metropolitan Railway, may be known to posterity mainly through the gently satirical verses of Sir John Betjeman and the white-slave-trading heroine of *Decline and Fall*.

Fashion, admittedly, left the City for Covent Garden and Bloomsbury in the seventeenth century, which it in turn abandoned in the eighteenth for Marylebone and Mayfair, and then proceeded to colonize Belgravia and parts of Kensington. But there, significantly, it stopped, refusing to exchange the squares and terraces of those districts for whatever detached gentlemen's residences Putney or Wimbledon might offer. Dulwich and Richmond, Hampstead and Highgate might seem exceptions, but they could be plausibly regarded less as villa suburbs than as country villages providentially convenient to central London. And in each it is the actual village portion—as in Church Row, Hampstead—that possesses the highest cachet, not the streets of vast detached dwellings of late Victorian and twentieth-century origin. In any event such suburbs, Hampstead in particular, are associated with artists and intellectuals, and hence not wholly proper. Perhaps eighteenth-century Hackney, with its City men commuting to their countinghouses in the coaches of that name, and early nineteenth-century Clapham, with its high-minded banking Evangelicals, or even Augustan Twickenham with its poets (or at least poet) fixed the association of suburban villas with people who were brainy or in trade or in other respects not quite the thing. We learn from Nancy Mitford's *Pursuit of Love* that even seemingly rural portions of Surrey are tainted by suburban associations.

In this London differed from every other English city. From its early development Edgbaston housed the wealthy and powerful of Birmingham, as Didsbury did for Manchester. No English provincial city—as distinct from county town, spa, or seaside resort—maintained a district that was at once fashionable, central, and densely built, comparable to London's West End or Edinburgh's New Town. But then, Nancy Mitford or Evelyn Waugh would have pointed out that residence in Birmingham or Manchester in itself was as bad as suburban. Certainly no provincial city possessed either a sizable population of leisured residents or urban attractions sufficient to outweigh the space, beauty, and freedom from industrial pollution their immediate surroundings could offer.

The disinclination of the governing class to move very far away from the West End was determined less by snobbery than by practical considerations. The richest and most powerful already had houses in the "real" country in which they spent much of the year, and would have had little incentive to pass the London season in the artificial rurality of suburbia. (A villa in Richmond, or farther up the Thames might offer a *third* residence for the summer but could never substitute for a house in Grosvenor Square.) If London lacked the heady concentration of pleasures to be found in the Vienna Altstadt or the *grands boulevards,* it could still offer what Dr. Johnson had called "all that life can afford." If Buckingham Palace could not rival the Hofburg in brilliance, Parliament could command the talent as well as the wealth and power of the realm. If London lacked the cafés and restaurants of Paris, its clubs were unrivaled anywhere. If London's theatrical life lagged behind Paris and its musical culture behind Vienna, its cultural life as a whole compared favorably with that of any other European capital, while the splendor of its social life was unsurpassed. Above all London was rich and held out the possibility of sharing in that wealth to the ambitious and the unscrupulous; Parisians could protest that even though London had money they had culture, but London's money then (like New York's or Houston's today) could buy the finest musicians, the most costly paintings, and if not always the finest minds, certainly very good minds indeed. London, too, was an *imperial* capital; and just as Vienna could and did attract the rich and the talented and the ambitious from Galicia and Bohemia and Transylvania to her streets, so London served as a magnet for the entire English-speaking world. For all its smoke-laden fogs (which despite the impression given by Dickens and old Basil Rathbone movies were at worst seasonal and intermittent), despite the high mortality rate (though never as high as that of Paris and Vienna), despite the sometimes unreliable drains, despite the dreary Sundays, London was where one wanted to be. And that London was not to be found in Ealing or Wandsworth or even St. John's Wood, but in drawing rooms in Belgrave Square, along Rotten Row, within the shops of Bond Street, in the clubhouses of St. James's Street and Pall Mall, and above all in the Palace of Westminster. To be within a gentleman's walking distance or a lady's easy carriage drive of all the above required one to live no farther north than Marylebone, no farther west than Belgravia. The Metropolitan District Railway of the late sixties made South Kensington just possible, but no more than that.

Yet however much the fashionable might sneer, however much the aesthetes might deplore villa suburbia, it provided for the great majority of the middle classes the ideal answer to their housing needs. The lower land values permitted a more generous allocation of land to each house and the allocation of as many rooms, just as spacious, on two or three floors as in the central areas would go into four or five and a basement. Such an arrangement—permitting kitchen, dining room, and drawing room to occupy the ground story, and all principal bedrooms the other—simplified life for those who could afford no more than one or two servants. Lower rents more than compensated for the extra expense of a season ticket to a London terminus.

The railways did all in their power to encourage the servant-keeping classes to reside along their lines, by establishing new competitive lines through the outskirts—particularly south of the Thames—and by providing whenever possible two London termini, one for the City and one for the West End. They offered a frequent service of trains at both peak and off-peak hours and arranged elaborate services over connecting lines that made it possible to get from anywhere to anywhere either by through train or by carefully arranged connections. With the exception of the Great Eastern, railways were reluctant to introduce services of workmen's trains in anticipation of demand.[1] Trains for full-fare third-class passengers and season-ticket holders in the higher classes were something else again.

The opening of the lines of the Underground system from the 1860s permitted through-running from most of the main lines into the heart of the metropolis. There were through trains from Windsor to Aldgate over the Metropolitan line, and from Southend to Ealing on the District. Today's Circle line trains were supplemented by Middle and Outer Circle trains bringing passengers from northern and western suburbs directly to Mansion House via Addison Road (today's Kensington Olympia) and Earls Court. Through trains ran from the northern suburbs to stations south of the Thames by way of the Metropolitan Widened Lines and a low-level station at Holborn Viaduct.[2] From inner suburbs omnibuses and trams gave an intensive service that carried far more passengers than the railways.[3]

When "the domestic economist finds that he is an actual gainer in pocket by sleeping in country air," reasoned the *Builder* in 1868, "the natural advantages of the latter mode of life will tell." Such considerations would, it thought, soon lead to the decentralization of both London and Paris, and the "dotting of a large area of country thickly over with houses, yet not so thickly as to form streets or towns." Sydenham, "covered by villa or cottage residences, each within its own inclosure of garden," offered the model for the future.[4]

The prediction proved more accurate for London than for Paris. "All people who can run away from the town to charming cottages or pretty villas, surrounded by well-planted and delightfully maintained gardens," César Daly had observed in 1855.

This practice of London residents, of living in the outskirts and using the town only for offices and shops, for the transaction of business, is becoming more and more general. The English merchant or manufacturer who has thus been able to divide his life in two, moving his home, his wife and his small children, into the verdure and under the trees, still keeping the active center of his commercial relations in London . . . has certainly done much to insure his own health and the moral and physical well-being of his family; he has even facilitated the success of his industrial or commercial operations, which demand that healthy nimbleness and promptitude of vision that the wholesome and sweet distraction of a happy family ought so much to help maintain.[5]

By the end of the Victorian era not only the merchant and industrialist but the small shopkeeper and clerk and even the artisan and semiskilled laborer were moving to the suburbs. If the lower middle and upper working classes did not find there charming cottages or genteel villas, they did benefit from lower rents and greater spaciousness than central London could offer. "The London of one hundred years ago may be said no longer to exist," thought one observer in 1909. There was "no parallel in any continental country" to her exclusively commercial center and rapidly growing residential suburbs.[6] Not just the more open surroundings but the form of the suburban house encouraged the exodus. "The revolt against basement houses . . . has emptied hundreds of houses by the simple process of the occupiers moving into the modern non-basement houses . . . further afield," George Head told the Surveyors' Institution in 1909. "The trend of sanitary science and medical advice is all in the same direction—away from the center, out into the fresh air." The mid-nineteenth-century suburbs were being abandoned for newer ones farther out. "Many find it more easy to reach their homes ten to fifteen miles from London Bridge than it was to reach their former houses which may have been less than half as distant."[7]

The social and aesthetic consequences were disturbing. Even the outspokenly anglophile Hermann Muthesius admitted that "the inner suburbs of London, most particularly those lying to the east and south, are covered by endless expanses of small houses, all exactly alike. The deadening uniformity that we noted in the terrace-houses of the city reaches its peak in the suburbs . . . in these districts for the less well-to-do there is nothing but houses and streets. . . . There are no bends, no variety, no squares, no grouping to relieve the unease that anyone who strays into these parts must feel."[8]

For Lewis Mumford, the more spacious and varied suburbs of the better off were even more to be deplored, because they encouraged the upper middle class to neglect its social responsibilities. "Here domesticity could flourish, forgetful of the exploitation on which so much of it was based. Here individuality could prosper, oblivious of the pervasive regimentation beyond." The dispersion of residence inhibited communal activity: "the wider the scattering of the population, the greater the isolation of the individual household . . . the more effort it takes to do privately . . . what used to be done in company often with conversation, song, and the enjoyment of the physical presence of others."[9]

To Jacob von Falke, the gradually increasing separateness and seclusion of the individual house as one moved toward the outskirts of an English town reinforced domestic privacy and strengthened the family. "The withdrawal into itself [Zurückgezogenheit] and intimacy of the English family, which will allow no outside eye to enter and even shuts off the house in the middle of the town from the street by the area and a railing, brings about wherever possible the still further separation of the house from the street and its activities by a front garden." That garden had "in fact no other purpose than to strengthen the private character of the house and to protect the family from the public world [vor der Oeffentlichkeit zu schützen]." Shorter terraces and semidetached houses were further steps toward the isolation of the single villa, hidden in its own garden[10] (fig. 70).

But if privacy and individuality were the suburban ideals, the reality all too often was as drab and uniform as districts nearer the center. "Merton is nearly all new, shabby and patchy—the type of a district that has never been quite sure whether it is growing up as a suburb or as a village," wrote G. W. Steevens in 1900. "Little glimpses of it are rural—a little grey bow-windowed coaching-inn, a tar-boarded mill by a black pool. . . . But most of it is too poor and bewildered even to be vulgar. . . . The jerry-built £40 houses spread out their terraces flauntingly; but . . . patches of rubber-strewn half-hearted green lie derelict between old and new." Closer to London, Balham had lost all of its rural qualities. "The last double-gated houses with stables are coming down . . . [and] in the streets that take off from the high road the villas . . . are like peas in a pod."[11]

Monotonous, interminable, ugly, London's vast suburban extent nevertheless had much to be said for it. "These little houses fulfil their purpose," Muthesius argued: "It is questionable whether their occupants would be housed in a manner more fit for human beings in tenement-houses. Here they have at least a measure of independence and quiet, they are nearer to the soil and in a home that is easily reached from the street, they cultivate their gardens and . . . know that they are masters in their own houses."[12]

Two suburbs in particular—Bedford Park and Hampstead Garden Suburb— anticipated Mumford's criticisms and attempted to devise a model for a new style of

70. *The separateness and seclusion of the individual house reinforced domestic privacy and strengthened the family.* Villa residences, Crystal Palace Park Estate. From *The Builder* 31 (1873): 367.

living that would combine the best of town and country rather than the worst. The former, laid out at Turnham Green, between Hammersmith and Chiswick and easily reached by the District Railway, dates from the 1870s. The latter, occupying ground purchased from Eton College north of Hampstead Heath, came into existence just before the First World War. Both employed architectural styles held at the time in high esteem in aesthetic circles: for Bedford Park a variant of Queen Anne, for Hampstead Garden Suburb the arts-and-crafts cottage style. Both provided facilities for community activity—preferably noncommercial—designed to appeal to the educated middle classes. Hampstead Garden Suburb was intended at the outset to house a mixture of social classes, but in practice came to be occupied by the same type of moderately well-to-do residents of a moderately intellectual and progressive bent that gave Bedford Park its character.[13]

The *Builder* in 1909 had its doubts about Hampstead Garden Suburb. "We should have felt a little more sympathy with the scheme . . . if there had been a rather less conscious effort at producing houses of the sort which the present generation has agreed to regard as picturesque; houses with high tiled roofs and small windows with small panes." It was sceptical about the high-mindedness of the operation:

There seems to be an idea . . . that the suburb is to promote a certain kind of social as well as building reform; . . . we overheard it explained to a visitor that "this was to be a place of social fellowship; not like the ordinary London suburb where you live next to a man for twelve or fourteen years and do not know him and do not want to know him." Whether that idea would be regarded in the light of an advantage incident to residence there may be a question.[14]

Here the writer put his finger on one of the qualities that made the unreformed stretches of villa suburbia so popular with their residents: the absence of a rich community life. It was precisely to avoid activities involving "conversation, song, and . . . the physical presence of others" that many chose suburban residence in the first place. It was just the qualities so condemned by Mumford that constituted the major attractions of suburban living, most especially the avoidance of contact with other classes. But the lower middle classes in particular wished to shun not merely people of different social status, but those of their own kind. The high garden wall and the tall hedge marking the boundary line in front were intended to cut the family off from all disturbing human contact, not just that of a socially compromising sort.

Paris

"It is certainly astonishing to find families in Paris willing to pay £1000 a year for a few rooms on a boulevard, when we know that at Neuilly, or Vincennes, they might have a whole house for one-tenth part of that sum," William H. White observed in 1877. "But ever since the world formed itself into communities—at Athens, at Rome, at Florence—the heart of a capital city has been thought by many men to contain all that makes life worth living; all the wit of one sex, and all the beauty of the other."[15] The consequence of such preference is something that everyone knows about Paris: that it is a densely built city of flat-residents, the antithesis of sprawling London. Its suburbs are, therefore, working-class and industrial, if anything more congested than the city itself.

Yet anyone approaching Paris from any direction today finds himself passing through mile after mile of communities of what look very much like detached single-family houses set in private gardens. The gardens are more likely than their London counterparts to grow vegetables rather than flowers, the lots tend to be smaller, and the whole scene has a more higgledy-piggledy look than either speculative or council estates in England. The signs of middle-class occupation are stronger toward the west and southwest than to the north and east, which look decidedly proletarian. The whole, though, looks remarkably like a Gallic version of villa suburbia. And the spectacle at the Gare Saint-Lazare at morning or evening or lunchtime rush hours, with heavily loaded trains serving a dense network of lines arriving and departing one after another, is not so different from the scene at Waterloo or Victoria.

To be sure, much of what one sees today is the product of the last quarter-century, during which one after another generalization about Paris and the French has had to be radically modified or discarded. Only the rash person today would venture to assert that the French hate foreign travel, scorn convenience foods, have no interest in domestic appliances, and shun the values of modern consumer society. But although French styles of living have altered tremendously since the 1950s, the history of villa suburbia in Paris goes back at least a century earlier.

The *Allgemeine Bauzeitung* for 1843 speaks approvingly of "a certain striving toward a *gemütlich* environment for residence" as characteristic of new buildings erected during the Restoration in the southwestern portions of Paris. Here could be found "very pleasing, tasteful façades, with large gateways, through whose railings can be seen small, neat courtyards or gardens, delightfully adorned with fountains, statues, lamp standards, flower stands, and the like."[16] Whether the passage refers to anything that a contemporary Englishman would have recognized as a suburban villa is unclear, but it does suggest a fashion for a dwelling at once elegant and unpretentious, with an emphasis on greenery and flowers, located in the direction from Paris in which villa development would shortly be taking place.

Beginning in 1819–20, the area bounded by the rues de la Rochefoucauld, de la Tour-des-Dames, and Saint-Lazare was laid out in lots on which were to be built private houses "so arranged as to preserve between each of them a considerable space which, by means of established regulations [*servitudes*] cannot in future be altered or diminished."[17] Mrs. Trollope, writing in 1835, spoke of "the endeavour to introduce *maisonettes,* or small houses calculated for the occupation of one family" into the neighborhood of the Madeleine.[18] It is doubtful whether such houses could be described as villas, for the streets in that neighborhood were densely built up, although there was often ample garden space in the rear.

In his description of a train journey from the Gare Saint-Lazare to Versailles in 1851, Sir Francis Head indicates that, whatever suburban development might have taken place, it was not visible from the railway. "As Paris has no suburbs, we were almost immediately in the open country," where he observed little beyond "fields and nursery-gardens." The landscape "was divided into little patches and long strips," with small vineyards besides; "in the immense plain nothing was conspicuous but the acropolis of Montmartre."[19]

The present sixteenth, however, was being visibly suburbanized. In 1855 a visiting Englishman "was much pleased with some newly-erected villas and cottages ornés . . . at Passy and Auteuil, in which a highly picturesque effect was produced by the employment of black and red brick and stone without any elaborate decoration. Some of these were in the Late Domestic French Gothic style." An item in the *Builder* for 1858 reported that the roads to the bois de Boulogne and Saint-Cloud had been "lined, with Aladdin-like rapidity, with little rural retreats,—nests, as it were, sheltered under the leafage of the wood"[20] (fig. 71). In 1860 César Daly proposed a whole new category of architecture, intermediate between that of town and country, "in the suburbs of large cities and along the lines of railway," which he called *suburban.* Now even the moderately well-to-do bourgeoisie were combining urban activity with the "restorative repose" offered by a second residence in the outskirts.[21]

In a description of the prospect to be had from the top of the Arc de Triomphe, *L'Illustration* for 1861 spoke of the "pleasant villages of Neuilly, Courbevoie, Suresnes, the suburban villas lining the river." The avenue de l'Impératrice (avenue Foch) was lined with "châteaux," "maisons italiennes," "donjons en miniature."[22] "The suburban villa is chiefly seen westward, in the vicinity of the Bois de Boulogne," wrote the *Builder* the same year; several good examples were to be found "between the Porte de Passy and Porte de la Muette. The composer Rossini resides in one of them." It observed that "since the completion of the railways . . . people have begun to live altogether out of town, and '*une jolie maison*

71. (opposite) *The roads to the bois de Boulogne and Saint-Cloud had been "lined . . . with little rural retreats,—nests . . . sheltered under the leafage of the wood."* Country house at Auteuil, near Paris. From *The Builder* 16 (1858): 759.

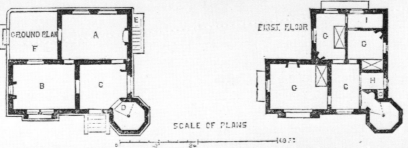

SCALE OF PLANS

COUNTRY HOUSE AT AUTEUIL, NEAR PARIS.——*M. Danjoy, Architect.*

A. Dining-room.
B. Saloon.
C. Vestibule.
D. Staircase.
E. Staircase for kitchen.

F. Terrace.
G. Bed-rooms.
H. Water-closet.
I. Dressing-room.

de campagne' is the frequent heading of advertisements." A fortnight later it returned to the subject:

> A few years ago there was no villa architecture, according to the English idea of it, in or about Paris, and to this hour you may leave the city, with little exception, choosing any road, and see nothing but the same straight line, unenlivened by the appearance of domestic life, the charm of well-cultivated gardens, and the occasional taste in architecture, that characterize the environs of London. However, at many of the towns and villages from which Paris is now easily accessible by railway, excellent specimens of architecture have sprung up; and woods and parks are rapidly undergoing the process of transformation analogous to that of the eligible building-sites, but with greater taste than in the environs of London.

Much of the activity lay beyond even the recently extended boundaries of Paris, as at Neuilly, and around the bois de Vincennes. "The *jardin à l'Anglais*' is now common; but garden and grounds attached to private houses are not attended to assiduously as in England."23

For Daly, the breaking up of "the great wooded estates around Paris into a multitude of small building plots" was a direct imitation of London. "As if by enchantment villas and cottages have been erected there: an elegant city has been formed in the ancient park of Neuilly, others at Vésinet, Passy, Auteuil, le Raincy, Billancourt, Villers, in the parks of Livry, Saint-Gratien, Bercy, of the duc de Trévise, at Villier-sur-Marne, and so on." He saw the new settlements as portending a decentralization that would relieve the pressure on accommodation in central areas, provide cheaper housing for the working classes, and lead to something like the functional division between commercial and residential districts that existed in London.24

Daly envisaged an exciting architectural future for the suburbs. Unlike an urban building, which had to subordinate itself to the lines and style imposed by adjacent structures, a detached villa could indulge in inventiveness or even eccentricity. Informal landscaping and the picturesque employment of flowers and foliage could enhance the aesthetic impact of the different buildings. Even if several villas could be seen at once, so long as they were adequately spaced, contrasts in size and style need not offend the eye, might even charm and delight.

The builders of London's suburbs had not, by and large, taken full advantage of such possibilities. The Eyre and Eton College estates in St. John's Wood and Primrose Hill, for instance, consisted of streets of nearly identical villas in neoclassical or Italianate dress. Their successors indulged in somewhat greater stylistic variety, yet the tendency for whole streets and districts to be built under the direction of a single speculating contractor led to much monotonous duplication. The aesthetically pleasing Bedford Park and Hampstead Garden Suburb managed a picturesque appearance while maintaining general stylistic consistency.

Parisian villa suburbia has, on the whole, triumphantly avoided both monotony and consistency and transcended the narrow boundaries of good taste. Only recently has there been large-scale development of housing estates on the English pattern. Piecemeal construction over time, house by house, has been more usual. The result is sometimes charming, often hilarious, rarely dull. Whoever wishes to escape from the tasteful uniformity of the typical Paris street need only set off by RER for Robinson or Saint-Germain-en-Laye to have his spirits and his faith in French individualism restored.

The dwellings that sprang up in Passy in the 1850s and early 1860s took aesthetic risks inconceivable a mile or two east: "Coloured materials are introduced with good effect," wrote one critic in 1861. "The mansard-roof, enclosing a lofty story, lighted by dormer-windows, richly sculptured in stone, and perhaps an attic over all, lighted by lucarnes ornamented in zinc, is very prominent. . . . Much taste is shown in the out-houses and lodges of villas, especially in the carved woodwork adapted from Germany and Switzerland." Enghien-les-Bains was "remarkable for the number of its houses directly imitated from the Swiss cottages."[25]

The plates and descriptions of César Daly's monumental *Architecture privée au dix-neuvième siècle,* which began to appear in the early 1860s, reveal a world distant from the severe rectitude of the boulevard Malesherbes or the rue Lafayette. The word *villa,* Daly explained, had come recently into use "to designate that class of construction, elegant rather than vast, sought by the bourgeoisie of moderate fortune" (fig. 72). Suburban architecture formed the "transition between the dwellings of town and country, uniting the artificial refinements and delicate comforts of the one with the freedom, space, and charms of the fields and parks that form the great attractions of the other." Villa suburbia reflected the rise to dominance of a "generally rich, cultivated, and enlightened bourgeoisie. It could serve to indicate

---

72. *The word villa had come recently into use "to designate that class of construction, elegant rather than vast, sought by the bourgeoisie of moderate fortune."* Suburban villa, second class, boulevard d'Argenson (à Neuilly), elevation. From *Architecture privée au XIXe siècle* 2, example D2, pl. 1.

the genius and the character of modern civilization, just as the temples of Egypt or Greece, the baths and amphitheaters of Rome or the cathedrals and castles of the Middle Ages help us to understand and penetrate into the spirit of the civilizations that have preceded ours." Comfort and freedom from the constraints of urban formality were its essential characteristics. It had greater variety of forms, more of the unexpected, reflected more of the individual imagination. Here he helps account for the startling contrast between the gray mediocrity of the ordinary Parisian street and the extravagant folly that so often rules the suburbs. Even a Frenchman eventually tires of *ordre, mesure,* and *bienséance.*[26]

The most favored suburbs adjoined the fashionable western reaches of Paris. The reconstruction and replanting of the bois de Boulogne in the 1850s and 1860s, and its subsequent use by the rich and elegant as their favorite promenade, enhanced the attractions of both Passy and Auteuil. "The price of land adjoining the Bois on all sides has been increased enormously," according to the *Builder* in 1869; "land, the value of which did not exceed from 1f.50c. to 6f. the *mètre,* is now worth from 20f. to 100 f. the *mètre.* . . . On the surrounding land 487 châteaux or expensive villas, the cost of which, with the furnishing, cannot be put at a lower average than 8,000*l.* each, have been built."[27]

Passy, wrote Adolphe Joanne in 1870, offered a fine view over the valley of the Seine, a healthy atmosphere, and the proximity of the bois de Boulogne. The convenience and the abundance of means of public transport encouraged a steady growth in its population. Immediately to the south, Auteuil provided "cool and peaceful shades, treasured by men who need repose." It resembled a "village in a comic opera; its streets are graveled like a *jardin anglais;* its houses and villas assume the architectural styles of every country and every age." The village was less a dormitory suburb than a summer resort: "As soon as the cold wind of autumn makes the yellow leaves fall, Auteuil begins to lose its population; by the coming of winter it is a veritable solitude. By contrast, the population doubles and triples with the return of spring; the deserted streets are suddenly covered with fine carriages; from every partly opened window comes the sound of a piano. . . . Most of these dwellings, more bizarre than elegant, more stylish than comfortable, villas and châteaux, are rented, their owners occupying them only during the winter, if they are not domiciled in Paris."[28]

Villa development continued during the early years of the Third Republic. "Even in the neighbourhood of the Arc de l'Etoile," it was reported in 1878, "there are now quite as many villas or small hôtels as there are maisons-à-loyer."[29] But the villas would soon be submerged by the expanding metropolis. By 1883 Passy was losing its semirural qualities. "Formerly, when land was cheaper, there were many isolated houses within the fortifications which stood in their own little parks, quite separated from others by groves of shady trees," recalled Philip Gilbert Hamerton:

> These little parks are becoming fewer every day. Where one villa stood thirty years ago three stand now, and sometimes half a dozen. Besides this, the old region for villas—Auteuil—is becoming a town like Passy. Enormous blocks of new houses, as large and lofty as any in the heart of Paris, are rising on the park lands and cutting them into formal streets. An old friend of mine had a delicious retreat at Auteuil—a small house in a large space of grass and grove. I went to find it this year, and found a block of buildings six storeys high and as long as the Hôtel du Louvre.[30]

A significant commuting population was also establishing itself beyond the fortifications. The *Continental Bradshaw* for April 1877 shows trains leaving both
Saint-Lazare and Montparnasse on the two lines to Versailles every hour on the hour
throughout the day, along with a half-hour regular-interval service from Saint-
Lazare to all points along the Petite Ceinture, which ran just inside the fortifications.
On 2 June 1867 the Gare Saint-Lazare sold no fewer than 159,742 tickets to suburban
destinations.[31]

In addition to the two lines of railway to Versailles (with a third, running from the
Gare des Invalides, added at the end of the century), there was a steam tram
operating from the pont de la Concorde along the banks of the Seine. "One may
note, after passing the fortification lines," the *Builder* remarked in 1899, "that
Paris . . . is spreading outward into small and undignified suburbs much after the
manner of London; streets lined with small shops and tenements, and where the
stone-fronted *maison de rapport* is unknown."[32]

Yet when all is said and done the suburbs of Paris are not like the suburbs of
London, and the Parisian bourgeoisie did not lose its preference for the life of the
boulevards over that of the private back garden. In 1930 Paul Cohen-Portheim
described Passy and Auteuil as "provincial towns, nay, to be correct, overgrown
provincial villages," with the intervals between the rapidly multiplying eight-storied
blocks of flats "occupied chiefly by little detached houses with gardens." The
residents were "well-to-do without being rich." Both inner and outer suburbs lay
beyond the realm of fashion. "One has one's house in Fontainebleau or St. Germain
(the *bourgeois* equivalent of the aristocrat's *château* in the country), of course, but
only for the summer months. A suburb, on the other hand, is a second-rate affair."[33]

For the most part the suburbs of Paris are not even unfashionably middle-class in
character, but unashamedly working-class. As high rents and the higher cost of
provisions resulting from the special customs duty (*octroi*) drove the poor outside
the city boundaries, industry followed. Unrestrained by the building and sanitary
regulations of the municipality, outside the zone of metropolitan improvements,
the working-class and industrial suburbs presented a picture of anarchic disorder.
Neither monumental square nor grand avenue gave focus or structure to districts
outside Paris. The governing intelligence that stamped its impression on the city
abandoned the suburbs to confusion and improvisation.[34]

The working-class suburbs of the Second Empire and early Third Republic were
more densely built and overcrowded than Paris proper. Not until the period between the wars did there develop working-class equivalents to middle-class villa
suburbia. The acute shortage of rental housing in the 1920s led large numbers of
the working poor to acquire tiny lots in the outskirts and build makeshift dwellings
for themselves. Over a period of ten years, land equivalent to one and a half times
the area of the city of Paris was turned into a kind of parody of villa suburbia, with
unpaved streets, no proper water supply or drainage, no municipal services.[35]

Since the Second World War there has been accelerated development in the
suburbs both of individual cottages and villas—of a far higher standard than those
of the inter-war period—and the spectacular proliferation of planned satellite
towns, *grands ensembles,* whose massive clusters of high-rise blocks dominate the
surrounding landscape.[36] The sheer hatefulness of these communities has produced a reaction in favor of the individual house with its garden, but economic and
political forces have required that they continue to be built.

Vienna

"Despite the favorable climatic and scenic conditions . . . Vienna does not possess the wreath of attractive gardens and scattered country houses that many far less well endowed [*stiefmütterlicher ausgestattete*] cities of northern and western Germany exhibit," wrote Anton Weber in 1905. "Just as housing in Vienna has taken the form of multistoried blocks of flats, so has the building of suburban dwellings been abandoned to speculation, so that single floors of 'villas' are rented and the gardens, even so meagerly proportioned, must be shared among many tenants."[37]

Today, even more than in 1905, what distinguishes Vienna from Paris quite as much as from London is the abruptness with which it ends and the country begins. A short tramride from the Ringstrasse brings one to the edge of the built-up area and the sudden appearance of vineyards. The built-up area itself can display sizable fragments of country villages engulfed by urban development—with low farm-laborers' cottages and farmhouses set along winding streets—but little evidence of an intermediate stage between rurality and intensive urban settlement.

The middle-class villa settlements along the lower reaches of the Wienerwald—Grinzing, Döbling, and Gersthof to the north; Hietzing, St. Veit, and Lainz west of Schönbrunn—offer abundant scenic and architectural delight but cover a relatively small area of Vienna and provide an even tinier proportion of its housing stock. Substantial structures in a variety of styles—as "representative" in their pretensions as anything in the Ringstrasse—loom over carefully tended but surprisingly small gardens and are ordinarily designed for more than one family each. The successful combination of Sezessionist decorative motifs with traditional building forms—the projecting turrets, the steeply pitched roofs with protruding gables, the contrasting textures of the *Heimatstil* in many instances—suggests the store of aesthetic possibilities that movement offered. Speculation there may have been, but the impression left by early twentieth-century villa suburbia in particular is one of creative adventure and individualism. The monotony and uniformity of London suburbia is nowhere to be found: villadom in Vienna housed a cultivated elite, and never became the normal environment of the unreflecting majority even among the prosperous (figs. 73–75).

The main line of railway leading from the Westbahnhof toward St. Pölten and Linz serves frequent stations where the original village core has been augmented by commuters' villas, but the village character predominates. Nowhere is there anything that a Londoner would recognize as a suburban housing estate, speculative or public. Across the Danube are some small-scale versions of the working-class *lotissements* of interwar Paris, but mostly postwar high-rise housing estates, less depressing than the Parisian *grands ensembles* only because they are fewer and smaller. Here, as to the southeast, industrial and working-class areas abut directly on farmland. The middle-class suburbia that constitutes so much of West Berlin and other German and Swiss cities finds no counterpart here. Even Budapest displays more extensive low-density suburban development from the interwar years.

How has Vienna escaped the curse or rejected the blessing of affluent, low-density suburbia? The explanation is clearly neither poverty nor the absence of a large and prosperous middle class. Nor does Vienna lack a tradition of detached residences set in gardens: the eighteenth century saw a great many suburban summer retreats built by noble and burgher alike. Such residences, however grand and however close to the City, were never considered as other than supplementary to the main palace or house within the walls. Yet they constituted more splendid

73. *(left) The impression left by villa suburbia is one of creative adventure and individualism. The monotony and uniformity of London suburbia is nowhere to be found.* Heimatstil villa, Sezessionist decoration. Corner of Naafgasse and Wallrissstrasse, eighteenth Bezirk, 1984. (Evelyn Benesch.)

74. *(below)* Wallrissstrasse, 1984. (Evelyn Benesch.)

75a–c. Beckgasse, thirteenth Bezirk, 1984. (Evelyn Benesch.)

models for detached suburban residences than anything in the vicinity of eighteenth-century London or Paris.

The appeal of a more relaxed style of living, away from artificial urban constraints, did not lack theoretical support. Romanticism, at least in the form that reached the English-speaking world, was mainly a German invention and in that guise was profoundly anti-urban.[38] A widespread bourgeois "villa-ideology" argued that a private and more intimate family life could best be pursued at a distance from the mass housing of the town.[39] Yet neither nobility nor bourgeoisie, artists nor intellectuals had by 1857 done much to put such ideals into practice in Vienna. In the following decades serious efforts were made to create a suburban environment along English lines but only a negligible proportion of those who could afford to build or rent a villa did so.

The failure of attempts by Ferstel and others to introduce the English single-family house into the City, Ringstrasse, or inner suburbs can be accounted for by the high cost of land. Such an obstacle did not exist beyond the Linienwall, and certainly not in the surrounding agricultural districts. Steam navigation came to the Danube in the 1820s and could have linked any number of riverside dormitory suburbs with the metropolis. Railways from the early 1840s penetrated areas that in England or France would have seemed ripe for housing development. From the 1860s tramways connected the City with the very edges of urban development and could, given any encouragement, have been extended beyond their then-existing or present termini. The flat agricultural land to the south and east could easily have been turned into low-density, low-cost suburbs, while the enchanting beauty of the Wienerwald and the Bisamberg––far superior by any objective standards to that of Highgate or Sydenham—could have attracted a more affluent clientele. That none of this happened has meant the preservation into our day of a green belt immediately accessible to the whole Viennese population. But a price was paid for such unspoiled surroundings—most notably in the high rents for overcrowded flats demanded of the working and lower middle classes. The vast majority of the population was never given the choice of a suburban alternative to their customary way of living. The upper middle and upper classes had such a choice, which they overwhelmingly rejected.

If London's architects longed for the opportunity to employ their skills and aesthetic imagination on the design of massive blocks of flats, their Viennese contemporaries longed to introduce English country cottages to the Lower Austrian landscape. Theophilos Hansen was commissioned in the 1860s to build a villa at Hohe Warte, in Unterdöbling, just north of Vienna. "Everyone who knows the immediate surroundings of Vienna will enjoy the noble panorama that unfolds from the Hohe Warte in Döbling over the Danube, the City of Vienna, and its surroundings, bounded by the lovely Kahlenberg," wrote Hansen in a description of the completed villa in 1865. He designed the dwelling for the occupation of two families, with additional space for guest rooms under the roof. The ground floor consisted of seven spacious living rooms and one service room. In front of the *salon* on the south side there stood an arcaded porch looking out over the garden and the entire city of Vienna. The dining room on the east side had a veranda with a view of the Danube and the Marchfeld beyond. The first floor contained another, similar flat.[40]

The isolated villa occupying a site of particular beauty was at most a portent of more extensive development. This latter came in 1873 with the laying of the cornerstone of the first villa in "Cottage," intended as a model suburban community in Währing. In many ways the equivalent of the contemporaneous Bedford Park, it had as its architectural advisor Heinrich von Ferstel. From the first the intention was to restrict residence to officials, officers, doctors, merchants and "persons of equal social status." Each villa was at the minimum to consist of one *Salon,* three *Zimmer,* two *Kabinette,* and a veranda on the first floor, with a kitchen, two more *Kabinette* and additional *Nebenräume* underneath.[41] Commercial establishments and blocks of flats were excluded. Ferstel did not himself design any of the villas but was responsible for the Casino, intended, like the Tabard at Bedford Park, as a community center with intellectual and artistic pretensions.[42]

Cottage served as the model for smaller developments in Hütteldorf, Hetzendorf, St. Veit, and Meidling. Individual villas, groups of villas, and low terrace housing began to appear during the seventies and eighties in other outer suburbs, mostly in connection with existing villages or clusters of housing. These were less an imitation of the old aristocratic hunting lodge and summer palace than expressions of the desire of the new *Grossbürgertum* for a "representative family dwelling-house of the English type."[43]

Neither Cottage nor its imitators were able to maintain the English principle of one family per house. The original intention had been to erect villas with kitchen and service rooms in the basement, reception rooms on the ground floor, and bedrooms upstairs. The Viennese habit of horizontal living proved too strong, and villas came to be designed for two families each, one occupying the ground floor and using the basement for service rooms, the other the first floor using the attic for *Nebenräume.* Externally the villas were as picturesque as could be desired, with irregular floor plans, balconies, wooden verandas, and stepped gables. Once the original area of Cottage had been completely built over in 1884, the focus of activity moved to Döbling where larger and more opulent family villas were erected. Further colonies were begun on the Kahlenberg and at Cobenzl, with varying success.[44] For even as modified, the limited supply of villa-type dwellings exceeded the demand. The *Builder* in 1884 spoke of "over-rash haste and miscalculation" having led to "acute crises" in the Austrian building industry. Pretentious developments on the outskirts of Vienna were "lugubriously deserted."[45]

In no way did such suburban developments, even when they included very large and expensive houses, threaten the social preeminence of the City and Ringstrasse. At most they were regarded as second-best opportunities for opulent living for those unable to find suitable flats in the Ringstrasse, where available building ground had by the 1880s been entirely occupied.[46] The *Builder*, noting the development of a "cottage quarter" in Währing, observed in 1881: "The style of architecture . . . finds little favour among the middle, or burgher, classes of the Austrian capital, most of its adherents being members of the official class, as well as artists and men following the literary profession."[47]

The period 1890–1914, which in London saw accelerated suburban development, saw a slowing of the movement in Vienna. The construction of the steam Stadtbahn in the last years of the century and the electrification of the tramways markedly improved the quality of transport within built-up areas, but did little to stimulate building beyond municipal boundaries. (Through running of trains from the Westbahn and the Franz Josefs-Bahn onto the Stadtbahn ought to have encouraged outer suburban development, but the fact that the original Stadtbahn termini—Hütteldorf-Hacking and Heiligenstadt—still roughly mark the edge of urban development suggests that it did not.) Individual villas by Otto Wagner and Sezessionist architects find their way into art histories, but the volume of new building was slight.[48]

In 1905 Cottage consisted of about 350 houses.[49] The census of 1910 showed no more than 5,734 single-family houses in the whole of Vienna, only 1.2 percent of the total number of units.[50] The comparable figure for London in 1911 was 60 percent.[51]

After 1918 economic depression and a fall in population, together with the impact of rent control, led to a virtual cessation of private speculative building. As in the surroundings of Paris, there appeared in the Viennese outskirts settlements of small, individually owned working-class cottages, sometimes built with financial assistance from the municipality, often by cooperative associations, but at times by the individual householders themselves.[52] Of new middle-class suburban housing there was very little. Since 1945 rising land prices together with the physical deterioration of much of the older villa housing has led to its replacement in many instances by new blocks of flats.[53] What remains is often of high aesthetic quality: the failure of villadom to become a mass phenomenon has saved it from the standardized monotony of its English counterparts. Villa suburbia remains the chosen environment for the exceptional few, not, as in London, the normal and preferred home for the many.

11

Working-Class Housing: Scarcity, Abundance, and Domestic Values

he paucity of reference to the working classes in this discussion of the city as home may suggest that privacy, intimacy, and domesticity were qualities too expensive for them to afford. With respect to the housing available to them in Paris and Vienna, and to a considerable extent in London, this may very nearly have been true: when the normal family dwelling consists of a single room, with perhaps a small separate kitchen, discussing the impact of *dégagements* and subdivided, specialized areas makes little sense. Neither was the question of the relative attractions of a flat in the Ringstrasse and a villa in Hohe Warte one that the ordinary Viennese worker had to face. As for neighborhoods segregated by social class, the luxury of choice of district was a middle-class privilege: the workers moved to whatever places economically stronger groups chose to avoid. Yet it would be a mistake to treat the working-class population of the three cities as a homogeneous group sunk in uniform misery, acted upon but not reacting to the challenges of the urban environment.

Studies of working-class housing before 1914, local and national, normally stress its inadequacy—overcrowded, overpriced, and insufficient—and note the failure of the free market to produce enough new housing to keep up with the growing population, much less bring average standards up to a level of decency. The most optimistic estimates show a degree of improvement far less than any overall rise in living standards.[1] But as one reads the dismal accounts the nagging objection emerges: conditions everywhere could not be worse than they were everywhere else. And the testimony both of contemporaries and of the buildings themselves suggests that for the working classes as for the middle classes, standards were higher in London than in Paris, in Paris than in Vienna. They were high enough to enable a significant minority of London's working classes to imitate middle-class patterns of behavior, much as the middle classes were shaping their own lives according to their notion of aristocratic manners.

In English urban districts as a whole the average number of occupants per house gradually fell from 5.75 in 1821 to 5.04 in 1911, but there are no comparable statistics on the average density per room.[2] Bertillon, to be sure, suggests that conditions in Paris were better than in London, but he does this by comparing statistics from Charles Booth on the worst districts in London with the average of whole arrondissements in Paris. In addition the unusually large proportion of one-person households in Paris makes her average rates of occupancy look unduly favorable.[3]

Perceptions as to what constituted intolerable overcrowding varied between classes and between countries. England, almost certainly having the least congestion, was more concerned with overcrowding as an evil than either France or Austria and was far ahead of any continental country in providing philanthropic and municipal housing. Until well into the twentieth century complaints about overcrowding—as distinct from high rents, lack of repair, absence of amenities—have tended to come more from middle-class reformers than from the poor themselves. Since most of what we know about working-class living conditions and attitudes comes to us by way of middle-class reformers it would be unwise to make too much of this point. Yet the frequency with which working-class tenants in London and Vienna sublet their already crowded accommodations suggests that, understandably, they preferred to sacrifice space to supplement their meager incomes. Privacy and the possibility of seclusion may seem necessities to the affluent, but dispensable luxuries to those living at the subsistence level.

It is necessary to keep separate three phenomena: overcrowding, working-class housing, and slums. Although there have been many overcrowded working-class slums, the three have not necessarily gone together. Sam Bass Warner has reminded us that "the condition of the poor in the post-war American city . . . reversed . . . the ingredients enumerated by the nineteenth-century slum symbol. Where the slum had been crowded with people now it was a place of empty lots, fires and housing abandonment."[4] Much depends on the definition of overcrowding. If proportion of land covered by buildings is the criterion, the Inner City of Vienna would qualify as intolerably overcrowded. Lewis Mumford has argued that the population per acre of New York's Upper East Side was such that its affluent residents were living in a slum without realizing it. Overcrowding, however defined, and working-class housing conditions need to be viewed in the context of the nature and health of the urban economy as a whole.

One point has to be made early on, if only because so much that has been written about the modern city assumes quite the opposite: congestion and high rents are indications of urban success, dispersal and low rents indications of urban failure. Leaving aside situations in which free choice is inhibited by laws or practices forcing racial or other kinds of segregation, a crowded neighborhood is one that has attractions sufficient to induce people to pay more for less space than they would find elsewhere. The attractions would typically be proximity to employment, but closeness to charitable institutions, places of entertainment, markets, or shops are frequent considerations. Overcrowded districts are not necessarily occupied by the poor, as Mumford's point about the Upper East Side reminds us. The higher rent paid for office space on Park Avenue than on the West Side indicates that multinational corporations, like oppressed workers, vote with their feet and their pocketbooks.

If the depopulated South Bronx of the late twentieth century is an emblem of urban failure, the congested Lower East Side of the early part of the century must be seen as an indication of urban success. Gillian Tindall has argued that the pavements of Bombay crowded with homeless immigrants reflect the comparative prosperity of that city:

> Many of the problems of present-day Bombay are directly attributable to her economic strength. . . . If Bombay had not continued commercially prosperous, if engineering works and petrochemical plants had not been added in this century to its older textile industry, if it did not have its own off-coast oil-field . . . then it would not have remained such a mecca for in-coming peoples, seeking work, seeking money, seeking life itself in an escape from the grinding, near-static poverty of India's rural heartlands.[5]

The relationship between the prosperity and the overcrowding of Hong Kong is evident; the "rabbit-hutches" in which the beneficiaries of the Japanese economic miracle too often live can be seen as a necessary consequence of that miracle. The concentration of buildings in Venice suggests how overcrowded it must have been when it was most prosperous. This would have been true of any premodern city except for those that failed to achieve their potential: they had open spaces in abundance, high vacancy rates, and low rents.

In more recent times housing shortages tend to occur in periods of prosperity, housing gluts in years of depression. One of the consequences of the depression that followed the stock market crash in Vienna in 1873 was a temporary easing of the housing shortage.[6] The catastrophic economic collapse after 1918 brought with it a corresponding improvement in statistics of domestic overcrowding, as a smaller population redistributed itself within the existing building stock. It was during the 1930s that middle-class Manhattanites moved from apartment to apartment every year for the fun of it. The Edwardian period, a time of economic crisis and one in which the long, late-Victorian rise in the general standard of living came to a halt, saw, for the first time, a temporary oversupply of working-class housing in London.

Just as it is those restaurants perceived as giving best value for money where tables are placed closest together, and it is during the January and July sales at Harrods that congestion reaches limits of absurdity, people will crowd together where the greatest concentration of attractions—good food, bargains, well-paying jobs, the prospects of growing rich beyond the dreams of avarice—are to be found. The poor paid excessive rents to live in substandard quarters in central London because there were more jobs there than elsewhere. Rents were higher in London than in provincial towns because wages were higher, and a greater variety of skills in demand there than elsewhere. The connection between prosperity and overcrowding may be unfortunate, the consequences deplorable, but it is far from astonishing.

Such an approach places both railway extensions and street improvements, regarded both in Victorian times and more recently as notable causes of urban congestion, in a somewhat different light.[7] The extension in the 1870s of the Great Eastern Railway from Shoreditch to Liverpool Street, to take a notable example, contributed to congestion in the City less by the displacements resulting from its construction than by the jobs created to build it and to operate the expanded train services from the new terminal. Indirectly it contributed to the expansion of employment—and hence immigration leading to more congestion—by enhancing the external economies of the City, making it an even more efficient money-making machine.

All this may account for but does not justify what happened. However desirable in the long run the transformation of the City into a device for facilitating banking, insurance, and corporate management, and increasing the gross national product, the unequal distribution of costs and benefits raises moral and political questions. Yet questions like "Ought the Great Eastern Railway or the City Corporation or Her Majesty's Government to have provided housing for those displaced and those attracted to London by improvements to its infrastructure?" are not the kind that the historian, in his capacity as historian, is qualified to answer. What he is equipped to answer, but has as yet failed to do, is the question why congestion did not become worse than it did; why—apart from particular areas—conditions in London not only failed to deteriorate but showed signs, over the long run, of improvement; why London did not move in the direction of Tokyo, Hong Kong, or Bombay, much less Calcutta.[8]

In Paris, too, the sharp rise in rents and overcrowding of the 1850s and 1860s were the consequence of immigration to take advantage of the expanded employment opportunities and the growing prosperity of the capital during the Second Empire, as much as of the displacements caused by Haussmann's demolitions. There, wrote the *Building News* in 1861, "families are crowded worse than in any Irish hovel"; "between Montmartre and Lavilette, a quarter has sprung up worse than Agar-town ever was," with "houses built of lumps of plaster from demolitions . . . roofed with old tin trays, tin cuttings and bits of painted table-covers."[9] This was an example of housing at its worst. More indicative of average standards was the response of an English saw-and-tool maker, one of a group of artisans selected by the Society of Arts to visit the Paris Universal Exhibition in 1867. He found "the general domestic condition of the French *ouvrier* greatly inferior to that of the British workman. If we speak of him with regard to his family comforts, adjudged by the English standard, 'home he has none.' " Taking as an instance an eight-foot-square flat at the top of a building in the boulevard Richard Lenoir, "he has a little bed that turns up, and a little table that lets down, which must be done alternately each night and morning in order to make room. He has a couple of small chairs, as many basins, plates, knives, forks, and table-spoons; a *pot à feu,* a tree planted in a tasty pot if possible, and a bird in a cage, nearly comprise his household goods."[10]

Housing conditions in Vienna were worse than in either of the other two capitals. "The working population is accommodated in houses of some architectural pretension . . . and with rather high rooms, in which, however, they are closely packed," Thomas Blashill told the RIBA in 1888. "Rates and taxes are exceedingly heavy, the cost of living high, and the conditions of life much harder than with us."[11] The *Builder* had reported excessive overcrowding in 1879. "Inhabitants were discovered living in thirty-four cellars."[12] As late as 1914 three-fourths of all flats in Vienna "consisted of only one or two rooms and a small kitchen. Families—even those with steady incomes—were crowded together in cramped and ill-ventilated quarters. . . . The homes of the poor were filled with lodgers, and public refuges for the homeless were chronically overcrowded." The *Kleinstwohnung,* which consisted of one room and a kitchen, with a possible smaller room in addition, "was the typical home of the laboring man and of the lower grade clerical worker." The somewhat larger *Kleinwohnung,* with two full-sized rooms, housed "the less prosperous shop-keeper and the better paid clerk" and constituted somewhat more than 9 percent of the total. The *Mittelwohnung,* slightly more than 12 percent of the total, housed "state officials, professional workers, and the main body of business men." *Grosswohnungen,* containing the equivalent of four large rooms or more, made up not quite 5 percent.[13]

In Paris in 1891 14 percent of the population lived in accommodations with more than two persons per room, "room" being defined as anything larger than a corridor, hence including antechambers and kitchens. In Vienna a comparable study in 1890 showed 28 percent living under such conditions. The category of single persons living alone was much higher in Paris, 30 percent as opposed to 5 percent. Bertillon was shocked at the extent of subletting in Vienna, "Single individuals . . . instead of living alone as in Paris . . . are lodged in Vienna in other households as subletters [*Aftermiether*] or as bed-tenants [*Bettgeher* or *Schlafleute*]." The contrast showed the higher degree of refinement of the Parisian, who, however poor, preferred solitude and privacy to the "promiscuité fâcheuse" of lodging with others.[14]

A later survey made in 1910 found comparable figures, with 32 percent of the Viennese population living more than two to the room. The *Bettgeher* "often sleeps in the same room with persons of the opposite sex." There were a total of 93,000 subtenants with separate rooms and 75,400 *Bettgeher*.[15] "In the Wollzeile, which is one of the principal streets of the City, I have seen a young shop-assistant, who had rented the end of a corridor to sleep, behind a curtain," wrote Victor Tissot in 1878; "in every street placards advertising 'beds for rent' swing in the wind."[16]

Vienna was by no means the worst European capital from the point of view of overcrowding. In Budapest the proportion living more than two to a room was an astonishing 71 percent.[17] Yet the Brookings Institution found Viennese housing standards low by European as well as American standards. It thought the early *Gründerzeit* blocks of workers' flats particularly bad, along with converted seventeenth- and eighteenth-century buildings, which, "as a result of minute subdivision, excessive age, and extreme overcrowding, have become conspicuous centers of misery." There were in addition "many dilapidated houses which are barely fit for human habitation" and "a considerable number of persons living in caves dug in railway embankments, in boats, in hiding places under the bridges."[18]

The overcrowding and housing shortage had been a constant since the late eighteenth century. The level of rents more than tripled between mid-century and 1914, faster than wages rose.[19] Despite marked expansion, the building industry could barely keep up with the growing population, and except for a minority of better-paid workers, no significant improvement in housing standards took place. Peter Feldbauer estimates that in 1914 nearly three-quarters of the Viennese population were inadequately housed.[20] E. Philippovich, who in 1894 made a careful survey of working-class tenements in Ottakring, Favoriten, and Brigittenau, found them wholly incapable of providing an environment for decent family life:

> One can go from flat to flat, yet all of them lack what we are accustomed to see as the basis for a healthy bourgeois life. The flat is only a shelter from bad weather, a place to spend the night, that by the cramped space into which people press themselves, by the lack of quiet and air and cleanliness, can never serve as a place of repose for the exhausted body. These flats offer no ease and no restorative comfort. They have no charm for anyone exhausted from labor. Anyone who has sunk into them or been born into them must degenerate in body or spirit, and wither or become depraved.[21]

The growth in working-class incomes in the early years of the twentieth century did not produce an increase in building production but merely raised the level of rents.[22]

The relative levels of wealth of the three countries may partly account for the differences in housing standards. The lower cost of land in greater London would also have worked to facilitate cheaper housing. Too much ought not to be made of this, since even in Vienna the price of land accounted for no more than 12 to 15 percent of the total cost of a working-class tenement, and in the years immediately before 1914 as little as 8 to 12 percent.[23] Contributing more to differentials in cost were the local building codes, most stringent in Vienna, least in London.[24] The "flimsy," jerry-built construction practiced by London's builders, of which contemporaries were forever complaining, did enable them to build and sell more cheaply and allowed house owners to make reasonable profits from lower rents than would have been conceivable in either Paris or Vienna. The mild English winters and the willingness of the English to endure cold indoors permitted builders to make little provision for insulation or other than primitive heating arrangements.

The nature of the London building industry, in which large numbers of small undercapitalized speculators were able to coexist with giants like Cubitt and William Willett, meant that there were always those willing to plunge into housing development whatever the economic climate. They went bankrupt with monotonous regularity, leaving rows of carcasses to be finished by the next generation of hopeful speculators, but the houses ultimately got built. The syndicates and companies that were responsible for building Paris and Vienna were not above overestimating the market themselves, but on the whole they behaved more rationally and cautiously and hence built more in response to than in anticipation of demand.

An article in the Vienna *Gemeindezeitung* in 1862 paid tribute to the responsiveness of the London housing industry to the demands put on it by its burgeoning population, with no assistance from the government. Paris and Vienna came off badly in comparison. "If one thinks, with what violence and extravagance in Paris, with what slowness and cumbersomeness in Vienna, an immensely smaller expansion of the city was achieved, one is astonished to see how in London things go forward almost as if by a law of nature and whole new districts appear, supplied with water and gas." In London everyone could find accommodation in the newer quarters according to his means and requirements, and the streets were more handsome and housing cheaper there than in any other great city. Rents, apart from the City itself, were about half what they were in Paris and in Vienna, "not only in the Inner City but in the more accessible parts of the suburbs," while the houses were both more comfortable and healthier than those of either of the other two cities.[25]

Builders could not have produced houses so lavishly had cheap land and cheap construction not been accompanied by cheap money. The building industry had access to capital at particularly low rates of interest, capital that was unlikely to be shifted into other areas. Mortgages at $4\frac{1}{2}$ and 5 percent gave a larger return than Consols, along with nearly as much security, being literally "safe as houses." Typically channeled from small, cautious middle-class investors through their solicitors, building mortgages tapped a source of capital that would never have been available for more speculative purposes. The thrift of the Victorian lower middle classes had as one socially beneficial consequence the abundant production of new urban housing, including much designed for working-class occupation.[26]

In France and Austria investors in housing expected a larger return, and housing had to compete with industrial and overseas investments for capital. In Paris the average return on building investment was estimated in 1910 at 6.61 percent; yet more and more capital was deserting such investments for opportunities overseas.[27] Builders in Vienna had long faced similar problems. In the years after 1848 house building had to offer a return of from 7 to 8 percent before it could divert funds from industry and bills of exchange. A 10 percent return was even aimed at in domestic investment. Interest rates fell thereafter, and the building boom that began in 1869 was financed at from 6 to 7 percent. Working-class housing, with its prospect of both greater wear and tear and nonpayment of rent, had to offer 2 or even 3 percent more. Mortgage rates fell in the eighties and nineties, to as low as 4½ percent in fashionable districts and from 6 to 8 percent in working-class neighborhoods like Ottakring and Meidling.[28] Yet capital was always liable to be withdrawn when more attractive investments appeared elsewhere.[29]

A comparable tendency for investors to desert building took place in England in the years just before 1914.[30] But this had followed a period of actual glut in the housing market and might have been no more than a temporary aberration had war, rent control, and a whole new set of public policies not intervened. New houses from the twenties onward have been either publicly subsidized or built as speculative housing for sale, not for rent. The average quality of housing, aesthetic considerations aside, has undeniably improved vastly since 1914, as it has in France and Austria. Yet housing in England had already achieved unmatched standards of space and sanitation in 1914, and it has maintained its relative superiority to this day. Though it would be foolish to deny the contributions made by the central government and local authorities, the level of expectations created by earlier generations of speculative builders needs equal recognition.

Another possible explanation is the leasehold system, which added to the accumulated savings of widows and orphans the vast capital resources of some of the wealthiest peers and private corporations of the realm. S. E. Rasmussen argued in *London: The Unique City* that the leasehold system was the major reason for the sprawling nature of London and the ubiquity of the individual private house.[31] Not having to purchase the freehold of the land, the builder needed to go to the capital market only to finance his construction costs. The practice of waiving rent payments for the early years of the lease further reduced his expenses. If, as sometimes happened, the landowner himself purchased improved ground rents in order to facilitate the development of his estate, or even if—as was more often the case—he extended the period of "peppercorn" rents to help builders over times of difficulty, he was investing even more capital in the cause of cheap urban housing. All this diminished the total demand for mortgage capital and served to keep the rate of interest on such capital down.

The discovery that there is no notable difference in density of layout, in the prevalence of single-family houses, in land values, or in the level of rents between English towns on the leasehold system and those where the freehold system prevailed has led historians to dismiss systems of land tenure as significant causal factors in urban development.[32] It is true that low interest rates on mortgages enabled speculators to develop freehold estates quite as cheaply as they could leasehold property. But the low level of mortgage interest was itself partly determined by the lower level of demand for such mortgages, since builders on leasehold estates had less need for them. To that extent the Grosvenors, Portmans, Portlands, Bedfords, Northamptons, and their fellow landlords in London; the Norfolks in Sheffield; the Calthorpes in Birmingham; the Derbys and Seftons in Liverpool, the Devonshires in Eastbourne were helping keep the cost of building down and thereby maintaining the relatively high standard of housing throughout England. Rasmussen's thesis would seem therefore, in a modified form, still valid.

Attempts to define the quality of life of the working-class or middle-class family need to place the dwelling in the context of the city as a whole and to consider the capacity of the city to fulfill the needs and aspirations of its residents. Gillian Tindall has done just that for Paris:

> The apparent paradox of contrast in the space devoted to external areas—café terraces, wide boulevards, vast *rond-points*—and that devoted to interior living, is actually causal: the existence of terraces and broad-walks has made it possible for the Parisian to keep his home a secluded eyrie if he so wishes, while the cramped, internal, secret quality of the traditional Parisian *ménage* has, in turn, made the external spaciousness essential.[33]

Conversely one might argue that it was the sheer awfulness of London that forced the Englishman to develop the home as a satisfactory refuge. Certainly no city, nor the men, women, and families who lived there, can be understood without reference to its public life, and more particularly to the pleasures that life has to offer.

If the nature of the London house, the layout of the London street, and the pattern of development that informed the Victorian metropolis encouraged withdrawal and seclusion, the structure of the Paris flat, the attractions of the Paris street, and the very nature of Paris itself called its residents out of doors. If the life of London lay hidden in its drawing rooms, inside its clubs, within the cozy subdivisions of its pubs, the life of Paris was there for all to see, and perhaps to join: in its promenades, its boulevards, and its streets.

THE CITY AS PLAYGROUND

12

London: Hidden Pleasures

have noted that as a rule family residences for well-to-do people will not be readily taken if over shops in a main street in London," E. T. Hall remarked in a paper to the Architectural Association in 1901:

It is strange that this objection does not hold in Vienna and Paris, where family suites in the heart of the cities are the rule, and are sometimes sumptuous. I suppose the difference lies in the temperament of the peoples. In England the mistress of the house and the family generally like to have the opportunity of being quiet; "a quiet evening at home" one constantly hears. . . . In France and Vienna the genius of the people is for bustle, vivacity, stir, and movement.[1]

Whether in pursuit of quiet or in terror of being thought to have some connection with trade, the Londoner goes to great lengths to isolate himself from institutions of business and pleasure. By contrast the archbishop of Vienna finds nothing compromising in there being a Pizzaland on the ground floor of his palace: his dignity does not depend on such external circumstances (fig. 76). By living in the Stephansplatz he has the most desirable address possible. For his predecessors to have chosen a residence as far from the center of things as Lambeth or Fulham is from London would have been unthinkable.

There is no easy way to account for the inward-looking quality of London. It may have something to do with the ingredients of fear and distrust in English society that sometimes seem to divide it into hostile classes with incompatible values and patterns of behavior. The dread of meeting someone unpleasant on the stairs might equally apply on the streets and in public places.

Or, as many Victorians argued, was the walled suburban villa no more than a normal escape from the pervasive unpleasantness of London? "Without touching at all upon the most crowded and filthy parts of London, one may see more in a walk from the Strand or Fleet-street to the Regent's Park than would suffice to make . . . [the Londoner] exclaim, 'What a miserable and disheartening accompaniment of all our boasted progress!'" wrote W. Robinson in 1869. "Such a reeking mass of mismanagement . . . the world has probably never seen."[2] How terrible a place *was* London in 1869? What would the foreign visitor have found there? How many of the attractions of today's London were already there? Were there others, absent today, that we would have enjoyed (fig. 77)?

76. *The archbishop of Vienna finds nothing compromising in there being a Pizzaland on the ground floor of his palace; his dignity does not depend on such external circumstances.* Shops in Archbishop's Palace, Stephansplatz, c. 1905. (Bildarchiv der Österreichischen Nationalbibliothek.)

Before attempting to answer those questions, let us rid ourselves of Dickensian and Chadwickian images. Whatever its sanitary inadequacies—and the worst had been taken care of by 1869—whatever the extent of poverty, by contemporary standards London was healthy and technologically advanced, and more remarkable for widely diffused moderate prosperity than for the extremes of riches and distress that existed there as elsewhere. There is, to be sure, evidence that the poverty that did exist in London was somehow more obtrusive than in continental cities. But we must assume that scenes of squalor and want did not prevent our visitor from enjoying London in 1869 any more than such scenes seriously interfere with our enjoyment of New York or Lisbon or Mexico City today. A selective blindness is a necessary attribute of the happy tourist.

If our hypothetical tourist had come from the Continent, his boat train would deposit him at either Charing Cross or Victoria (fig. 78), both of them brand-new, and the former, apart from its soaring trainshed, looking much as it does today. If he had come from America his ship would probably have docked in Liverpool, so his boat train would have brought him to the incongruous combination of the ramshackle with the monumental that constituted Euston until the 1960s. A railway hotel would have awaited him at each terminus, the still-functioning Charing Cross Hotel or the Grosvenor at Victoria for the continental visitor, the now vanished Euston for the American (fig. 79). Apart from these, or the Great Northern at King's Cross and the Great Western at Paddington that we still have today—the longevity of railway hotels is a happy feature of late twentieth-century travel—he would have had his choice of long-departed hotels converted from one or more terrace houses (of which Brown's is an untypical survival) or one of the new monster hotels, notably the Langham at the foot of Portland Place or the Westminster Palace in Victoria Street.

Once checked in, he would have found facilities not altogether different from those of today: gas lighting instead of electric, and bath and lavatory down the hall, but these latter of a sort we would recognize; hydraulic passenger and luggage lifts would operate in the larger establishments, and an abundance of servants would more than make up for the absence of tea- and instant-coffee-making devices in the rooms or shoe-polishing machines in the corridors.

77. **Transport map of late Victorian London. Baedeker,** *London,* **1892.**

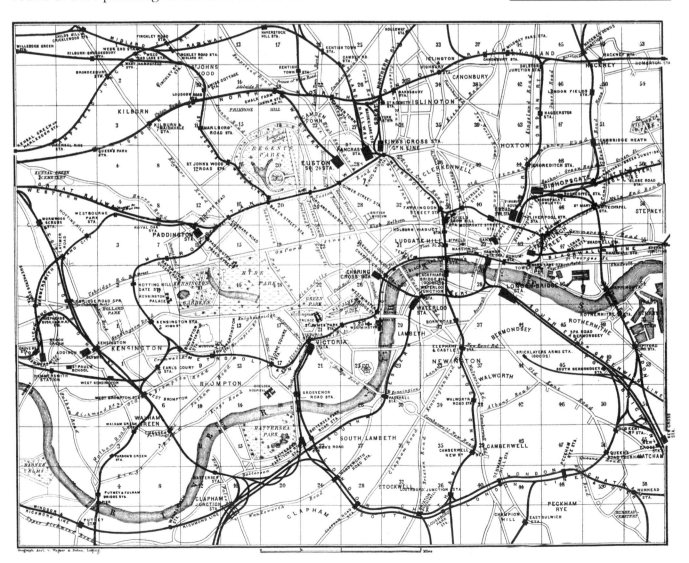

BROOM, 421.

VICTORIA STATION, S.W.

78. *His boat train would deposit him at either Charing Cross or Victoria.* Victoria Station, early twentieth century. (Museum of London.)

Exploring London would not be so different from today, either. The fact that all vehicles in the streets were horse-drawn made essential the wearing of boots and the services of crossing-sweepers, but the tourist would be spared the unpaved streets of contemporary American cities or having to brave traffic in the absence of foot pavements, as he often would on the Continent. If he grew tired of walking, he could hail a cab or a passing omnibus, the latter stopping to pick up passengers anywhere along the route. Buses were, then as now, double-deckers, but the upper deck was open to the weather, as it remained long into the motorized era. Or he could, depending on his destination, experience the thrill of riding the world's first underground railway, by then operating from Farringdon Street in the City via King's Cross and Paddington to Notting Hill, South Kensington, and a just-opened extension to Westminster.

The steam underground would bring him within a short walk of the South Kensington Museum—the present Victoria and Albert—and the Horticultural Exhibition occupying the site of the present Natural History Museum all the way north to

Kensington Gardens (fig. 80). Other cultural attractions would be the British Museum, much in its present form, the National Gallery in Trafalgar Square, and the Soane Museum in Lincoln's Inn Fields.

Orchestral concerts would be performed at the St. James's Hall Piccadilly. If our tourist were lucky enough to be in London during the season, he could hear Italian opera at Covent Garden, although in a manner inferior to both present Royal Opera House standards and those of the best continental companies. As for the theater, the present Drury Lane, Haymarket, Adelphi, Vaudeville, Old Vic, and several others long since demolished would offer an evening's entertainment. Shaftesbury Avenue and Charing Cross Road were not yet cut through the slums of Soho and St. Martin-in-the-Fields, so he would find the theater district more concentrated in the Strand–Covent Garden area than it is today. But his English friends would probably have advised him to avoid the theater entirely, except perhaps for a Shakespearean production at the Lyceum. The advice would be given on aesthetic as well as moral and social grounds: for the quality of the plays, productions, and performances in London at this period was lower than it ever has been before or since. The visit to London of the Comédie Française in the 1870s would come as a revelation of the potential of the theater as an art form and encourage agitation for a subsidized national theater. But for the moment the opportunity to see drama of serious literary quality intelligently acted was yet another reason to slip over to Paris for a fortnight's visit.

If our tourist was interested in urban architecture, and sufficiently catholic in his

---

79. *A railway hotel would have awaited him at each terminus.* Charing Cross Hotel, 1865. (Guildhall Library. Photo Godfrey.)

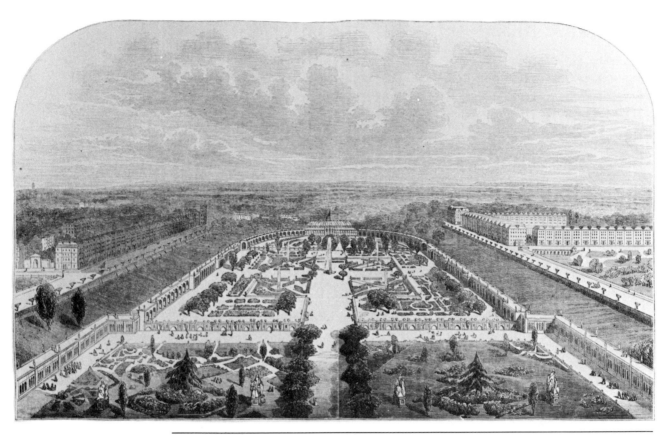

80. *The steam underground would bring him within a short walk of the Horticultural Exhibition.* View of the Estate of the Commissioners for the Exhibition of 1851. From *The Builder* 17 (1859): 457.

tastes to respond both to the picturesque and to the productions of a deliberate classicism, he would have riches at his disposal that we must envy. The City still contained all of Wren's churches, including many that would shortly be sacrificed to the demands for new office space as well as those that were to be lost in the Second World War. Apart from that, it would have consisted of a mixture of converted late Stuart red-brick and Georgian gray-brick houses, early Victorian stucco commercial buildings, and an assortment of modern, massive stone structures, monumental in concept and imaginative in design.

Proceeding westward, he would find a greater proportion of old to modern than in the City, where soaring land values encouraged rebuilding to high and expensive standards. Here, along the Strand, north through Covent Garden and St. Giles's to Bloomsbury, west through Soho toward Mayfair, Marylebone, and St. James's, could be found remnants of seventeenth-century suburban growth overlaid by an essentially Georgian urban fabric. On estates with ambitious ground landlords, modern stucco facing and plate-glass windows might attempt to disguise the seventeenth- or eighteenth-century origin of the building. Along major thoroughfares and on particularly valuable sites, wholly new structures would have arisen to testify that this was now the Victorian age. But to picture the West End in the 1860s it is necessary to imagine duplicated and multiplied Bedford Square and Montague Street, Harley Street and Gloucester Place, and Soho with the porno bookshops replaced by sober Victorian shop fronts.

Much of this vast area was still residential. Nursemaids with their charges walking the graveled paths of the locked garden squares, tradesmen making deliveries to kitchen staffs behind area railings, carriages depositing ladies making morning calls gave the more favored areas a domesticated character that in their present form as publishers' offices and tourist hotels we can barely conceive (fig. 81). Of course it would have been the rarest of tourists in the 1860s who went to Bloomsbury or Marylebone to admire the architecture. But anyone not wholly enslaved by contemporary aesthetic dogma must have recognized the quiet, orderly, wholesome quality of the residential West End.

Our particular tourist would be among the first able to enjoy the promenade along the Thames, now that the Victoria Embankment was approaching completion. The still new Houses of Parliament and the older Adelphi Terrace and Somerset House lent aesthetic distinction to the riverfront, long hidden from view.

Still farther to the west, either north or south of the Park, the visitor would see modern domestic architecture at its most splendid, inhabited by families of wealth and fashion during the season, if somewhat melancholy during the autumn and winter months when left to the care of skeleton domestic staffs. The royal parks themselves would have possessed all the attractions they do today: even the most churlish of Victorian London-haters admitted that its parks were treasures that would have graced any city.

---

81. *Nursemaids with their charges walking the graveled paths of the locked garden squares, tradesmen making deliveries to kitchen staffs behind area railings, carriages depositing ladies making morning calls gave the more favored areas a domesticated character.* Corner of Torrington Square and Torrington Street, looking toward Keppel Street, 1850. G. Scharf. (British Museum.)

Beyond the parks, beyond Kensington and Bayswater, lay the real country, or at least what had once been real country and was only now being visited by the speculative builder. If our tourist had left his train at Kensington High Street or Gloucester Road, he would be within a short walk of market gardens and nurseries, survivals of country villages, and stretches of Georgian ribbon development. If he had taken one of the frequent North London suburban trains from Broad Street Station to Hampstead Heath, then larger in extent than today, and walked steadily up the hill he would find himself not in today's Hampstead Garden Suburb or Golders Green but in genuine rolling countryside. The Victorians complained about the sprawling extent of the built-up area, but from our perspective the "green belt," although threatened at every point, was still remarkably accessible to the town.

So far, so good, particularly because his perambulations have taken him mainly to the west and north, and he has neglected to explore the mews and courts that lay behind some of the attractive and respectable street frontages. But his exertions in pursuit of beauty and culture have left him tired, thirsty, and hungry. What is he to do? For practical purposes, his best recourse is to hail a cab and demand to be taken back to his hotel. He might find a bench or decide to abandon dignity and sprawl on the grass in one of the parks, but elsewhere there would be no place to sit without payment of some sort, and even then no place that he (or certainly she) would find at all pleasant. A public house would be out of the question, while the occasional ostensibly respectable eating establishment would be entered with justifiable misgivings (as in the early 1950s) (fig. 82). Nor would he be particularly well fed at his hotel, although there the service and surroundings would be as genteel as he could desire (fig. 83). For meals composed with imagination and prepared with care, as

82. *The occasional ostensibly respectable eating establishment would be entered with justifiable misgivings.* Coffee shop in Holborn, 1833. G. Scharf. (British Museum.)

83. *At his hotel the service and surroundings would be as genteel as he could desire.* London Bridge Terminus Hotel, late 1860s. Lithograph by Robert Dudley. (Museum of London.)

for drinkable wines, he would need a letter of introduction to a member of one of the better clubs or, best of all, to someone wealthy enough to employ a French chef of his own. Were he really adventurous, he might try one of a number of small restaurants in and around Soho and Leicester Square, patronized mostly by resident foreigners, but his English friends would do their best to dissuade him. Spiers and Pond had opened up a few restaurants at places like the new Cannon Street Station and would shortly create in the Criterion at Piccadilly Circus a multi-storied mecca for respectable wining and dining (fig. 84). But such monster restaurants were, one suspects, at best up-market anticipations of the later Lyons Corner Houses—perfectly satisfactory places to dine, but not worth crossing the Channel to experience.

All this brings us to the crux of the difficulty: Victorian London was admirably equipped to provide the higher pleasures, with its museums, learned societies, architectural treasures, and areas of natural beauty. But as for the lower pleasures, if eating and drinking and playgoing can be so described, it was ill-prepared to satisfy the wants of the visitor. And even the museums, exemplary though they were, were closed on Sunday.

As references to the London season, locked garden squares, and French chefs in private employ have already suggested, London had abundant resources available to those in privileged positions. For the visitor with access to the right people, there

84. *Spiers and Pond would shortly create in the Criterion a multi-storied mecca for respectable wining and dining.* The Criterion, Piccadilly Circus. From *The Builder* 29 (1871): 527.

were pleasures sufficient to dazzle most Europeans and any American. For the tourist arriving with nothing but a letter of credit and a Murray's Guide, London could, particularly on a wet Sunday, seem a dreary place indeed.

"Why with the majority of travellers does Paris inspire liveliness and a desire to remain in town?—London, sadness and a desire to quit it?" William H. White asked in 1877.3 "London," wrote Théophile Gautier, "may become Rome, but it will certainly never become Athens: this last fate is reserved for Paris. In the first we have gold, power, material development in the highest degree; a gigantic exaggeration of all that can be done with money, patience, and will; the useful, the comfortable; but the agreeable and the beautiful, no."4

Hermann Muthesius turned the indifference of the Londoner to cultural attractions into a kind of virtue. He admitted that the long journeys from the suburban dwelling to town "make social life difficult, complicate visits to the theatre and to concerts and the physical effort that such journeys entail effectively restricts all visits to the inner city." Yet urban amusements, even of a high cultural nature, were best tasted sparingly. Suburban pleasures, centered on the home, had moral advantages over the more sophisticated offerings of the capital. "An evening of music-making at home, an evening's reading *en famille* is more rewarding to thoughtful natures than three visits a week to the concert-hall or opera-house."5

The Viennese coffee house and the Paris café were always being celebrated as among the glories of the two capitals. It was not until well into the twentieth century that the English middle classes discovered the virtues of the London pub. Georgian poets might, in the years just before 1914, refresh themselves on a walking tour in a country inn, but London pubs did not become acceptable middle-class hangouts for both sexes until the Second World War. For the Victorians, public houses were not a healthy part of popular culture, but a problem, like back-to-backs and unventilated drains (fig. 85).

Europeans must think the English "the most besotted of nations," wrote one critic in 1854. "Were our publicans, like the traiteurs of Paris, providers of well-cooked dinners and repasts at moderate prices, there might be some reason for their excessive numbers . . . the Parisian goes out for his luxuries, the Cockney enjoys them at home; and it is only the want of domestic comforts that fills our tap-rooms."6 Dr. Johnson's remark about the tavern chair being a throne of human felicity must have struck Victorian readers as just another example of the good lexicographer's amusing perversity of opinion. One ate in inns while traveling, but didn't expect to enjoy it. Kitty and Lydia Bennett's cold meat, salad, and cucumber at the inn were not much relished by the more rational members of their family. The fare provided by railway refreshment rooms seems to have been even more detestable. Trollope never describes his characters as actually enjoying the meals they take at the railway hotels at Paddington and King's Cross while breaking cross-country journeys. To dine well, it was necessary to do so at home or at one's club.

The descent of foreign tourists on London for the 1851 exhibition was awaited with some trepidation. "Those who know anything of foreigners on the Continent will perceive the necessity of providing them with viands suitable to their tastes," wrote one Londoner in February 1851. "The general construction and management of . . . our coffee-shops are also very faulty, compared with the *cafés* of France and Germany (fig. 86). Whatever opinions we may have respecting the personal habits of foreigners, their cafés are generally noted for cleanliness and comfort." By

85. *For the Victorians, public houses were a problem, like back-to-backs and unventilated drains.* Public house, corner of Tottenham Court Road and Grafton Street, 1839. G. Scharf. (British Museum.)

86. *(opposite, above) "The general construction and management of . . . our coffee-shops are also very faulty."* Coffee house, Museum Street, 1844. G. Scharf. (British Museum.)

87. *(opposite, below) "The Holborn Restaurant was the first of any size to astonish the Londoner with its comparative luxury, cleanliness, and good cooking."* Holborn Restaurant, From *The Builder* 48 (1885).

contrast some London eating houses were "so objectionable in these points as to prevent decently-attired persons from frequenting them. The place is often dirty, and the attendants slovenly." In 1901 E. T. Hall recalled the time "that outside a club or a chophouse there was hardly a place where one could get a decent meal, and certainly no place where one could take a lady except it were to an hotel." Apart

from "one or two Italian cafés . . . the Holborn Restaurant was the first of any size to astonish the Londoner with its comparative luxury, cleanliness, and good cooking"[7] (fig. 87).

London also lagged behind Paris and American cities in the provision of luxury hotel accommodation. "In 1834, before the completion of the London and Birmingham Railway, the hotels of London . . . either resembled, and indeed were, one or two private houses run together . . . or they were local inns, built for the cheap accommodation of coach passengers," the *Builder* recalled in 1880 (fig. 88). "City-ward there were . . . inns of a somewhat Shakespearian stamp—Green Dragons, and Bulls, and Griffins, and the like, in which external wooden galleries looked down on the inn yard, and gave access to the separate bedrooms." The railway both doomed the coaching inns to rapid obsolescence and closure and brought about a new kind of hotel, often directly connected with the station itself.[8]

The same journal had in 1860 hailed such hotels as "one of those striking conceptions which distinctively mark the civilization of the age, so far as it is justly considered that judicious arrangements for bodily comfort and convenience are absolutely essential for healthy mental exertion and truly pleasurable enjoyment." The Grosvenor Hotel at Victoria Station that opened that year offered "seven stories above the ground floor, the two first containing suites of drawing, dining, and bedrooms, and other accommodation for separate families." A bathroom was provided on every floor, "except the topmost one for the servants." The ground floor contained "private sitting and other rooms and offices, . . . a large dining-room for wedding and other parties, and a ladies' coffee-room" at one end, "and at the other, which may be considered as the bachelors' end . . . the gentlemen's coffee-room, adjoining which . . . is a smoking-room." A lift was provided for passengers and luggage. Altogether the hotel formed "almost a little town under one roof"[9] (fig. 89).

For the London gentleman, married or single, the want of cafés and restaurants and boulevards and agreeable places of public resort was to a considerable degree made up for by the facilities of his club. "One is aware of the particular role that in England, and especially in London, the societies known under the name of clubs play," wrote the French architect Hittorff in 1860. "Their number is considerable, and in the finest streets and main squares of the capital they present a succession of large and magnificent palaces, with a monumental effect." Daly had earlier exclaimed over their luxury and comfort, "to the point even, as in the *Reform Club,* of using machines to bring up to the different floors objects which it would be inconvenient to encounter on the stairs."[10]

The English often accounted for the development of the club as providing an economical place for the young bachelor to dine. Thus A. Hayward in 1853, discussing the recent concentration in London of "a vast variety of formerly untransportable luxuries," instanced "the improvement and multiplication of Clubs" as "the grand feature of metropolitan progress." In them "a man of moderate habits can dine more comfortably for three or four shillings (including half a pint of wine) than he could have dined for four or five times that amount at the coffee houses and hotels, which were the habitual resort of the bachelor class . . . during the first quarter of the century."[11]

It was not only bachelors who used the clubs. To Hittorff, their popularity among married men demonstrated the fragility of the supposed sanctity of the English home. "These constructions of stone and marble where floods of light sparkle"

Hickinbottom's BRITISH HOTEL.

John Hickinbottom,

respectfully informs the Nobility and Gentry, that he has fitted up and opened an Hotel, in the most fashionable Style, distinguished by the Name of the British Hotel, No 88, Jermyn Street, St James's: Adapted as well for the Accommodation of Families as Single Gentlemen.

He ventures to solicit the Company of the Nobility & Gentry as his Charges will be moderate, & the most minute Attention paid in every respect to their Convenience.

88. *"In 1834 . . . the hotels of London . . . resembled, and indeed were, one or two private houses run together."* Hickinbottom's British Hotel, 88 Jermyn Street. (Guildhall Library. Photo Godfrey.)

89. *The modern hotel was "one of those striking conceptions which distinctively mark the civilization of the age."* The Grosvenor Hotel, Pimlico. From *The Builder* 19 (1861): 375.

were frequented day and night by "many heads of family, to the detriment of their domestic happiness." Clubs by their very comforts encouraged "the cult of egoism, the abandonment of family virtues, the exclusive taste for material pleasures, and a deplorable laxity of morals of which the whole nation will someday feel the baneful consequences"[12] (fig. 90, colorplate 5).

Daly was more inclined to praise than condemn the club, which he saw as the natural product of the Englishman's desire for society and his fear of encountering people of inferior social class. "In that country, the different classes of society are separated by fixed boundaries [*une délimitation tout à fait tranchée*], which is related to a variety of causes that one wouldn't be able to modify without commotions and terrible fights, and which the conservative spirit of the nation has up to now prevented from surmounting." The social mixture of a Parisian café would be intolerable to an Englishman:

> It is probably this fear that everyone has of compromising himself with a person of a rank too inferior to his own . . . that has made almost impossible the organization of those places of public meeting so common in France, where the natural gaiety of the inhabitants manifests itself almost without restraint, and where the presence of women prompts, down to individuals of the lowest class, that grace and that proverbial politeness, qualities that contrast so strongly with the awkwardness and rudeness of the lower classes of other nations, whose manners, however, could not be softened except by more frequent contact with the polite classes of society, who are urged by those very faults to keep themselves even more aloof [*que ces défauts même engagent à se tenir encore plus en réserve*].

Daly suggests that the English lower classes, unlike the French, could not comport themselves decently in a mixed social setting. English tourists in Paris were always being charmed and astonished at the universal reign of good humor and good manners, something they were not used to at home. Whatever the patronizing tone of Daly's interpretation—that mingling with the middle classes would improve working-class manners—his contrast between social harmony in France and social division in England raises questions. For it was the Parisian working classes who were to throw up barricades eight years later, not the Chartists. The persistent English middle-class *fear* of the working classes was again and again proved unjustified, whereas the polite French workman was perfectly prepared to rebel against established authority. It may be simplistic to assume any relationship between behavior in a boulevard café and readiness to engage in revolutionary activity, but the contrast between the political docility—and often political sophistication—of the English working classes and their presumed inadequacies of public manners remains puzzling. The answer may lie more in middle-class perceptions than in working-class behavior, but that still leaves the question of how such perceptions developed.

90. *Clubs by their very comforts encouraged "the cult of egoism, the abandonment of family virtues, the exclusive taste for material pleasures, and a deplorable laxity of morals."* Morning room, Army and Navy Club. (Guildhall Library. Photo Godfrey.) See also colorplate 5.

For Daly the social differences, real or imaginary, would doom any attempt to import the Parisian café to London:

> It is once again that same aristocratic spirit that has kept the custom of cafés from establishing itself in England. If absolutely necessary, each café could perhaps have addressed itself to a certain class, one to the aristocracy, one to the upper bourgeoisie, and so forth; but that would have limited its clientele to a small number of persons; and besides, the English would not easily put up with a situation which would not absolutely prevent the stranger from coming in to join them. The cafés, which have for the past few years added so much to the fame of Paris, and whose splendor is an object of astonishment for all foreigners who visit this fine capital, will never acclimatize themselves in London, unless there is a great revolution in manners.

The London club by its very nature avoided such dangers and met the needs of a large class of male society for food, drink, and companionship:

> Even away from home, the Englishman wishes to make himself, so to speak, inaccessible to everyone except people of a rank equal to his own. This distinction between individuals, combined with the *comfort* to which the English are accustomed at home, makes it easily understandable that English soil is eminently suited for the development of clubs, and one understands in the same way that in France, where distinctions of fortune and of title are easily forgotten, where the spirit of sociability, the love of conversation and gaiety, are carried to such a high degree, and where besides general politeness facilitates relations between persons of different classes, cafés have prospered as much as clubs in England.[13]

Clubs offered their members reading rooms with newspapers and magazines from home and abroad, a library, a café, a smoking room, a card room, rooms for conversation and formal meetings. "One dines there, one invites one's friends, whom one can receive with all the advantages of luxury, comfort, and perfect service, for a relatively minimal expense." The Reform Club was, for its members, "hotel, restaurant, café, reading room, *cercle de conversation,* etc., but all this done in a discreet, dignified, honorable, and distinguished manner. No vulgar commotion [*pas de bruit vulgaire*], but throughout a well-managed household [*la bonne tenue d'une grande maison*] and select company."[14]

The club served as an extension of, or substitute for, the private house and if anything carried its principles of organization to even higher degrees of refinement. Ladies and children were not merely relegated to separate floors and rooms but excluded altogether. There were separate dining rooms for members and guests, and a greater subdivision of specialized public rooms than any but the very rich could achieve in their own homes. Membership was arranged so as to bar not only the socially unacceptable but those of incompatible politics or opinions or interests. That the very excellence of the clubs, by attracting the rich, the powerful, and the clever, impoverished public life for the rest of society, that they served even further to banish women from occasions of rational conversation is only to say that they conformed to the general tendency of late Georgian and Victorian England to institutionalize inequality.

"His nature is inventive, and he has proved, in private dwellings, and in the club, that other form of private house, that the achievement of the comfortable was easy for him," wrote a French visitor to London in 1865 of the skills of its speculative builders. But they did not extend from the private to the public sphere. Englishmen were "little concerned about comfort away from home."[15]

If sparing in physical comforts, places of public amusement in London did what they could to keep the classes decently apart. "There is scarcely a theatre in London the approaches to which are not superior to those of the theatres in Paris," boasted the *Building News* in 1862, "for here the visitors to pit, boxes, and galleries are separated, and have distinct ways for entering and leaving; whereas across the channel the same doorway serves for all . . . and even, in the French Theatre, the visitors to boxes and galleries descend the same staircases." It would have none of the argument that the superior manners of the French lower orders made segregation unnecessary: "a French mob is no better than an English one." The French thought otherwise. "A theater belongs to everyone," wrote G. Davioud, "and every spectator must be able to move about as he would in his own home."[16]

The one public amusement London had in abundance was shopping. "It is only through the principal thoroughfares, such as Oxford-street, Regent-street, or the Strand, where the shops and the throngs of people afford some amusement, that the pedestrian would care to loiter in London," wrote Alexander Payne in 1872.[17] The pseudonymous Marquis de Vermont described the route of the fashionable lounger through the West End in 1823:

> What sauntering indifference is displayed in the steps of the well-dressed pedestrians, who at the accustomed moment commence their daily pilgrimage from the top of Bond-street to the end of Pall Mall! Some stop at the fruit-shops, and, careless of consequences, run up a bill for early strawberries, forced peaches, and pine-apple ices. . . . Some empty their purses in bidding for useless baubles at the splendid auction-rooms of Phillips and Christie. Some are attracted by the grotesque prints exhibited at the windows of the caricature-sellers . . . scarcely any can resist the varied temptations which shops of every possible kind hold out to the vanity or the wants of the passers by. [Fig. 91]

Gentlemen walked; ladies came in carriages.

> The ladies who occupy the splendid equipages which so thickly fill the same streets . . . [seem] not less anxious than they to have recourse to every possible stimulus which novelty offers. . . . At the panoramas, bazaars, milliners', perfumers', and, above all, at the jewellers' shops, what strings of these carriages are seen . . . this favourite recreation, which your ladies call *shopping,* is often the cause of serious injury to the fortunes of their husbands.[18]

There were as many as fifteen "bazaars," devoted mostly to shops selling items of female dress, at the time in London. The arcade, even more popular in Paris than in London, provided an enclosed environment for shopping. The Burlington Arcade, built in 1818–19, contained in 1828 "milliners, hosiers, glovers, shoemakers, hairdressers, hatters, tobacconists, jewellers, a goldsmith, an optician, a wine merchant and a book-seller."[19]

From the 1820s Regent Street began to rival Bond Street's preeminence in the luxury trade. The western part of Oxford Street, Holborn, the Strand, Ludgate Hill, and Cheapside were other major shopping streets. The new availability of cheap plate glass and the use of iron columns and bressummers to support the walls above made possible the modern shop-front, and added window-shopping to pedestrian pleasures[20] (fig. 92). "Assuredly there are few whose memory cannot carry them back to the old shop fronts of the metropolis," remarked the *Art-Union Journal* in 1848. "They remember the small dingy panels, the heavy frame-work, like the gratings of a prison, and the miserable attempts at display of wares, more calculated to repel than to invite purchasers." Now the "improved and improving taste of the people" was being gratified by the displays within the "plate glass, rich mouldings, and splendid pillars, in the shops in Regent-street, the new Strand, and Ludgate-hill."[21] Such magnificent shop fronts "form one of the most prominent indications of the grandeur and wealth of the metropolis," wrote *Chambers Journal*:

> Enormous plate-glass windows, gilded or polished brass frames, expensive mirrors, polished mahogany frames, and all sorts of fancy woodwork; sometimes crystal columns, and generally a singular covering of iron Venetian blinds, which roll up and down by intricate machinery, like a stage curtain displaying . . . the gorgeous scenery within—these are the necessary decorations of a fashionable London shop of the middle of the nineteenth century.[22]

The pleasure of admiring such displays and acquiring the treasures in the shop behind might give blameless solace to the otherwise sequestered suburban house-wife. It might induce the overseas tourist to prolong by a few days his stay in

91. *"Scarcely any can resist the varied temptations which shops of every possible kind hold out to the vanity or the wants of the passers by."* Messrs. Harding Howell & Co, Pall Mall. Colored aquatint, published 1809 by Ackerman. (Museum of London.)

92. *The new availability of cheap plate glass made possible the modern shopfront and added window shopping to pedestrian pleasures.* Group of women admiring window display at Swan & Edgar's, Piccadilly Circus, early twentieth century. Detail of photograph of Quadrant from Piccadilly Circus. (Guildhall Library. Photo Godfrey.)

London. But if the former had inevitably to return to her domestic duties in Wimbledon or Dulwich, the latter would soon succumb to the temptation of hailing a cab for Charing Cross and boarding the next boat train for Paris.

13

Paris: The Garden and the Street

t this Easter-time," wrote the *Architect* in 1881, "the man is always to be envied who finds himself able to take a week in Paris. After a winter spent in the cold, damp smoke of London, there can scarcely fail to come to him a sense of pleasure and relief. . . . On this one spot of the earth's surface the spirit of incomparable elegance has . . . effectually settled."[1] Let us accompany the escaping Londoner or the bored American during the Easter holidays of 1881 to see what he would find when he got there.

It requires even less of an effort of the imagination to do so than for Victorian London, since the Paris of the 1880s had already achieved the outward appearance and could offer the inner satisfactions of the city of the 1980s. Haussmann's successors had completed his major projects, and the transformations were losing their original appearance of rawness and novelty and coming to give the illusion that they had existed from all eternity.

Arriving at the present Gare du Nord, designed by Hittorff and opened in 1863, he would pass beneath sculptural representations of Mercury, Neptune, and Jupiter, and personifications of eight foreign cities served by the Chemin de fer du Nord on his way to cab or omnibus. Already 5,800 cabs existed in 1864, while the omnibus ran over 31 different routes, charging a uniform fare of 30 centimes inside and 15 on the roof, the former with transfer privileges.[2] "We Londoners may well envy the Parisians the cheapness, regularity, and rapidity of their omnibus service, its well-arranged and numerous waiting-rooms, the politeness of the conductors, and the comfort especially of the more newly-constructed carriages," the *Builder* would write in 1882.[3]

Contemporaries were agreed that Parisian buses were more comfortable, and the service better organized, than in London. The American James Jackson Jarves had in 1852 pronounced them "superior to all others that I have seen." Armrests guaranteed each passenger adequate space to himself, and once all seats were occupied no more people were allowed to board.[4] London conductors were, on the other hand, notorious for enticing unwary passengers on board even if the bus was crowded past capacity.[5] Paris had as early as 1662 enjoyed a regular bus service, with seven carriages, offering six seats apiece, running a regular service along each of three routes. Such a precocious enterprise was abandoned in 1675, and the modern omnibus first appeared in Paris in 1828, one year before it came to London. A variety of concerns operated vehicles with such names as *tricycles, favorites, béarnaises, dames blanches, dames réunies, constantines, batignollaises, gazelles,* and *hirondelles,* but a single company acquired a monopoly in 1855.[6]

Bateaux-mouches began plying the Seine in 1867,[7] and a tramway, authorized in 1854, connected Boulogne, across the Seine from Sèvres, with the place de la Concorde.[8] The only rail rapid transit within Paris was the Chemin de fer de Ceinture, which linked all the railways entering the city by a line running just inside the fortifications. Trains ran at half-hour intervals out of the Gare Saint-Lazare and took about two hours to complete the entire circuit. Adolphe Joanne urged all visitors to Paris to ride the Ceinture to gain a sense of the topography of its surroundings, taking a second-class ticket in order to benefit from the better view from the upper level of the *impériale.* By a "happy innovation," the newest carriages were provided with glass windows that could be raised and lowered at will.[9] The opening of the Métro in the early years of this century provided direct radial routes from the outer arrondissements and so deprived the Ceinture of most of its clientele. A few years before the line lost its regular passenger service in the early 1930s, an English eccentric sent the *Railway Magazine* an account of an afternoon spent traveling around it from Auteuil to Auteuil, during which no more than two persons disturbed the solitude of his first-class compartment.[10] Today, save for passengers from Channel ports being shunted from the Gare du Nord to the Gare de Lyon on the rare through-carriage, the only people using any portion of the line travel on the ancient electric shuttle service between Pont Cardinet and Auteuil.

Proposals for an English-type steam underground or an American-type elevated appeared at intervals from 1871 on.[11] Nothing of the sort appeared to disfigure central Paris until the possibility of an electrified system brought about the present Métro, largely underground. It did not, like the London Underground, extend its lines to distant suburbs, but remained a strictly urban undertaking.

Our visitor in 1881 would hesitate to submit himself to the uncertainties of public transport but would instead choose a cab and direct it to one of the three monster hotels: the Louvre, the Grand, or the Continental (today's Intercontinental). The oldest was the Louvre, at the place du Palais-Royal, which opened in 1855. The ground floor and the mezzanine were from the outset given over to the department store that eventually took over the entire building. Already in 1878, "scarcely anything of the original caravanserai has been left . . . and eventually, the hotel . . . will be wholly disestablished," wrote George Augustus Sala, "and linen-drapery, hosiery, and haberdashery will reign supreme in the vast saloons where they used to charge such very high prices for such very indifferent luncheons and dinners." He was about as happy to see the hotel disappear, although "the vast dimensions of its principal apartments, the splendour of the decorations and furniture . . . made the Hôtel du Louvre in its youth a rarity and a phenomenon. It was twice as dear, moreover, as any other existing hotel."[12]

It was followed in 1862 by the Grand Hotel on the boulevard des Capucines, directly across from the site of the new Opéra. With seven hundred bedrooms, it was managed by the same company as the Louvre, and it is still very much in operation. It had two vast dining rooms where, at six o'clock, a table d'hôte would be served. Cesena described both hotels as "true private monuments, worth visiting for that reason alone." But one would find there neither quiet nor economy: "day and night, there is noise and agitation."[13] The Continental, on the rue de Rivoli, occupying the site of the Ministry of Finance destroyed by the Commune, was the new luxury hotel of the seventies.

If money was an object, the visitor would have his choice of lodgings at every level of price and comfort, in every quarter of the city. "Nowhere is existence cheaper than at Paris for those who know how to manage," Augustus Hare assured his readers in 1887. "A bachelor who does not mind mounting five pairs of stairs may have a charming little apartment for about 1*l.* a week."[14] As early as 1828 Richard's *Véritable conducteur parisien* estimated that there were more than five hundred *hôtels garnis* charging from as little as two francs a night to as much as fifty for a room or suite, depending on the district.[15]

For both families and single men planning a long visit on a strict budget, the "pension de famille" offered an economical alternative. They were not to be found in the high-rent areas around the western boulevards, but were frequent in Saint-Germain-des-Prés and near the Champs-Elysées. Cesena thought them particularly suitable to single ladies of small means, traveling without a chambermaid. Those near the Champs-Elysées were popular with English, American, and Russian ladies.[16]

After reading so much about the splendor and attention to individual comforts in Paris hotels, it is refreshing to find the damning account in Rowland Strong's *Where and How to Dine in Paris.* "Paris is a city of hotels, the majority of them bad," he wrote at the end of the century. "There is hardly a third-rate town in Germany or Italy, to say nothing of Switzerland which is not better provided with hotel accommodation than Paris." By 1900 the demands of the international tourist had multiplied, but Paris, in its hotels as in so much else, had moved little beyond its achievements under the Second Empire. Baths were a particular problem.

> Ten years ago it was impossible to obtain a bath at any of the Paris hotels, excepting one or two of the very best, without going through some extraordinary proceedings which are indeed still necessary in every establishment today not of the first rank. The bath had to be ordered in the early morning, and then a strange vehicle, something between a fire engine and an automobile, would make its approach, accompanied by men in special costumes, recalling that of the Royal Humane Society, London, and armed with indiarubber piping and other outlandish instruments. A great copper bath would then be transported into the patient's bedroom and the men passing water up the staircase in buckets from hand to hand filled it, and subsequently emptied it the same way.

Strong warned his readers against the "old-fashioned, grimy barrack-like . . . hotels with a totally fictitious reputation for comfort" to be found south of the boulevard de la Madeleine and west of the rue de la Paix. "Avoid those places if you value your lives and reputations. . . . They are expensive, their proprietors are thievish and curmudgeonly." He recommended, among expensive hotels, the new Ritz and the older Bristol, both in the place Vendôme, the hotels du Rhin and de Londres, and the Continental. "It is impossible for me to recommend the cuisine of these huge houses, though I have known people who had a kind of horrible longing for it. One of my friends, after a quarrel with his wife, always took her to lunch or dine at the *table d'hôte* either of the Grand, the Continental, or the Terminus. It was the peace-offering she best appreciated, and for him a very sufficient penance."[17]

The new hotels of the twentieth century lacked nothing that technology could supply to ease the life of the traveler. Yet neither then nor earlier did the world come to Paris primarily to enjoy the luxuries of its hotels. However satisfactory the lodgings of our Easter visitor in 1881, he would almost certainly have left them as soon as he had unpacked to explore the "real" Paris, probably first in a café.

The institution that best epitomizes the peculiar character of Paris, even, or perhaps especially, to the person who has never been there, is the café (fig. 93, colorplate 6). "All quarters of Paris have their cafés," a guidebook of 1828 tells us, where refreshments were to be had from dawn until midnight. "The old establishments maintain themselves by a well-founded reputation and a clientele of numerous *habitués* who come every evening . . . while the new ones try to achieve suc-

93. *The institution that best epitomizes the peculiar character of Paris is the café.* Grand Café du XIXe Siècle, boulevard de Strasbourg, 1861. (Musée Carnavalet.) See also colorplate 6.

94. *"All quarters of Paris have their cafés . . . the new ones try to achieve success by the sumptuousness of their decoration."* Le grand salon de Frascati. (Musée Carnavalet.) See also colorplate 7.

cess by the sumptuousness of their decoration"[18] (fig. 94, colorplate 7; fig. 95). They were especially plentiful in the boulevards, at the Palais Royal, along the Champs-Elysées, and in the neighborhood of railway termini. In the morning one could have *café au lait,* tea, or chocolate with bread and butter; and throughout the day a chop, a steak, cold meats, and eggs.[19] "Never was luxury of gilding, of mirrors, of rich satins, of downy cushions, of costly adornments, carried to a more Oriental excess than in the newly-constructed *cafés* of Paris," wrote Mrs. W. P. Byrne in 1859. "Neither taste nor expense has been spared, and the result is positively dazzling."[20]

"It is particularly in the evening that one has ices and sorbets," explained Amédée de Cesena in 1864; "but it is principally from three to five o'clock that one has, standing up, cakes and pastries," accompanied by a glass of Bordeaux, Madeira, or Malaga.[21] The most famous of the *glaciers* was Tortoni's, in the boulevard des Italiens. On a hot summer evening in 1835 Mrs. Trollope and her party "were fortunate enough to secure the places of a large party that were leaving a window in the upper room at Tortoni's." The scene was "totally un-English. . . . Both the rooms above, as well as those below, were quite full of gay company, each party sitting round their own little marble table, with the large *carafe* of ice." She found "the brilliant light within, the humming crowd without,—the refreshing coolness of the delicate regale . . . incontestably French."[22] The Champs-Elysées were noted for *cafés chantants*. An English visitor described one of them in 1855:

I entered a "café chantant," a place where coffee, ices, lemonade, sherbet, &c. can be imbibed to the sound of music and the strains of syrens, who, decked out in white muslin flowers and jewellery, occupy a raised and gaily decorated stage in the open air, the public being seated at small tables in front of the proscenium. Plants and variegated lamps are arranged at intervals, and give a fairy-like look to the whole.[23]

The café represented lightness and frivolity; the restaurant was something very serious indeed. "At the salas of your *restaurateurs,*" wrote Sir Charles Darnley in 1823, "I remark . . . *'que c'est une affaire bien sérieuse que le diner';* and I daily see twenty or thirty persons deeply occupied in the discharge of this important duty, scattered about at detached tables, and swallowing their meat in impenetrable silence."[24] Except at fixed-price restaurants, all such establishments had, "apart from their vast public rooms, extremely comfortable private dining rooms where one can talk of business or pleasure in an uninterrupted *tête-à-tête*. In these *boudoirs* as in the *salons* everything is neat, comfortable, elegant, sometimes even sumptuous." Lunch was served from nine in the morning until one, dinner from two until six or seven.[25]

Mrs. Trollope was as much impressed by their respectability as by their abundance. "Hundreds of these houses exist in Paris, and all of them are constantly furnished with guests. But this manner of living, so unnatural to us, seems not only natural, but needful to them. They do it all so well—so pleasantly!" At a *prix-fixe* establishment in the Palais Royal she found the dinner "extremely good, and as varied as our fancy chose to make it, each person having privilege to select three or four plats from a carte that it would take a day to read deliberately." She was struck by "the number of strange-looking people, and the perfect amenity and good-breeding which seemed to reign among them all." Most of the other diners were French, although there were a few German families and "many English, chiefly gentlemen." That the French patronized restaurants as a matter of course, not merely as an occasional treat, showed again how different they were from the English. "What a singular mode of existence is this, and how utterly inconceivable to English feelings!"[26]

95. "Never was luxury . . . carried to a more Oriental excess than in the newly constructed *cafés* of Paris." Café de la Banque de France, 1850. (Musée Carnavalet.)

The tremendous variation in price and pretension of Parisian restaurants, from the very expensive such as Beauvillier's in the rue de Richelieu, where Sir Charles Darnley regularly dined in 1823,[27] the Trois Frères Provençaux, Véry's, and Véfour's—all in the Palais Royal—and the Café Anglais in the boulevard des Italiens to the vast establishments where one dined for two francs or under suggests both the extent of the moderately well-to-do population and the success with which its desires were catered to.[28] How well an English tourist of modest means could take advantage of such circumstances is indicated by the account of "D.W.R." of his stay in Paris in the summer of 1855. A *maison meublée* in the rue Neuve Saint-Augustin, near the rue de la Paix, provided a bed-sitting room for 3 francs a day. (At 25 francs to the pound, that would make the rent roughly 2s. 6d.; the 2-franc fixed-price dinner would be a mere 1s. 8d., cheap even by Victorian standards.)

> During my stay I dined usually at one restaurant, "Courrieux, au Grand Gastronome," in the Passage Choiseul [running south from the rue Neuve Saint-Augustin and paralleling the rue Sainte-Anne] (where a very good dinner is given for 1 franc 60 centimes, plus 2 sous to the *garçon*), and seldom before seven or eight o'clock, when my day's work or pleasure was over. I breakfasted where I happened to be at ten o'clock—sometimes cheaply, but oftener the reverse; and I found these two meals sufficient except as regards thirst; but cool beverages are plentiful in Paris, and I was not too proud to step into a wine-shop, and get two sous of wine, which, mixed with a demi-siphon of eau de Selz, is a most refreshing drink.[29]

In 1864 meals at first-class fixed-price restaurants could be had at between three and four francs. Second-class establishments charged between 2 fr. and 2 fr. 50 c. "One generally prefers those of the Palais Royal, the passage de l'Opéra, and the passage Jouffroy." The outstanding à la carte restaurants were still the Trois Frères Provençaux and the Café Anglais. At either one could "dine as a gourmet . . . on succulent dishes with exquisite wines. . . . But one can hardly dine there at less than 25 fr."[30] In 1870 Adolphe Joanne added the café Riche in the boulevard des Italiens to the "restaurants of exceptional quality, those which one does not enter except with the intention of dining *seriously,* without worrying about the amount of the bill."[31]

At the other extreme was the chain of "*Restaurants Duval,* which are admirably managed and very moderate in price. These establishments are scattered all over the town, and a list of them is found on the card . . . on which the waitress (dressed in a costume) marks articles as they are ordered."[32] Rowland Strong thought they gave good value for money; he especially commended their beefsteaks. "The prices at Duval's vary slightly . . . according to the quarter in which they are situated. The white-capped hospital nurses who serve you are alike in each of them." They were "only useful for the simplest form of luncheon or dinner. But there are people, from the provinces mostly, and sometimes parents who are giving a treat to their children home from school, who order quite long banquets." G. W. Steevens was less indulgent. "This is the ABC shop of France. . . . The food is not nice, and it is not filling at the price. But the Parisian eats of it with joy and saves his sou."[33]

Every generation was convinced that the quality of cookery was on the decline. "The Art of Cookery is slowly but surely deteriorating and degenerating," wrote George Augustus Sala in 1878. "It is every day becoming more difficult to secure the services of really accomplished cooks, for the reason that first-rate *chefs* can always command much larger salaries in London, in Berlin, in Vienna, in St. Petersburg, in

New York, and in San Francisco, than they can obtain in Paris." Yet Rowland Strong, twenty years later, looked back to the seventies as a gastronomic golden age. "For a decade at least, Paris, as a dining centre, has been on the decline. . . . The old classical traditions of cooking . . . have been gradually giving way before a modern impressionism, in which are reflected the more bustling manners of the present generation, its yearning for intense and rapid emotions."[34]

The quality of its meals, the splendor of its decorations, and the cheapness of its accommodations cannot in themselves account for the hordes of Easter visitors or the seeming "law of nature that he who finds himself with money should go to Paris to spend it."[35] It was not so much all the good things that Paris contained as what Paris was. "From the moment he sets foot in Paris the stranger knows that he is among an artistic, elegant, affable, polite, obliging people, who bring sensibility and taste to all things," wrote J. Amero in *L'Illustration* for 1861. "Arriving in London, he feels himself in a large warehouse of coffee, sugar, tea, cinnamon bark and ginger."[36] Of course this was nonsense, just as the English view of Paris as a sinkhole of impiety, frivolity, and vice was nonsense. Yet it suggests a more fundamental truth: that it was the manners and customs of the Parisians themselves that endowed the city with its peculiar charms. Certainly watching Parisians as they use and enjoy Paris is one of the great delights of being there.

"To a foreigner," wrote Augustus Hare, "half an hour spent on the boulevards or on one of the chairs in the Tuileries gardens has the effect of an infinitely diverting theatrical performance." For Amédée de Cesena, Paris was "perpetually animated by the continual movement of a population of promenaders and idlers who have the air of being continually on holiday." One reason Paris was "so much more amusing to a looker-on than London," thought Mrs. Trollope, "is, that it contains so many more people, in proportion to its population, who have nothing in the world to do but to divert themselves and others."[37] There is little reason to believe that Paris had a class of *rentiers* larger than London's, but, despite the loungers of Bond Street and Pall Mall, the leisure class in London spent more of its leisure out of public view.

What made Paris special, thought Amédée de Cesena, was its *exterior* quality, caused by "the tastes and ideas of a society . . . predisposed to live much more out of doors than indoors, and to display itself as often as possible in public promenades, in the *salons,* at the theater."[38] If cramped living quarters helped to push Parisians into public places, the city was wonderfully well equipped with institutions to render unnecessary the elaborate domestic machinery required for genteel existence in London. "We of England and America," observed Henry T. Tuckerman, "instinctively revolve about a permanent centre, hallowed and held by the triple bond of habit, love, and religion." Not so the Parisians:

> Imagine . . . we dwelt in a kind of metropolitan encampment, requiring no domicile except a bedroom for seven hours in the twenty-four, and passing the remainder of each day and night as nomadic cosmopolites: going to a café to breakfast, a restaurant to dine, an estaminet to smoke, a national library to study, a *cabinet de lecture* to read the gazettes, a public bath for ablution, . . . a thronged garden to promenade, a theatre to be amused, a museum for science, a royal gallery for art, a municipal ball, literary soirée, or suburban rendezvous, for society.[39]

On Sundays the activity outdoors and in public places of amusement was at its most intense, a fact that either scandalized or enchanted English visitors. "The decent classes among us are quiet people, with comfortable homes, from which we rarely stir on the Sabbath," wrote George Augustus Sala; "whereas the Parisians, in a vast number of cases, have no homes at all that can be called comfortable, and are an excessively noisy, restless, and inconsequential race, who can only find happiness out of doors."[40]

It is a commentary on English popular behavior in the late Georgian and Victorian period that nothing impressed English visitors to Paris more than the decorum and good humor with which all classes of society behaved in public places. "At your theatrical performances of all sorts . . . not a word escapes the lips of the giddiest or most ignorant of the audience; and every body seems to listen with equal attention," wrote Sir Charles Darnley in 1823. "At your public libraries and subscription reading-rooms, the same decorum is observed."[41] Mrs. Trollope was amazed at the good manners of the patrons of restaurants, and thought, "what din, what unsocial, yet vehement clattering would inevitably ensue!" if similar establishments were to appear in London. But in Paris everything was "perfectly respectable and well arranged": "during this hour of rest and enjoyment all differences seem forgotten; and however discordant may be their feelings, two Frenchmen cannot be seated near each other at table without exchanging numberless civilities."[42]

From the context of both quotations, it would appear that a degree of roughness and crudity in public manners was taken for granted in London not only among the lower orders, but among the middle and upper classes as well. The superficial elegance of Regency and late Georgian England ought not to mislead us into thinking that the age of Squire Western and Captain Mirvan was over or that the exquisite manners of the Dandy were other than exceptional. The general testimony was that *all* classes of Frenchmen behaved better than their English counterparts.

Yet it was the fact that roughly the *same* standards of public behavior could be expected from all classes that impressed English visitors the most. "In France, a politeness of manner, together with an equality of classes, exists, of which many of the results upon the *ouvriers* and lower orders of the *bourgeoisie* claim the notice of those Englishmen who desire to promote kindly relations between the several orders in their own country," observed the *Builder* in 1861. "Certain forms and expressions of politeness which the Englishman either neglects to his 'inferiors,' or can observe only at his disadvantage, are common to and amongst all persons in France."[43]

Perhaps in no way did and do Parisians show their good breeding more heroically than in their manner of dealing with boorish English and American visitors. "The manner of visiting the French capital . . . by the large majority of our countrymen, simply fills us with shame," exclaimed the *Builder* in 1864. "Their demeanour in the streets of Paris is often not what a good patriot should desire."[44] How the myth of French rudeness to foreigners ever established itself is a minor mystery, and how anyone who had spent as much as a day in New York City could find anything to complain of in the surliest Parisian is a greater one.

Evidence of the different relationships between classes in England and France can be found in the reports of artisans sent by the Society of Arts to the Paris Universal Exhibition of 1867. A cabinetmaker among the group observed that "in Paris the man in his blouse could sit and enjoy the society of the upper class in a grand *café;* but he is not at all surprised that it is not so in England, because there are people in his own trade with whom he finds it impossible to associate out of the shop; how much more were they separated from the educated and refined."[45]

Theodore Zeldin reports on a survey made in the 1960s among French workers, in which no more than 21 percent expressed an interest in a specifically working-class culture. Seventy percent thought that *culture* meant *communication*. "They welcomed education as an escape from their isolation, to help them achieve dignity."[46] Despite its inadequacies, the universal state educational system that France (and Austria) were achieving in the course of the nineteenth century made communication between individuals and between classes easier than it was (or is) in England. Similarly migration to Paris seems to have been more of a civilizing (or "socializing") experience than migration to London. Whatever the desires of the Victorian middle classes to impose their standards of behavior on the working classes, they didn't succeed. The aim of the French Revolution to create a single nation came closer to fulfillment.

Paris, particularly as remade in the Second Empire, played a role in the process. It was not so much the way Haussmann's improvements broke up existing working-class *quartiers,* for they left most of them nearly intact. It was rather the way they provided a concrete focus for civic and national pride, and the extent to which they gave Paris places where all classes could congregate for pleasure, most notably in the modern *street.*

The Paris street as we know, use, and enjoy it today is a creation of the Second Empire. When the Marquis de Vermont pictured the English gentleman enjoying himself he made him stroll down Bond Street, along Piccadilly, and on to Pall Mall through St. James's Street: eminently urban streets in the heart of the West End. When Sir Charles Darnley sought to portray a Parisian equivalent he chose the Tuileries Gardens, the Palais Royal, and the Champs-Elysées: either protected environments within Paris or a semirural promenade without. The reason is self-evident: since the Westminster Paving Act of 1751 and with the subsequent multiplication of local improvement authorities, it had been possible to walk through the West End for pleasure; until the great sanitary operations of the nineteenth century, the ordinary Paris street was something to be avoided (figs. 96 and 97).

Nothing impressed Louis-Sébastien Mercier more about London in the 1780s than its foot pavements. London was surrounded by roads, "very neatly maintained, with sidewalks; so that from everywhere one leaves the City, without the impediment of mud, as in the suburbs, barriers, and villages of Paris." He thought the great fault of Paris its narrow streets, in which, due to the absence of protected footways, "every day people perished. . . . Enlarge the streets at whatever price, or London will always make Paris feel ashamed."[47]

From the 1860s to our own day Paris has used the street to blur the distinctions between indoors and out. From the dispenser of fresh shellfish outside restaurants to the pavement stalls which the *grands magasins* themselves set up outside their establishments, French life overflows the confines of mere buildings and comes out to mingle with the life of the streets (fig. 98). Yet until Haussmann set to work on them, the sheer foulness of the Paris street made such blurring, such mingling unthinkable.

"Every day brings . . . fresh conviction that a very considerable portion of the enjoyment of life is altogether destroyed in Paris by the neglect or omission of such a degree of municipal interference as might secure the most elegant people in the

220

96. *Since the Westminster Paving Act of 1751 it had been possible to walk through the West End for pleasure.* Suffolk Street, 1824. G. Scharf. (British Museum.)

97. *(opposite, above) Until the great sanitary operations of the nineteenth century, the ordinary Paris street was something to be avoided.* Le désagrément d'aller à pied. (Musée Carnavalet.)

98. *(opposite, below) French life overflows the confines of mere buildings and comes out to mingle with the life of the streets.* Carrefour de Buci, 1984. (Evelyn Benesch.)

world from the loathsome disgust occasioned by the perpetual outrage of common decency in their streets," exclaimed Mrs. Trollope in 1835.[48] Sir Francis Head, returning to Paris in 1851 for his first visit in nearly forty years, recalled the streets of the Restoration city. The "rude ill-constructed pavement of round stones for carriages, horses, and foot-passengers" had running down its center "a dirty gutter, which, in heavy rain, looked like a little trout stream". By night the streets were

lighted, inadequately, by a "picturesque line of large, frail, creaky, cranky, crazy-looking lanterns . . . suspended over the middle of every street."[49] Mrs. Trollope complained of the "profound darkness of every part of the city in which there are not shops illuminated by the owners of them with gas."[50]

An examination of photographs taken of the streets of *Vieux Paris* during the 1850s confirms the impression of contemporary visitors that, however picturesque and rich with historical associations, they must have done more to disgust than to charm (fig. 99). The slimy paving stones, bespattered with filth, the leprous walls of the houses, the darkness—for the sun can rarely have penetrated such narrow confines—would have repelled any pedestrian whose sensibilities had not been

99. *The streets of* Vieux Paris *during the 1850s must have done more to disgust than to charm.* Marville, rue Bernard de Palissy, sixth arrondissement. (Musée Carnavalet. Photo Lauros-Giraudon.)

100. *When the well-to-do of London made their move to the West End, they saw to it that their new quarters were supplied with broad, well-drained streets, with pavements reserved for pedestrians, and with spacious, landscaped squares.* Bloomsbury Square, June 1828, showing devices for watering and sweeping the carriage way. G. Scharf. (British Museum.)

deadened by familiarity. We today in an immensely richer, incomparably cleaner Paris delight in perambulating similar narrow passages in the inner arrondissements. But it would be a mistake to assume that an exploration of the same streets in the 1840s would have provided comparable satisfactions. Just as Macaulay contrasted the pleasures of an early Victorian jaunt to the Lake District or the Highlands of Scotland with the fear and horror evoked by travel through the same districts in 1685, we may be grateful that we can enjoy Paris after Haussmann's cleansing operations.

"For people accustomed to the splendors of life, is there indeed anything more ignoble than the tumult, the mud, the cries, the bad odor, the narrowness of populous streets?" asked Balzac in 1834.[51] The eagerness with which those who could afford it moved out of central Paris, first to the Marais and the Ile Saint-Louis, then to the faubourgs Saint-Germain and Saint-Honoré, suggests that even in the seventeenth century, *Vieux Paris* had few charms. When the well-to-do of London made their contemporary move to the West End, they saw to it that their new quarters were supplied with broad, well-drained streets, with pavements reserved for pedestrians, and with spacious, landscaped squares (fig. 100). In Paris, however magnificent the *hôtels* that went up in the new districts, less was done to create a pleasant *total* environment. From the narrow streets of the Marais and faubourg Saint-Germain one sees a mixture of great houses and small: the great ones lie hidden behind plain stone walls, with only a soberly ornamented *porte cochère* to suggest the splendors across the courtyard (fig. 101). The *hôtels*, with their private

223

101. *Plain stone walls, with only a soberly ornamented* porte cochère *to suggest the splendors across the courtyard.* Rue de Babylone, 1984. (Evelyn Benesch.)

pleasure grounds, deliberately turned their backs on the street. The streets themselves remained without attractions: stinking, dirty, narrow, plain, dangerous. One arranged to move from one protected enclosure to another: the *porte cochère* permitted one to be safely inside the carriage or sedan chair before emerging into the street, and not to have to descend until it passed through another *porte cochère* into the courtyard of another *hôtel.* One could and did live pleasantly in eighteenth-century Paris, but only by insulating oneself from the city itself, above all from its streets.

Of course the vast majority of Parisians—not just the working classes but most of the *bourgeoisie*—were in no position to create special protected environments for themselves. What happened in the nineteenth century, and was already beginning to happen by the 1830s, was the contrivance by the moderately well-to-do of an urban style of living that gave them some of the satisfactions that only the extremely rich had enjoyed before 1789. The new blocks of flats with their marble chimneypieces and mirrors, their rich carpets and cleverly arranged *dégagements* gave their private lives a degree of comfort. Outside, the street was turned from a passage of horrors into an attraction in itself, contributing to the pleasantness of life. Eighteenth-century Paris had *contained* pleasures, contained them in profusion; by the 1850s Paris was beginning to embody pleasure, making public and generally available what had before been the privileges of the few. London, too, was in the same period engaging in the democratization of aristocratic pleasures, but the contrast was less sharp: pleasure in eighteenth-century London had been less exclusive than in Paris, while it became less universally accessible in the nineteenth.

The introduction of the raised foot-pavement was already making life safer for the pedestrian in the 1830s. First installed in the rue de l'Odéon in 1781,[52] they were still rare in the 1820s, "when one had to hop from stone to stone in the fond hope of escaping wet shoes" and was tormented too "with the terror of being run over by carts, fiacres, concous, cabs, and wheelbarrows." By 1835 Mrs. Trollope felt inclined to "bless with an humble and grateful spirit the dear little pavement

Plate 1. *(above)* Westbourne Terrace, Hyde Park. Lithograph by G. Hawkins after J. Johnston, c. 1850–55. (Museum of London.)

Overleafs

Plate 2. Cheapside looking west, Mansion House to left. T. Shotter Boys. (Guildhall Library, City of London—Bridgeman Art Library.)

Plate 3. Kohlmarkt, 1900. Watercolor by Richard Moser. (Museen der Stadt Wien.)

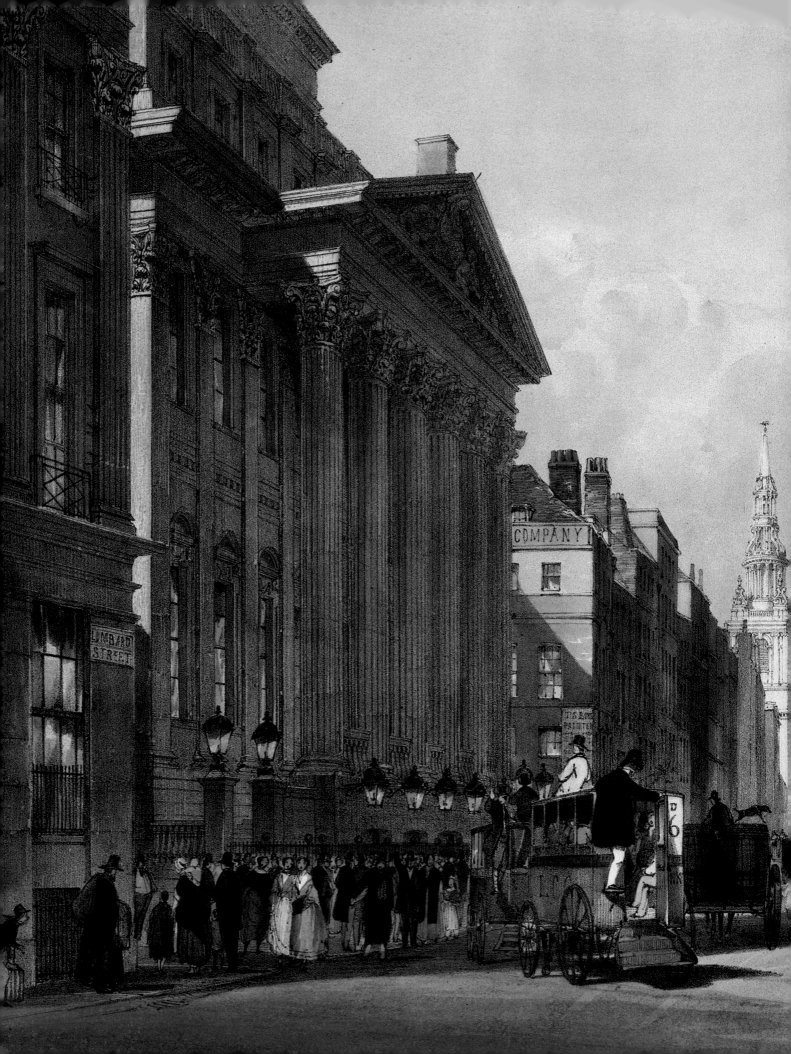

WIEN I.
"KOHLMARKT"

RICHARD MOSS
1900.

which . . . borders most of the principal streets of Paris now." Admittedly they were narrower than the "enormous esplanades on each side" of Regent and Oxford streets, but she was confident that "in a few years . . . it will be almost as easy to walk in Paris as in London."[53]

But even with the *trottoirs* and the gas lamps that now projected, at some distance from one another, from the walls of the houses, few of the streets of pre-Haussmann Paris could have been attractive to the genteel pedestrian.[54] Before 1789 one could have walked for pleasure only in the private gardens many landowners made available to the public, in the royal promenades such as the Tuileries and Luxembourg Gardens and Champs-Elysées, and along the *grands boulevards*. The gravel walks of Parisian parks, so unsatisfying to the Londoner accustomed to the freedom of the grassy lawns of his parks, would, by their dryness and cleanliness, have been delightful alternatives to the slimy stones of the streets.

The closing years of the eighteenth century produced, in Paris, a new building type—the shopping arcade—to supplement the parks and gardens as agreeable promenades for the idle bourgeoisie. Glazed roofs provided light by day, and gaslights gave illumination by night. They could be kept clean and safe from the intrusion of both wheeled traffic and the rabble and were in every respect a vast improvement on the open street. Richard's guidebook states that 137 such "protected ways" (*chemins abrités*) existed by 1828, citing for richness and magnificence the passages Vivienne, Colbert, de l'Opéra, Choiseul, and Véro-Dodat. "In bad weather they serve, like the Palais Royal, as promenades and places of rendez-vous"[55] (fig. 102).

The most complex, ambitious, and successful enclosed environment in early nineteenth-century Paris was the Palais Royal. Built for Cardinal Richelieu, it became the property of the duc d'Orléans in 1672. In the 1780s the then-duke, Philippe-Egalité, had the courtyard and its surrounding galleries developed for commercial purposes. It immediately became the concentration of fashion and intellect, the *centre du plaisir* that the western boulevards were to be a century later. In 1823 Sir Charles Darnley found there a "gay crowd formed of persons presenting the utmost diversity of character." Frenchmen of all sorts mingled with foreign tourists, "who come hither to stare at the articles displayed in the many-coloured shops,—to eat ice—dine—drink coffee—to be cheated in purchasing clothes, books, or trinkets—to lose their money at the gaming-tables, or their health at some of the various temples of vice which abound in these purlieus."[56] "All the world . . . is taken to look at the Palais Royal," Mrs. Trollope reported the next decade, with "its restaurans [*sic*], its trinket-shops, riband-shops, toy-shops . . . and all the world of misery, mischief, and good cheer which rises *étage* after *étage* above them"[57] (fig. 103).

Outside such enclosed environments the streets themselves were shunned by aristocracy and bourgeoisie alike. Jeanne Gaillard finds in the novels of Balzac a world in which the bourgeoisie has abandoned the street to the populace and shuts itself into its shops and dwellings.[58] Certainly snobbery and a desire to maintain a physical distance from socially inferior groups played a role in the bourgeois preference for "enclosed urban structures," but the sheer unpleasantness of the street played another.

The greater importance of the latter is suggested by the rapidity with which the bourgeoisie abandoned the Palais Royal and the *passages* for the new streets and boulevards of the Haussmann era. Now properly drained, cleaned, and lighted,

102. *(opposite) "In bad weather they serve, like the Palais Royal, as promenades and places of rendez-vous."* Marville, Passage de l'Opera, between 1856 and 1865. (Musée Carnavalet. Photo Lauros-Giraudon.)

103. *(above) "All the world . . . is taken to look at the Palais Royal."* Palais Royal, from court-yard. (Musée Carnavalet.)

such streets would multiply and diversify the hitherto highly restricted possibilities for outdoor pleasures. Paris became and remained an "out-of-doors city" whose boulevards were its sitting rooms.[59] The eagerness with which the Parisian used the facilities for promenading, lounging, and window-shopping offered by the new streets could be accounted for in part by domestic overcrowding, but it also testified to possibilities markedly absent in the older Paris.

By 1878 the elegant throngs had abandoned the Palais Royal. "Fashionable civilisation spreading westward, spreading to innumerable new boulevards, spreading to the Parc Monceaux, overrunning the Champs Elysées, and threatening to overlap the Bois de Boulogne, has contemptuously pronounced the Palais Royal to be situated, as things go, *dans un pays impossible,*" according to George Augustus Sala. "The great restaurateurs, Véfour excepted, have deserted the arcades of the Palais Royal for the western boulevards. The cafés are, socially and intellectually, only the shadows of their former selves." By the end of the century Rowland Strong could recommend its restaurants only to "people who do not object to dining in company with ghosts. . . . Personally I would as soon take my meals in the catacombs."[60]

The Palais Royal was not replaced by similar structures but, successively, by various stretches of boulevard and clusters of streets, first on the right bank, then on the left. Such thoroughfares offered the pleasures of movement and variety and the possibility of seeing from, and being seen in, a splendid carriage (fig. 104). The taking over of broad avenues by motorized through traffic has made our century return to the comparative quiet and seclusion of narrower streets for its favored

227

104. *Such thoroughfares offered the pleasures of movement and variety.* Boulevard scene. *Le Figaro Littéraire,* 1888. (Musée Carnavalet.)

promenades. But until the coming of the motor car the triumph of the boulevard seemed inescapable and permanent.

When the *grands boulevards* were laid out in the 1670s and 1680s, they ran mostly through open fields. Only in the eastern stretches did the boulevards du Temple, des Filles-du-Calvaire, and de Beaumarchais skirt an urbanized quarter. Since that quarter was the Marais, those boulevards became the favored resort of its rich and noble inhabitants. Intensive building development along the route of the boulevards did not come until the Revolution, when confiscated lands ·of ecclesiastical and noble owners came onto the market.

By the Restoration the boulevards were acquiring a more urban character. Sir Charles Darnley found a scene of "general gaiety" similar to that at the Palais Royal. "The carriages in the centre are filled with elegant and well-dressed women," he wrote, "and under the shade of lofty trees on each side, numerous parties of merry pedestrians hasten forward, while picturesque groups . . . appear seated on chairs near the *Café Hardi.* . . . Further on, the stalls covered with books, prints, and baubles . . . arrest for a moment the lounger's attention." The whole mixture of "well lighted coffee-houses, . . . shops, hotels, baths, panoramas, theatres, puppet-shows, fountains, and triumphal arches" foreshadowed the exhilarating qualities that would make the new Haussmannian streets such an economic and urbanistic success.[61]

By 1864 the *beau monde* had moved west to the boulevards des Capucines, des Italiens, and Montmartre: "there they display themselves in all their luxury and all their animation," wrote Amédée de Cesena. Especially along the south side of the boulevard des Italiens, "a long open-air room where waves of humanity follow one another, a room that is enlivened in the evening by the resplendent brightness of innumerable jets of gas and by the happy bursts of laughter coming out of . . . restaurants where one sups, cafés where one has ices." Here the spectacle achieved its greatest intensity. "I don't believe that there is in the world a living panorama comparable to that offered by . . . the Paris that begins at the *Café Riche* and ends at the *Café de la Paix*."[62]

For Adolphe Joanne, the popular character of the *grands boulevards* reflected the political and moral nature of France. Just as the public promenades of St. Petersburg, Vienna, and Berlin embodied in their regularity the spirit of absolutism, and those of London the studied elegance of an aristocratic society, the Parisian boulevards represented French egalitarianism. It was the mixture of classes participating in their splendors and pleasures that gave them their special quality, that of a brilliant theater in which all Frenchmen could fraternize[63] (fig. 105).[63]

By 1930 the western boulevards had lost all of their elegance and most of their significance. Paul Cohen-Portheim looked back to their "golden age" under the Second Empire, when they "must have resembled the Ringstrasse in Vienna at the turn of the century." Since those days Paris had turned its attention elsewhere. "The new generation takes its walks in the Avenue du Bois and lives far out. . . . The better sort of foreigner leaves the Boulevards to the . . . provincials of every country and the sellers of indecent postcards. . . . Society . . . by day . . . is to be seen in the west, at night its meeting-place is now Montmartre." The boulevards had adapted themselves to a changed world. "New shop-fronts have sprung up everywhere,"

---

105. *The mixture of classes participating in their splendors and pleasures.* Boulevard du Temple, before Haussmann's alterations. (Musée Carnavalet.)

with "lots of shoe-shops, travel bureaux and men's outfitters catering for a well-to-do but not ultra-smart or discriminating public." There were "masses of cinemas, and an orgy of electric signs." The increased traffic that the motor car had brought insured that they would "never again be a place to lounge about in."[64]

In addition to refurbishing "the" boulevards, Haussmann created wholly new ones and embellished the old *boulevards extérieurs* (figs. 106 and 107). His whole program of *percées* was an attempt to insert the vitality of the *grands boulevards* into decaying and even moribund sections of the older city. That the attempt was neither universally nor uniformly successful is less remarkable than that it had the success it did. Even today, to recapture what the boulevard des Italiens must have been like a century ago, one could do worse than visit the busier stretches of the boulevards Saint-Michel, Saint-Germain, and Montparnasse.

Deserted plazas, shunned pedestrian precincts, and crime-ridden parks throughout America testify to the inability of open spaces in themselves to create urban theater: the stage must somehow attract a cast to perform upon it. The *Building News* predicted a bleak future for Haussmann's improvements:

Let us assume a parallel case: let us . . . fancy a builder . . . cutting a wide street from Whitechapel Church through Bethnal-green, and building shops equal in size and splendour to those of Regent-street, running a belt of similar buildings round our metropolis, and attempting to found a new "Bond-street" between the Mother Red Cap, at Camden Town, and the Swiss Cottage. He might leave an open square here and there, he might put up a fountain, he might put balconies to all the floors, and build the houses of stone, but he could not make the Belgravians drive down there. . . . We know the difficulty of drawing visitors to New Oxford-street; we know that the aristocracy but rarely shop farther eastward than Wells-street or Berners-

106. *In addition to refurbishing "the" boulevards, Haussmann . . . embellished the old* boulevards extérieurs. Marville, boulevard d'Enfer, later boulevard Saint-Jacques. (Musée Carnavalet. Photo Lauros-Giraudon.)

107. Marville, boulevard de l'Hôpital. (Musée Carnavalet. Photo Lauros-Giraudon.)

street, and seeing this . . . we do not anticipate great results from the new streets in Paris.[65]

In fact the new streets in Paris had greater luck in attracting both businesses and customers for such businesses than any one of the successors of Regent Street. "In Paris, if they form a new street in which the ground-floors of the houses are shops . . . they are sure to meet with occupiers," G. Herbert West told the RIBA in 1871.[66] The response of commercial purveyors of popular amusements to the splendid frontages and wide pavements in turn called forth the crowds that gave the whole life and meaning. The congestion in the flats above the shops and in the streets behind the boulevard further encouraged their occupants to leave their cramped homes to join the crowd outside.

Combining the attributes of the street and the park, the boulevards wisely allowed the streetlike qualities to predominate. "The English have invented the *house,* the French have invented the *street,*" wrote Philip Gilbert Hamerton. "The French are the first people who have thoroughly understood the street and realised a conception of it which has become a model of excellence."[67] By adding the commerce and density of the old Paris street to the greenery and spaciousness of the original boulevards, the new boulevard achieved a wholly new urban form: the perfected street, a concrete representation of urbanity itself.

The Champs-Elysées, as reshaped under the Second Empire, was the most spectacular of such creations. "The stranger who enters Paris for the first time by this monumental approach is for the moment stupefied at the aspect of so much magnificence," wrote *L'Illustration* in 1861; "on either side . . . this forest of venerable trees. . . . Ahead the place de la Concorde with its statues, its fountains, its marble horses and its granite needle; to the right, the great Palace of Industry; to the left kiosques, enchanted gardens, charming mansions." The avenue was as significant for being a human spectacle as it was for its horticultural and architectural splendors (fig. 108). Here the *beau monde* came to display itself. "This avenue sees the latest fashion born. . . . It is today what the *Cours-la-Reine* was in the last century."[68]

Yet for all the talk about fashion, the easternmost section of the Champs-Elysées had by the 1870s become "a people's park . . . now the most popular holiday resort of Paris."[69] English visitors were here as elsewhere astonished at the good behavior of the crowds. "There are no railings higher than six inches; and yet no flowers at Kew or the Crystal Palace are more valuable than these suffice to protect day and night," wrote one Englishman. Toward the side of the rue du Faubourg Saint-Honoré could be found "revolving circuses, . . . various kinds of juvenile amusements, cafés, summer music halls, dahlia beds, fountains. . . . On fine days the wide tree-shaded walks are crowded with pedestrians . . . the whole thing is as orderly as could be wished."[70]

Supplementing the new streets and boulevards were *squares*—so called in French—and both relandscaped and totally new parks, also modeled on the English. Like their London namesakes the squares were landscaped enclosures, separated from the surrounding carriage ways by iron railings, but unlike them open to

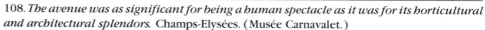

108. *The avenue was as significant for being a human spectacle as it was for its horticultural and architectural splendors.* Champs-Elysées. (Musée Carnavalet.)

109. *"The fine gardens of the past, which were only for the pleasures of a few, are today replaced by . . . elegant squares which everyone can enjoy."* Square of the Arts and Sciences. From *The Builder* 32 (1874): 1049.

the public at large. The transformation of the former royal parks of Boulogne and Vincennes, at the western and eastern extremities of the city, gave Paris its first real *jardins anglais.* With the opening of the boulevard Malesherbes and the development of the present seventeenth as an expensive residential neighborhood, the parc Monceau—originally laid out by the duc d'Orléans in 1778—was reduced in size and relandscaped to enhance the attractiveness and value of the surrounding dwellings. In the northeastern outskirts a former quarry was converted into the parc des Buttes Chaumont, which had more in common with the Chinese gardens described by Sir William Chambers that were designed to provoke emotions of astonishment and terror than with the placid landscapes of London parks.

"Paris has been developing into Arcadia, and has left us far behind," admitted the *Builder* in 1869.[71] It would become "the meeting place for literary, artistic, and elegant Europe, a focus of attraction, of seduction for the whole world," exulted César Daly. He contrasted the new parks and promenades with the private gardens of the ancien régime: "the fine gardens of the past, which were only for the pleasure of a few, are today replaced by magnificent parks and elegant squares which everyone can enjoy"[72] (fig. 109).

Social distinctions in the use of such attractions inevitably established themselves. The bois de Boulogne became the preserve of fashion, the parc Monceau of middle-class respectability, while the Buttes Chaumont and the bois de Vincennes were left to the common people. On weekdays, "by some curious tacit agreement among the classes," the Champs-Elysées were "the playground of the rich. On Sundays the mob comes."[73] Even the boulevard cafés, often cited as triumphs of "modern democracy," where "a simple workman, for his thirty centimes, while having his coffee, is reflected in mirrors that Louis XIV would not have been able to procure,"[74] practiced informal but effective segregation. The Maison Dorée offered its fashionable customers special rooms facing the side streets so that they wouldn't have to mix with people who wandered in from the boulevard.[75] Yet the myth of equality was a powerful one, and the English were surely right to view Paris as a more public city, more welcoming to the stranger, less obsessed with class, than their own capital.

14

Vienna: Display and Self-Representation

nlike Paris and London, Vienna was very much off the regular tourist circuit in the nineteenth century. A general European guidebook published in 1843, which listed 200 hotels in London, could find in Vienna only two hotels strictly speaking—the Erzherzog Karl and the Kaiserin von Oesterreich—and five *Gast-höfe*.[1] Though the third largest city in Europe, the capital of a major empire and great power, it lay too far east of the major line of tourist traffic up the Rhine through Switzerland into Italy to be visited by any but the most adventurous foreigner.

The most likely occasion for a visit from our imaginary tourist would have been the World's Fair of 1873. By that time the Ringstrasse had taken shape and Vienna could pride itself on presenting the face of an up-to-date world metropolis. The Orient Express still lay ten years in the future, but the Compagnie Internationale de Wagons-Lits (not the present concern) already provided a sleeping car service from Paris, so the trip could be made in some comfort. Arriving at the Westbahnhof, our tourist from London or Paris would, then as now, be able to take a tram directly to the Ring by way of the Mariahilferstrasse. Beginning in 1865 a growing network of lines radiated outward to serve both inner and outer suburbs. Although they did not enjoy today's reserved track in the Ringstrasse, the roadway was more than ample to accommodate the trams as they made their dignified way around the new boulevard.[2] Or the visitor could avail himself of a speedy two-horse cab, whose curtained and mirrored interior an admiring Frenchman compared to a small drawing room, lacking nothing but a washbasin and a clock. He was less taken with Viennese buses. Divided into smoking and nonsmoking compartments on the same level, they were "horrible, bulging, dirty, [and] damp."[3]

Once he had been deposited at his Ringstrasse or City hotel, the tourist would need to use buses and trams only for excursions to Schönbrunn or Grinzing and cabs only for occasions of state. Practically every tourist attraction would be within easy walking distance; business and pleasure for the well-to-do resident were similarly concentrated in the old City and the Ring. Lacking the vastness of London and the filth of Paris, Vienna was, as it still is, a pedestrian's city. Even the Stadtbahn of the 1890s and the U-Bahn of the 1970s, the latter especially, seem more matters of prestige than necessity. Line no. 1 of the Underground manages to get from one terminus close to the edge of the built-up area on one side of Vienna to the other at a new suburban development on the opposite edge in a mere eighteen minutes.

In 1873 the tourist would never have heard of Kagran and feel no inclination to visit Favoriten. Once he had inspected the exhibits at the *Weltaustellung* in the Prater, he would find ample amusement in Ring and City. To be sure, with the exception of the Opera House, the major public buildings of the Ringstrasse were as yet uncompleted, but the Ring had already become a street of palaces. He would have had no problem finding suitable accommodation for himself, because a number of world-class luxury hotels had just opened in time to greet the visitors to the exhibition.

A quarter-century earlier Ludwig von Förster and Theophil Hansen had designed the 300-room National Hotel in the Taborstrasse in the inner suburb of Leopold-stadt. Eight furnaces and a steam engine produced heat, brought spring water to all floors, and performed useful functions in kitchen and laundry. An underground icehouse provided refrigeration and cool drinks.[4] An English visitor, shortly after the Revolution of 1848, was not impressed. "Imagine a building four or five stories high, with a frontage of ten or fifteen, nay, twenty and forty windows,—as, for instance, the great National Inn, in the Leopoldstadt." Even for a hotel, he thought the vast size "fraught with much inconvenience."[5]

What became in 1871 the Grand Hotel, at Kärntner Ring 9, was originally de-signed, by Karl Tietz, as a block of flats, although with ultimate conversion to a hotel in mind. The *Allgemeine Bauzeitung* thought it met all the requirements of a "first-class hotel of a world metropolis." Its decorations and facilities "stood, in a word, at the height of the age."[6] The 1873 exhibition called forth the erection of three major hotels: the Britannia in Schillerplatz, the Austria in the Schottenring, and the Metro-pole at Franz Josefs-Kai. The first two proved commercial failures, the Britannia being taken over by the Ministry of Justice, and the Austria converted to police head-quarters. Another hotel built for the exhibition, the Donau, facing the Nordbahnhof, was converted into flats. Only the Metropole survived, to end its life in ignominy during the Second World War as the local headquarters of the Gestapo.[7]

The stock market crash of 1873 and the subsequent weakening of the Viennese economy contributed to the failure of such luxury hotels, as did the competition provided by the Imperial, converted from the palace of the duke of Württemberg, across the Kärntner Ring from the Grand, and described in 1877 as "now the favourite hostelry of crowned heads, their heirs-apparent, and ambassadors"[8] (figs. 110 and 111).

Our visitor would therefore have had a wider choice of luxury accommodation in 1873 than he would have had at most times before or since. He would have been able to catch glimpses of the Austrian aristocracy without leaving his hotel: if the new hotels of London and Paris were left to the middle classes and to foreign tourists, the luxury establishments of the Ringstrasse were used by the local aristoc-racy for social occasions.[9] Stepping out of the Grand or the Imperial between three and five any afternoon, he would find himself in the midst of the Ringstrasse Corso, in which "every branch of society, from the great world, to the *demi-monde,* to the

110. *The Imperial "now the favourite hostelry of crowned heads, their heirs-apparent, and ambassadors."* Hotel Imperial, grand staircase from the mezzanine. (Kunsthistorisches Institut der Universität Wien. Photo Johanna Fiegl.)

111. Entrance to the Palais Württemberg shortly before it became the Hotel Imperial. (Kunsthistorisches Institut der Universität Wien.)

'quarter world,' as well as the world of diplomacy and the court," could be observed promenading between the Schwarzenbergplatz and the corner of the Kärntner Strasse.[10]

A color lithograph of 1908 purports to show the actual Corso, with all the famous people identified. Princes and princesses, counts and countesses mingle with professors from the university, singers from the opera, journalists, and figures from the world of high finance. The man with the low, artistic-looking hat, toward the right in the front row, is Gustav Mahler, director of the Court Opera. Toward the rear, just to the right of the motor car, with a white beard, is *Oberbaurat* Otto Wagner. There are, to be sure, a great many people *we* would like to see included who are absent: Freud, Schnitzler, Klimt, Hofmannsthal. But the symbolic significance of both the lithograph and the street scene it represented is immense. The Ringstrasse provided the stage for the intellectual and artistic achievements that made Vienna, in the years just before 1914, our century's nearest approach to the Athens of Pericles or the Florence of the Medici (fig. 112, colorplate 8).

Vienna, with its harsh winters, could not indulge the year round in outdoor life as much as Paris. Nor, apart from the Ringstrasse, did it have the profusion of broad avenues suitable for conspicuous promenading. The proportion of its population able to devote its time to public idleness was smaller. A French visitor in 1899 reported little movement in the streets apart from morning and evening, when shops and offices opened and closed.[11] Yet for all the obstacles which its climate and street plan posed, Vienna placed greater stress on public life than Paris, im-

112. *A color lithograph of 1908 purports to show the actual Corso.* Ringstrasse Corso. Water color by Theo Zasche. From Reinhard E. Petermann, *Wien im Zeitalter Kaiser Franz Josephs I* (Vienna, 1908). (Kunsthistorisches Institut der Universität Wien.) See also colorplate 8.

mensely more than London. In part this was a consequence of its position as Residenzstadt, the seat of the imperial and royal court, with all the associated circles of officialdom and aristocracy.

City, which in a London context connotes philistinism, crass vulgarity, and single-minded devotion to the pursuit of wealth, to the Viennese ear has overtones of elegance, refinement, and luxury. So far *City* to a Viennese would be roughly equivalent to *West End* or *Mayfair* to a Londoner. But the Schwarzenbergplatz is not Grosvenor Square, the Herrengasse not Park Lane, and the manners and values of those who lived in the one differed profoundly from those who lived in the other.

The triumph of Habsburg absolutism not only deprived the old Viennese *Bür-gertum* of its independence but took from the old feudal aristocracy its political functions. It could justify its wealth and privileges not on the basis of services it performed for society—as the English aristocracy could—but on the basis of the splendor and conspicuousness with which it lived. To maintain a position based on symbolic rather than functional grounds, it was necessary to invest every aspect of behavior with high ceremonial content. The consequences were awesome: the permanent "self-representation" demanded a formalized manner of moving, speaking, and dressing. The style of living of the nobility had to be appropriate not only to its own social standing but to the absolutist regime itself.[12]

The regime was no longer an absolute monarchy when the Ringstrasse was laid out, but the aristocracy of the later period felt equally constrained to live in a punctilious, splendid, and public fashion. Since no two members of that aristocracy were precisely equal, it was as important to establish and maintain one's position in the social hierarchy as it had been in the Versailles of the duc de Saint-Simon. The building forms of City and Ringstrasse palaces served that end, as did an ostentatious and formalized manner of living by those who lived in them.[13]

It is the necessity for *Selbstdarstellung,* the presentation of oneself, the acting of a role, that most sharply differentiates the Austrian aristocrat in Vienna from the English aristocrat in London. This is not to say that the English upper classes ignored questions of precedence, proper form, and the need to look the part. One wore ceremonial robes at coronations and the opening of parliament, one appeared in Rotten Row at the appropriate hour, one cultivated habits of speech and behavior to distinguish oneself from the rank just beneath. But it was on the whole easier to take one's social position for granted in England than in Austria, to indulge in eccentricities, to be careless or even slovenly in dress, without jeopardizing one's position in society.

This was true not just for individuals but for the upper classes as a whole. For the English aristocracy was, and was seen to be, a *working* aristocracy, performing political and administrative functions as ministers of state, members of parliament, justices of the peace, ambassadors, civil servants, administrators of vast agricultural and urban estates. They were essentially useful and only accidentally ornamental. With some reason, they felt secure in their position. By contrast, it is not only in hindsight that the precariousness of the whole Dual Monarchy, the anachronistic and top-heavy apparatus of privilege and inequality that characterized it, and its vulnerability to demands for national independence, democratic self-rule, and social justice are apparent. Just as Franz Joseph himself suppressed his personal preference for a life of modest withdrawal in order to perform the ceremonial functions deemed necessary to the survival of the empire, so his courtiers, civil

Plate 4. Grabengasse. Aquatint by Erwin Pendl. (Museen der Stadt Wien.)

Plate 5. *(above)* Morning Room, Army and Navy Club (Guildhall Library, City of London—Bridgeman Art Library.)

Plate 6. *(opposite, top)* Grand Café du XIX^c Siècle, boulevard de Strasbourg, 1861. (Musée Carnavalet.)

Plate 7. *(opposite, bottom)* Le grand salon de Frascati. (Musée Carnavalet.)

Plate 8. Ringstrasse Corso, c. 1908. Watercolor by Theo Zasche. (From Reinhard E. Petermann, *Wien im Zeitalter Kaiser Franz Josephs I,* Vienna, 1908.)

servants, and aristocracy sacrificed whatever yearnings they may have felt for a life of private domesticity to the needs of state and society.

Appearance along the "town-side" of the Kärntner Ring between three and five in the afternoon, to display oneself, see and be seen, acknowledge and be acknowledged, was one such duty, to oneself, one's class, and one's sovereign[14] (fig. 113). The Corso was by no means composed exclusively of the high nobility. The *demi-monde,* the substantial bourgeoisie, and upper bohemia were there as well, observing and mimicking the display and rituals of their social superiors. On Sunday afternoons the middle classes took over the Ringstrasse. Today court and aristocracy have vanished, the Corso has democratized itself and moved from the Kärntner Ring to the Kärntner Strasse, but the stress on *Höflichkeit* and correct behavior persists in all levels of Viennese society. From the courtly fashion in which the shopkeeper greets his customers to the way the coffee-house waiter, formally attired, bears on a tray the cup of coffee and the glass of water with the spoon carefully balanced on top, life in Vienna to this day reflects the spirit of the manners of its once-ruling class.

For the great majority of Viennese its public places—the parks and promenades, cafés and *Keller*—were more than additional places to display their finery, meet their friends, and fill vacant hours. Given the conditions of domestic overcrowding

113. *Appearance along the "town-side" of the Kärtner Ring to display oneself, see and be seen, acknowledge and be acknowledged, was one such duty.* Polite encounters at the Sirk-Ecke, looking toward Opernring. *Neue Illustrierte Zeitung,* 1873. (Museen der Stadt Wien.)

of all but the upper reaches of society, they were the necessary extensions of, or substitutes for, the home (fig. 114). "The café and the *brasserie* are for the inhabitant of Vienna a second home [*chez soi*] . . . the regular customer [*Stammgast*] ordinarily spends three or four hours a day at the *brasserie,* the wine shop, or the café," reported Victor Tissot (fig. 115). The number and luxury of the cafés astonished even a French observer. Everyone went: men, women, priests, children. At four in the afternoon it was hard to find a seat. The quality of service was already legendary.

114. *They were the necessary extensions of, or substitutes for, the home.* Interior of Café Griensteidl. (Bundesdenkmalamt Wien.)

115. *The café and the* brasserie *are for the inhabitant of Vienna a second home.* Café Griensteidl. Aquatint by R. Völkel. (Museen der Stadt Wien.)

"The Viennese waiter is the king of *garçons de café*. . . . He is exported throughout Germany, where he is sought for his promptitude, his politeness, his good humor, his honesty."[15] The *Builder* was "lost in wonder at the skill and the costliness and the labour involved in . . . these very necessary places of public amusement."[16]

The Ringstrasse cafés were as important monuments of Viennese culture as the museums and theaters and educational establishments. No longer the centers of ideological discussion they had been before 1848, cafés acquired social rather than political functions. The "family café" became an important type in the 1870s, and special features were added to attract ladies.[17] The great decrease in the number of cafés in Vienna, first in the interwar period and continuing since the last war, gives retrospective confirmation to the interpretation that they served to make up for inadequate housing. Their decline exactly paralleled the rising standards of spaciousness and comfort of the ordinary Viennese dwelling.[18]

Karoline Pichler devoted a scene in her *Zeitbilder* to an encounter between two young gentlemen at an outdoor café in the Volksgarten one summer evening in the 1830s. One has returned from several years of travel in the East, the other has just arrived from dinner at the Erzherzog Karl in the Kärntner Strasse. "But so late? It is past seven?" queried the first. "Quite right. We sat down at the table at half-past-five," explained the other, proud of the sophisticated lateness of his mealtimes. The first remained astonished at such advanced customs. The second assured him that Vienna had changed unbelievably in his absence. "But it was certainly necessary.

Mein Gott! We used to be pitifully behind Paris in these respects! Only think how our restaurants, our coffee houses looked, if you compared them with those in Paris."[19] Fifty years later Victor Tissot judged Vienna to be, after Paris—a long way, to be sure—the city where one fared best as to food. The best restaurants were in the hotels. Sacher's came closest in quality to the great Parisian restaurants. At a lower level were the *brasseries* where for 2 fr. 50 c.—roughly two shillings—the Viennese dined on "a plate of meat, a vegetable, and a pudding." The last constituted, as it still does, "the great triumph of Viennese cuisine. What variety, what originality in the preparation of those jam-fritters, those chocolate eclairs, those rice puddings flavored with red wine." The Viennese, like the Parisian but unlike the Londoner, was accustomed to dining out *en famille.* Dinner was from one to three, supper from seven to eleven. "The theaters close at ten o'clock, one doesn't eat until after the show. . . . A Viennese who has gone with his wife and children to the theater would be negligent if, that evening, he didn't take his family to supper in a restaurant; the pleasure is doubled, as is the expense"[20] (fig. 116).

The theater in Vienna played an even more serious role in cultural and social life than it did in Paris, and incomparably more than in Victorian London. In the years before 1848 only the high aristocracy had the privilege of occupying the first two rows of boxes in the Kärntnertor and Hofburg theaters. Here social segregation was enforced not by the pocketbook but by law. One furnished one's box according to

116. *"The theaters close at ten o'clock, one doesn't eat until after the show."* **After the theater in a Viennese restaurant.** (From Reinhard E. Petermann, *Wien im Zeitalter Kaiser Franz Josephs I,* Vienna, 1908.)

one's taste and means and used it to receive visitors as well as to observe the stage.[21] If the Ringstrasse was a theater writ large, so the theater strictly speaking served as a microcosm of the greater Vienna. The conspicuous positions of the State Opera and the Burgtheater reflect their symbolic and practical importance for city, society, and regime.

Long before their demolition, the City walls were a favorite promenade. Pichler describes the exodus from the Inner City on a warm summer evening in the 1830s:

> Everybody deserted the houses, the narrow streets, and streamed in private carriages, in hired cabs and communal vehicles [*Miets- und Gesellschaftswagen*], on foot, on horseback out into the fresh air. As a visible sign that the inner, genuine City had become too confined for its growing population, an almost unbroken line of strollers moved through many more gates than earlier out past the fortifications.[22]

Once onto the ramparts they found what Mrs. Trollope thought "probably, the most beautiful town promenade in the world."[23] Both the walls and the surrounding glacis had long since been converted into recreation grounds (fig. 117). The large proportion of the Ringstrasse zone devoted to parks and landscaped areas surrounding public buildings enabled it to continue to act as a circle of green repose as well as a place of public resort.[24] The Augarten and the Prater in Leopoldstadt provided further open spaces.

If the landscaped glacis had served as a recreation ground for all levels of society, the lower orders were tacitly excluded from the parks of the Ringstrasse that replaced it. The frequenters of the Volksgarten and the Stadtpark came from the upper middle classes, officials, officers, shopkeepers, as well as members of the rich *Grossbürgertum*. Before 1848 the Volksgarten had been the resort of the high nobility, particularly in its "Aristocratic Corner," for which an entry fee had to be paid. From the 1860s the high aristocracy retired to their favored portion of the Prater.[25]

The *Builder* styled the Prater as "*par excellence, the Hyde Park of Vienna.*" On the first day in May "the newest shape in carriages, the last 'sweet thing in bonnets,' the most correct cut of coat *à l'Anglais,* is then to be seen, walking, riding, or driving up and down, much the same as the *habitués* of our [Rotten] Row."[26] Pichler describes the first mild day of a February in the 1830s when the Prater offered "the spectacle of long rows of glittering equipages, elegant riders, and here and there a stroller." The *ton* was not diminished by the presence of the lower orders, who instead "flocked in these hours . . . especially on Sundays to Hernals, which is a sort of pilgrimage site . . . and to the many small inns in Lerchenfeld."[27]

The use of the outdoors for fashionable social and recreational purposes was not confined to the area outside the walls. The streets of the City, narrow and confined as they were, provided stages for *Selbstdarstellung*. The Paris street of the ancien régime served, from the point of view of the wealthy, mainly as a carriage route from one protected environment to another; the street in Vienna was an integral part of the pleasure of the Inner City.

The different forms taken by the Parisian *hôtel particulier* and the Viennese *Palais* reflect different attitudes toward their surroundings. The former looked out not onto the street but onto an inner courtyard and, wherever possible, a private garden. This inward-looking quality gives the Parisian *hôtel* its special character: "the street is for the rabble, but the center of the block [*l'îlot*] is for the *seigneur*," as

117. *Both the walls and the surrounding Glacis had long since been converted into recreation grounds.* Promenading along the Wasserglacis. (Museen der Stadt Wien.)

Jean-Pierre Babelon explains it. In Vienna both the dwelling and the street were "pour le seigneur." The main reception rooms of a City palace invariably look out onto the street. The wall of an *hôtel* facing the rue de l'Université or the rue Saint-Dominique is austere and forbidding, with only the restrained decoration around the *porte cochère* to hint at the rococo extravagances that lie behind. "It is a hidden world, occupied by a society that does not care to display its pomp before passers-by."[28] The street façade of a town palace by Fischer von Erlach or Lucas von Hildebrandt is alive with figurative sculpture, from the caryatides and atlantes flanking the entrance door and supporting the *piano nobile* to the heroic statues standing along the cornice. The interior garden, which in the Marais and Saint-Germain-des-Prés might cover a much larger area than the house itself, did not exist in Vienna. Gardens were for the summer house in the *Vorstadt*; City land was too valuable to be so squandered.

There is reason to believe that the contrasting attitudes toward the street reflected contrasting realities: that the street in Vienna was pleasanter, or at least less disgusting, than the Parisian street. It is generally unwise to use the figures placed in architectural engravings as independent documentary evidence. Yet the scenes of street life with which Salomon Kleiner enlivened his views of Vienna published between 1724 and 1737 are so varied and rich with incident that they demand to be taken seriously, if only as idealized representations.[29] Idealized, but not stylized. All classes of society are represented, engaged in many different activities. A military parade marches round the Peterskirche; a market is in progress in the Neuer Markt; carriages of varying states of splendor, carts carrying barrels, baskets, and merchandise share street space with sedan chairs, riders on horseback, and pedestrians. Children play, dogs fight, clergy observe, gentlemen with swords bow politely to one another, ladies carrying fans engage in light conversation. A funeral procession moves past the archbishop's palace, at the Wollzeile corner of which a print seller is carrying on her business. Workmen repair the pavement in front of the Palais Liechtenstein. Laborers, shoppers, and passers-by look on with interest as two market-women tear each other's hair. Clearly there was a great deal to watch, not all of it either genteel or uplifting. And the prints show the people watching, both pedestrians and those looking out of the windows of the houses and palaces.

What made a street in Vienna a more amusing place both to be in and to observe from a drawing-room window than a Parisian street? The appearance of a horse-drawn street-watering cart in a view of Favoriten, and in others paviors and the occasional street sweeper suggests that greater efforts were made to keep the

118. *The authorities had every motive to keep the streets of the Inner City in a clean and decent condition.* Sterngasse, c. 1911, from corner of Judengasse. Note the immaculate pavements. (Bildarchiv der Österreichischen Nationalbibliothek.)

streets reasonably clean. "Vienna is perhaps the city in the world where they water the streets and the pavements the most," wrote Ulysse Robert in 1899.[30] Such a practice was of long standing, antedating the sanitary reforms of mid-century. Mrs. Trollope in the 1830s was vastly impressed by the "perfect freedom from filth, or external annoyance of any kind," in the streets of Vienna:

> How the thing is managed passes my comprehension; but neither in the streets of the city, [nor] on its noble and widely spreading ramparts . . . is any sight or scent to be met that can either offend the senses or shock the feelings in any way. What renders this the more extraordinary is, that the population is extremely dense, the streets narrow, and the system of drainage, though greatly superior to that of Paris, immeasurably inferior to that of London. Yet you may walk through every street and lane of Vienna with impunity.[31]

If the proliferation of *passages* in Paris testified to the bad state of its streets, their failure to establish themselves in Vienna is further evidence that people could walk for pleasure along its ordinary shopping streets. Geist, who lists twenty-nine *passages* in Paris, could find only one, the Ferstel Passage (1856–60) linking the Freyung with the Herrengasse, in the Austrian capital.[32]

The authorities had every motive to keep the streets of the Inner City in a clean and decent condition, given the high status of its residents (fig. 118). With offensive trades and non-essential members of the working classes banished to the suburbs, the City had to be maintained in a condition appropriate to a restricted upper-class neighborhood. That the Ringstrasse supplemented but did not replace the Graben and the Kärntner Strasse as fashionable promenades suggests that the streets of the City were, or at least were perceived as, pleasant places to walk, acceptable extensions of the reception rooms that looked out onto them.

It is difficult to disentangle cause and effect in this connection. Did the public nature of life in Vienna encourage its governors to make the streets pleasant for people of quality, or did the people of quality use the streets because they were kept pleasant? Just as within a City flat the comfort and convenience of family and service rooms were willingly sacrificed to enable yet another salon to be seen through folding doors, *Vorstadt* and *Vorort* may have been neglected in order that City and Ringstrasse could be made into a set of breathtaking reception rooms for metropolis and empire. No city in Europe is better suited for a life of public self-representation.

THE CITY AS DOCUMENT

15

Architecture as
Historical Evidence

n assumption underlying this book has been that a work of art is also a historical source, that the city, as the largest and most characteristic art form of the nineteenth century, has something to tell us about the inner nature of that century. The notion that a century has an "inner nature" is itself a nineteenth-century idea, one that has in recent years been subject to critical scrutiny. Sir Ernst Gombrich in particular, while accepting the "Hegelian intuition that nothing in life is ever isolated, that any event and any creation of a period is connected by a thousand threads with the culture in which it is embedded," questions whether such connections are sufficiently tight and coherent to justify the concept of the *Zeitgeist.* He would accept the reality of movements but not of periods. "Hegel saw all periods as movements since they were embodiments of the moving spirit," one which "manifested itself in a collective, the supra-individual entities of nations or periods." Gombrich argues that such a notion has "blocked the emergence of a true cultural history."[1] He would have the historian concentrate on individual artists and on coherent movements and abandon the search for an all-encompassing spirit of the age, uniting the divergent ideas, values, and institutions of the time under a single umbrella.

Two books by David Watkin, *Morality and Architecture* and *The Rise of Architectural History,* question the relevance of history to the study of architectural developments. Like Gombrich, Watkin argues that individual works of art can better be understood as products of particular artists, as responses to particular situations, or—if they are to be placed in a broader perspective—in the context either of a well-defined movement or a particular aesthetic tradition. Attempts to relate them to contemporary intellectual, economic, social, or political movements or conditions will rarely illuminate and probably mislead.

If Gombrich and Watkin explicitly deny the relevance of history to art, the writings of most urban historians implicitly deny the relevance of art to history. If questioned they might plausibly respond that a knowledge of the outward appearance of cities contributes little to an understanding of them as social, economic, and political entities: that a city may or may not be a work of art, but its aesthetic qualities have nothing to do with it as an arena for political conflict, social change, and economic development. A working-class tenement does not become less overcrowded, disease-ridden, and oppressive to its occupants by being in the Elizabethan rather than in the Tuscan mode.

Yet neither urban historian nor art historian dare overlook any kind of evidence. The notion of the *Zeitgeist* remains a useful myth for the working historian, to keep him on the alert for patterns and correspondences that he might otherwise overlook. That Hegel's or Burckhardt's or Pevsner's formulation of the nature of a particular age turns out to be inadequate or misleading does not in itself demonstrate the futility of a *search* for the *Zeitgeist,* only that that spirit is more elusive than once was thought. Knowledge of the fundamental character of an age, like truth and goodness, may be unattainable in an absolute sense, but is a legitimate goal toward which to strive. What is wrong is to take for granted that we know what it is going to be before we find it.

Perhaps the search will prove as ultimately sterile as the Scholastic's pursuit of Aristotelian essences. I think not, if only because common experience teaches otherwise: presented with an unfamiliar building or painting or piece of music or fragment of prose we can usually guess fairly accurately both its approximate date and the cultural tradition to which it belongs. That we are sometimes surprised, particularly by the creations of the greatest artists, does not invalidate the general truth that what is produced in a particular time and place tends to bear a family resemblance to its neighbors and contemporaries. The more simple-minded attempts to express such underlying relationships—baroque diplomacy, Jewish physics, bourgeois poetry—need not discredit the search for the unifying characteristics.

David Watkin correctly points out some of the difficulties involved in relating architecture to contemporary ideology:

> A Baroque style of interior decoration adopted on the continent to glorify absolute monarchy and the Catholic Church could be adopted at Chatsworth in the 1680s by the avowed enemy of those institutions, the archetypal Whig and Protestant 1st Duke of Devonshire; similarly, the Painted Hall at Greenwich looks like an apotheosis of absolute monarchy and the Catholic Church but is, of course, exactly the reverse.[2]

But the *Zeitgeist* is not to be confused with "school of thought" or "partisan ideology." It rather consists of just those assumptions and presuppositions that are taken for granted by Catholics and Protestants, Whigs and Tories, Marxists and liberals, in any given historical period. Such unspoken assumptions give unity and coherence to a period and are what enable us to speak of historical periods at all. The similarities displayed by Stalinist, Nazi, and New Deal architecture tell us nothing very important about the respective ideologies of the three countries but do say something about the 1930s.

To accept Watkin's challenge: the shared assumptions of the late seventeenth century would include the importance of structure, hierarchy, classical antiquity, reason, geometry, experience, an ordered universe governed by a Supreme Being. For Europe after 1848, common assumptions were the importance of history, development, evolution, progress; the existence, whether for good or evil, of nations, with specific cultural traditions; the existence of discoverable laws governing human behavior, economics, society, politics; the high importance of individual responsibility; the existence of a universal moral code (whether derived from supernatural authority or discoverable through reason and experience); the reality of racial differences; the susceptibility of social evils to rational analysis and amelioration through public policy or individual effort or both.

Many of the absurdities in which Watkin has caught otherwise respectable architectural historians come from their determination to relate their subject to something called the Industrial Revolution, thereby dismissing as irrelevant all architectural design that failed to express the new technology: that is to say, practically everything that was actually built down to the end of the nineteenth century, and most of what was built, in England at least, before 1939. Since their evidence conflicted with their theory, they discarded the evidence. Urban historians have with more reason clung to the identification of the modern metropolis with something called the "industrial city." Many cities—Bradford, Pittsburgh, Essen—were undeniably products of the new techniques of manufacture, and all were affected by the technology and wealth that the industrial centers produced. Yet London, Paris, and Vienna—to name but three—had long antedated the Industrial Revolution and were affected by it at most indirectly.

Richard Sennett has pointed out that the great population growth in the nineteenth century took place not in the new industrial cities, but in the established capitals, where "trade, finance, and bureaucracy remained the main activities."3 Peter Feldbauer has shown how political and commercial factors outweighed industrialization in accounting for Vienna's growth even in the later years of the century.4 At the very least, as Maurice Agulhon points out in a recent volume on the modern French city, "the connection between urbanization and industrialization is neither exclusive nor simple."5

Yet it is hard to know what label to substitute for "industrial." The unsatisfactory nature of all attempts to devise a theory of urban structure and development can partly be accounted for by the different purposes for which cities exist. In addition to the city as factory, there is the city as fortress, palace, *salon,* office, temple, monument, toy, barracks, school, revolutionary cell, expression of abstract idea. No city has ever been exclusively any one of the above, but the proportions in the mixture have varied greatly, both from city to city and from period to period in the same city.

Such difficulties say more about the inadequacies of existing analytical categories than about the inappropriateness of the city as a subject for historical inquiry. There is no shortage of evidence, either documentary or monumental. Nor can the sources be dismissed as stemming from an effete or unrepresentative minority. In the building of a city the links between political, social, economic, technological, aesthetic, and even intellectual history are obvious and inescapable. Whatever may have been true of earlier periods, if we wish to understand Western culture in the nineteenth and twentieth centuries, its cities are a good place to begin.

16

The Beautiful

In Search of a
Nineteenth-Century
Aesthetic

he capital cities of the nineteenth century certainly ought to reveal what that century considered beautiful. A painting might reflect no more than the private fancies of a single artist, a country house no more than the eccentricities of the landowner who commissioned it. But a city in its public buildings necessarily reflects the aesthetic values of the regime, in its private structures the taste of those economically strong enough to participate in "the market."

The historian ventures at his peril into the realm of nineteenth-century architectural studies. He will find there a great deal of work on particular architects, something on individual movements and aesthetic theories, but nothing at all of the consensus on stylistic categories that can be found in the scholarly literature on every century until the nineteenth. The time is long past when the bulk of nineteenth-century architecture could be dismissed as "ugly," because it failed to conform either to eighteenth-century or twentieth-century aesthetic orthodoxy. Nor can the attempts of those like Sir Nikolaus Pevsner to give it coherence by seeing in it a single school of twentieth-century architecture struggling to be born satisfy any longer.

It now seems obvious that if we are to understand nineteenth-century architecture, we have to take nineteenth-century architects seriously, as seriously as we take their predecessors and those of our own day. Just as we do not criticize the architects of Byzantium for not building in the manner of the fifth century B.C., or reproach Romanesque architects for failing to make use of Gothic constructional techniques, we need to judge the architecture of the 1850s by the standards of the 1850s, the 1880s by those of the 1880s. But that is where the trouble begins.

For it is by no means clear what the standards of either the 1850s or the 1880s were. The wholesale denigration of nineteenth-century architecture was not something that began in the twentieth century. There is no need to turn to Lewis Mumford or Sigfried Giedion when Pugin or Ruskin or Morris could be as memorably scathing and dismissive of the attempts of their contemporaries to provide firmness, commodity, and delight.

A more intractable problem has to do with questions not of aesthetic judgment but of stylistic definition. That nineteenth-century architecture was disliked by contemporaries as well as by their grandchildren need not worry us unduly: most

254

earlier stylistic categories, from "Gothic" on, had begun as terms of abuse. The annoying thing about nineteenth-century architecture is that neither its friends nor its enemies can agree on a name for whatever it is they are defending or attacking.

Sometimes names assigned particular styles by contemporaries have stuck or been reappropriated by later architectural historians: Queen Anne or neo-Grec, for instance. Other times twentieth-century historians have applied labels—like "Strict Historicism" or "Stripped Classicism"—that contemporaries would not have recognized. Yet no one has yet come up with a system of categorization that applies to Europe as a whole, in the way that "baroque" or "the International Style" do. What applicability does Queen Anne have to Italian architecture, or *Vormärz* to English? Finally there are styles to which nobody has bothered to give names at all. What name shall we give to the dominant school of domestic architecture in Paris in the decades before the Second Empire: the symmetrical, plaster-coated, Mansard-roofed buildings with external shutters that come after the plain, anonymous style of *le vieux Paris* and before the stone frontages of the Haussmann years? It is to be seen everywhere and is easily recognizable for what it is, but no one has dignified it with a label (fig. 119).

The fault may not lie at the door of the architectural historian's profession but may be inherent in the subject itself. Heterogeneity and incoherence, the battle of the styles, uncertainty about direction, confusion about aims may make nineteenth-century architecture unsusceptible to lucid analysis. Some Victorians, bemused by the visual confusion that they saw around themselves, hoped that future historians would be able to perceive a pattern where they could only apprehend chaos. We have had nearly a century to gain perspective, but even at a distance it still looks pretty chaotic.

Even so, some things are beginning to seem less confused, some patterns are emerging. First of all, we must not exaggerate the degree of diversity, the rapidity of change, the intensity of the battle of the styles. When we think of nineteenth-century architecture as characterized by an anarchic array of incompatible styles, we really mean the English-speaking nineteenth century. France and Austria indulged in far fewer experiments outside their respective classical traditions and were particularly reluctant to do so in Paris and Vienna, where dignity and correctness were seen as especially important. Follies and experiments might be indulged in in the countryside or suburbia but were unthinkable in town. In the whole of the vast Ringstrasse zone, for instance, there were no more than four major buildings in the Gothic style—the Votivkirche, the Rathaus, the Sühnhaus, and the Academic Gymnasium—each of them an exceptional case, with a special reason to justify departure from the classicism that alone was suitable for buildings with representative pretensions.

The divergence of English and continental practice in this regard may suggest that the nineteenth century had not one architectural history but several. After a cosmopolitan eighteenth century in which a dominant style was subject to no more than minor national and local modifications, and before the general triumph in the twentieth century of a vulgarized Bauhaus style, independent national and regional styles developed. Some historians are discovering certain qualities unifying seemingly disparate national developments, but one's first impression is that different drummers were being heard in Paris, Vienna, and London.[1]

Such stylistic variations suggest that nationalism may have been a more impor-

tant aesthetic determinant than economics, technology, or broader social forces. For with travel facilitated and made cheaper, and the proliferation of technical and illustrated periodicals, the architects of any one country had at their disposal more plentiful and more accurate information on foreign developments than ever before. Cheaper means of transport lessened the dependence on local building materials, while mass-produced ornament diminished the importance of local traditions of workmanship. If, as was then generally believed, architecture reflected the broad historical forces of the day, it ought to have responded to the population growth, urbanization, industrialization, and development of liberal and capitalistic institutions and ideologies that affected Europe as a whole, in much the same way in different cities and countries. But it did not.

A direct comparison of the domestic architecture of early Victorian London with *Vormärz* Vienna and the Paris of Louis-Philippe is made difficult by the fact that in neither of the continental cities were buildings of the *size* and *shape* of the standard London terrace house being built any more. Vienna had long since and Paris had fairly recently stopped putting up narrow houses, two to three windows wide, on the medieval scale. In both cities the standard dwelling now occupied a block of more generous width and greater height. As a consequence, the architect could plan a single, large, impressive doorway, with the possibility of massive decoration, rather than have the problem of his London contemporary of integrating a row of individual entrances into the structure. Above the ground-floor level, the problem was more nearly the same as in a London terrace, with the grouping and framing of windows and the indication of the different floor levels the obvious tasks.

Neither Vienna nor Paris built, in those years, anything like the elaborate set pieces of the Regent's Park or Belgravia terraces, with their detached rows of columns or extruding porticoes.[2] Though the individual building units were larger than in London, the uniform groupings into terraces and squares in the British metropolis gave its architects scope for compositions of a vastness that surpassed anything then going up on the Continent. Unified ownership and management of leasehold estates helped make this possible, along with the size and organization of some firms of building contractors. But despite the continuance of such conditions into the high Victorian period, builders gradually ceased taking advantage of them.

Public architecture came to be more sharply differentiated from domestic and strove toward a higher level of assertiveness. The *Allgemeine Bauzeitung* for 1850 used the recently completed British Museum to illustrate the move from Regency to early Victorian standards of architectural judgment (fig. 120). Taste had much changed in the nearly thirty years since the new Museum buildings were commenced, "and what people would then have called extravagant ornamentation now seems self-evidently required." The exterior of a museum ought to be a work of art appropriate to the treasures of art and science that it contained. Yet despite the sums lavished on the British Museum, its only ornament was the Ionian columns along its frontage, while its other sides were faced with naked brickwork, with no attempt at architectural design. The whole had an "impoverished, incomplete appearance." It

London

119. *(opposite) The dominant school of domestic architecture in Paris in the decades before the Second Empire: the symmetrical, plaster-coated, Mansard-roofed buildings with external shutters.* Marville, rue du Faubourg Montmartre. (Musée Carnavalet. Photo Lauros-Giraudon.)

120. *Taste had much changed in the nearly thirty years since the new Museum buildings were commenced, "and what people would then have called extravagant ornamentation now seems self-evidently required."* The British Museum from Great Russell Street. (Guildhall Library. Photo Godfrey.)

suggested how far aesthetic expectations had been raised since the 1820s. Had it been completed at that time, "such sobriety would have been to an extent pointed out as a characteristic fault of a period that lies behind us. Today people expect from buildings of every sort far more ornamental treatment than they then required even from monumental structures."[3] It found New Oxford Street an instance of the improvement in taste since Regent Street was laid out. "Not only is a tolerable ornamentation brought into life . . . we also observe better lines, finer proportions . . . an approach towards style, that earlier building lacked."[4]

The houses that went up during the fifties and sixties in South Kensington reflected the changed aesthetic. "Italianate" in style, they made use of classical ornamental features to emphasize the separateness of each unit of the terrace. South Kensington, with its juxtaposition of cultural institutions and opulent residences, was London's closest approach to the Ringstrasse, and its domestic architecture shared certain features of the residential blocks in Vienna. The most important of these was the high degree of articulation in the façade, whereby each story was treated differently within a design that united the whole. The focus in both was on the richly decorated *piano nobile;* but whereas in Vienna this meant that the most important personage in the building lived behind the first-floor windows, in South Kensington it meant this is where the grand reception rooms are to be found.[5]

Writing in 1891 Robert Kerr looked back at the state of architecture and architectural taste as it had been at the middle of the century. The new Houses of Parliament were "exceedingly magnificent in the mass, graceful in proportion, bright in aspect, and abundantly elegant in detail." He praised the British Museum for its monumental design, but observed that "Blore's weak Italian frontage to Nash's much better Greek quadrangle" for Buckingham Palace "was not admired by anybody." What were admired were the new clubhouses in Pall Mall by Barry, Burton, and Smirke. "The façade of the new Station of the Great Northern Railway at King's Cross, designed, or rather non-designed, by the engineer, was regarded with shame as a demonstrative manifestation of the most absolute and abased philistinism" (fig. 121). So much for what came to be seen as a landmark in the development of functionalist architecture. Of the building that would be the most extravagantly admired by the coming orthodoxy, he wrote: "The Exhibition Building, although ostentatiously called 'the Crystal Palace,' made no pretensions to architectural merit. . . . A shelter of iron-work and glass became recognised as the proper thing for future Great Exhibitions; but, whether we call it a Crystal Palace or a Greenhouse, nothing has come out of it to this day which can be called an aesthetic architectural advance with new materials."[6]

121. *"The façade of the new Station . . . at King's Cross . . . was regarded with shame."* King's Cross Station. From *The Builder* 9 (1851): 739.

Each building type had its appropriate style. Gothic, despite attempts by its supporters to make it a new universal style, was regarded as most particularly the style for churches. Starting in the 1860s but especially in the seventies and eighties, the Queen Anne style dominated domestic building. Using classical decorative motifs but renouncing classical proportions and principles of symmetry, it sought quaintness rather than correctness. Associated with it were the "crude-looking half-timbering, tile-hung and rough stone walls" of the "Old English Revival."[7] Professor Kerr in 1891 characterized the still widespread Queen Anne: "Ornamental gables . . . with all kinds of dormers by way of supplementaries. . . . Huge chimney stacks . . . wooden bay windows . . . paltry doorways and incomprehensible little windows enter their protest against dignity without, and 'nooks' and 'ingles,' twisted passages, breakneck steps for the sake of the questionable pleasure of surprise, and tipsy arrangements generally, carry out the same scheme of artistic merriment within."[8] The first duke of Westminster had as much as possible of his estate in Mayfair rebuilt in such a fashion. Just before his death in 1899 his judgment on a building scheme for Duke Street was "the more red brick the better."[9]

Yet no one style totally dominated, even in a single decade or in a single street. "Nothing is more striking in London than the utter confusion and want of plan in the place," Alexander Payne complained in 1872. "One man has his warehouse or shop built in Classic; his neighbour adjoins thereto a Gothic building . . . Regent-street is the only street of any architectural pretensions . . . which has anything like similarity or unity of design about it."[10]

The nineties saw two contrary developments. On the one hand, the hunger for the picturesque, the irregular, and the colorful called forth riotous and assertive additions to the streets, "lofty structures of brick, stone, and terracotta, with salient gables, turrets, and chimneys."[11] On the other, a genuine classical revival began that would dominate the early twentieth century. The long-scorned eighteenth century came into its own, and the French Beaux Arts tradition no longer seemed an unwarrantable restraint on the individual imagination. "Town planning" came into vogue, and the virtues of symmetry and uniformity were rediscovered.

Writing in 1936, the young Nikolaus Pevsner could hardly contain his indignation at the consequences. "Just about 1900 . . . England . . . receded into an eclectic Neo-Classicism, of great dignity sometimes, but with hardly any bearing on present-day problems and needs. For country houses and town houses Neo-Georgian or Neo-Colonial became popular; in public buildings, banks and so on, solemn rows of colossal columns reappeared . . . Burnham's Selfridge Building of 1909 illustrates this tendency at its worst."[12] Associated with the return to classicism was a revival of the Regency hankering after urban magnificence: the Admiralty Arch, the Victoria Monument, and Aston Webb's new façade for Buckingham Palace embody the new assertiveness, the desire for the grandiose, the formal, the specifically urban. That such aspirations were also expressed in the Oxford Street façade of a mere department store dismayed the purists of the 1930s but was totally appropriate for Edwardian London, indulging in unashamed self-adornment.

Paris   Two things impressed the observant visitor to Paris during the second half of the nineteenth century: the magnitude of the physical and structural changes, and the persistence throughout of a single aesthetic. As England moved giddily from style to style, France remained loyal to the austere classicism it had chosen in the seventeenth century, and which had served it well ever since. This is not to say that a building in the 1890s was indistinguishable from one dating from the 1830s, but that the two could stand side by side with no sense of incompatibility. The absence from French architectural discussions of the snide remarks about the eighteenth century that disfigure otherwise sensible Victorian criticism suggests a profession at ease with its past and with itself. The nineteenth-century architect revered his predecessors from the ancien régime, studied their works, and strove to develop his own style within the tradition they had bequeathed him. That style grew more richly ornamented than earlier taste had allowed, but the ornaments were drawn from the classical repertoire, and buildings maintained their traditional proportions.

Until the wrenching changes that began in the late 1950s, Paris, whatever the transformations wrought by Henri IV and Napoleon III, whatever the impact of the steam locomotive and the motor car, and however individual the character of each *quartier,* was never other than recognizably itself. That specialists are unable to date, even to the extent of assigning a century, large numbers of its streets and buildings—the exhaustive *Dictionnaire historique des rues de Paris* is filled with entries like "vieille maison" and "vieux hôtel"—suggests a wonderful permanence of building techniques and of ideas as to what a house ought to look like.[13]

Adolf Loos himself could not have faulted the normal pre-nineteenth-century façade for unnecessary ornament. Even the accents that lend interest to the Georgian terrace house in London were lacking: doorframes, fanlights, pilasters, pediments, ornamental cornices, balustrades, rustication—to say nothing of the decorative area railings or lamp standards. There was little if any differentiation between stories, often without string courses to separate them. The windows are as lacking in "eyebrows" as the notorious structure in the Michaelerplatz.

Nor did the *hôtels* of the aristocracy and wealthy bourgeoisie provide much of an exception to the timeless uniformity of the streets. Often faced with the same plaster coating as their less pretentious neighbors, the street walls would be windowless and unadorned save for the *porte cochère.* Churches and other public buildings would be exceptions to the extreme sobriety of most private street façades but, with their classical dress, would contrast with their surroundings by their greater outward splendor, not by the style in which that splendor was expressed. Only Gothic structures that had survived unmodernized, mostly churches, could shock the taste of the eighteenth-century connoisseur.

The *Allgemeine Bauzeitung* in 1843 may have been misled by the uniform whitewashed façades into underestimating the age of the physical fabric of Paris. "Whoever undertakes an architectural ramble through the streets of Paris," it wrote, "will be astonished at how few buildings date from before the latter half of the seventeenth century." Unlike the picturesque streets of German cities, those of Paris were mostly "of a plain and monotonous appearance." To someone used to the decorative extravagances of baroque Vienna, Paris looked mean and unassertive. The neoclassicism of the Revolutionary and Napoleonic eras did little to enliven the streets. "The houses from this period have a chilly and icy quality like the period itself, and the long, uniform, barracklike frontages resemble the strict rule of the autocrat, but also his majesty and power."[14]

By 1843 all that had changed. Since the July Revolution, and more especially during the previous six or seven years, a transformation had taken place in domestic architecture. Just as London during the same decade was rejecting the Regency in favor of the Italianate, Paris was demanding greater richness of decoration; a new stress on comfort, light, and air; a striving for luxury and refinement not only in the dwellings of the rich but for those of modest means. "The sculptors . . . now cover with the creations of their often uncontrolled imagination all surfaces of the façade from top to bottom."[15] (fig. 122).

"Hardly twenty-five years ago, it was necessary to go back to the previous century to find any notable houses in Paris," wrote Adolphe Lance in the *Moniteur des architectes* for 1847–48. "Twenty-five years ago . . . [a street of] private dwellings, stripped during the Revolution of the compromising luxury of exterior ornaments, was still what the hideous [*affreuse*] architecture of the Empire had made it: an ugly wall with square openings serving as windows." Significantly he criticized not eighteenth-century architecture but that of the Empire, and that chiefly for its want

122. *"The sculptors . . . now cover with the creations of their often uncontrolled imagination all surfaces of the façade from top to bottom."* Ein Miethaus in Paris. From *Allgemeine Bauzeitung* 8 (1843), fig. 1.

of proper ornament. "One ought not to look there for that modest simplicity with which good taste sometimes adorns itself, but the nakedness of destitution [*la nudité de dénûment*], the saddest and most tiresome appearance, that of impotence and misery." The architecture that had in recent years embellished the new quarters in Paris derived its inspiration, he thought, from the pre-Revolutionary tradition, which gave the dwellings "a little of their past splendor, a little of the grace that they had lost. They no longer had to assume the appearance of a prison, as under the Terror, nor to resemble barracks, as under the Empire. The times had changed."[16]

Much that came to be associated with the architecture of the Second Empire was already in the course of development by the 1840s. The abandonment of stucco for surface decoration, the wrought-iron balconies, the combination of large-scale uniformity with subtle variations in details could already be found in the private *hôtels* and *maisons à loyer* to the north and west of the *grands boulevards*. Early in the Second Empire, C. F. Hayward described the new Parisian style. Its main characteristics were "delicacy of detail . . . everything in low relief; mouldings of a flat Greek character, often applied with the spirit of Gothic freedom; and constant use of ornamental carving" (fig. 123). In the proper light many streets of Paris today look like Victorian steel engravings. To Hayward, at the time such streets were going up, "a Parisian façade seems to be a drawing in stone, full size, literally an immense lithograph. A large, flat mass of stone wall, with few slightly projecting blocks, is carried up in the street line, and on it is engraven with a chisel the design of the architect, to scale, the projection of the pilasters and strings being about the proportion of the thickness of the ink lines on the paper design"[17] (fig. 124).

Hayward was here in a sense anticipating Neil Levine's argument that Labrouste designed the façade of the Bibliothèque Sainte-Geneviève to resemble a page in a printed book.[18] Previous centuries had left the wall a tabula rasa; the architects of the Second Empire used it as a slate on which to write and draw.

Hayward found the drawing "deficient in boldness and almost in outline at any distance." Here his views were in accord with the then-orthodox view that scorned the works of the brothers Adam, for instance, for the shallowness and littleness of their designs. One English critic thought that "the too free and frequent use of ornament, and too great a number of details, often spoil French buildings, and take away from them all expression of energy."[19] Another found "the emanations of French architects . . . weak; the detail of their buildings is *pretty* we allow, but . . . flat and insipid—a frittering away of ideas in incised stone."[20]

Kerr thought English architects superior in "muscular power," French in "feminine grace." Particularly characteristic of the "new French manner" was the "extreme delicacy with which projections are handled,—tending towards feebleness as compared with the bold and heavy work of the English school, and only redeemed by the perfect precision of both design and workmanship."[21] The absence of the articulation of façade characteristic of the otherwise very different London town house and Viennese *Mietpalast* is very noticeable in Second Empire blocks. "The ordinary street-architecture of Paris, above the *entresol,* is remarkable for the equality of its stories; and little attention is given to grouping stories together," wrote the *Builder* in 1864.[22]

The Victorians had no inhibitions about speculating on national character. "If English art is free, varied, but often queerly whimsical, it is because the English

123. *"Delicacy of detail . . . everything in low relief; mouldings of a flat Greek character, often applied with the spirit of Gothic freedom; and constant use of ornamental carving."* Rue Neuve des Capucines 6. From *Revue générale de l'architecture* 13 (1855), pl. 48.
124. *(opposite) "A Parisian façade seems to be a drawing in stone, full size, literally an immense lithograph."* Rue de la Victoire 98. From *Revue générale de l'architecture* 16 (1858), pl. 35.

character loves liberty above all things," wrote Lawrence Hervey in 1870. "If French art, in its timid sameness, has the oneness of massive creation, it is for a psychological reason." The French combined the qualities of Descartes and Louis XIV. "The history of France is the history of centralisation . . . of *leading ideas*. Politics, literature, science, and art have always in France revolved round centres. French

Echelle de 0,01ᵉ pour mètre.

military monarchies, the French Academy, and French schools of art, show how readily Frenchmen will sink their individualities in behalf of an idea." A French building grew organically out of "*one* idea. Every portion, every ornament of the building . . . subserve that idea or purpose."[23]

The events of 1870 and 1871 made it harder to see the French as slavishly subservient to centralized authority. Yet the Ecole des Beaux Arts and its influence over architectural practice survived 1871 and were not utterly overthrown until 1968. Once the ruins wrought by the bombardment and civil war were cleared away, and once the Third Republic embarked on its own urbanistic and architectural projects, it became clear how little effect political change had had on the concept of what was beautiful and fitting.

"Parisian architecture . . . is not a senseless conglomeration of nice decorative features and details," insisted Joseph A. Stark, a former student at the Beaux Arts, in 1879. It had harmony, unity, system, and direction. Apart from the impact of their academic training, Parisian architects were enabled, by the vast scale both of the buildings they had to design and the urban landscape in which they worked, to think in broad and universal terms: in the Burkean sense, of the Sublime. "Where the canvas stretched before the architectural artist is large, he will feel a sense of liberty to let his genius fly. . . . Large and decisive features of design will be possible, reducing long and high façades into a few distinct but harmonising figures." The worth of details "is increased in proportion to the frequency of their occurrence. . . . The regular rotation of a well-chosen detail becomes . . . a feature."

Stark here put his finger on an essential quality of the Parisian townscape: its repetition of details, stretching as far as the eye can see. The arcades of the rue de Rivoli, the straight ranks of identical trees in the Tuileries Gardens, the interminable succession of the same features in every boulevard: not just the same block of flats—the same in dimensions, color of stone, architectural style, and general effect—but the same street furniture—lamp standards, fixed benches, bus stops, Métro entrances, the same grills protecting the roots of the same trees—the same cafés with the same tables, chairs, menus, the same awnings advertising the same apéritif. . . . Depending on one's point of view such qualities either exhilarate or depress, but for better or worse they are Paris.

Sartre's vision of Hell in *Huis Clos,* with its endless corridors leading to an infinity of windowless rooms, furnished in the style of the Second Empire, is not all that different from the captious response of someone who has had, in Paris, all the good taste, the classical restraint, the carefully contrived vistas that he can stomach. And were Paris nothing but its architecture and the layout of its major thoroughfares, such a response would be more frequent than it is. Fortunately the anarchic individualism, the capacity to astonish, and the diversity of character concealed by the standardized and repeated architectural features are such that one must be very easily bored to find Paris tedious.

Stark finds "*contrast within general harmony*" the key to the effectiveness of Parisian architecture. On the large scale, he saw "power, breadth, magnificence," on the small, "refined beauty, serene or playful. . . . The qualities of the individual buildings become . . . the character of the whole street and of the whole city. Cornices and roof-lines, ranging at nearly uniform elevation, furnish grand perspective-lines which are strengthened . . . by the uniformity of the stone and roof tints." Such architectural features combined with "bright bits of flowers and . . . the soothing green of the trees to [create] a picture such as few cities can present."[24]

Yet while the dominant effect remained one of graceful consistency within the rules of classicism, by the 1880s such rules were beginning to be challenged and stretched, if not yet repudiated. Uniformity came to seem boring. Windows acquired new shapes. Architectural experiments in the developing area north of the parc Monceau portended a freer use of classical motifs, more varied and individualized façades.[25] Modifications in building regulations in 1882 and 1884 permitted greater projections from the main façade and allowed the use of bay windows (fig. 125).[26]

By 1900 a curious divergence in direction between French and English architectural developments was taking place, prefiguring the plot line of *Summer and Smoke*. After decades in which English muscular originality could be contrasted with French subservience to rules, it began to be clear that the old generalizations no longer applied. England, having come to regard the products of aesthetic indi-

125. *Uniformity came to seem boring. Windows acquired new shapes. Modifications in building regulations permitted greater projections from the main façade.* Apartment block, place de Passy, built c. 1893, sixteenth arrondissement, 1984. (Evelyn Benesch.)

vidualism that constituted the Victorian heritage with a mixture of distaste and embarrassment, was embarked on a classical revival that was producing buildings as correct, as balanced, and as well-mannered as anything that emerged from the Ecole des Beaux Arts. France was entering a period of self-indulgent experimentation, in which individual expression counted more than good taste, exuberance than restraint, dramatic movement than serenity and repose.

One phase of the changed aesthetic climate was Art Nouveau, called "le modern style" by the French. But more was involved than the exotic and sinuous productions of that school. Windows grouped themselves in unconventional ways; walls bulged and receded as far as the relaxed building regulations allowed. The experiments with combinations of material, asymmetry, and informality might be seen as a delayed equivalent to the English Queen Anne. Free play of fancy enlivens any street dating from the late 1880s to 1914. The exhibition of 1900 allowed full scope for the exponents of the sculptural approach to the urban façade. While praising "that facility and freedom in modelling which is so remarkable a quality of modern French architecture," the *Builder* in 1900 wondered "whether there is not too much modelling—too constant a recurrence of curves and scrolls everywhere . . . the constant introduction of nude figures balanced on the edge of a cornice or escutcheon, and hanging their feet out in the air . . . becomes a mannerism which is repeated rather too often."[27] For an English publication to urge restraint on the French, a reversal of roles, if not an aesthetic revolution, must have taken place.

The pont Alexandre III, the Gare d'Orsay, and the Hotel Lutétia exemplify the new freedom, as Paris loosened the bonds of classicism and strove, if not to repudiate, at least to transcend its Haussmannite heritage. If the boulevard Sébastopol was the showcase of the new Paris of the 1850s, the avenue de l'Opéra that of the 1870s, the representative street of early twentieth-century Paris was the boulevard Raspail (fig. 126). "If we measure the distance that separates the façades of the avenue de l'Opéra from those of the boulevard Raspail, we shall become aware . . . of the efforts of our Parisian architects during a quarter-century," exulted Raymond Escholier on the eve of the First World War. "It amounts to building . . . the new City, renouncing Doric, Ionic, Corinthian orders . . . using the latest materials, the most modern discoveries . . . to embellish our façades, no longer mechanically or by contrivance, but artistically, sculpturally." While London was rediscovering, in the Aldwych and Kingsway, the attractions of balance and consistency, Paris was experimenting with the picturesque. "Our age has too lively a taste for liberty," thought Escholier; "it is too much in love with diversity to content itself with a geometrical and uniform design. If French taste cannot give up its strong classical stamp . . . neither does it mean, at the present time, to abdicate its native tendencies of individualism."[28]

Shortly after Escholier wrote those lines the artistic evolution of Paris, like so many other developments in France and throughout Europe, came to an end, never to be resumed. When, after wars, depressions, social and economic upheavals, it became possible, in the late 1950s, to subject Paris to fundamental physical alterations, the assumptions that had seemed self-evident to Labrouste, Daly, Haussmann, and Escholier no longer had enough vitality to make them seem worth refuting. That much of the Paris of Henri IV and Louis XIV, not to speak of that of Louis-Philippe and Louis Napoleon, survives is the result of a

126. *The representative street of early twentieth-century Paris was the boulevard Raspail.* Boulevard Raspail looking south from Sèvres-Babylone, 1984. Hotel Lutétia to left. (Evelyn Benesch.)

series of economic and political accidents, not of conviction as to its transcendent value. But survive it does, as virtually nothing does of the London of James I and Charles II, and less and less of that of George IV and Victoria.

Vienna

The history of Vienna as a work of art similarly came to an abrupt halt in 1914. How it would have developed had war not come and had some means been devised to reconcile the economic and cultural advantages of the Habsburg empire with the national aspirations of its subjects, no one can know. Physically Vienna retains much of the fabric of the city of 1914. As such it offers a wealth of evidence for the changing ideas about how an Imperial Residence ought to look from the era of Maria Theresa to that of Franz Joseph.

Maria Theresa and Franz Joseph, together with their subjects, thought that an imperial residential city ought to look like what it was: a concentration of wealth and power, learning and taste. To that end they employed the resources of a florid and expressive classicism with lavish prodigality. Nothing comparable to Perrault's rejection of the baroque or Lord Burlington's revival of Palladianism occurred to restrain the exuberance of the architect or the desire for self-glorification of the patron. Whether erecting a church or a palace, a monastery or a bourgeois dwelling, a hospital or a theater, the aim was to create the most splendid and impressive structure that the money available could buy. Structural solidity was taken for granted, but it was important for the building to look, as well as be, designed for the ages, to proclaim to posterity the grandeur of the age that erected it. Massiveness of scale and correctness of proportions were as desirable as in Paris, but such qualities alone were not enough to satisfy the aspirations of the Viennese: the decorative capabilities of the sculptor and the painter, the mason and the plasterer had to be utilized to the utmost. Adolf Loos could have chosen no city in the world in which his equation of ornament with crime would have seemed more outrageous, more radically subversive of the assumptions that underlay its very being, than Vienna.

The reaction of the Sezessionist movement to the decorative excesses of Ringstrasse Vienna had been anticipated a century earlier by the reaction against the baroque during the reign of Joseph II, and the move toward an even plainer architecture in the period of the French Revolution and the Napoleonic Wars. The plainness and austerity of Viennese architecture between 1780 and 1848 must be understood as being such more in comparison with what went before and after than in absolute terms. Just as no Austrian monarch would have allowed himself to occupy anything as unpretentious as Kensington Palace or Kew, none of his moderately prosperous subjects would have put up with residence in the equivalent of Gower or Baker or Harley street. If the standard domestic architecture of the 1830s calls to mind that of the Regency in London, the two reached that state from opposite directions: the Viennese by a process of self-denial, the Londoners by one of self-indulgence. What in London was the unprecedented use of ornament to achieve monumental street façades was, in its Viennese context, a stripping away of all but the minimum of traditional decoration to achieve a restrained and economical architecture.[29]

Similarly the architectural monuments of the Sezession can be seen more as attempts to devise new kinds of ornament than as rejections of ornament as such. Even Adolf Loos achieves, through his use of costly materials, an impression of opulence. The Viennese eye, like the Viennese palate, has been so indulged with richness and variety that the mere reduction to a moderate degree of ornament can give an impression of ascetic restraint.

In the four decades between the demolition of the interior fortifications and the founding of the Sezession, neither restraint nor asceticism played much of a role in Vienna. The Ringstrasse provided unprecedented opportunities for the new young architects to realize their dreams of beauty and expressiveness, unconstrained by considerations of frugality or outmoded notions of aesthetic simplicity. The many surviving monuments of the age of Maria Theresa and her immediate predecessors challenged the architects of the 1860s and 1870s to emulate and surpass them in splendor and magnificence.

Victorian architects deliberately rejected the eighteenth century. Both contemporary French and Austrian architecture, by contrast, looked to their respective national eighteenth centuries for inspiration. In Vienna this meant the palaces and public buildings of Lucas von Hildebrandt and Fischer von Erlach, father and son, massive, dramatic, rich with figurative sculpture, employing all the forms of Italian baroque to glorify and celebrate church and regime and those who ruled. The monster blocks that lined the Ringstrasse used their eighteenth-century vocabulary to convey a modern message.

For their architects, a part of that message was joyful repudiation of the limitations that the Metternich regime had imposed on their creative imagination. Since 1809 Viennese architecture had been kept under the strict control of the *Hofbaurat,* so that the austere neoclassicism that had begun as a generally accepted fashion was maintained as the visual expression of reactionary politics. Other styles, in particular those associated with Romantic nationalism, were stigmatized as politically subversive.[30]

Functionalism, simplicity, and economy, far from being, as the Bauhaus was later to preach, novel requirements of democracy and socialism, were here the stylistic demands of a regime of reaction and repression.[31] With ornament reduced to a minimum, early nineteenth-century buildings were characterized by a marked absence of articulation or indeed of any differentiation between one part of the façade and another.[32] Such simple, standardized, undifferentiated forms seemed to an increasingly restive architectural profession unsatisfactory both for their want of variety and because their poverty of visual elements kept them speechless. To the Romantics, striving to portray ever more complex truths in words and images, the official architecture of *Vormärz* Vienna seemed pathetically tongue-tied, neglecting the ability of shapes, textures, and forms to convey information and express ideas.

"There is perhaps not one branch of the liberal arts and sciences cultivated in the *Kaiserstadt* . . . that has made greater advances during the last twenty years than architecture," wrote the *Builder* in 1866; "the great political storm of 1848 . . . has had the largest influence on the taste of the Viennese for architectural beauty. . . . In consequence of the new political organisation of the monarchy fresh life and vigour were instilled into the public mind."[33] In its origins Viennese historicism was a *revolutionary* style, whereby architects like Ludwig von Förster, Ferdinand Fellner, August von Siccardsburg, Eduard van der Null, and Theophil Hansen took advantage of their new freedom to create forms that would express the spirit of their age. The town-expansion schemes gave them the opportunity to put their theories into practice and replace the old "barracks" style with one that would raise even the block of flats to the level of serious art[34] (fig. 127).

By 1873 enough of the Ringstrasse had taken shape for the French architect and critic J.-L. Pascal to hazard an appraisal. He found "lofty and spacious constructions, heavy with walls, . . . powerful cornices, detached columns, projecting balconies, substantial chain-courses, rich window-frames, gold ornaments, sculptures" (fig. 128). The result was a "solidity and grandeur of which none of our new streets in Paris could give an idea." He attributed it to familiarity with the vast scale of the buildings in the City, "where, on the old narrow streets there rise large palaces of the past century." The new blocks imitated such buildings. "The block of flats gives externally the appearance of a vast residence," he observed. "Many medium-sized proprietors united in order to have a fine façade embracing their flats in a single composition."[35]

One new feature was the recessing of the window behind the surface of the external wall—something that in London had taken place in the early years of the eighteenth century.[36] By lending yet another plane to the already thickly layered façade, the practice both added to the three-dimensional quality of the architecture and reminded the viewer of the extreme thickness and solidity of the walls. The neoclassical façades of earlier structures, with the window panes at the surface, came to look flimsy and insubstantial as well as bare and inartistic by contrast.

By the 1880s new residential architecture was employing even richer external decoration, ransacking the repertoire of baroque design to produce ever more dramatic effects (fig. 129). The wall ceased to be a flat surface but became the

127. *The town-expansion schemes gave them the opportunity to replace the old "barracks" style with one that would raise even the block of flats to the level of serious art.* Building on the corner of Schottenring and Börsegasse, 1984. (Evelyn Benesch.)

128. *(opposite) "Lofty and spacious constructions, heavy with walls... powerful cornices, projecting balconies, substantial chain courses, rich window frames... sculptures."* Neuthorgasse 10, corner of Werderthorgasse, Ludwig von Zettl, architect. (Kunsthistorisches Institut der Universität Wien. Photo Johanna Fiegl.)

ground for sculptured extravagances, made particularly effective by the shadows cast by the strong Viennese sunlight (fig. 130). The "history" evoked in such façades was more a general impression of past traditions than something to be read carefully. Here one must distinguish between the specific references of the Ringstrasse monuments of the eighties—such as the University and the Town Hall—and the exuberant use of historical forms by suburban architects, for whom the façade was a kind of decoration to be chosen by the owner, with no necessary organic relationship to the building that lay behind.[37] Architectural forms which in the hands of serious designers in the sixties had intellectual content by the eighties became frivolous disguises, intended to flatter the social ambitions of modest suburban flat-dwellers.

Everyone could take pleasure in as much decoration as the building owner could afford. The French architect Paul Sédille described a typical Viennese façade in 1884:

The monumental-looking portals with double columns and sculptures and rich cornices; the columned windows, with caryatides and pediments, the other stages adorned with friezes and decorations of all kinds, often with paintings on a gold ground; the balconies carried by columns or winged figures; the entablatures with

129. *By the 1880s new residential architecture was employing even richer external decoration.* Dapontegasse, 1984. (Evelyn Benesch.)

130. *(opposite) The wall ceased to be a flat surface but became the ground for sculptured extravagances.* Schottenring 21. (Kunsthistorisches Institut der Universität Wien. Photo Johanna Fiegl.)

many consoles and crowned with balustrades and statues, are the usual *motifs*. . . . Add to these the square or circular angle pavilions dominating the lateral wings, and above all the overhanging chambers . . . and you will have some idea of the appearance of these vast habitations, suggesting reminiscences of the Italian palaces of the Renaissance, which . . . strike the visitor with astonishment.

Deeper relief and bolder projections were employed in Vienna than in Paris (fig. 131). The Viennese architect could "give life to his façades by advanced masses, detached columns, large balconies, or small chambers corbelled out; and . . . he can *silhouette* his façades by pavilions raised upon them, pediments and accentuated gables, turrets, cupolas, roofs of all kinds"[38] (fig. 132).

Thomas Blashill, visiting Vienna in the late 1880s, was struck by the role of figurative sculpture in creating a lively, varied, and informative street architecture.

In one of the private buildings, I counted one hundred and fifty figures of large size on its four faces; and, if a street census were taken . . . they would certainly equal the population of a respectable market town. . . . Statues stand in lines on ground-floor cornices and on the balustrades over chief cornices; the spandrils of circular-headed openings are filled with figures in high relief. On pediments, large and small, broken or entire, they recline after the manner of Twilight and Dawn in the Medici Sacristy at Florence. . . . Caryatides and Atlantes are, however, the great characteristic feature of Viennese architecture [fig. 133]. They . . . support the chief cornices; they flank the

131. *(above, left) Deeper relief and bolder projections were employed in Vienna than in Paris.* Dapontegasse, 1984. (Evelyn Benesch.)

132. *(above, right) The Viennese architect could "give life to his façades by advance masses . . . large balconies, or small chambers corbelled out . . . pavilions raised upon them, pediments and accentuated gables."* Building on the corner of Schottenring and Bör-segasse, Wilhelm Fraenkel, architect, 1870, 1984. (Evelyn Benesch.)

133. *(opposite) "If a street census were taken . . . they would certainly equal the population of a respectable market town."* Figurative sculpture on façade of Schubertring 9–11. Ludwig von Zettl, architect, 1865. (Kunsthistorisches Institut der Universität Wien. Photo Johanna Fiegl.)

windows . . . they support the pediments over doorways . . . one feels a sense of incongruity when some slim figure stands placidly under an impossible load, or when a prodigy of muscular development does not simply bear but hoists his end of the pediment, turning his face to the wall for that purpose. Indeed, I am not sure that such objects are at best altogether cheerful to look upon.[39] [Figs. 134 and 135]

It is hard to examine the increasing exuberance and activity of the Viennese façade as the seventies move into the eighties, the eighties into the nineties, without sympathizing with the opinion of the Sezession that enough was enough (fig. 136). After a winter spent consuming *Rindfleischsalat, Rostbraten Esterhazy mit Serviettenknödeln, Tournedos Maria Theresia, Salzburger Nockerln, Kaiserschmarrn,* and *Palatschinken* with nuts, chocolate sauce, and whipped cream, one went to Karlsbad to drink the cleansing waters and submit to the regime of a plain, wholesome diet, so as to be able to resume the pleasures of the Viennese kitchen on one's

278

134. *(opposite)* "*Caryatides and Atlantes are . . . the great characteristic feature of Viennese architecture.*" Grillparzerstrasse 6. Wilhelm Stiassny, architect, 1884. (Kunsthistorishes Institut der Universität Wien. Photo Johanna Fiegl.)

135. *(above)* Palais Pallavicini, Josefsplatz (Ferdinand von Hohenberg, architect, 1783.) (Evelyn Benesch.)

136. *It is hard to examine the increasing exuberance and activity of the Viennese façade without sympathizing with the opinion of the* Sezession *that enough was enough.* Produktenbörse, Taborstrasse 10, c. 1900. (Bildarchiv der Österreichischen Nationalbibliothek.)

return to the capital. Had the architectural consequences of the Sezession been comparable, an interlude of austerity to restore the digestive functions and prepare the twentieth century for a resumption of decorative experiment, all would have been well. As it has happened, war and poverty in the short term, aesthetic indoctrination in the long, have reduced us to a permanent diet of boiled potatoes and mineral water.

17

Architecture as Language: Representation and Instruction

 o far the stylistic evidence provides little support for the hypothesis of an underlying unity for nineteenth-century European civilization. Whatever common concerns and shared experiences England, France, and Austria had, they did not express themselves in the outward appearance of their respective capitals. National and local traditions of building and urban design operated seemingly independently of one another to produce cities as unlike as could be imagined.

Yet however different the outward garb, London, Paris, and Vienna in the century after Waterloo responded to and reflected assumptions and convictions shared by the makers of all three. One was that architecture was a language, capable of expressing complex and important ideas. Another was that such ideas ought to be directed to the service of public good and private morality.

The notion of architecture as language has in recent years returned to vogue. In reaction to the hostility to associationism that for so many decades dominated architectural theory, Post-Modernists are today urging that the architect use his craft to express clear ideas in a common language. "We see a babble of tongues, a free-for-all of personal idiolects, not the classical language of the Doric, Ionic and Corinthian Orders," complains Charles Jencks. "Where there once were rules of architectural grammar, we now have a mutual diatribe between speculative builders; where there once was a gentle discourse between the Houses of Parliament and Westminster Abbey, there is now across the Thames, the Shell Building shouting at the Hayward Gallery, which grunts back at a stammering and giggling Festival Hall."[1] For Robert Venturi, the aridity and boredom of recent architecture stems in large measure from its deliberate avoidance of symbols and associations:

> The forms of Modern architecture have been created by architects and analyzed by critics largely in terms of their perceptual qualities and at the expense of their symbolic meanings derived from association. . . . Early Modern architects . . . rejected eclecticism and style as elements of architecture as well as any historicism that minimized the revolutionary over the evolutionary character of their almost exclusively technology-based architecture.[2]

There was nothing esoteric or arcane about the meaning expressed by nineteenth-century buildings. Their style, ornament, structure, and inscriptions were intended to speak clearly not just to other architects or scholars, but to the ordinary man or woman. Rationalists—at the time mostly Gothic revivalists—argued that the exterior should indicate the structural qualities of the building; that its load-bearing walls be visible and seen for what they were: not plastered over, not pretending to be stone while actually brick. The façades at King's Cross and the Gare de l'Est, expressing the shapes of the trainsheds behind them, the visible iron columns supporting the roof of the Bibliothèque Sainte-Geneviève were admired by modern functionalists even at periods when the Victorian aesthetic as a whole was misunderstood and reviled. But at the time such structures were built, people were assumed to be interested in more than the principles of stress and support of civil engineering.

Where did the trains go? Allegorical female statues representing Rouen, Amiens, Beauvais, and the like answered that question quickly enough to anyone approaching the Gare du Nord (fig. 137). (Anyone approaching Blackfriars Station in the latter years of its existence expecting to be taken to Dresden or Baden-Baden or St. Petersburg would have suffered prompt disillusionment.) What would he find when he reached his destination? Murals representing the local customs and characteristics of the provinces reached from the Nordwest Bahnhof in the imperial waiting-rooms would have answered that question, at least for the emperor and his entourage. Whom ought we to thank for making possible railways in the first place? Statues of Watt and Stephenson that still guard the entrance to the East Station in Budapest provide the answer for travelers from that city.

Inscriptions, murals, and statues could convey useful information and suggest

137. *Allegorical female statues representing Rouen, Amiens, Beauvais, and the like.* The Gare du Nord from the boulevard de Strasbourg, 1984. The grander figures at the cornice represent Berlin, Warsaw, Paris, London, and Vienna. (Evelyn Benesch.)

elevating subjects for contemplation. The particular style of the building might indicate what went on inside—often by a *historical* reference. In Vienna, the Gothic of the Votivkirche evoked the piety of the High Middle Ages, the Greek of the Parliament buildings Athenian democracy, the Northern Gothic of the Rathaus the independence of the medieval commune, the Renaissance of the University humanistic scholarship. In London the Houses of Parliament represented the Ancient Constitution, the Law Courts the Common Law, the Queen Anne of Pont Street and Cadogan Square the comfort and hospitality of the seventeenth-century manor house. The building Ludwig von Förster designed for Albert von Klein in 1862, still standing in the Praterstrasse, along whose upper story stand twelve sandstone figures representing the twelve different branches of industry carried on by its owner, served both to convey information and shed luster on a wealthy industrialist[3] (fig. 138). The pictorial decorations that enliven Harrods Food Halls add an educational as well as an aesthetic dimension to a shopping expedition.

That architecture was a language was a truism endlessly repeated. "The history of architecture is the history of the world," proclaimed Pugin in 1843. "The belief and manners of all people are embodied in the edifices they raised."[4] In 1892 N. J. W. Westlake reminded the Architectural Association that "the higher architecture is . . . a language for the expression of thought. . . . In ancient times it expressed the ideas of the period in the idiom of the period."[5] Pevsner expressed the situation thus: "every building creates associations in the mind of the beholder, whether the architect wanted it or not. The Victorian architect wanted it."[6]

In his presidential address to the RIBA in 1904, John Belcher pursued the analogy between architecture and writing further:

> Architecture must tell its tale; it has its message to deliver. Like a musical score it expresses a great deal more than meets the eye. . . . Architecture is the prose of inarticulate but beautiful thought and feeling. Sometimes it tells of the commonplace in life; rising higher it speaks of domestic peace and happiness; and yet again in more stately diction it sets forth the grander and larger purposes of life. It recounts the past, records the present, and holds up ideals for the future. But only when it is enriched from the sister arts of sculpture and painting can it tell the tale with the fulness of eloquence and power.[7]

Here Belcher made explicit a conviction implicit in historicist theory: architecture and its associated arts could convey the maximum of beauty, morality, and truth only if they combined to form a *Gesamtkunstwerk*.

What messages were buildings, cities, and other works of art expected to transmit? What meaning did they possess, what ideas did they contain? What can a city, in its capacity as a work of art, accomplish? What can art do, apart from existing in its own right? It can tell a story, or many stories. It can establish a mood. It can reinforce selected virtues. It can surprise and delight by unexpected juxtapositions of forms, textures, colors, and movements. It can soothe and reassure by repetition of familiar forms, textures, colors, and movements. It can stand for, or *represent,* ideas, qualities, institutions. English critics placed great stress on the expressive qualities of buildings, German theorists on their representational qualities.

Regent Street, the Ringstrasse, the place de la Concorde, like contemporary representational painting and sculpture, take for granted that art is not self-contained and independent, not simply about itself, but about things outside itself:

138a–b. *The building in Praterstrasse, along whose upper story stand twelve sandstone figures representing twelve different branches of industry served both to convey information and shed luster on a wealthy industrialist.* Ludwig von Förster, architect, 1862. (Evelyn Benesch.)

politics, ideas, morals, emotions, institutions, history. The notion of the self-sufficiency of art was a by-product of Romanticism, and a common enough heresy, but a heresy nonetheless, one held by an articulate minority, but with little influence on the way buildings and cities were actually designed and erected. The conviction that art had meaning, that such meaning was related to the great world outside art narrowly defined, and that good art could be distinguished from bad less by its formal qualities than by the extent to which it told the truth about the outside world and lent support to high moral principles, affected urban layout, the external appearance of buildings, and their interior plans.

The Ringstrasse, for instance, is "about" monarchy, empire, law, science, music, painting, sculpture, scholarship, order, joy, movement, commerce, war, industry, horticulture, thrift—not necessarily in that order. As an ideological statement, it is seen by Hannes Stekl as conveying the values of centralized monarchy,[8] while Carl Schorske sees in it the values of a confident bourgeois liberalism.[9] Actually it contains both, being the product of an age when, for a time, the values of monarchy, aristocracy, and bourgeoisie seemed fundamentally compatible.

Today such values are at best on the defensive, at worst obsolete and irrelevant, yet we respond to the Ringstrasse, which embodies such values, with affection and delight: the physical achievement of its builders has proved more enduring than their didactic intentions. Absolutism, multinational empires, authoritarian theology, a hierarchical social structure, even the liberalism of the 1860s have long since ceased to command general assent. We are of course used to responding aesthetically to a work of art while rejecting the intellectual foundations on which it was created. Henry Adams did not really worship the Virgin Mary while at Chartres any more than we adopt the tenets of the Mayan religion while wondering at the monuments of Uxmal. Yet just as an understanding of the intellectual life of early thirteenth-century France contributes to an aesthetic apprehension of Chartres, an awareness of the intentions of their builders can intensify our pleasure in Vienna, Paris, and London.

The relationships among urban form, ideology, and *Zeitgeist* are hard to pin down. Each generation lives in the city built by its predecessors. Renaissance Florence was medieval Florence embellished with a few classical buildings and disguised with a few more classical façades. Victorian London was mostly Georgian, Edwardian London almost entirely Victorian. Yet even attempts to relate the *changes* introduced in different periods to the dominant ideology of the ruling classes turn up paradoxical anomalies.

Lewis Mumford's category "The Baroque City" is undeniably suggestive: certain parts of certain cities in certain periods *have* displayed qualities of balanced magnificence, controlled movement, dramatic expression, and axial symmetry, frequently with the intention of glorifying an individual, an ideology, a dynasty, a social class. Yet some of the most effective instances of urban baroque come centuries later than the period ordinarily assigned the style by art historians. Mumford himself carries it up to about 1850, well after neoclassicism, industrialization, bourgeois liberalism, and Romanticism—to name but a few movements—ought to have rendered it wholly obsolete. Long after 1850 Edwardian London and twentieth-century Washington provided examples of baroque design and planning more ambitious than anything the age of the Counter-Reformation or of absolutism had achieved. Baroque as an architectural style does not necessarily accompany baroque arrangements of streets and open spaces: eighteenth-century Vienna was a city of baroque palaces lining medieval streets; Haussmann's Paris had a baroque street pattern but classical architecture. Although the baroque is supposed to represent absolutism, Louis XIV chose classicism as the dominant style for his reign; the baroque revival in Ringstrasse Vienna coincided with the liberal era of the Dual Monarchy. The spurt of baroque display in late Victorian and Edwardian London came *after* the Third Reform Bill and coincided with the New Liberalism, Fabianism, and the rise of the Labour party. The City Beautiful in America flourished during the age of populism and progressivism. Vienna during the age of Metternich, which one would have thought the epitome of embattled absolutism, saw an almost total absence of new public building or urban embellishment, and a timidly restrained architecture in what did go up.

Yet some connections between architectural form and the society it serves can be perceived. One notable instance is the theory and practice of *representational* architecture. Of all the aesthetic conventions of the nineteenth century, none strikes us today as odder or more embarrassing than the one that made the external form and structure correspond to the social status of the occupant. Social and economic hierarchies continue to exist, in capitalist and socialist societies alike, but we try to avoid giving them obvious visual expression. Even distinctions based on merit are stigmatized as "elitist." The universal adoption of denim as appropriate garb for everything from hard physical labor to attendance at the opera suggests the pervasiveness of the myth of equality and a disinclination to make distinctions of dress on the basis of class, function, or occasion. The difficulty of identifying the nature of a modern building on the basis of its architecture results from similar inhibitions. Rosalie Colie once recalled her disappointment on a long motor trip at finding that what from a distance looked enticingly like a Howard Johnson's turned out to be a Lutheran church. There are ways of distinguishing an IBM branch office from a nursery school, a council house from a speculative dwelling, but such ways are furtive and guilt-ridden, and subvert architectural orthodoxy.

The nineteenth century felt no such guilt and acted under no such inhibitions. The wealth of stylistic devices it had at its disposal enabled it to make its architecture more blatantly expressive of social distinctions than had earlier centuries. In eighteenth-century London a "first-rate" house differed from a "fourth-rate" one in matters of size and scale, not constructional material or decoration. By the late nineteenth century the contrast between a block of luxury flats in Kensington and a model dwelling in Stepney, or between a working-class suburban terrace and Fitzjohn's Avenue was expressed in every structural and aesthetic device available to the designer. That an age when clothing—particularly of men—ceased to serve as an outward indicator of wealth and class should indulge in such extravagance of individual display through architecture was a paradox noted by contemporaries. Whatever the cause, the tendency of architecture and urban structure to reflect, even to exaggerate, the distinctions of contemporary society contributed wonderfully to the diversity of appearance of Vienna and Paris no less than London.

Even César Daly, disciple of Fourier, exponent of individual equality as the leading characteristic of modern French society, was fascinated by the ways in which architecture could express social hierarchy. In the first volume of the *Revue générale de l'architecture* he showed how the design of a military barracks might reflect the distinctions and relations of the institution that it housed, in which "order, measure, and unity would flow from the hierarchy and create variety. . . .

The rooms of the soldiers would be of a perfect simplicity . . . the apartments of the officers would be of a richness and of an importance proportional to their rank; these differences would be revealed externally as well as internally."[10]

"Representational" architecture did not merely depict a hierarchical social structure but provided a stage on which the kind of life appropriate for those at the top of the hierarchy could most conspicuously be pursued. The key word is *conspicuously,* for the representative life-style stood opposed to the pursuit of privacy and domesticity. A representative dwelling, lacking corridors and service stairs, was one in which privacy was liable to constant interruption. The conviction that individual privacy and domestic withdrawal were inconsistent with nobility and royalty persisted longer in Austria than it did in either France or England.

With the decline of the military functions and independence of the landed aristocracy and the simultaneous rise of the absolute monarch, the Austrian nobility came to derive its power and standing from its participation in the rituals and ceremonies of the imperial and royal court. Courtly manners, formalized patterns of behavior, and splendor in dress and in architectural surroundings grew in importance as real power diminished, hence the representational significance of all outward appearance. In a society at once rigidly hierarchical and fiercely competitive, constant attention to details was essential to enhance or even maintain one's position.[11]

All of Vienna lay within the immediate sphere of influence of the court. Courtly display served as a model and ideal not merely for the nobility in their town and suburban palaces, but for the greater bourgeoisie as well. The "Liberal Era" from 1860 on saw the affluent bourgeoisie imitate with assiduity the manners of the court nobility. The stress on the impressive entrance to the Ringstrasse block, the grand public hall and staircase, and—within the flat—the emphasis on reception rooms at the expense of kitchen, bedroom, and accommodation for the family reflected the extension into private bourgeois life of the values and priorities of absolutism (fig. 139).[12]

The Ringstrasse successfully conveyed the idea that it was occupied by individuals and institutions of more than ordinary importance, that what went on behind the massive and highly ornamented walls had to be taken very seriously indeed. Even those areas devoted to pleasure—the opera, the theaters, the cafés and restaurants and parks—were not to be approached in a mood of thoughtless frivolity. The architecture, heavy, solid, and uniform, evokes emotions of awe, wonder, and fear more readily than affection and delight.

Carl Schorske has argued that, coinciding as it did with the granting of a liberal constitution and the rise to power of a self-confident middle class, the Ringstrasse ought to be seen as a monument to a resurgent bourgeoisie. Between 1859 and 1866, "the substance and meaning of the Ringstrasse program changed, responding to the will of a new ruling class to erect a series of public buildings expressing the values of a *pax liberalis.*" Unlike the Altstadt which expressed the power of emperor, church, and aristocracy, "in the new Ringstrasse development, the third estate celebrated in architecture the triumph of constitutional *Recht* over imperial *Macht,* of secular culture over religious faith."[13]

There is much to be said for such an interpretation. The Ringstrasse contains two unquestionably bourgeois monuments: the Stock Exchange and the Town Hall. The Gothic style of the latter suggested the triumph of municipal liberties in both the

Middle Ages and the present[14] (fig. 140). The University had, certainly, in the age of Metternich, contained subversive elements, but by the time it moved into its present building next to the Schottentor it had become a source of pride to the regime as a center of sound scholarship. The opera, theater, concert hall, and museums, however enthusiastically patronized by the bourgeoisie, represented historically the tradition of court and aristocracy.

Finally there came the massive extensions to the Hofburg itself, whose execution dates mostly from *after* the period of liberal ascendancy but whose plans go back to that period. The intention was to link the expanded palace and the art and natural history museums with triumphal arches spanning the Burgring.[15] The relationship between the New Hofburg and the two court museums as planned, and even as it actually stands, assumes a symbiosis between "culture" and "monarchy." The bourgeoisie are nowhere in sight.[16]

The question remains whether the monuments of the Ringstrasse—imperial and royal or bourgeois—can better be understood as expressing the triumph of the latter or the persistence of the former. "Vienna's Ringstrasse district was . . . a vast public salon in which the different layers of high society met without mixing," Arno J. Mayer has written, arguing that "the conventions of this cohabitation were fixed, not by the ambitious yet insecure bourgeois, but by the self-assured aristocrat . . . the urban space . . . favored the continuing pre-eminence of the aristocracy."[17] Particularly favorable to aristocratic domination was the "relentlessly historical" style of the monuments that lined the Ringstrasse.

It was not so much the historical nature of the architecture—*all* architecture of the period was historical—as the particular historical references and reminiscences of the monuments and buildings that render suspect the interpretation that they express specifically bourgeois values. Ritual, hierarchy, leisure, extravagance, all expressed in a style closely associated with eighteenth-century absolutism, are not virtues one would have expected a bourgeoisie truly confident in itself to espouse. Speculation about what a Ringstrasse that genuinely celebrated bourgeois values—thrift, diligence, sobriety, worldly asceticism, the Invisible Hand, never dipping into capital, the rational allocation of resources—might have looked like can only make us grateful for the failure of the bourgeoisie really to put its stamp on the street.

On the face of it monumentality in itself would seem to be inconsistent with sensible capitalistic practice. It involves the diversion of savings from productive investment to the creation of works of art for public enjoyment, the glorification of one or more abstract qualities, and the satisfaction of individual or corporate vanity. Yet one of the most pervasive developments in nineteenth-century cities generally was the growing number of groups, institutions, and activities deemed appropriate for monumental treatment. What had once been the peculiar privilege of the spiritual and secular masters of society became a universal indulgence.

Renate Wagner-Rieger has argued that, in the period of early historicism which she dates from 1830 to 1860, it became possible for all building types to strive toward monumentality.[18] The social barriers that had long separated one architec-

---

139. *The stress on the impressive entrance to the Ringstrasse block, the grand public hall and staircase reflected the extension into private bourgeois life of the values and priorities of absolutism.* First-floor vestibule, Dr. Karl Lueger-Platz 2. (Kunsthistorisches Institut der Universität Wien. Photo Johanna Fiegl.)

290

tural genre from another were now being breached as successfully as those in the realm of literature, which had, for instance, long restricted tragedy to kings and princes, comedy to the bourgeoisie. If the bourgeoisie and common man could aspire to tragic status, so could the buildings where they lived and worked aspire to monumentality.

César Daly specifically cited monumentality as a proper goal for domestic architecture in 1840. Not only did it lose its exclusive association with high social rank, but it was unaffected by the otherwise crucial distinction between the public and the private. In 1862 he returned to the notion of monumentality, but he was then concerned more specifically with monuments strictly speaking, unique objects commemorating something or representing some general idea.[19] In his *Architecture privée,* he wrote of the monument as an instrument of patriotic unification, of national inspiration:

> The public monument, the monument which addresses itself to *everybody,* which belongs to the *nation* . . . needs to satisfy the *general, national* sentiment of beauty. . . . Finally, beauty, as *everyone conceives it,* must shine on the face of our *public* buildings, like glory on our army, holiness on our religion, loyalty on all acts of national life. . . . The beauty of a public monument ought to be a dazzling and direct emanation of the living genius of society, a profession of aesthetic faith by the race.[20]

The private dwelling, fortunately, did not have to bear the weight of such national and moral responsibilities.

And yet private as well as public architecture was involved in the making of Paris, itself the greatest of all national monuments, the most eloquent testimony to the achievements of French civilization. The effect, both individually and in the aggregate, of the representative blocks of dwellings that were lining the new streets of the capital was monumental in precisely the sense defined by Daly. The boulevard de Sébastopol, the boulevard Malesherbes, the future avenue de l'Opéra, though dedicated to private residence and private business, were designed to elicit quite the same surge of civic and national pride that the place de la Concorde, Notre Dame, and the Louvre called forth. Paris had its share of private retreats, hidden back courtyards, narrow passages, and unpretending side streets in its older quarters, colonies of bourgeois villas in its outlying suburbs, where it put aside its full-dress uniform. But no city anywhere has taken more seriously its duties to look and behave throughout as if the eyes of the world were on it and the honor of the nation at stake.

Vienna, by concentrating its monuments along the Ringstrasse, and by employing shamelessly theatrical architectural techniques, achieved a higher emotional intensity in its center than can be found in any single part of Paris. But such a piling up of institutions embodying the power, learning, and creativity of the empire; such prodigality of grandiloquent façades, heroic statuary, dramatic scenic compositions meant, inevitably, that there was less to go around elsewhere. While the inner and outer suburbs of Vienna are always decent and frequently pleasing in aspect, and far from wanting in instances of heightened aesthetic incident, they do not display the consistent monumentality that Paris achieves throughout.

---

140. *The Gothic style of the [Town Hall] suggested the triumph of municipal liberties both in the Middle Ages and the present.* The New Town Hall, Vienna. From *The Builder* 35 (1877): 980.

To listen to most Victorians, London, by such standards, was nowhere at all. "Contrasted with Paris, or many other continental cities, London fails to maintain its dignity," complained the *Builder* in 1857. "A most happy position is lost for want of grand leading routes; a noble river mutilated through sheer neglect; and many majestic buildings sacrificed, simply because they cannot be viewed at the right *coup d'oeil*. Every artist has made up his mind that this is a most lugubrious, if not an unhappy, metropolis."[21]

The new Houses of Parliament, and the as yet uncompleted Victoria Embankment would in due course provide London with a succession of monumental structures along the Westminster bank of the Thames that would be both impressive in themselves and eminently visible. By 1914 not only the Embankment, but Whitehall, the Mall, and Trafalgar Square itself would have consciously adorned themselves in dress of state. Yet the attempts of the late Victorians and Edwardians to provide London with its share of triumphal ways and open spaces would do little to disguise the major thrust of their concerns: the home and the quality of life lived there. Even for the new London County Council, its most enduring and valuable monuments would be neither Kingsway nor the Aldwych nor certainly County Hall, but its housing estates. Implicit in its scale of priorities was the conviction that the city ought primarily to be a means of promoting the welfare and ennobling the morals of its citizens.

It was accepted in Vienna and Paris as well that architecture, whether in the form of individual buildings or in the mass, could not only convey information, represent the social and political structure, and express the aspirations of owner and occupier, but serve as an ethical agent, a means of exhortation, a moral statement to the world at large.

The concept of "social control," whereby the dominant class makes deliberate use of institutions and amenities such as schools, public baths, libraries, philanthropic housing, and organized sports to inculcate certain values and patterns of behavior among members of subordinate classes, thereby rendering them less dangerous to the established order, has been much explored in recent years.[22] The notion offers a promising tool for understanding how cities were intended to be used, so long as we do not confine its meaning to explicit devices by one social class to influence another. Many of the institutions, many of the visual forms and structural shapes of London, Paris, and Vienna were intended less to influence particular classes than to convey a moral message to society as a whole. Their intended audience was not limited to the residents of the cities but included provincial visitors, foreign tourists, visiting heads of state, and, extremely important, posterity. Keeping the submerged proletariat content, or at least acquiescent, was but one of the functions architecture and urban design had to perform. When a national or imperial capital was involved, the task grew all the more ambitious. If, as Pericles tells us, Athens was the school of Greece, Paris thought of itself as the school of civilized humanity. As such, it was necessary that it look the part.

It is legitimate to ask, if difficult to answer, how far attempts to use architecture and urban design for moral and political purposes actually worked. To what extent do buildings and planned environments in fact affect human behavior? Do individual bedrooms promote individualism? Do high garden walls encourage autonomous family life? Do social centers promote a sense of community? Do working-class blocks of flats from interwar Vienna encourage a sense of workers' solidarity and promote the class struggle? Do the baroque churches of Vienna, their façades adorned with gesturing saints—exhorting, bearing witness, representing Divine Truth—strengthen religious conviction? Does the statue of Maria Theresa facing the Hofburg serve as the call to patriotism, dynastic loyalty, and imperial pride that it was intended to be?

However sceptical we have become about the ability of room arrangements to affect morals or of didactic art actually to teach, the nineteenth century still clung to the high hopes of the Enlightenment for the possibilities of human betterment. Art in particular seemed to possess the capacity to elevate both taste and morals, and the vision of an entire city filled with objects of beauty designed to do both raised the highest of hopes. The strident and assertive qualities that made Victorian architecture so hateful in the eyes of early twentieth-century aesthetes represented deliberate efforts to turn it into an instrument for popular enlightenment. "There are some old architects still alive, who have not abandoned the orthodox faith of their pupilage . . . [that] it is only the *cognoscenti* who can enjoy a good thing," remarked one critic in 1870. "The efforts of such men were little calculated to raise the public taste." The "simple elegance" of a "chaste brick house in St. James's-square" could speak to the cultivated minority, but would have no impact on the ordinary person. Victorian architects had instead moved to "real designs, in which a positive ornamental and artistic effect was attempted," but even these "could not impress the population, which had been deprived of its proper instruction in art." Medieval revival architecture had helped to educate the public eye by its bold use of color and "minute features of form." Urban architecture had an important role to play in "the great movement for industrial training. Abstract art, the art of *cognoscenti* and *dilettanti,* is not enough . . . there must be something tangible, which the tradesman and artisan can appreciate."[23]

Belief in the capacity of art to bring spiritual improvement to the masses was widely held. To adorn a city with works of art was to educate and uplift its inhabitants. "The liberal diffusion of art in public places and in the streets educates the people through their eyes, forms their taste, imbues the masses with a feeling for beauty by a spectacle that every day polishes manners and elevates the soul," wrote César Daly.[24]

There was in the 1850s a considerable movement, led by the Prince Consort, to bring art and enlightenment into the lives and consciousness of the English working classes. The 1851 exhibition had this as a principal aim, and so did the subsequent development of South Kensington as a cultural center.[25] The *Builder* for the first of January 1859 reported with satisfaction the presence of a large number of working-class visitors at the British Museum during the Christmas holidays. "The conduct of all was admirable, and . . . no case of intoxication or ill-behaviour was noticed . . . although it must be admitted that some passed by the rare objects collected here in a somewhat hurried manner . . . not even the most careless can pass through these galleries without gathering wholesome materials for future thoughts."[26]

But it was the home on which the Victorians placed their firmest hopes for moral regeneration, not just of the workers, but of all classes of society. The French, too, saw the family as the bastion of public morality and used the walls of the *salles des mariages* of the different Paris arrondissements to instruct those entering into the

141. *The French, too, saw the family as the bastion of public morality and used the walls of the* salles des mariages *to instruct those entering into the married state as to their domestic and civic duties.* M. Moreau de Tours, *Sacrifice à la Patrie, Mairie* of the second arrondissement. From *The Builder* 77 (1899).

married state as to their domestic and civic duties. The marriage chamber of the *Mairie* of the second arrondissement, for instance, was adorned with paintings of "ancient Gauls, labourers and warriors . . . grouped into compositions symbolising 'Marriage,' 'The Family,' and 'Sacrifice for One's Country' " (fig. 141). At the sixth one could find "Equality Presides at the Accomplishment of Civic Duties," "The City of Paris offers to Liberty the sacrifice of children slain in fighting for her," and "Fraternity extinguishes Hate and leads Peace to dwell with men."[27]

18

The City as
the Embodiment
of History

he forms that were created, the language used, the ideas expressed, the institutions monumentalized, the values inculcated shared one unifying characteristic: they were employed and perceived by a culture that thought *historically*. A sense of history gave the nineteenth century the organizing principle—a way of relating discrete facts, ideas, and images one to another—that Christian Aristotelianism had given the High Middle Ages, a vision of classical antiquity had given the Renaissance, and Euclidean geometry the seventeenth century. Perhaps even more so, for scholasticism, humanism, and rationalism had at best provided unifying syntheses for a tiny intellectual elite, while the vast majority lived within whatever world view popular culture furnished. But the spread of free and compulsory education and the achievement of something approaching universal literacy in the nineteenth century brought a knowledge of history to a far larger proportion of the European population than had earlier been influenced by Thomas Aquinas or Petrarch or Descartes. Bancroft and Michelet and Treitschke did succeed in imposing their patriotic interpretations of national development on the consciousness of their generation. Macaulay's *History of England* did supersede the last fashionable novel on the tables of young ladies. And that fashionable novel would itself have been as likely as not a historical novel; even if set in the contemporary world, it would have made use of historical allusions and treated the present as part of history.

The days of Hamlet in a powdered wig and Lady Macbeth in a hoopskirt were succeeded by Shakespearean productions aiming at literal fidelity to the dress and surroundings of the age in which the play was supposed to take place. The replacement of Whigs and Tories—defined by their respective attachment to such unchanging principles as Monarchy, Church, the Liberties of Englishmen—by Liberals and Conservatives—defined by their respective attitudes toward the desirable rate and direction of historical change—reflected a new attitude toward change itself. No longer was it equated with flux and disorder but with growth and development; no longer did it portend the unknown but turned out itself to be susceptible to rational analysis and hence to human control. Even mathematics, through the developing science of statistics, now put demographic, economic, and social changes into manageable tables and graphs. The prospect of future change not only ceased to frighten but came to reassure, as the idea of progress, or purposeful change in a desirable direction, came to dominate the Western consciousness.

Above all this looms the figure of Hegel. However special or even perverse some of the specific portions of Hegelian philosophy, the assumptions that underlay his thinking, the kinds of questions he posed, influenced the ideas not only of his avowed disciples but of those, like Burckhardt, who vehemently opposed him. Beyond that, in an attenuated or distorted form, they came to influence the far greater number of people who had never read Hegel and the even greater number who had never heard of him. We are dealing, that is to say, less with the issues over which they argued, than with the unspoken assumptions, shared by all save the outer fringes of thought, that for Carl Becker constituted the history of ideas.[1]

Françoise Choay rightly sees history as one of the two forces competing for the soul of the nineteenth century, the other being an amalgam of science, engineering, and an Enlightenment tradition dominated by Bentham and Fourier.[2] Although she points out that the two forces often coexisted within the same person, as with Viollet-le-Duc, Baltard, César Daly himself, she nevertheless sees the position of the engineer as essentially modern, that of the historically trained architect as consisting of a preoccupation with the past. She is, on a more sophisticated plane, under the same misapprehension that made Pevsner see historicist art as the imitation of earlier styles. The mistake is to confuse history with antiquarianism, to define it as "the study of the past" rather than as a way of perceiving: past, present, and future; art and science; man and nature; church and state; the good, the true, and the beautiful. History for the nineteenth century was no mere field of research, still less a way of escaping from the present, but a pervasive mode of thinking, a world view, a means of coping with and mastering the multitudinous facts, images, and ideas with which the contemporary consciousness was being bombarded. That our own age has for the most part rejected such a world view, that today even professional historians often try to make sense of their findings by moving outside history—in particular to the models of the social sciences—does not lessen its importance as a key to the thought and behavior of the nineteenth century.

The new constructional materials at the disposal of its builders, the triumphs of its engineers, the discoveries of its scientists, and the applications of its technologists unquestionably affected much of the life and thought of the time. The fallacy is to assign these effects a different order of importance from those brought about by other forces: population growth, urbanization, nationalism, religious revivals, Romanticism, utilitarianism, socialism, imperialism, racism, feminism—the whole panoply of phenomena that give the period its peculiar flavor. All of the above *may* somehow turn out to be the consequences of technological advance rather than independent causal elements, but this has yet to be demonstrated. Until it is, it would be prudent to ask what specific effects technological change did have on nineteenth-century cities and to refrain from reproaching their rulers and builders for failing to employ and glorify the new technology in all their works. Above all, let us not make Whiggish distinctions in applying the term *modern:* the new Houses of Parliament were quite as modern as the Crystal Palace, the Midland Grand Hotel as the St. Pancras trainshed; all were profoundly of their time.

History played at least as important a role as technology in shaping the consciousness and determining the conduct of the ordinary European during the century preceding 1914. (By *history* I mean not objective historical forces, in a Marxist or any other sense, but patterns of thought, systems of categorizing, modes of perception associated with the study and interpretation of human history as practiced in the post-Hegelian world.)

First, he had immensely more information, and more accurate information, about events, institutions, and societies both in his own past and in that of the non-European world. The work done by the Bollandists and antiquaries, philosophes and popularizers in clearing away the rubbish of myth and conjecture and establishing soundly based chronologies had, from the late eighteenth century on, been carried forward and brought to a higher level of sophistication by the scholars, mostly at German universities, who changed history from a branch of literature to a scientific profession. Their discoveries and interpretations gradually but pervasively filtered down into textbooks, magazine articles, and novels, and all the other places where the nonhistorian picks up his ideas about what the past was like and how it came to be the present.

Second, and this applies to a much smaller group of the population, he became at least faintly aware that the study of history involved not the transmission of traditional lore, but the critical examination of evidence, and that such evidence was to be found in "sources" or documents, which could take the form of narrative manuscripts, but more often took wildly varied shapes: coins, inscriptions, legal codes, account books, paintings, statues, buildings. Anything, indeed, written or made or altered by human hand could, if properly questioned, be made to reveal something about the past.

Third, he understood that there was likely to be a family resemblance linking one with another the sources or documents from any given time and place: that the Latin used by tenth-century Norman monks was going to be recognizably different from that used by fourteenth-century Italian humanists. More tantalizing, if harder to demonstrate, was the discovery that such resemblances crossed the boundaries separating genres, that there were links between the art and philosophy, politics and economics of a particular age, giving it *as a whole* a distinctive shape or flavor. This conviction about the interconnectedness of things and the organic unity of a given society at a given time was perhaps more an act of faith than a discovered truth, but it was one held with determination by most intellectuals, and taken for granted by the unreflective. It had a strong effect on the kind of art that the nineteenth century produced and the way that art was perceived and enjoyed.

Fourth, *everything* had a history, and nothing could be properly understood unless its history was known. The search for the origin of modern American liberties in the forests of Gothic Germany, the use of philology as the key to the nature of existing languages, the ubiquitous search for the *Urtext* make much nineteenth-century scholarship seem faintly absurd from a late twentieth-century posthistorical vantage point, but absurd or not, the search for *origins* and the tracing backward of causal development then seemed central to an understanding of the present. If the nineteenth century was convinced that family resemblances provided links connecting things contemporary with one another, it was equally convinced of the importance of links of cause and effect through time.

Fifth, a sense of the interconnectedness of things, both in time and in space, meant that a thing to be properly understood had to be seen in its particular historical *context*. Nothing could be studied in isolation, either from the society of which it formed a part, or from the lines of causation connecting it with its particular ancestry.

Sixth, change was inevitable, and the course of historical development, while it might be slowed or deflected, could not be permanently halted, much less reversed. This assumption was less widely shared, particularly in central and eastern Europe, and among certain popes, than the preceding ones. But the assumption of the inevitability of change was more widely held after the French and Industrial revolutions than before.

Finally, history in practice during the nineteenth century was almost always national history. The ecumenical approach of Bossuet and Voltaire was abandoned by an age that was genuinely convinced of the centrality of the growth of the nation-state to an understanding of the past.

Such assumptions came under explicit attack in certain advanced intellectual and aesthetic circles in the nineties and early years of our century, and they came less and less to characterize the thinking of the Western world from the catastrophe of 1914 onward. There is no easy answer to Carl Schorske's lament of the absence of any unifying factor to help make sense of the twentieth century,[3] but I would suggest that the deliberate abandonment of history by large groups of artists and intellectuals, and the happy unconcern of the ordinary man with things historical may provide one negative way of defining our age. That we can no longer assume either a knowledge or a sense of history even among cultivated people today makes, by contrast, the pervasive historicism of the nineteenth century all the more striking and significant.

What evidence of a dominant historical sense can be found in nineteenth-century London, Paris, and Vienna? How much awareness of history is there in the writings of nineteenth-century architects, critics, and observers of urban phenomena?

To begin with, the widespread diffusion of hard historical *knowledge* is everywhere evident. Robert Kerr, writing in 1864, accounted for the variety of historical styles then being used by the "unprecedented degree to which the English public have lately become imbued . . . with the character of virtuosi . . . fifty years ago . . . the entire kingdom could not have clubbed together so much of this kind of knowledge . . . as go to the furnishing at the present day of one second-rate head . . . all the world's a museum, and men and women are its students." He denied the fashionable assertion that the nineteenth century lacked a style of its own. "Our age . . . has a very notable style of its own . . . the style of this miscellaneous connoisseurship . . . the style of instinct superseded by learning."[4]

The professionalization of architectural education, in which architectural history played a central role, the establishment and proliferation of architectural journals, in which lavishly illustrated articles on historical subjects took up more space than reports on contemporary building, insured that the architect would possess a working knowledge of the major historical styles. Illustrated newspapers and the Baedekers and Murray's Guides, which tourists taking advantage of cheap and rapid railway travel carried dutifully with them, helped diffuse a simplified form of the same knowledge. An architect could justifiably expect his public to recognize the difference between Gothic Revival churches in the Decorated and Perpendicular styles, between French and German Renaissance, between Jacobean and Queen

Anne. If he combined elements from different historical styles in a single façade, he could expect his audience to recognize the fact and to judge his skill and historical sense accordingly.

"Although it is impossible not to recognize, in the art displayed in the shops of the Viennese tradesmen, the existence of an acquaintance with every period and style of art, it is . . . only with the architects of Vienna . . . that there can be said to exist a steadfast adherence to the best art of any time," wrote the *Builder* in 1883.[5] The same journal found some palliation of the destruction of the historical record involved in the overenthusiastic restoration of Gothic churches in the resulting increase of historical knowledge: "To some extent, restoration . . . meant the destruction or impairing of the historical . . . value of a building. But . . . restoration included an investigation and development of the history of the structure . . . and brought out facts in connexion with the history of the building dealt with . . . such as constituted a real addition to our critical knowledge of this type of architecture."[6] N. J. W. Westlake, addressing the Architectural Association in 1892, suggested that "the great knowledge of the various styles which have [*sic*] been diffused by the successive study of them" would enable the architects of the day "to form a clear and intelligent knowledge of the capacities of each, as though we could speak many languages and choose that which best expresses our thoughts, even if we lacked a mother tongue." In the ensuing discussion, Owen Fleming objected that architectural style was the collective and unconscious product of an age. "Each century had its own individual style, but he [Fleming] did not think that any of the persons who created that style were aware of what they were doing; they acted . . . without any consciousness of 'inventing.'"[7]

But it was precisely the possibility of unconscious stylistic creativity that the new historical awareness had taken from the nineteenth-century architect, just as it had from the painter or poet or statesman. Having once tasted of the fruit of history, they could not recapture the innocence of an earlier age. Yet what art lost in spontaneity it gained in richness of reference and wealth of allusion. Able to draw on the whole store of accumulated historical knowledge, it had vocabularies and grammars in which to express more complex thoughts than the single styles of previous centuries had permitted. How far it realized such possibilities is another question, but the means were there as never before.

In addition to the knowledge that an educated subject of Victoria or Louis Napoleon or Franz Joseph could bring *to* a building—where his grandparents might feel no more than a "pleasing gloom" or "sensations of awe"—came his ability to acquire knowledge *from* a building. He could approach a piece of architecture as a historical source and learn from it something about the age that produced it. Much of the early preservationist movement sought to protect ancient buildings not because of their beauty—for often, in contemporary eyes, they had little—but in their capacity as historical records, as documents of how men had built and lived in past ages. "Large and useful buildings are . . . the clearest types with which the history of a people is written," observed Geheimrat Ritter von Wiebeling of Munich in the 1830s. "The intellect of a great nation is most correctly judged by the exhibition of its taste," George R. Burnell reminded the RIBA in 1865. He found an analogy "between the forms of faith, and the principles of philosophy, on the one side, and the style . . . given to architecture on the other."[8]

Burnell suggested that architecture not only gave information about a past age but provided the key to that age as a whole. "The 'spirit of the age' is in some measure a novel expression," John Stuart Mill wrote in 1831. "I do not believe that it is to be met with in any work exceeding fifty years of antiquity. The idea of comparing one's age with former ages, or with our notion of those which are yet to come, had occurred to philosophers; but it was never before the dominant idea of an age."[9] The notion continued to dominate European thought for the rest of the century. "So truly is architecture a reflection and monument of a people, that never yet a work worthy the name of noble art was produced by a man not fulfilled with the spirit of his age," wrote James Knowles, Jr., in 1855; "and for learning the character of our own day, where shall we find a better school than the streets and shops?"[10] The belief that history gave each period a unifying essence strengthened the efforts of the nineteenth century to make its cities worthy reflections of the spirit of their own time.

Earlier artists had been unconsciously moved by the *Zeitgeist*; those of the nineteenth century strove deliberately to express it. Earlier critics had judged works of art by standards that they thought were eternal but in fact reflected current aesthetic fashions; those of the nineteenth century were aware of the relativity of standards and judged works of art on the basis of their appropriateness to the times. The loss of innocence as to the immutability of aesthetic, not to speak of moral and political values, contributed to a self-consciousness both in art and criticism, in which everyone was dimly aware that History was speaking through him.

"In giving expression to a building the architect must not only consider what are the uses to which it is to be applied, but he must consult the spirit of the age in reference to these uses," advised Samuel Huggins in 1851. "The same institution may . . . assume a different aspect or character with the march of intellect and progress of society, and will require a different plan and a different character of expression in consequence." Buildings of all sorts had to be made deliberately and consciously *Victorian*.[11] Friedrich von Schmidt, the architect of the Vienna Town Hall, insisted that what was particularly characteristic of its style (late medieval northern Gothic) was that it expressed the spirit of the *modern* age.[12] Employing historical models, far from indicating the creative poverty of the nineteenth century, enabled it to use the language of the past to make a statement to and about the present.[13]

The architect and critic who saw most clearly the impact of the new historical consciousness on architectural practice was César Daly. In his books and in the pages of the *Revue générale de l'architecture* he made explicit the unspoken assumptions of his less reflective contemporaries, as he strove to relate architecture to the course of universal history. The past had, he argued, seen periods of organic synthesis—like fifth-century Greece and the High Middle Ages—in which artistic forms, ideology, and social institutions were consistent within themselves and with one another, and periods of transition marked by confusion and contradiction.[14] The whole of Western cultural history since the breakup of the medieval synthesis had been characterized by fragmentation and inconsistency. He foresaw a new synthesis emerging which would bring an architecture as expressive of its age as the Greek and the Gothic had been of theirs, but until that happened the arts would be as heterogeneous and diverse as the civilization that produced them.

Daly's particular theory is of less interest than the mode of thinking he employed to arrive at it, and his manner of placing architectural evidence into an historical context. Aesthetic values, like all ideas, were relative to the period of history in which they were found. "One does not really possess an idea, even that of the *House,* unless one knows its history." He dissociated himself from the assumptions of the neoclassicists, for whom "Greek and Roman works of art are not . . . simply expressions of the ancient system of ideas, that is to say, of the intellectual and moral state of a civilization destined to give way to a higher civilization . . . but manifestations of a sense of *absolute beauty."* Architecture was a language, and the key to that language was history. The architect had to be able to select motifs from the past, "thereby associating in his compositions the past with the present." For his own age in particular, one couldn't become an eminent architect without a profound knowledge of history. "No art lives as much by *tradition* as architecture."[15]

Just as the study of geology had achieved its current state of knowledge through becoming a historical science, just as the study of language required a knowledge of its history, so the architect had to look to the records of the past if he was to master his art. "Our architecture is as rich in archaic details of often doubtful meaning as geological formations are of fossils representing lost species, and languages of words whose original sense has been forgotten or altered." The analogy with historical geology and philology reflects an awareness of the connectedness of seemingly disparate disciplines and of the role of history in providing the connections. "Geologists make rapid progress in paleontological studies, investigating the characters and the habits of extinct species in order to complete, if it is possible, the picture of the entire evolution of organic life on our planet; and on their side philologists do everything possible to lay out the picture of linguistic evolutions." Despite Daly's insistence on the confused and disorderly state of knowledge and the arts in the modern world, one can understand his confidence that a new organic synthesis lay in the near future: one to which history would hold the key.[16]

Throughout his writings Daly stressed the subordination of architecture to the particular character of the age for which it was erected. "*Our domestic architecture results from our manner of living."* The very beauty of an eighteenth-century *hôtel particulier* came from the way it reflected the structure of the household and the nature of the society of the time, in particular the skill with which it embodied and represented a way of life and scheme of values based on hierarchy.[17] Nineteenth-century architecture would have to respond with equal skill to nineteenth-century needs and find external forms to represent nineteenth-century values.

Daly's friend the conservative journalist J. Barbey d'Aurevilly, reviewing in 1861 Daly's *Symbolisme dans l'architecture,* stressed the centrality of history to his philosophy of art. To push his ideas to their logical conclusion would demonstrate that Art was in fact "History idealised."[18] The alternative to art for art's sake was, therefore, not art in the service of an ideology—what a later generation would call commitment, or *engagement*—but art as the expression (or representation) of History, as manifested in the spirit of the age.

Daly developed his view of history with particular reference to domestic architecture and the family, arguing that the plan of the dwelling necessarily responded to the mode of existence imposed by the particular civilization, its appearance to the dominant sense of art, and that in its totality it made "a thousand revelations on public taste, on the customs and manners of the family, and it offers innumerable insights into the character of social relations."[19] He was convinced of the necessity of an architecture appropriate at once to the material conditions and intellectual values of his age, one that would enter into the feelings of the century [*pénétrer . . . dans les entrailles du siècle*] and contribute to its physical and spiritual needs. He rejected classicism on the grounds that "our sensibility [*notre sentiment*] is not identical to that of antiquity." Even more alien to the spirit of the age was the Gothic revival: "the genius of our civilization is in total reaction to the feudal and fanatical genius that characterizes the Middle Ages." The rationalist school, as he termed those who looked to the civil engineer for leadership, would deprive architecture of all its poetry.[20]

The appropriate architecture for the age, one that reflected and expressed its philosophical diversity and its abundance of historical knowledge, was eclecticism: "An eclectic atmosphere totally envelops the modern world, all lungs breathe it, and, mixed with our blood, it operates on the heart and mind of each of us, giving its particular color to our feelings and ideas, art and science, religion, philosophy and politics."[21] Eclecticism was not the basis for the best imaginable architecture, one comparable to that of the ancient Greeks or the High Middle Ages, but it was the *only* one appropriate to the nineteenth century as it actually was. Nor would it remain unchanged, for it would evolve along the same lines that the course of history would take. Architecture's incoherence and uncertainty of direction since the Middle Ages reflected the character of the modern age quite as appropriately as the Gothic had reflected that of the thirteenth century: "modern Art has been, by its lack of originality, by its revivals [*renaissances*] and its hesitations, the exact representation of the lack of fixed and determined social ideas that has characterized the world since the Middle Ages."[22] It was not just the architects of the Second Empire whose lack of originality reflected their age, but Bramante and Palladio and Perrault and Mansard and all who worked within the classical tradition. Only with the nineteenth century had historical development reached the stage in which the revival of historical styles one after the other could be replaced by an architecture in which the whole historical repertoire was available to the artist for exploitation.

The period that had come closest to a new synthesis analogous to that of the age of Pericles or the High Middle Ages was that of Louis XIV, which had "a unity of spirit and a general harmony of things appropriate to characterize a period of national apogee," in which literature, painting, music, and dance, along with the forms of etiquette reflected "number, weight, and measure." But the Regency and reign of Louis XV reacted against and destroyed the precarious unity of the preceding age. "Grace succeeded gravity, comfort and caprice in social life and in architecture were substituted for order and majesty. It was the reign of Women." From such new impulses came, among other consequences, new domestic comforts. Less admirable was the frivolity of the rococo. In vain did serious architects protest against its capriciousness: the new feminine dominance of taste replaced the rule of Vitruvius by that of Fancy. The new sobriety and balance of the style of Louis XVI arrested the excesses of the tendency and provided a basis for the developments of the following century.[23]

Here again Daly made explicit assumptions more generally characteristic of the thought of his time, presenting a Hegelian thesis-antithesis-synthesis dialectic, with the hieratic rationalism of the age of Louis XIV producing the graceful, sensual, feminine reaction of the age of Louis XV, and the art of Louis XVI synthesizing the best of both. Equally characteristic of French attitudes was his treatment of the eighteenth century. In contrast to the necessity that every Victorian Englishman felt to condemn that age for its coldness, its reliance on rules, its immorality, its dreariness, Daly saw it as an important and praiseworthy stage in the development of modern civilization. There is none of the denigration, none of the patronizing superiority, none of the venom that cheapen Victorian art history whenever it deals with the Georgians.

Yet France had a revolution in 1789 and England did not. And that revolution constituted a total repudiation of the ancien régime and its institutions, one that no subsequent regime, royal or imperial, has been able to reverse. Contemporary British history, by contrast, showed continuity and organic development, with monarchy, aristocracy, the legal system, weights and measures, county boundaries—all the external forms of life—remaining what they had been. Any dramatic alterations in the fundamental structure of things—decimal currency, the annihilation of Rutland and Middlesex—lay far in the future. By comparison France seemed, from across the Channel, a byword for instability.

Yet in the realm of the arts the situation was reversed. The poetic revolution of Lamartine and Hugo and Vigny was mild and cautious compared with that of Wordsworth and Coleridge and Southey: a few liberties taken as to the placing of caesuras, an expansion of the permitted vocabulary, and greater latitude of subject, but maintaining the Alexandrine couplet as the form of expression. In painting, admittedly, the French were more adventurous, although none in the *early* nineteenth century more so than Turner. But in architecture the French maintained aesthetic continuity at a time of political discontinuity. It was not simply a matter of the Gothic revival never really getting off the ground, despite Viollet-le-Duc, but of the unbroken line of development that classicism took. In England even those working within the classical tradition felt it necessary to sneer at the brothers Adam, just as every literary critic had to demonstrate that, like Willoughby, he admired Pope no more than was proper. The French did not wait until the brothers Goncourt to treasure the arts and letters of the eighteenth century: they had never ceased to regard them as an important and valuable part of the national cultural tradition.

Continuity, the maintenance of traditional values, taste broadening down from precedent to precedent: French architectural history showed the qualities the Victorians admired in their own constitutional history, while English architectural history presented the chaotic appearance of French constitutional history. Just as no one of the political revolutions succeeded in creating anything like the general acquiescence that 1689 had produced in England, but rather added yet another splinter group, so each new aesthetic revolution added to the number of irreconcilable camps of English architects. Its Greeks, Romans, Goths, and Elizabethans were its Bourbons, Orleanists, Bonapartists, Jacobins. If the English of the 1760s had their sixty religions and their one sauce, the subjects of Victoria were as fragmented in their worship of beauty. The French, to be sure, had their opposing schools, and Viollet-le-Duc held views different from those of Henri Labrouste; but so did the English have their political parties, each loyal to monarchy, church, and constitution. On fundamentals French architects were agreed, as were English politicians.

Both societies used history to understand themselves and their world; the French found in history things that the English did not. Victorianism can be understood as an attempt to find a valid *alternative* to the eighteenth century; contemporary French culture was able to live with its eighteenth-century heritage very comfortably indeed.

The contrasting attitudes manifested themselves not only in the styles in which new buildings were erected but in the way old buildings were treated. The Victorians went to some effort to adapt Georgian buildings in London to make them acceptable to modern taste. It was, for example, a policy of the Grosvenor and Bedford estates that, on the renewal of long leases, radical modernization of the façades be undertaken. The Bedford estate in the 1850s and 1860s plastered over Georgian fronts, added bedroom stories, and installed plate-glass windows. The Grosvenor estate imposed rusticated plasterwork on ground stories, heavy window dressings on upper stories, and, most noticeably in the better streets of Mayfair, extended Kensington-like porches over the entrances. The strange doorframes that the Bedford estate gave the west side of Gower Street in the seventies and eighties were its way of attracting gentlemen private residents to houses that, in their original Georgian dress, had descended to the status of lodging houses and private hotels. The elaborate refacing of the greater part of Russell Square in 1899 and 1900 constituted an ambitious attempt to raise its social standing by bringing it up to date architecturally. Such policies cannot be dismissed as the aesthetic vagaries of eccentric dukes but were honest efforts to satisfy the requirements of the affluent householder, who had to be enticed to remain in or return to streets of eighteenth-century origin, and resist the attractions of modern houses in Kensington, Bayswater, Hampstead, and the better railway suburbs.

Something of the sort seems to have been done by house owners in the older section of Paris in the years around 1852 to compete more effectively for tenants with the newer areas to the west and northwest. César Daly spoke in 1840 of how "old houses, putting off their ragged garments, dress themselves anew, and strive to regain an air of youth."[24] But the impression one gets today in perambulating streets of eighteenth-century origin in Paris is that, once one looks above the shop fronts, no fundamental alteration of façades has taken place. The remodeling Daly spoke of was most likely internal modernization: the installation of antechambers, the addition of servants' stairs, or more cosmetic changes in paneling, plasterwork, and the marble chimneypieces and mirrors that so impressed the subjects of Louis-Philippe. More often, because the migration of the affluent to more spacious neighborhoods proved on the whole irreversible, the alterations took the form of partitioning large rooms into rabbit warrens, so that a larger number of poorer tenants could be accommodated in the space abandoned by middle-class families. For such tenants, the addition of street façades in the latest architectural fashion would have been an unnecessary extravagance. For the genuine aristocracy in their *hôtels* in Saint-Germain, the effacement of the external architectural expression of the ancien régime would have been morally unthinkable even if they had had the money to indulge in such follies.

In Vienna eighteenth-century architectural dress was not only not despised but positively admired throughout the nineteenth century. The splendid new blocks of flats of the Ringstrasse were left to the nobility of newer creation and the upper bourgeoisie, who were not lucky enough already to have baroque residences of their own. Some buildings in the City did have extra floors added and façades altered, but a high proportion of them retained their original outward appearance.

Gründerzeit architecture itself strove less to provide a modern alternative to the baroque than to push baroque decorative forms to their logical extreme. The dominant neo-Grec of the Second Empire and Third Republic likewise served more to extend and develop eighteenth-century forms than to repudiate them. What both *Gründerzeit* and neo-Grec did repudiate was the plainness and sobriety of the neoclassical *Vormärz* architecture of the Biedermeier era on the one hand and the Revolutionary and Napoleonic period on the other. For the dominant eighteenth-century style—baroque in Vienna, classical in Paris—Ringstrasse Vienna and Haussmannite Paris had nothing but admiration, and a desire not only to emulate but to surpass in splendor and taste.

That the French and the Austrians should feel pride in and affection for the architectural monuments of the recent past, whatever their attitudes toward the political and social climate in which they had been erected, is not surprising. Only in the China of the Maoist Cultural Revolution was the *art* of the prerevolutionary past seen as irremediably tainted by the ideology of that past. The Hermitage and the Kremlin and GUM are no less objects of Russian national pride today because of their czarist origins, any more than Colonial Williamsburg suggests to Americans shameful memories of subservience to Hanoverian kings. It is the Victorian English attitude toward their Georgian heritage that needs to be accounted for.

Not by the wildest stretch of the imagination can Victorian England be regarded as having experienced a Cultural Revolution or as lacking awareness of the value of its national artistic traditions. The Gothic Revival, the liturgical extravagances of the Oxford movement, the popularity of the novels of Sir Walter Scott, the Pre-Raphaelite phenomenon, to go no further, suggest a society obsessed with the past in general and its own in particular. It is the selective nature of its attitude to the past and its ambivalent attitude toward the eighteenth century that call for examination.

Even here it would be unwise to overstate the case. Thackeray's *Virginians,* the young Macaulay and his sisters reading *Sir Charles Grandison* aloud to one another, the repeated performances of Handel's *Messiah* with ever-larger massed choruses, the popularity of *The Vicar of Wakefield,* the Johnsonian cult, the veneration of Edmund Burke—certainly the Victorians found much to enjoy and admire in Georgian civilization. But there was condescension and amusement even in their admiration: not, perhaps, so very different from the way we, until recently, looked on the Victorians. It was how quaint! how amusing! how typical! rather than the awe and respect with which they entered a Gothic cathedral or attended a performance of Shakespeare. If the Victorians felt affection for some aspects of the eighteenth century, they could never quite take it entirely seriously.

Eighteenth-century London, though, was neither amusing nor quaint, and demanded being taken seriously. For one thing there was so much of it, and most of what there was was not, to their eyes, especially prepossessing. Whereas eighteenth-century Paris conjured up visions of the *hôtels* and gardens of Saint-Germain-des-Prés and the place de la Concorde, and eighteenth-century Vienna the Karlskirche and the palaces of the Herrengasse, eighteenth-century London evoked visions of Gower Street and its likenesses: plain, smoke-begrimed, and dreary. A constitutional monarchy kept poor by a watchful parliament could give London none of the adornments which the absolute rulers of the Continent bestowed on their capitals. The dullness of the Hanoverian courts did nothing to counteract the preference of the English aristocracy for country pleasures. The wealthy citizens were more likely to emulate their aristocratic betters by building country seats than by building splendid town residences. The Church of England did not try to rival the continental Catholic church as a patron of the arts.

The result was a London lacking in architectural set pieces calculated to awe and astonish. Its virtues—understatement, quiet good taste, and sanitation unrivaled at the time—lacked the immediate appeal to the senses of the gesturing saints on the parapets of Viennese churches or the towering dome of the Invalides. And the comparative virtues of Georgian London in the areas of sanitation and spaciousness of layout were just those areas in which the Victorians could justly afford to be condescending if not censorious, for in such respects they could and did surpass their grandparents. In plumbing, sewerage, water supply, street lighting, paving, transport, the Victorians could look with pitying smugness at their benighted past. It was in the realm of material progress more than in the fine arts that Georgian London excelled, and here Victorian London easily outstripped it. It took a later generation to appreciate the less immediately apparent urbanistic achievements of the Georgian planners and builders of London. And by then it was too late, for most of those virtues had already been obliterated either by the Victorians or their bungling successors.

If the Victorians found little of visual delight in London, they were becoming aware of its historical dimensions. The popularity of topographical guidebooks, in which antiquaries like E. Beresford Chancellor described the former appearance of different London neighborhoods, listed the famous residents of particular streets, and related events to the places they occurred suggests a widespread eagerness to see behind the commonplace present to a romantic past. To the historian today trying to recapture the appearance of Victorian London such volumes can be frustrating and maddening: only by inadvertence do they pause in their interminable passages on literary and historical associations to reveal anything about what the streets or neighborhoods looked like at the time. But they are evidence for a kind of historical sense among the Victorian reading public: perceiving the ghosts of former residents walking their streets, the shadows of earlier buildings behind the existing façades. The notion of history that it reveals is an unsophisticated one: that of a costume drama set in a highly colored past quite separate from the humdrum present. Anecdotal rather than analytical, it made no effort to relate one event to another or to place the individual streets and buildings in a broader urban context. Yet the interest in *associations* that linked particular parts of London to pieces of literature and names and events from the past represented a first step in the direction of genuine historical inquiry.

Somewhat more sophisticated were the official efforts to foster patriotism or enhance popular awareness of the national cultural heritage by erecting commemorative monuments or restoring buildings of historical interest. Even the destruction of the past proceeded according to deliberate historical principles. The clearances required by the Metropolitan Improvements of London and Haussmann's boulevards in Paris swept away much of the historical fabric of the two cities yet nonetheless reflected a kind of historical awareness. By clearing surrounding buildings away to expose and make prominent selected monuments—what he called *dégagement*—Haussmann made them more visible, better available for study, better able to dominate the townscape.[25] The Tour Saint-Jacques, restored in 1853 and conspicuously isolated at the junction of the boulevard de Sébastopol and the rue de Rivoli, typifies his policies (fig. 142).

A similar impulse was at the same time taking works of art from their original locations in archeological sites, churches, and private houses and placing them in museums, where they would be classified according to historical and stylistic categories. The aim in both cases was partly historical, partly aesthetic: the selection of a work of art of certified merit and its separation from its less important surroundings. Such a process of judgment, selection, and classification for didactic purposes was in accord with broader contemporary tendencies toward specialization and segregation, in particular the separation of art from crafts, classical from popular music, architecture from building. The human mind has in all times and places attempted to impose an intelligible structure on disorderly reality; what was new in the nineteenth century was the predominantly historical nature of the categories imposed.

The destruction of substantial portions of individual churches in the name of restoration that characterized the Victorian attempt to transform the actual medieval survivals into an idealized representation of the Gothic was consistent with contemporary scholarly practice.[26] Just as the pious editors of George Washington's correspondence corrected the grammar and deleted expressions unworthy of the father of his country, so Viollet-le-Duc restored Gothic churches to a state of ideal perfection they had never attained in the Middle Ages. The scholarly and architec-

142. *The Tour Saint-Jacques conspicuously isolated at the junction of the boulevard de Sébastopol and the rue de Rivoli.* Boulevard de Sébastopol, looking north. (Musée Carnavalet.)

tural conventions of the nineteenth century were not ours, but neither were they stupid or inconsidered; whatever their faults, nineteenth-century historians and historicist architects cannot be accused of approaching the past with trembling passivity. It is their active collaboration with the builders of the past that gives such energy and originality to their works of both restoration and emulation.

The widespread diffusion of historical habits of thought and of hard historical knowledge affected the way the nineteenth century built anew in its cities as well as the way it dealt with the old. It gave its architects a degree of choice unavailable in any previous generation. Freed from the necessity of working within a single dominant style, they could choose to imitate or take elements from any style of the past, or to mix elements from a number of historical styles, as seemed most appropriate to the task at hand. Rightly or wrongly, they believed that their knowledge of history had liberated them from its constraints.

The twentieth century, while consciously rejecting history as an organizing principle, yet retains the historicist conviction that certain styles are appropriate to our age and that others are not. Even "post-Modern" architects assume that they must work essentially within the Bauhaus tradition, at most introducing an occasional allusion to an earlier style. The seeming inability of the architectural profession today to respond to unmistakable popular rejection of the Bauhaus aesthetic stems in part from its failure to question the formula: one century, one style. The anti-historicist practice of contemporary architects is based on philosophically historicist assumptions. They are the slaves of history—or rather a view of history—not its masters.

The physical destruction of the surroundings involved in the isolation of historical monuments might suggest that the nineteenth century was unaware of the importance of context. Though it did violence to the principle in such instances, it nevertheless honored it in theory. Just as the meaning of every historical fact depended on the time and place of its occurrence, each new building, each new street, each new neighborhood had to be viewed in its spatial and temporal context. The nineteenth century saw the city as not only extended in space but extended in time, not as an isolated phenomenon but as something that would, with modifications, endure into the future, as it had from the past, like Burke's vision of the British Constitution.

Nineteenth-century cities show strange juxtapositions and startling discontinuities. In London in particular, changing fashions as to building materials and styles, and a tendency both toward higher ceilings and a greater number of stories led to sharp breaks in the building line whenever a new structure was inserted into an existing street. In Paris the intersection of a Haussmann-era street with an older neighborhood can produce notable contrasts in scale and texture. The suburbs of Vienna are enlivened by the appearance of tall *Gründerzeit* buildings next to one- and two-story survivals from the original village street. Yet such breaks in architectural uniformity provide a sense of historical development, and serve as living records of that change, just as the intrusion of a basaltic dike in a limestone cliff records a volcanic event in the geological past.

What one never finds in a nineteenth-century city is evidence of attempts to obliterate the past entirely and proceed as if the world had been created yesterday, like our recent efforts at comprehensive redevelopment. Haussmann cleared away the slums of the Ile de la Cité, the Office of Woods and Forests pulled down the rookery of St. Giles, and Franz Joseph had the inner fortifications of his capital removed: yet all three projects, once they had been completed, left many links with the past to preserve a sense of historical continuity.

Vienna treated its past with greater solicitude than either London or Paris, in that it never engaged in street improvements involving more than the bare minimum of destruction. Individual buildings were, to be sure, replaced by others, and arrangements were made for the eventual widening of narrow streets. Yet the main danger to historic buildings was not public policy but rising land values, which worked to make replacement a profitable option.

It may be unnecessarily kind to the memory of Baron Haussmann to defend his trail of destruction by pointing out how much more ruthless the town planners of the 1960s were. His moderation, it could be argued, resulted from limited resources, not from latent preservationist principles. Yet the difference between a Haussmann *percée* and the totally rebuilt areas such as the Front de Seine, the place d'Italie, and the purposeful devastation of the nineteenth arrondissement is not merely one of scale and extent. For not only did Haussmann's broad new ways attach themselves with care and success to adjacent segments of the original Paris, but they themselves took the form of *streets*—streets widened and glorified and idealized, but streets nonetheless—while a central principle of twentieth-century town planning has been the destruction of the street.[27] Superblocks, limited-access motorways, pedestrian precincts, elevated walkways, sunken plazas, people-movers: every device that human ingenuity could contrive has been used to render unnecessary the street, combining wheeled, hoofed, and pedestrian traffic, commerce and residence, business and pleasure, movement and repose.

A Haussmannized boulevard was appropriate dress for a city based on *historical* principles; a *grand ensemble* or superblock or completed urban renewal project is appropriate punishment for a century that has turned its back on history and sought its salvation in the social sciences. History is inclusive, unsystematic, and untidy: it dare exclude *no* evidence; no aspect of the human experience is alien to its concerns. (Here, to be fair, I am defining history as Herodotus wrote it, not the more restrictive kind that Thucydides inaugurated.) A street comes from somewhere and is going somewhere else; it has both movement and direction. The Anti-Street—or whatever expression will serve to encompass the manifestations of recent town-planning theory and practice—is intended not for becoming but for being, not for motion but for repose. It seeks to approximate in glittering reality the Ideal Type of the social scientist, in which exceptions to the rule, muddle, and human diversity have been rigorously excluded. It stands outside time, outside history, just as any properly formulated law or abstract theory stands aloof from the flux and confusion of day-to-day experience. Just as social scientists are divided into departments of economics, sociology, political science, and so on, according to the particular aspect of human behavior in which they specialize, so the properly constituted Anti-Street—let us use the word, on the analogy of anti-matter, to stand for the anti-city of our own day—is neatly divided into residential areas, recreational precincts, manufacturing zones, cultural centers, shopping plazas, and the like. It is human experience ordered and methodized.

Not that Haussmann's perfected street, or boulevard, is human experience in its raw chaotic form; but the principles of organization are more akin to the working concepts of the practicing historian than the mathematically precise categories of the social scientist. There are, for instance, separate ways for wheeled and non-wheeled traffic, pedestrians and service vehicles. Sidewalks are partly for walking, partly for lounging at café tables. In the facing buildings business will occupy the street level, residence the upper floors. Aesthetically, individualized decorative features will be maintained within the overriding rules of classical design. The variety of possible behavior in a well-conducted Parisian street is not infinite, any more than a single work of history tries to encompass the whole of human experience: it is simply greater than that of any part of the Anti-Street.

The nineteenth-century city strove to be a *Gesamtkunstwerk,* a vast opera to which all of the arts made their due contribution, but in which each subordinated itself to the artistic vision of the whole. The specifically Wagnerian connotations of the word can best be ignored, although it is symptomatic of the embarrassment the mid-twentieth century felt at the very notion of the *Gesamtkunstwerk* that Bayreuth after 1945 ignored Wagner's specific instructions on scenic effects in its productions, with overwhelming critical approval. Meyerbeer or early Verdi may be more appropriate analogies for the remade Paris and Vienna. The point is that just as a multitude of human activities went forward simultaneously along the Ringstrasse or a Parisian boulevard, so all of the arts were employed in their embellishment. The sculptor, the painter, the horticulturist all gave of their best, while the poet spoke in the theater, the musician in concert hall and opera house and in the bands in the parks performing Strauss and Lanner. National politics in the Parliament building, municipal politics in the Town Hall, scholarship in the University, capital investment in the Stock Exchange, flirtation at the *Sirk-Ecke:* the Ringstrasse provided an arena for all aspects of the lives of the favored few who lived along it and frequented its promenades and institutions. Insofar as it stood as a concrete representation of History, it was history as written at the time, in which the lives of the poor and inarticulate received less than their due. But it was not narrowly political and diplomatic: social history, art history, intellectual history, economic history were all more than amply represented.

One would have to range farther afield in Third Republic Paris to get a comparably comprehensive sense of French history, while London's historical treasures were even more scattered and less easily recognizable for what they were. Yet unsatisfactory as *any* single word or phrase is to characterize such diverse and dynamic cities as London, Paris, and Vienna were in August 1914, to think of them as embodying History—meaning both particular national traditions and a shared mode of perceiving reality—may be marginally less misleading than a label referring either to industrialization or to a momentarily triumphant bourgeoisie. That such traditions and modes of perception were about to be shaken and transformed, if not totally obliterated, renders the surviving remains of the three cities both poignant and instructive to our own age.

The current mood of reactionary preservationism—which may turn out to be part of a revolution in sensibility and thought comparable to early-nineteenth-century Romanticism—makes us better able to enter into the thought processes of the builders and designers of cities before 1914. We are discovering that they knew how to create not only a more beautiful, but a more livable, urban environment than we can today. We no longer feel ourselves superior to an age that regarded a house not as a machine for living but as an intellectual and moral statement and a city as a total environment in which the individual might achieve self-fulfillment.

The new visual aesthetic may have fruitful consequences for both urban history and urban policy. It is already turning us from the selective Whig approach that saw the whole of the nineteenth and early twentieth centuries moving inexorably toward some now discredited architectural doctrine or school of town planning. Disenchantment with our cities today can help us better understand the mood of rejection that, as in the London of the 1830s or the Vienna of the 1890s, led to earlier discontinuities in urban and architectural attitudes and policies. If it forces us to use our eyes more carefully when looking at the physical evidence of existing cities for what they can reveal about their makers and to reexamine our assumptions about urban morphology and dynamics, it can only enhance our understanding of what has given particular cities their particular forms. Now that the very survival of the city has been called into question, a heightened awareness of the pleasures that persist in some of them can only make us more perceptive as urban historians, more grateful as city dwellers.

NOTES

Preface

1. Parts of the preface and chapter 1 are taken from Donald J. Olsen, "The City as a Work of Art," on *The Pursuit of Urban History,* ed. Derek Fraser and Anthony Sutcliffe (London: Edward Arnold, 1983), pp. 264–85.

Chapter 1. Urban Virtue and Urban Beauty

1. Johan Huizinga, *Homo Ludens* (London: Paladin, 1970), p. 201.
2. Horace Walpole to George Montagu, 1 September 1760, in *Horace Walpole's Correspondence,* ed. W. S. Lewis and Ralph S. Brown, Jr. (New Haven: Yale University Press, 1941), 9: 295. *The Collected Essays, Journalism and Letters of George Orwell* (Harmondsworth: Penguin Books, 1970), 1:218.

Chapter 2. The Monumental Impulse

1. Hubert Ch. Ehalt, "Schloss- und Palastarchitektur im Absolutismus," in *Architektur und Gesellschaft von der Antike bis zur Gegenwart,* ed. Hannes Stekl (Salzburg: Wolfgang Neugebauer, 1980), p. 239.
2. "To build new streets, to plan fresh thoroughfares, would disturb some church, destroy some oratory, inconvenience some marquis, or displace some convent." Frederic Harrison, *The Meaning of History* (London: Macmillan, 1930), p. 428.

Chapter 3. The Remaking of London

1. Much of this section is taken from my introduction to David Owen, *The Government of Victorian London, 1855–1889,* ed. Roy MacLeod (Cambridge, Mass.: Harvard University Press, 1982), pp. 1–15.
2. "It was practically a modern city . . . a far more agreeable, more civilised, more splendid city than Paris." Harrison, *Meaning of History,* p. 419.
3. Sir John Summerson, *Georgian London* (Harmondsworth: Penguin Books, 1962), p. 181. John Nash and J[ohn] White, *Some Account of the Proposed Improvements of the Western Part of London,* 2d ed. (London, 1815), p. xxxvii.
4. Summerson, *Georgian London,* pp. 189–90.
5. Hermione Hobhouse, *A History of Regent Street* (London: Macdonald and Jane's, 1975), p. 51; Tallis quoted on p. 60.
6. Donald J. Olsen, *Town Planning in London: The Eighteenth and Nineteenth Centuries* (New Haven and London: Yale University Press, 1982), p. 60.
7. E. M. Forster has written a vivid account of the collapse of one of the bankers—Henry Thornton—who just managed to survive it. *Marianne Thornton* (New York: Harcourt Brace Jovanovich, 1956), pp. 109–29.
8. C. W. Chalklin, *The Provincial Towns of Georgian England* (Montreal: McGill-Queen's University Press, 1974), pp. 140–46.
9. For the immediate impact of the collapse of 1825 on ground rents, see, e.g., James Noble, *The Professional Practice of Architects* (London, 1836), pp. 99–105; Hermione Hobhouse, *Thomas Cubitt, Master Builder* (London: Macmillan, 1971), pp. 172–84. For the low cost of suburban building land in the 1920s and 1930s, see Alan A. Jackson, *Semi-Detached London* (London: George Allen & Unwin, 1973), pp. 92, 225, 253, 301, 303, 317.
10. One notable exception was South Kensington from the 1840s onward. On the Alexander estate at Thurloe Square, between 1840 and 1846, 149 new houses produced ground rents of nearly £1,200 per annum, or around £120 per acre. Yet on the nearby Smith's Charity estate, C. J. Freake was able to acquire building land in the early 1840s for Onslow Square for slightly more than £50 per acre. Greater London Council, *Survey of London,* vol. 41, *Southern Kensington: Brompton* (London: Athlone Press, 1983), p. 69. In 1853 Brompton Hospital purchased the freehold of four acres from the earl of Harrington at £4,000 per acre (p. 139). The Gunter estate of 63 acres was let on building leases between 1850 and 1878 at a total rent of £5,890, or about £39 10s. per acre (pp. 228–29). The commissioners of the exhibition of 1851 were able, in 1851, to purchase the freehold of the Gore House estate at £2,300 per acre, but subsequent purchases were more expensive. Greater London Council, *Survey of London,* vol. 38, *The Museums Area of South*

Kensington and Westminster (London: Athlone Press, 1975), p. 54. The parts of the commissioners' estate let for residential building fetched an average ground rent of £400 per annum per acre (p. 62).

11. *Builder* 29 (1871): 421.

12. Again, South Kensington, developed from the 1840s to 1860s as a district of urban mansions grouped into terraces and squares, was a conspicuous, anachronistic exception.

13. [Samuel] Leigh, *Leigh's New Picture of London* (London, 1818), pp. 33–34.

14. J[ohn] Britton, *The Original Picture of London, Enlarged and Improved,* 26th ed. (London, [1826]), pp. 22–23.

15. "Many of the parish vestries . . . were of the 'open' variety, where all male ratepayers were entitled to attend the often disorderly meetings. But in the great new suburbs 'close' or 'select' vestries were more common, and here membership and power were restricted to a group of from thirty to a hundred of the 'principal inhabitants,' who had usually been originally nominated in a local act of Parliament, and who filled vacancies by making further nominations as they pleased." Francis Sheppard, "The Crisis of London's Government," in David Owen, *The Government of Victorian London, 1855–1889,* p. 24.

16. *Builder* 24 (1866): 808–09.

17. Ibid. 71 (1896): 487.

18. Ibid. 22 (1864): 679.

19. Edward I'Anson, "Some Notice of Office Buildings in the City of London," *Papers Read at the Royal Institute of British Architects, Session 1864–65,* pp. 25–26.

20. *Builder* 24 (1866): 810.

21. *Allgemeine Bauzeitung* 15 (1850): 276.

22. For the methods of the London speculative builder, see Summerson, *Georgian London,* pp. 69–79; H. J. Dyos, *Victorian Suburb* (Leicester: Leicester University Press, 1961), pp. 122–37; H. J. Dyos, "The Speculative Builders and Developers of Victorian London," in *Exploring the Urban Past,* ed. David Cannadine and David Reeder (Cambridge: Cambridge University Press, 1982), pp. 154–76; Hobhouse, *Thomas Cubitt,* pp. 260–80. For the operation of the leasehold system see Olsen, *Town Planning in London,* pp. 29–38. For the estate management practiced by the earl of Bedford in connection with the original development of Covent Garden, see Greater London Council, *Survey of London,* vol. 36, *The Parish of St. Paul Covent Garden* (London: Athlone Press, 1970), pp. 25–37.

23. *Allgemeine Bauzeitung* 15 (1850): 276. Unless otherwise indicated, all translations of quotations from German and French sources are my own.

24. César Daly, in *Revue générale de l'architecture* 13 (1855), col. 149.

25. *Builder* 10 (1852): 683.

Chapter 4. The New Paris

1. Harrison, *The Meaning of History,* p. 422.

2. H. Monin, *L'état de Paris en 1789* (Paris: D. Jouast, 1889), pp. 11–12.

3. Pierre Couperie, *Paris through the Ages* (London: Barrie & Jackson, 1970), n.p.

4. Edward I'Anson, "On the Recent Improvements in Paris," *Papers Read at the Royal Institute of British Architects, Session 1858–59,* p. 41.

5. Reprinted in *Builder* 20 (1862): 747.

6. Monin, *L'état de Paris en 1789,* p. 13.

7. Anthony S. Wohl, *Endangered Lives: Public Health in Victorian Britain* (London: J. M. Dent & Sons, 1983), p. 81.

8. Frances Trollope, *Paris and the Parisians in 1835,* 2d ed. (New York: Harper & Brothers, 1836), p. 77.

9. Louis-Sebastien Mercier, *Parallèle de Paris et de Londres* (Paris: Didier-Erudition, 1982), p. 140.

10. *Building News* 7 (1861): 897.

11. Couperie, *Paris through the Ages,* n.p.

12. *Builder* 8 (1850): 110.

13. Trollope, *Paris and the Parisians in 1835,* p. 80.

14. Richard, *Le véritable conducteur parisien* (Paris, 1828; facsimile ed., Paris: les Yeux Ouverts, 1970), p. 25.

15. Monin, *L'état de Paris en 1789,* pp. 15–16.

16. Adeline Daumard, *Les bourgeois de Paris au XIXe siècle* (Paris: Flammarion, 1970), p. 230.

17. Trollope, *Paris and the Parisians in 1835,* p. 192.

18. Quoted in Adeline Daumard, *Maisons de Paris et propriétaires parisiens au XIXe siècle, 1809–1880* (Paris: Editions Cujas, 1965), p. 30.

19. *Builder* 5 (1847): 430.

20. Ibid., 431.

21. César Daly, in *Revue générale de l'architecture* 1 (1840), col. 166.

22. Raymond Escholier, *Le nouveau Paris: La vie artistique de la cité moderne* (Paris: Editions Nilsson, n.d. [c. 1913]), pp. 1–2. Jeanne Gaillard, *Paris, la ville 1852–1870* (Paris: Editions Honoré Champion, 1977), p. 2.

23. Gaillard, *Paris, la ville,* pp. 34–35, 38–40.

24. Amédée de Cesena, *Le nouveau Paris* (Paris: Garnier Frères, 1864), pp. 3–4.

25. Baron Haussmann, *Mémoires* (Paris: Guy Durier, 1979), 1:54–55.
26. Gaillard, *Paris, la ville,* pp. 38–40.
27. *Builder* 60 (1891): 45. For a critical analysis of the principles underlying the works of Haussmann, see Françoise Choay, "Pensées sur la ville, arts de la ville," in *La ville de l'âge industriel: Le cycle haussmannien,* ed. Maurice Agulhon, vol. 4 of *Histoire de la France urbaine,* ed. Georges Duby (Paris: Seuil, 1983), pp. 168–74.
28. Henry T. Tuckerman, *Maga Papers about Paris* (New York: G. P. Putnam & Son, 1867), pp. v, 17.
29. *Revue générale de l'architecture* 13 (1855), cols. 134–37.
30. *Builder* 16 (1858): 257.
31. *Paris nouveau illustré,* p. 27, supplement to *L'Illustration* 38 (1861).
32. Reprinted in *Builder* 20 (1862): 748.
33. *Builder* 16 (1858): 814; 17 (1859): 344.
34. *Revue générale de l'architecture* 18 (1860), cols. 88–89.
35. X. Feyrnet, in *L'Illustration* 38 (1861): 114.
36. Edward R. Smith, "Baron Haussmann and the Topographical Transformation of Paris under Napoleon III," pt. 4, *Architectural Record* 22 (1907): 497–500.
37. *Builder* 19 (1861): 693.
38. Baron Haussmann, quoted in *Paris nouveau illustré,* p. 38.
39. *Builder* 19 (1861): 693.
40. *Paris nouveau illustré,* p. 38. X. Feyrnet, in *L'Illustration* 38 (1861): 115.
41. Ibid. 38 (1861): 114.
42. Quoted in *Paris nouveau illustré,* p. 38.
43. X. Feyrnet, in *L'Illustration* 38 (1861): 114. "Les percements projetés dans Chaillot et l'achèvement des avenues rayonnant autour de la place de l'Etoile compléteront le *West-End* du Paris nouveau." Baron Haussmann, 13 August 1861, quoted in *Paris nouveau illustré,* p. 38.
44. César Daly, in *Revue générale de l'architecture* 20 (1862), cols. 187–88.
45. Reprinted in *Builder* 20 (1862): 748.
46. *Paris nouveau illustré,* p. 26.
47. César Daly, in *Revue générale de l'architecture* 21 (1863), col. 246.
48. Ibid. 21 (1863), cols. 246–47.
49. Ibid. 21 (1863), cols. 247–48.
50. Amédée de Cesena, *Le nouveau Paris,* pp. 1–2, 7, 35.
51. *Builder* 24 (1866): 837, 903.
52. Jacques-Guillaume Legrand, in *L'Illustration* 49 (1867): 107.
53. *Builder* 26 (1868): 95, 508.
54. Adolphe Joanne, *Paris illustré en 1870 et 1877* (Paris: Hachette, n.d.), pp. xi–xii.
55. Quoted in *Builder* 30 (1872): 180.
56. "The fall of the Empire . . . did not substantially affect the course of architectural history in France as it might have done elsewhere." Robert Kerr, in James Fergusson, *History of the Modern Styles of Architecture,* 3d ed., ed. Robert Kerr (New York: Dodd, Mead, 1899), 1:305.
57. Anthony Sutcliffe, *The Autumn of Central Paris: The Defeat of Town Planning, 1850–1970* (London: Edward Arnold, 1970), p. 321.
58. Maxime du Camp, *Paris: Ses organes ses fonctions et sa vie dans la seconde moitié du XIXe siècle* (Paris: Hachette, 1875), 6:341–42.
59. *Builder* 35 (1877): 1142.
60. George Augustus Sala, *Paris Herself Again in 1878–9,* 2d ed. (London: Remington, 1879), 2:344.
61. *Builder* 37 (1879): 705, 1366.
62. Marcel Roncayolo, "La production de la ville," in *La ville de l'âge industriel,* ed. Agulhon, p. 78.
63. *Builder* 42 (1882): 635–36.
64. Emile Rivoalen, in *Revue générale de l'architecture* 39 (1882), cols. 258–59; 40 (1883), col. 66.
65. *Builder* 64 (1883): 200.
66. Philip Gilbert Hamerton, *Paris in Old and Present Times* (London: Seeley, 1892), p. vi.
67. Kerr, in Fergusson, *History of the Modern Styles of Architecture,* 1:303.
68. Anthony Sutcliffe, *Towards the Planned City: Germany, Britain, the United States and France 1780–1914* (Oxford: Basil Blackwell, 1981), pp. 154–62.
69. See in particular Steen Eiler Rasmussen, *Towns and Buildings* (Liverpool: Liverpool University Press, 1951), pp. 160–71.

Chapter 5. The Vienna of Franz Joseph
1. Thomas Blashill, "The Recent Development of Vienna," Royal Institute of British Architects, *Transactions,* n.s. 4 (1888): 37.
2. *Allgemeine Bauzeitung* 1 (1836): 8.
3. Elisabeth Lichtenberger, *Wirtschaftsfunktion und Sozialstruktur der Wiener Ringstrasse,* vol. 6 of *Die*

Wiener Ringstrasse: Bild einer Epoche, ed. Renate Wagner-Rieger (Vienna: Hermann Böhlaus Nachf., 1970), p. 23.

4. Frances Trollope, *Vienna and the Austrians* (London: Richard Bentley, 1838), 1:280–81.

5. Renate Wagner-Rieger, *Das Kunstwerk im Bild,* vol. 1 of *Die Wiener Ringstrasse: Bild einer Epoche,* ed. Wagner-Rieger (Vienna: Hermann Böhlaus Nachf., 1969), p. 82.

6. *Allgemeine Bauzeitung* 1 (1836): 7.

7. *Builder* 21 (1863): 734.

8. Hans Bobek and Elisabeth Lichtenberger, *Wien: Bauliche Gestalt und Entwicklung seit der Mitte des 19. Jahrhunderts* (Graz: Hermann Böhlaus Nachf., 1966), pp. 23–24.

9. Ibid., pp. 24–25.

10. Blashill, "The Recent Development of Vienna," pp. 37–38.

11. Peter Feldbauer, *Stadtwachstum und Wohnungsnot: Determinanten unzureichender Wohnungsversorgung in Wien 1848 bis 1914* (Vienna: Verlag für Geschichte und Politik Wien, 1977), p. 33.

12. Ibid., pp. 29–31.

13. Arno J. Mayer, *The Persistence of the Old Regime* (London: Croom Helm, 1981), p. 42.

14. Bobek and Lichtenberger, *Wien,* pp. 119–20.

15. Ibid., pp. 26–27; Renate Goebl and Peter Parenzan, "Die Wohnbauten der Zeit von etwa 1770 bis 1840," in Kunsthistorische Arbeitsgruppe "GeVAG," *Wiener Fassaden des 19. Jahrhunderts: Wohnhäuser in Mariahilf* (Vienna: Hermann Böhlaus Nachf., 1976), pp. 28–30.

16. Bobek and Lichtenberger, *Wien,* p. 64. See also Elisabeth Lichtenberger, *Die Wiener Altstadt: Von der mittelalterlichen Bürgerstadt zur City* (Vienna: Franz Deuticke, 1977), pp. 141–42.

17. Victor Tissot, *Vienne et la vie viennoise,* 19th ed. (Paris: E. Dentu, 1878), p. 137.

18. *Builder* 8 (1850): 255.

19. *Beilage zur Allgemeinen Bauzeitung. Ephemeriden,* no. 10 (August 1845), p. 255; no. 2 (May 1846), p. 17; no. 7 (May 1847), p. 137.

20. Renate Wagner-Rieger, *Wiens Architektur im 19. Jahrhundert* (Vienna: Österreichischer Bundesverlag für Unterricht, Wissenschaft und Kunst, 1970), p. 80.

21. For the widespread nature of such conversions, see map 2, "Der Beginn des Miethauswesens 1566," in the map portfolio of Lichtenberger, *Die Wiener Altstadt.*

22. Wagner-Rieger, *Wiens Architektur im 19. Jahrhundert,* p. 43.

23. *Builder* 8 (1850): 255.

24. *Beilage zur Allgemeinen Bauzeitung. Ephemeriden,* no. 11 (January 1848), p. 243.

25. Trollope, *Vienna and the Austrians,* 1:319.

26. Tissot, *Vienne,* p. 137.

27. *Wiener Zeitung,* 25 December 1857, quoted in Peter Haiko and Hannes Stekl, "Architektur in der industriellen Gesellschaft," in *Architektur und Gesellschaft von der Antike bis zur Gegenwart,* ed. Stekl, p. 258.

28. *Notizblatt der Allgemeinen Bauzeitung,* January 1858, pp. 141, 145. An English translation of the decree is to be found in Frederick R. Farrow, "The Recent Development of Vienna," Royal Institute of British Architects, *Transactions,* m.s. 4 (1888): 28.

29. Haiko and Stekl, "Architektur in der Industriellen Gesellschaft," p. 258.

30. Wagner-Rieger, Introduction, *Das Kunstwerk im Bild,* p. 87.

31. Lichtenberger, *Wirtschaftsfunktion,* p. 34.

32. Ibid., p. 34.

33. Carl E. Schorske, *Fin-de-Siècle Vienna: Politics and Culture* (London: Weidenfeld and Nicolson, 1980), pp. 32–36.

34. Ibid., pp. 32–33.

35. The Vienna correspondent of the *Augsburger Allgemeine Zeitung* emphasized in 1858 that the wide streets cut through central Paris would be unthinkable in Vienna. Elisabeth Springer, *Geschichte und Kulturleben der Wiener Ringstrasse,* vol. 2 of *Die Wiener Ringstrasse: Bild einer Epoche,* ed. Wagner-Rieger (Wiesbaden: Franz Steiner, 1979), p. 119. The jury examining the schemes for the town expansion submitted that year summarily rejected any that called for extensive destruction of existing buildings, and praised any that managed to avoid all but a minimum of demolition, even at the junction between City and Ringstrasse zone (pp. 123, 125, 126, 129).

36. *Builder* 23 (1865): 411.

37. Lichtenberger, *Wirtschaftsfunktion,* p. 18.

38. *Builder* 35 (1877): 582.

39. Wagner-Rieger, Introduction, *Das Kunstwerk im Bild,* p. 88.

40. "Prize Competition for a General Improvement Plan of the City of Vienna," reprinted in Arthur Cawston, *A Comprehensive Scheme for Street Improvements in London* (London: Edward Stanford, 1893), pp. 123–24.

41. Schorske, *Fin-de-Siècle Vienna,* pp. 72–74.

42. Wagner-Rieger, *Wiens Architektur im 19. Jahrhundert,* p. 252.

Chapter 6. The Process of Urban Embellishment

1. Both the well-known blocks of municipal workers' flats—Karl Marx-Hof, George Washington-Hof, and the rest—of the twenties and early thirties and the even more extensive provision of public housing since the war necessarily involved the destruction of older, substandard buildings. Yet the impact on the existing street pattern and character of the affected neighborhoods was notably less drastic than that of comparable redevelopment schemes in London and Paris.

Chapter 7. The Building and the Dwelling

1. Edward Shorter, *The Making of the Modern Family* (New York: Basic Books, 1975), p. 228.
2. Richard Sennett, *The Fall of Public Man* (Cambridge: Cambridge University Press, 1977), pp. 11, 20.
3. Huizinga, *Homo Ludens,* p. 228.
4. Richard Weiss, *Häuser und Landschaften der Schweiz,* 2d ed. (Erlenbach-Zürich: Eugen Rentsch, 1973), p. 1.
5. *Building News* 3 (1857): 181.
6. [Gillian Tindall], "Expatriates' Paris," in *The Paris Spy,* ed. Raymond Rudorff (n.p.: Anthony Blond, 1969), p. 233.
7. Marquis de Vermont and Sir Charles Darnley, Bart. [pseuds.], *London and Paris, or Comparative Sketches* (London: Longman, Hurst, Rees, Orme, Brown, and Green, 1823), p. 262. Hermann Muthesius, *The English House* (New York: Rizzoli, 1979), p. 7.
8. Robert Kerr, *The Gentleman's House* (London: John Murray, 1864), p. 77.
9. Hermann Muthesius, *The English House,* p. 9.
10. Stefan Muthesius, *The English Terraced House* (New Haven and London: Yale University Press, 1982), p. 3.
11. Ibid., p. 1.
12. Francis E. Masey, quoted in *Builder* 56 (1889): 32.
13. Harrison, *The Meaning of History,* p. 449.
14. Reprinted in *Notizblatt der Allgemeinen Bauzeitung,* vol. 5, no. 11 (1862), p. 216. See also Stefan Muthesius, *The English Terraced House,* pp. 5–6.
15. Hermann Muthesius, *The English House,* pp. 138–40.
16. *Builder* 80 (1901): 81.
17. Ibid.
18. Hermann Muthesius, *The English House,* pp. 144–45.
19. Michel Jean Bertrand, *Architecture de l'habitat urbain: La maison, le quartier, la ville* (Paris: Dunod, 1980), pp. 42, 63. See also William H. White, "On Middle-Class Houses in Paris and Central London," Royal Institute of British Architects, *Sessional Papers 1877–78,* p. 23; Michel Gallet, *Paris Domestic Architecture of the 18th Century* (London: Barrie & Jenkins, 1972), pp. 63–67.
20. Hélène Lipstadt, "Housing the Bourgeoisie: César Daly and the Ideal Home," *Oppositions,* no. 8 (Spring 1977), pp. 35–36.
21. Trollope, *Paris and the Parisians in 1835,* p. 189.
22. César Daly, in *Revue générale de l'architecture,* 1 (1840): col. 199.
23. *Allgemeine Bauzeitung* 8 (1843): 51.
24. *Architect* 10 (1873): 168; 18 (1877): 285.
25. Hamerton, *Paris in Old and Present Times,* pp. 314–17.
26. Lipstadt, "Housing the Bourgeoisie," pp. 35–36.
27. Escholier, *Le nouveau Paris,* pp. 20–21.
28. *Allgemeine Bauzeitung* 12 (1847): 237.
29. Bobek and Lichtenberger, *Wien,* p. 213.
30. See, for instance, map 9 in map portfolio of Lichtenberger, *Die Wiener Altstadt.*
31. Bobek and Lichtenberger, *Wien,* pp. 61–62, 213.
32. Wagner-Rieger, *Wiens Architektur im 19. Jahrhundert,* p. 44.
33. Trollope, *Vienna and the Austrians,* 1:357–58.
34. *Allgemeine Bauzeitung* 12 (1847): 238. *Builder* 8 (1850): 255.
35. Wagner-Rieger, *Wiens Architektur im 19. Jahrhundert,* p. 206.
36. Wagner-Rieger, Introduction, *Das Kunstwerk im Bild,* p. 92.
37. Mayer, *The Persistence of the Old Regime,* p. 192.
38. Wagner-Rieger, *Wiens Architektur im 19. Jahrhundert,* p. 212.
39. Schorske, *Fin-de-Siècle Vienna,* p. 49.
40. R. v. Eitelberger and Heinrich Ferstel, *Das bürgerliche Wohnhaus und das Wiener Zinshaus* (Vienna: Carl Gerold's Sohn, 1860), p. 21.
41. Ibid., pp. 19, 13.
42. Klaus Eggert, *Der Wohnbau der Wiener Ringstrasse im Historismus: 1855–1896,* vol. 7 of *Die Wiener Ringstrasse: Bild einer Epoche,* ed. Wagner-Rieger (Wiesbaden: Franz Steiner, 1976), pp. 6–9.
43. Norbert Wibiral and Renata Mikula, *Heinrich von Ferstel,* vol. 8, 3 of *Die Wiener Ringstrasse: Bild einer Epoche,* ed. Wagner-Rieger (Wiesbaden: Franz Steiner, 1974), passim.

Chapter 8. Inside the Dwelling

1. Hermann Zinn, "Entstehen und Wandel bürgerlicher Wohngewohnheiten und Wohnstrukturen," in *Wohnen im Wandel,* ed. Lutz Niethammer (Wuppertal: Peter Hammer, 1979), pp. 14, 15–16.
2. Lewis Mumford, *The City in History* (Harmondsworth: Penguin Books, 1961), p. 328.
3. Zinn, "Entstehen und Wandel," p. 16.
4. Mumford, *The City in History,* p. 329.
5. Zinn, "Entstehen und Wandel," pp. 19–20.
6. Quoted in William H. White, "On Middle-Class Houses in Paris and Central London," p. 23.
7. Louis-Sébastien Mercier, *Tableau de Paris* (Amsterdam, 1782; reprinted, Geneva: Slatkine Reprints, 1979), 2:185–86.
8. "German Domestic Architecture, and its Influence on the Social Condition of the Country," translation in *Builder* 11 (1853): 598.
9. Zinn, "Entstehen und Wandel," pp. 20–21.
10. W. G. Hoskins, *Provincial England: Essays in Social and Economic History* (London: Macmillan, 1963), p. 144; quoted in Shorter, *The Making of the Modern Family,* p. 42.
11. Mark Girouard, *The Victorian Country House* (New Haven and London: Yale University Press, 1979), p. 31.
12. Stefan Muthesius, *The English Terraced House,* p. 45.
13. Hermann Muthesius, *The English House,* p. 79.
14. Kerr, *The Gentleman's House,* p. 124.
15. Hermann Muthesius, *The English House,* p. 79.
16. Kerr, *The Gentleman's House,* p. 30.
17. Robert Kerr, "Observations on the Plan of Dwelling-Houses in Towns," *Journal of the Royal Institute of British Architects,* 3d ser., 1 (1894): 216.
18. Kerr, *The Gentleman's House,* p. 481.
19. Stefan Muthesius, *The English Terraced House,* pp. 86–97.
20. César Daly, in *Revue générale de l'architecture* 13 (1855), cols. 145–46.
21. Jacob von Falke, "Das englische Haus," in *Zur Cultur und Kunst* (Vienna, 1878), p. 60.
22. Kerr, *The Gentleman's House,* pp. 104–05, 101, 111, 129.
23. Ibid., pp. 119, 127.
24. Leonore Davidoff and Catherine Hall, "The Architecture of Public and Private Life: English Middle-Class Society in a Provincial Town 1780 to 1850," in *The Pursuit of Urban History,* ed. Fraser and Sutcliffe, pp. 327–45.
25. George Gissing, *In the Year of Jubilee* (London: Lawrence and Bullen, 1894), 3:212.
26. Hermann Muthesius, *The English House,* p. 70.
27. Priscilla Robertson, *An Experience of Women* (Philadelphia: Temple University Press, 1982), pp. 136–39.
28. Karoline Pichler, *Zeitbilder* (Wien: Österreichischer Schulbücherverlag, 1924), p. 18; first edition Vienna, 1839–41.
29. Falke, "Das englische Haus," pp. 63–64.
30. Robertson, *An Experience of Women,* p. 175; César Daly, in *Revue générale de l'architecture* 13 (1855), cols. 145–46.
31. Hermann Muthesius, *The English House,* pp. 71, 93.
32. Kerr, *The Gentleman's House,* p. 160.
33. César Daly, in *Revue générale de l'architecture* 13 (1855), col. 146.
34. Ibid. 15 (1857), col. 345.
35. Kerr, *The Gentleman's House,* pp. 227, 233.
36. Hermann Muthesius, *The English House,* p. 95.
37. Ibid., p. 70.
38. Stefan Muthesius, *The English Terraced House,* p. 46.
39. Hermann Muthesius, *The English House,* p. 96.
40. M. J. Daunton, *House and Home in the Victorian City* (London: Edward Arnold, 1983), p. 281.
41. Stefan Muthesius, *The English Terraced House,* p. 145.
42. *Builder* 97 (1909): 328.
43. Stefan Muthesius, *The English Terraced House,* pp. 183–91.
44. Hermann Muthesius, *The English House,* pp. 70, 83.
45. Kerr, *The Gentleman's House,* pp. 73–74, 200.
46. Hermann Muthesius, *The English House,* p. 235.
47. César Daly, in *Revue générale de l'architecture* 1 (1840), cols. 591–92. Hermann Muthesius, *The English House,* p. 235.
48. Gissing, *In the Year of Jubilee,* 3:70–71.
49. César Daly, in *Revue générale de l'architecture* 1 (1840), col. 199. *Building News* 3 (1857): 181.
50. Jean-Pierre Babelon, *Demeures parisiennes sous Henri IV et Louis XIII* (Paris: le Temps, 1977), p. 94.
51. A.-L. Lusson, in *Revue générale de l'architecture* 7 (1847–48), col. 167.

52. César Daly, in *Revue générale de l'architecture* 1 (1840), col. 199.
53. Ibid., cols. 168–69.
54. *Allgemeine Bauzeitung* 8 (1843): 51–54.
55. *Building News* 3 (1857): 181.
56. *Allgemeine Bauzeitung* 8 (1843): 52–54.
57. César Daly, in *Revue générale de l'architecture* 10 (1852), col. 401.
58. César Daly, *L'architecture privée au dix-neuvième siècle* (Paris, 1870–72), 1:15.
59. *Builder* 23 (1865): 113.
60. Gaillard, *Paris, la ville,* pp. 73–74.
61. Daly, *L'architecture privée au dix-neuvième siècle,* 1:10.
62. *Allgemeine Bauzeitung* 8 (1843): 52.
63. César Daly, in *Revue générale de l'architecture* 10 (1852), col. 401.
64. *Builder* 13 (1855): 637.
65. White, "On Middle-Class Houses in Paris and Central London," pp. 26–27. Sala, *Paris Herself Again in 1878–9,* 1:317.
66. *Building News* 3 (1857): 181.
67. *Allgemeine Bauzeitung* 8 (1843): 52. César Daly, in *Revue générale de l'architecture* 10 (1852), col. 401.
68. White, "On Middle-Class Houses in Paris and Central London," pp. 26–27.
69. Hamerton, *Paris in Old and Present Times,* p. 318.
70. [Gillian Tindall], "Expatriates' Paris," p. 234.
71. Michel Gallet, *Paris Domestic Architecture,* p. 86.
72. *Literatur- und Anzeigeblatt für das Baufach. Beilage zur allgemeinen Bauzeitung* 6 (1860): 288–93; quoted in Eggert, *Der Wohnbau der Wiener Ringstrasse im Historismus,* pp. 8–9.
73. *Builder* 46 (1884): 940. Falke, "Das englische Haus," p. 53.
74. Blashill, "The Recent Development of Vienna," p. 38. Tissot, *Vienne et la vie viennoise,* pp. 453–54.
75. Charles O. Hardy, *The Housing Program of the City of Vienna* (Washington, D.C.: Brookings Institution, 1934), p. 15.
76. Tissot, *Vienne et la vie viennoise,* p. 455.
77. J.-L. Pascal, in *Revue générale de l'architecture* 30 (1873), col. 208.
78. Tissot, *Vienne et la vie viennoise,* p. 455.
79. Daunton, *House and Home in the Victorian City,* p. 280.
80. Ferdinand Fellner, *Wie soll Wien Bauen* (Vienna, 1860), pp. 1–18; quoted in Eggert, *Der Wohnbau der Wiener Ringstrasse im Historismus,* pp. 7–8.
81. *Allgemeine Bauzeitung* 12 (1847): 242.
82. Ibid. 31 (1866): 341; quoted by Hannes Stekl in Franz Baltzarek et al., *Wirtschaft und Gesellschaft der Wiener Stadterweiterung,* vol. 5 of *Die Wiener Ringstrasse: Bild einer Epoche,* ed. Wagner-Rieger (Wiesbaden: Franz Steiner, 1975), pp. 328–29.
83. Wibiral and Mikula, *Heinrich von Ferstel,* p. 154.
84. *Allgemeine Bauzeitung* 29 (1864), 3.
85. Lichtenberger, *Wirtschaftsfunktion,* p. 43; Frederick R. Farrow, "The Recent Development of Vienna," Royal Institute of British Architects, *Transactions,* n.s. 4 (1888):34–35.
86. Lichtenberger, *Wirtschaftsfunktion,* pp. 43–44.
87. Bobek and Lichtenberger, *Wien,* p. 220.
88. Ibid., p. 106.
89. Hardy, *The Housing Program of the City of Vienna,* pp. 15–16.
90. F. Leonhard, "Städtische Miethäuser," in *Wien am Anfang des XX. Jahrhunderts,* ed. Paul Kortz (Vienna: Gerlach & Wiedling, 1905), 2:425.

Chapter 9. Social Geography

1. For the social vicissitudes of Bloomsbury, see Gladys Scott Thomson, *The Russells in Bloomsbury* (London: Jonathan Cape, 1940), pp. 37–54, 354–67; Donald J. Olsen, *Town Planning in London,* pp. 108–25; and Donald J. Olsen, *The Growth of Victorian London* (London: B. T. Batsford, 1976), pp. 129–37.
2. Greater London Council, *Survey of London,* vol. 39, *The Grosvenor Estate in Mayfair,* Part 1, *General History* (London: Athlone Press, 1977), pp. 30–31, 85–86.
3. Summerson, *Georgian London,* p. 186.
4. Olsen, *Town Planning in London,* pp. 113–16.
5. Greater London Council, *Survey of London,* vol. 39, *The Grosvenor Estate in Mayfair,* Part 1, *General History,* pp. 40–41.
6. Edward I'Anson, "On the Valuation of House Property in London," *Papers Read at the Royal Institute of British Architects, Session 1872–73,* p. 40.
7. Stefan Muthesius, *The English Terraced House,* p. 237.
8. *Builder* 71 (1896): 487.

9. Ibid. 35 (1877): 519–20.

10. Hermann Muthesius, *The English House,* p. 135.

11. Kerr, "Observations on the Plan of Dwelling-Houses in Towns," pp. 208–09.

12. Greater London Council, *Survey of London,* vol. 39, *The Grosvenor Estate in Mayfair,* Part 1, *General History,* pp. 93, 98–99.

13. Ibid., pp. 100–01.

14. For the relationship between public policy and the contraction of the supply of privately rented houses, see Daunton, *House and Home in the Victorian City,* pp. 286–307.

15. *Architect* 10 (1873): 141.

16. Monin, *L'état de Paris en 1789,* pp. 15–16.

17. Adeline Daumard, *Maisons de Paris et propriétaires parisiens au XIXe siècle, 1809–1880* (Paris: Editions Cujas, 1965), p. 84.

18. Sutcliffe, *The Autumn of Central Paris,* pp. 322–23, 150–52.

19. *Builder* 8 (1850): 110.

20. Daumard, *Maisons de Paris,* pp. 86–87.

21. *Allgemeine Bauzeitung* 8 (1843): 49–50.

22. Gaillard, *Paris, la ville,* pp. 17–18.

23. *Revue générale de l'architecture* 2 (1841), cols. 570–72.

24. Quoted ibid., col. 576.

25. Gaillard, *Paris, la ville,* p. 18.

26. *Allgemeine Bauzeitung* 8 (1843): 49.

27. Quoted by Perreymond in *Revue générale de l'architecture* 2 (1841), col. 577.

28. *Builder* 7 (1849): 176.

29. Among significant "conceptions et représentations nouvelles de la ville" during the age of Haussmann, Marcel Roncayolo includes the contemporary medical opinion that "tout ce qui est mouvement, circulation est sain; tout ce qui stagne est malsain." "Le modèle haussmannien," in *La ville de l'âge industriel,* ed. Agulhon, p. 93.

30. A.-L. Lusson, in *Revue générale de l'architecture* 7 (1847–48), cols. 166–67.

31. Sennett, *The Fall of Public Man,* p. 297.

32. Gaillard, *Paris, la ville,* pp. 43–44, 35.

33. Pierre Lavedan, *Histoire de l'urbanisme,* vol. 3, *Epoque contemporaine* (Paris: Henri Laurens, 1952), p. 115.

34. Gaillard, *Paris, la ville,* pp. 35–36, 75.

35. *Revue générale de l'architecture* 13 (1855), cols. 136–37.

36. Ibid. 13 (1855), cols. 43–44.

37. Gaillard, *Paris, la ville,* pp. 97–98.

38. Ibid., p. 78

39. *Building News* 7 (1861): 86. *Builder* 42 (1882): 212–13.

40. César Daly, in *Revue générale de l'architecture* 20 (1862), col. 167.

41. Edward R. Smith, "Baron Haussmann and the Topographical Transformation of Paris under Napoleon III," pt. 3, *Architectural Record* 22 (1907): 369–72.

42. Gaillard, *Paris, la ville,* pp. 97–98.

43. Ibid., pp. 91–96.

44. Georges Riat, *Paris* (Paris: Librairie Renouard, 1904), pp. 5–6, 7–8.

45. César Daly, in *Revue générale de l'architecture* 10 (1852), col. 596.

46. *Building News* 7 (1861): 86.

47. *Builder* 19 (1861): 278.

48. Gaillard, *Paris, la ville,* pp. 84, 110–11.

49. Daumard, *Maisons de Paris,* pp. 90–92.

50. Gaillard, *Paris, la ville,* p. 83.

51. Cesena, *Le nouveau Paris,* p. 44.

52. Ibid., pp. 44–45, 47–48.

53. Joanne, *Paris illustré en 1870 et 1877,* p. lv.

54. Sutcliffe, *The Autumn of Central Paris,* pp. 168–70.

55. Marguerite Perrot, *La mode de vie des familles bourgeoises, 1873–1953* (Paris: Librairie Armand Colin, 1961), p. 266.

56. Sutcliffe, *The Autumn of Central Paris,* p. 173.

57. Ibid., p. 170.

58. Sisley Huddleston, *In and About Paris* (London: Methuen, 1927), pp. 172–73.

59. Paul Cohen-Portheim, *The Spirit of Paris* (London: B. T. Batsford, 1937), pp. 20–21, 22. First published in Germany, 1930.

60. Huddleston, *In and About Paris,* pp. 140–41. Cohen-Portheim, *The Spirit of Paris,* p. 10.

61. Jean Bastié, *La croissance de la banlieue parisienne* (Paris: Presses Universitaires de France, 1964), pp. 425, 428–29.
62. Richard Cobb, *The Streets of Paris* (London: Gerald Duckworth, 1980), pp. 10, 50.
63. Bobek and Lichtenberger, *Wien,* pp. 24–25.
64. Elisabeth Lichtenberger, *Die Wiener Altstadt,* p. 14.
65. Trollope, *Vienna and the Austrians,* 1:313–15.
66. Lichtenberger, *Die Wiener Altstadt,* pp. 134–36.
67. Lichtenberger, *Wirtschaftsfunktion,* p. 16.
68. Bobek and Lichtenberger, *Wien,* pp. 65–66.
69. Ulysse Robert, *Voyage à Vienne* (Paris: Ernest Flammarion, [1899]), p. 37.
70. Franz Baltzarek et al., *Wirtschaft und Gesellschaft,* p. 91.
71. Lichtenberger, *Wirtschaftsfunktion,* pp. 61–63.
72. Hannes Stekl, in *Wirtschaft und Gesellschaft,* ed. Baltzarek et al., p. 280.
73. Baltzarek et al., *Wirtschaft und Gesellschaft,* p. 95. See also Lichtenberger, *Wirtschaftsfunktion,* p. 54.
74. Lichtenberger, *Wirtschaftsfunktion,* pp. 61–63; Schorske, *Fin-de-Siècle Vienna,* pp. 54–58.
75. Stekl, in Baltzarek et al., *Wirtschaft und Gesellschaft,* p. 336; Schorske, *Fin-de-Siècle Vienna,* p. 51.
76. Lichtenberger, *Wirtschaftsfunktion,* p. 38.
77. Renate Goebl, Elisabeth Klemm, and Hellmut Lorenz, "Die Wohnbauten der Hochgründerzeit (1865/70 bis 1880/85)," in *Wiener Fassaden des 19. Jahrhunderts,* Kunsthistorische Arbeitsgruppe "GeVAG" (Vienna: Hermann Böhlaus Nachf., 1976), pp. 50–52.
78. Robert, *Voyage à Vienne,* pp. 202–04.
79. Lichtenberger, *Wirtschaftsfunktion,* p. 52.
80. Lichtenberger, *Die Wiener Altstadt,* pp. 225–26.
81. Lichtenberger, *Wirtschaftsfunktion,* pp. 93–94.
82. Ibid., p. 99.
83. Ibid., p. 128.
84. Ibid., p. 196.
85. Ibid., p. 212. That Lichtenberger felt compelled to use the English words *downtown, suburbs,* and *shopping-centers* suggests how alien the phenomena still were in Austria.
86. Bobek and Lichtenberger, *Wien,* pp. 343–45.

Chapter 10. Villa Suburbia
1. John R. Kellett, *The Impact of Railways on Victorian Cities* (London: Routledge & Kegan Paul, 1969), pp. 376–81.
2. Alan A. Jackson, *London's Local Railways* (Newton Abbot: David & Charles, 1983), includes detailed descriptions of the suburban services offered by the different railways from Victorian times to the present.
3. H. J. Dyos, *Victorian Suburb,* pp. 66–69, 74–75.
4. *Builder* 26 (1868): 403.
5. César Daly, in *Revue générale de l'architecture* 13 (1855), cols. 57–58.
6. *Builder* 97 (1909): 327.
7. Ibid. 96 (1909): 337.
8. Hermann Muthesius, *The English House,* p. 146.
9. Mumford, *The City in History,* pp. 563, 582.
10. Falke, "Das englische Haus," p. 50.
11. G. W. Steevens, *Glimpses of Three Nations* (New York: Dodd, Mead, 1900), pp. 11–13.
12. Hermann Muthesius, *The English House,* p. 146.
13. Andrew Saint, *Richard Norman Shaw* (New Haven and London: Yale University Press, 1976), pp. 201–02.
14. *Builder* 97 (1909): 89–90.
15. Royal Institute of British Architects, *Sessional Papers 1877–78,* p. 64.
16. *Allgemeine Bauzeitung* 8 (1843): 48.
17. François Thiollet, *Choix de maisons, édifices et monuments publics de Paris et des environs* (Paris, 1838), supplement describing the district known as "la Nouvelle Athènes," quoted in Pierre Lavedan, *Histoire de l'urbanisme à Paris* (Paris: Hachette, 1975), p. 365.
18. Trollope, *Paris and the Parisians in 1835,* p. 188.
19. Sir Francis Head, *A Faggot of French Sticks; or, Paris in 1851* (New York: George P. Putnam, 1852), p. 219.
20. *Builder* 13 (1855): 428; 16 (1858): 757.
21. César Daly, in *Revue générale de l'architecture* 18 (1860), cols. 34–35.
22. Supplement to *L'Illustration* (1861): *Paris nouveau illustré,* p. 26.
23. *Builder* 19 (1861): 695, 729.
24. César Daly, in *Revue générale de l'architecture* 20 (1862), cols. 182–83.
25. *Builder* 19 (1861): 695, 729.
26. César Daly, *L'architecture privée au dix-neuvième siècle,* 1:19–21.

27. *Builder* 27 (1869): 277.
28. Joanne, *Paris illustré en 1870 et 1877,* pp. 244, 254.
29. *Builder* 36 (1878): 31.
30. Hamerton, *Paris in Old and Present Times,* p. 333.
31. Camp, *Paris* 1:306.
32. *Builder* 77 (1899): 189.
33. Cohen-Portheim, *The Spirit of Paris,* pp. 103–04.
34. Bastié, *La croissance de la banlieue parisienne,* pp. 15–16.
35. Ibid., pp. 32–33.
36. Ibid., p. 33. Norma Evenson, *Paris: A Century of Change, 1878–1978* (New Haven and London: Yale University Press, 1979), pp. 238–53.
37. Anton Weber, "Familienhäuser und Villen," in *Wien am Anfang des XX. Jahrhunderts,* ed. Kortz, 2:427.
38. For the anti-urban tradition in nineteenth-century German thought, see Andrew Lees, "Perceptions of Cities in Britain and Germany, 1820–1914," in *The Pursuit of Urban History,* ed. Fraser and Sutcliffe, pp. 151–65.
39. Haiko and Stekl, "Architektur in der industriellen Gesellschaft," p. 296.
40. Theophilos Hansen, in *Allgemeine Bauzeitung* 30 (1865): 1.
41. Bobek and Lichtenberger, *Wien,* pp. 92–93.
42. Wagner-Rieger, *Wiens Architektur im 19. Jahrhundert,* pp. 215–16. See also Wibiral and Mikula, *Heinrich von Ferstel,* p. 155.
43. Bobek and Lichtenberger, *Wien,* pp. 102–03, 217.
44. Wagner-Rieger, *Wiens Architektur im 19. Jahrhundert,* pp. 216–17.
45. *Builder* 46 (1884): 223.
46. Lichtenberger, *Wirtschaftsfunktion,* p. 99.
47. *Builder* 40 (1881): 627. "Zumindest für den Winter blieb das Wohnen im Mietwohnhaus in der Stadt charakteristisch für das Grossbürgertum. Familienhäuser wie sie für England typisch sind, gab es nur in den Villenvierteln Hietzings und Döblings und in biedermeierlicher Tradition im weiteren Umland von Wien, und diese Häuser wurden damals meist nur als Zweitwohnung mit Sommercharakter angesehen." Baltzarek et al., *Wirtschaft und Gesellschaft,* p. 91.
48. Bobek and Lichtenberger, *Wien,* p. 118.
49. Weber, "Familienhäuser und Villen," p. 441.
50. Hardy, *The Housing Program of the City of Vienna,* p. 6.
51. Stefan Muthesius, *The English Terraced House,* p. 3.
52. Bobek and Lichtenberger, *Wien,* pp. 139–40; Hardy, *The Housing Program of the City of Vienna,* pp. 68–72.
53. Bobek and Lichtenberger, *Wien,* pp. 193–95.

Chapter 11. Working-Class Housing: Scarcity, Abundance, and Domestic Values

1. For the current state of scholarly debate on English working-class housing, see Anthony Sutcliffe, "In Search of the Urban Variable: Britain in the Later Nineteenth Century," in *The Pursuit of Urban History,* ed. Fraser and Sutcliffe, pp. 234–63. For Paris and France generally, see Yves Lequin, "Les citadins et leur vie quotidienne," in *La ville de l'âge industriel,* ed. Agulhon, esp. pp. 313–15. For Vienna, see Feldbauer, *Stadtwachstum und Wohnungsnot,* and "Wohnungsproduktion am Beispiel Wiens (1848–1934)," in *Wohnen im Wandel,* ed. Niethammer.
2. Stefan Muthesius, *The English Terraced House,* p. 4.
3. Jacques Bertillon, *Essai de statistique comparée du surpeuplement des habitations à Paris et dans les grandes capitales européennes* (Paris: Chaix, 1894), p. 15.
4. Sam Bass Warner, Jr., "The Management of Multiple Urban Images," in *The Pursuit of Urban History,* ed. Fraser and Sutcliffe, p. 390.
5. Gillian Tindall, *City of Gold: The Biography of Bombay* (London: Temple Smith, 1982), p. 19.
6. Feldbauer, *Stadtwachstum und Wohnungsnot,* pp. 148–50.
7. See H. J. Dyos, "Railways and Housing in Victorian London," and "Some Social Costs of Railway Building in London," in *Exploring the Urban Past,* ed. David Cannadine and David Reeder (Cambridge: Cambridge University Press, 1982), pp. 101–25; and Kellett, *The Impact of Railways on Victorian Cities,* pp. 337–46.
8. John Burnett, *A Social History of Housing 1850–1970* (London: Methuen, 1980), examines both rural and urban, working-class and middle-class housing. Anthony Wohl, *The Eternal Slum: Housing and Social Policy in Victorian London* (London: Edward Arnold, 1977), deals rather with the Victorians' moral and political perception of the problem and their response than with the slums themselves. Daunton, *House and Home in the Victorian City,* makes a strong case for the improvement of working-class housing conditions during the period 1850–1914 but does not deal directly with London. Anthony Sutcliffe, while pessimistic on the whole, admits that "average housing standards, including the housing of manual

workers, greatly improved as a consequence of the rise in real earnings after mid-century" ("In Search of the Urban Variable: Britain in the Later Nineteenth Century," p. 253). "Any secular *deterioration* in housing conditions would have been confined to the poorest, central districts of the largest cities. . . . It would be dangerous to speculate on whether any such deterioration did indeed occur" (p. 259).

9. *Building News* 7 (1861): 897.
10. *Builder* 26 (1868): 22.
11. Blashill, "The Recent Development of Vienna," p. 38.
12. *Builder* 37 (1879): 1200.
13. Hardy, *The Housing Program of the City of Vienna,* pp. 2, 8.
14. Bertillon, *Essai de statistique comparée du surpeuplement,* pp. 4, 7, 28, 19, 21.
15. Hardy, *The Housing Program of the City of Vienna,* p. 19.
16. Tissot, *Vienne et la vie viennoise,* p. 454.
17. Bertillon, *Essai de statistique comparée du surpeuplement,* p. 28.
18. Hardy, *The Housing Program of the City of Vienna,* p. 5.
19. Feldbauer, "Wohnungsproduktion am Beispiel Wiens," pp. 318–19.
20. Feldbauer, *Stadtwachstum und Wohnungsnot,* pp. 204–07, 210.
21. Quoted in Bobek and Lichtenberger, *Wien,* p. 60.
22. Feldbauer, "Wohnungsproduktion am Beispiel Wiens," pp. 320–22.
23. Feldbauer, *Stadtwachstum und Wohnungsnot,* pp. 242–44; "Wohnungsproduktion am Beispiel Wiens," p. 325.
24. For the London building acts and those of German cities, see Hermann Muthesius, *The English House,* p. 74; for the Vienna building codes of 1883 and 1893 see Bobek and Lichtenberger, *Wien,* p. 46; for the impact of Vienna's regulations on housing costs, see Feldbauer, *Stadtwachstum und Wohnungsnot,* pp. 258–59.
25. Reprinted in *Notizblatt der Allgemeinen Bauzeitung,* vol. 5, no. 11 (1862), p. 214.
26. H. J. Dyos, "The Speculative Builders and Developers of Victorian London," pp. 166, 172.
27. Bastié, *La croissance de la banlieue parisienne,* p. 189.
28. Feldbauer, *Stadtwachstum und Wohnungsnot,* pp. 262, 263–65.
29. Feldbauer, "Wohnungsproduktion am Beispiel Wiens," pp. 330–32.
30. Daunton, *House and Home in the Victorian City,* pp. 100–01.
31. Steen Eiler Rasmussen, *London: The Unique City* (Cambridge, Mass.: MIT Press, 1967), pp. 405–16.
32. See, for instance, Daunton, *House and Home in the Victorian City,* pp. 64–77.
33. [Tindall], "Expatriates' Paris," p. 233.

Chapter 12. London: Hidden Pleasures
1. *Builder* 80 (1901): 81.
2. W. Robinson, *The Parks, Promenades & Gardens of Paris* (London: John Murray, 1869), p. 114.
3. White, "On Middle-Class Houses in Paris and Central London," p. 51.
4. *Caprices et Zigzags,* paraphrased in *Builder* 10 (1852): 683.
5. Hermann Muthesius, *The English House,* p. 10.
6. *Builder* 12 (1854): 96.
7. Ibid. 9 (1851): 128; 80 (1901): 81.
8. Ibid. 39 (1880): 66.
9. Ibid. 18 (1860): 755.
10. Jacques-Ignace Hittorff, in *Revue générale de l'architecture* 18 (1860), col. 184. César Daly, ibid. 1 (1840), col. 328.
11. A. Hayward, *The Art of Dining,* based on 1853 ed. (London: John Murray, 1883), pp. 122–23.
12. Hittorff, in *Revue générale de l'architecture* 18 (1860), col. 184.
13. César Daly, in *Revue générale de l'architecture* 1 (1840), cols. 328–29.
14. Ibid. 15 (1857), cols. 343–44.
15. G. Davioud, in a report on the theaters of London prepared for the prefect of the Seine, printed in *Revue générale de l'architecture* 23 (1865), cols. 247; 117–18, 127.
16. *Building News* 9 (1862): 308. G. Davioud, in *Revue générale de l'architecture* 23 (1865), col. 123.
17. *Builder* 30 (1872): 61.
18. Vermont and Darnley, *London and Paris,* pp. 34–35.
19. Sir Nikolaus Pevsner, *A History of Building Types* (London: Thames and Hudson, 1979), pp. 261–62, 264.
20. Samuel Knight, "The Influence of Business Requirements upon Street Architecture," *Sessional Papers Read at the Royal Institute of British Architects, 1876–77,* pp. 16–17.
21. Reprinted in *Builder* 6 (1848): 117.
22. *Chambers Journal,* 15 October 1864, quoted in advertisement for Bunnett & Co., in *Builder* 22 (1864): 767.

Chapter 13. Paris: The Garden and the Street

1. *Architect* 25 (1881): 283.
2. Cesena, *Le nouveau Paris,* pp. 186–87, 196, 201–04.
3. *Builder,* 42 (1882): 380.
4. [James Jackson Jarves], *Parisian Sights and French Principles* (New York: Harper & Brothers, 1852), pp. 20–21. See also *Builder* 9 (1851): 711.
5. Charles Dickens, "Sketches by Boz," quoted in J. Joyce, *The Story of Passenger Transport in Britain* (London: Ian Allan, 1967), p. 119.
6. Camp, *Paris: Ses organes ses fonctions et sa vie,* 1:254–56, 257–59.
7. Joanne, *Paris illustré en 1870 et 1877,* pp. lxxxv–lxxxvi.
8. David H. Pinkney, *Napoleon III and the Rebuilding of Paris* (Princeton: Princeton University Press, 1972), pp. 167–68.
9. Joanne, *Paris illustré en 1870 et 1877,* pp. 1069–71.
10. *Railway Magazine* 56 (1925): 236–37.
11. Evenson, *Paris: A Century of Change,* pp. 91–105.
12. Sala, *Paris Herself Again in 1878–9,* 1:158–60.
13. Cesena, *Le nouveau Paris,* pp. 157–58.
14. Augustus J. C. Hare, *Paris* (London: Smith, Elder, 1887), 1:11.
15. Richard, *Le véritable conducteur parisien,* p. 39.
16. Cesena, *Le nouveau Paris,* pp. 52–53.
17. Rowland Strong, *Where and How to Dine in Paris* (London: Alexander Moring, n.d. [c. 1900]), pp. 11–12, 17–19, 20–21.
18. Richard, *Le véritable conducteur parisien,* p. 51.
19. Joanne, *Paris illustré en 1870 et 1877,* p. lxii.
20. [Mrs. W. P. Byrne], *Realities of Paris Life* (London: Hurst and Blackett, 1859), 1:80–81.
21. Cesena, *Le nouveau Paris,* p. 164.
22. Trollope, *Paris and the Parisians in 1835,* p. 356.
23. *Builder* 13 (1855): 416. See also Cesena, *Le nouveau Paris,* p. 680.
24. Vermont and Darnley, *London and Paris,* p. 25.
25. Richard, *Le véritable conducteur parisien,* p. 53.
26. Trollope, *Paris and the Parisians in 1835,* pp. 245–46.
27. Vermont and Darnley, *London and Paris,* p. 25.
28. For the luxury restaurants of the 1830s see Sala, *Paris Herself Again in 1878–9,* 1:264.
29. *Builder* 13 (1855): 374–75.
30. Cesena, *Le nouveau Paris,* pp. 161–63.
31. Joanne, *Paris illustré en 1870 et 1877,* p. lx.
32. Hare, *Paris,* 1:15.
33. Strong, *Where and How to Dine in Paris,* pp. 93–94. Steevens, *Glimpses of Three Nations,* pp. 170–71.
34. Sala, *Paris Herself Again in 1878–9,* 1:262. Strong, *Where and How to Dine in Paris,* pp. 27–28.
35. Steevens, *Glimpses of Three Nations,* p. 150.
36. *L'Illustration* 38 (1861): 171.
37. Hare, *Paris,* 1:5. Cesena, *Le nouveau Paris,* p. 679. Trollope, *Paris and the Parisians in 1835,* p. 248.
38. Cesena, *Le nouveau Paris,* p. 680.
39. Tuckerman, *Maga Papers about Paris,* pp. 25–26.
40. Sala, *Paris Herself Again in 1878–9,* 1:68.
41. Vermont and Darnley, *London and Paris,* pp. 23–24.
42. Trollope, *Paris and the Parisians in 1835,* pp. 246–47.
43. *Builder* 19 (1861): 101.
44. Ibid. 22 (1864): 699.
45. Ibid. 26 (1868): 21.
46. Theodore Zeldin, *France 1848–1945: Ambition and Love* (Oxford: Oxford University Press, 1979), p. 273.
47. Mercier, *Parallèle de Paris et de Londres,* pp. 57, 60. "La plupart de tous les abords de Paris, larges routes comme étroites, aux approches des barrières sont sales. L'homme de pied est les trois quarts de l'année harassé et abîmé dans la boue et par le gros pavé" (p. 98).
48. Trollope, *Paris and the Parisians in 1835,* p. 77.
49. Head, *A Faggot of French Sticks,* p. 24.
50. Trollope, *Paris and the Parisians in 1835,* p. 80.
51. Honoré de Balzac, *La duchesse de Langeais,* quoted in Bertrand, *Architecture de l'habitat urbain,* p. 158.
52. Pierre Lavedan, *Histoire de l'urbanisme à Paris,* p. 288.
53. Trollope, *Paris and the Parisians in 1835,* pp. 187–88. For the deplorable consequences of the absence of *trottoirs* from Parisian streets, see Johann Friedrich Geist, *Passagen: Ein Bautyp des 19. Jahrhunderts*

(Munich: Prestel-Verlag, 1969), pp. 90–92. By 1849 181,000 out of 420,000 meters of Paris streets had been provided with raised footways.

54. François Bédarida and Anthony R. Sutcliffe, "The Street in the Structure and Life of the City: Reflections on Nineteenth-Century London and Paris," in *Modern Industrial Cities,* ed. Bruce M. Stave (Beverly Hills: Sage Publications, 1981), pp. 27–28.

55. Richard, *Le véritable conducteur parisien,* p. 24. Geist lists no more than twenty-nine *passages* in Paris, including seven erected after 1830, according to his criteria, which exclude other than independent glazed shopping arcades, lighted from above. London, with thirteen examples, had the second largest number. Geist, *Passagen,* pp. 121–28.

56. Vermont and Darnley, *London and Paris,* pp. 104–05.

57. Trollope, *Paris and the Parisians in 1835,* p. 243.

58. Gaillard, *Paris, la ville,* pp. 525–26.

59. *Architect* 1 (1869): 149.

60. Sala, *Paris Herself Again in 1878–9,* 1:24–25. Strong, *Where and How to Dine in Paris,* p. 97.

61. Vermont and Darnley, *London and Paris,* pp. 105–06.

62. Cesena, *Le nouveau Paris,* pp. 680–81.

63. Joanne, *Paris illustré en 1870 et 1877,* pp. 43–44.

64. Cohen-Portheim, *The Spirit of Paris,* pp. 31–33.

65. *Building News* 7 (1861): 86.

66. *Builder* 30 (1872): 23.

67. Hamerton, *Paris in Old and Present Times,* p. 308.

68. *Paris nouveau illustré,* p. 26. Much of the article is taken from Edmond Texier, *Tableau de Paris* ([Paris, 1852]), 1:3–5.

69. *Builder* 32 (1874): 1048.

70. Robinson, *The Parks, Promenades & Gardens of Paris,* pp. 4, 7–8.

71. *Builder* 27 (1869): 437.

72. César Daly, in *Revue générale de l'architecture* 21 (1863), cols. 128–29.

73. Sala, *Paris Herself Again in 1878–9,* 1:287–88.

74. *Revue générale de l'architecture* 22 (1864), col. 299.

75. Gaillard, *Paris, la ville,* p. 526.

Chapter 14. Vienna: Display and Self-Representation

1. Eggert, *Der Wohnbau der Wiener Ringstrasse im Historismus,* pp. 347–48.

2. Walter Krobot et al., *Strassenbahn in Wien* (Vienna: Josef Otto Slezak, 1983), pp. 19–25.

3. Tissot, *Vienne et la vie viennoise,* pp. 199, 202.

4. *Beilage zur Allgemeinen Bauzeitung. Ephemeriden,* no. 11 (January 1848), p. 243.

5. *Builder* 8 (1850): 255.

6. *Allgemeine Bauzeitung* 31 (1866): 340; 36 (1871): 244–45.

7. Eggert, *Der Wohnbau der Wiener Ringstrasse im Historismus,* pp. 348–54.

8. *Builder* 35 (1877): 582.

9. Stekl, in Baltzarek et al., *Wirtschaft und Gesellschaft,* p. 338.

10. Tissot, *Vienne et la vie viennoise,* pp. 202–03.

11. Robert, *Voyage à Vienne,* p. 206.

12. Ehalt, "Schloss- und Palastarchitektur im Absolutismus," pp. 197–98.

13. Stekl, in Baltzarek et al., *Wirtschaft und Gesellschaft,* pp. 337–38.

14. Ibid., pp. 339–40.

15. Tissot, *Vienne et la vie viennoise,* pp. 246, 241–43.

16. *Builder* 44 (1883): 197.

17. Stekl, in Baltzarek et al., *Wirtschaft und Gesellschaft,* p. 338.

18. Lichtenberger, *Wirtschaftsfunktion,* pp. 155–56.

19. Pichler, *Zeitbilder,* pp. 246–47.

20. Tissot, *Vienne et la vie viennoise,* pp. 251–52.

21. Hannes Stekl, *Österreichs Aristokratie im Vormärz* (Vienna: Verlag für Geschichte und Politik, 1973), pp. 146–47. As late as 1900 the ordinary burgher knew better than to purchase tickets for the first two ranks of the Burgtheater and the Opera, even if he could afford them; just as he forwent dinners at the Sacher and the Bristol and ices at Demel, leaving such pleasures to those of higher station. Otto Friedländer, *Letzter Glanz der Märchenstadt: Das war Wien um 1900* (Vienna: Molden-Taschenbuch-Verlag, 1976), p. 136.

22. Pichler, *Zeitbilder,* p. 245.

23. Trollope, *Vienna and the Austrians,* 1:280.

24. Wagner-Rieger, Introduction, *Das Kunstwerk im Bild,* p. 95.

25. Stekl, in Baltzarek et al., *Wirtschaft und Gesellschaft,* pp. 342–43.

26. *Builder* 23 (1865): 411.

27. Pichler, *Zeitbilder,* p. 322.
28. Babelon, *Demeures parisiennes sous Henri IV et Louis XIII,* p. 120.
29. For the documentary value of the street scenes in the engravings, see Elisabeth Herget, Nachwort to *Das florierende Wien,* by Salomon Kleiner (Dortmund: Harenberg Kommunikation, 1979), p. 294.
30. Robert, *Voyage à Vienne,* p. 36.
31. Trollope, *Vienna and the Austrians,* 1:282.
32. Geist, *Passagen,* p. 307.

Chapter 15. Architecture as Historical Evidence
1. Sir Ernst Gombrich, "In Search of Cultural History," in *Ideals and Idols* (Oxford: Phaidon, 1979), pp. 46, 50.
2. David Watkin, *The Rise of Architectural History* (London: Architectural Press, 1980), p. 183.
3. Sennett, *The Fall of Public Man,* p. 130.
4. "Die enorme Bevölkerungszunahme und das beschleunigte Stadtwachstum dürften demnach auch während der sogenannten Hochgründerzeit in beträchtlichem Ausmass durch die politische Funktion Wiens als Reichshaupt- und Residenzstadt mitbestimmt worden sein. Eine grosse Rolle hat in dieser Zeit zweifellos auch der Ausbau Wiens zum Finanz-und Organisationszentrum der Monarchie gespielt." Feldbauer, *Stadtwachstum und Wohnungsnot,* p. 33.
5. Agulhon, *La ville de l'âge industriel,* p. 9.

Chapter 16. The Beautiful
1. See, for instance, Barbara Miller Lane, "Government Buildings in European Capitals 1870–1914," in *Urbanisierung im 19. und 20. Jahrhundert,* ed. Hans Jürgen Teuteberg (Cologne: Böhlau Verlag, 1983), pp. 517–60; and Barbara Miller Lane, "Changing Attitudes to Monumentality: An Interpretation of European Architecture and Urban Form 1880–1914," in *Growth and Transformation of the Modern City,* pp. 101–14.
2. Stefan Muthesius, *The English Terraced House,* p. 14.
3. *Literatur- und Anzeigeblatt für das Baufach. Beilage zur Allgemeinen Bauzeitung* 4 (1850): 54.
4. *Allgemeine Bauzeitung* 15 (1850): 277.
5. Greater London Council, *Survey of London,* vol. 38, *The Museums Area of South Kensington and Westminster,* p. 308.
6. Robert Kerr, in James Fergusson, *History of the Modern Styles of Architecture,* 3d ed., ed. Robert Kerr (New York: Dodd, Mead, 1899), 2:126–29.
7. Stefan Muthesius, *The English Terraced House,* p. 234.
8. Kerr, in Fergusson, *History of the Modern Styles of Architecture,* 2:159.
9. Greater London Council, *Survey of London,* vol. 39, *The Grosvenor Estate in Mayfair,* Part 1, *General History,* p. 53.
10. *Builder* 30 (1872): 62.
11. *Building News* 71 (1896): 689.
12. Sir Nikolaus Pevsner, *Pioneers of the Modern Movement* (London: Faber & Faber, 1936), p. 166.
13. "La maison modeste continue d'être bâtie selon un processus qui remonte au moyen âge, et qui a subi bien peu de transformations. . . . C'est la raison pour laquelle ces édifices sont si difficiles à dater." Jean-Pierre Babelon, *Demeures parisiennes sous Henri IV et Louis XIII,* p. 69.
14. *Allgemeine Bauzeitung* 8 (1843): 48.
15. Ibid. 8 (1843): 48–49. Much of the article is plagiarized from César Daly, in *Revue générale de l'architecture* 1 (1840), cols. 166–67.
16. Adolphe Lance, in *Moniteur des architectes* 1 (1847–48): 129–30.
17. *Builder* 13 (1855): 604.
18. Neil Levine, "The Book and the Building: Hugo's Theory of Architecture and Labrouste's Bibliothèque Ste.-Geneviève," in *The Beaux-Arts and Nineteenth-Century French Architecture,* ed. Robin Middleton (Cambridge, Mass.: MIT Press, 1982), pp. 139–73.
19. *Builder* 13 (1855): 604; 16 (1858): 814.
20. *Building News* 9 (1862): 332.
21. Kerr, *The Gentleman's House,* p. 378.
22. *Builder* 22 (1864): 219.
23. Ibid. 28 (1870): 280. For a recent interpretation, see Anthony Sutcliffe, "Architecture and Civic Design in Nineteenth-Century Paris," in *Growth and Transformation of the Modern City* (Stockholm: Swedish Council for Building Research, 1979), pp. 89–100.
24. *Builder* 37 (1879): 1424–26.
25. E. Rivoalen, in *Revue générale de l'architecture* 39 (1882), cols. 33–34.
26. Sutcliffe, "Architecture and Civic Design in Nineteenth Century Paris," p. 98.
27. *Builder* 78 (1900): 361.
28. Escholier, *Le nouveau Paris,* pp. 23, 11–12.

29. For the unusually late persistence of the baroque in Vienna, and its gradual supercession by a form of neoclassicism in the late eighteenth century, see Wagner-Rieger, *Wiens Architektur im 19. Jahrhundert,* pp. 11–12.
30. Elga Lanc and Eckhart Vancsa, "Die Wohnbauten der Frühgründerzeit (1840 bis 1865)," in Kunsthistorische Arbeitsgruppe "GeVAG," *Wiener Fassaden des 19. Jahrhunderts: Wohnhäuser in Mariahilf,* pp. 37–38.
31. Wagner-Rieger, *Wiens Architektur im 19. Jahrhundert,* pp. 82–83.
32. Eggert, *Der Wohnbau der Wiener Ringstrasse im Historismus,* pp. 52–53.
33. *Builder* 24 (1866): 111.
34. Wagner-Rieger, *Wiens Architektur im 19. Jahrhundert,* p. 141.
35. J.-L. Pascal, in *Revue générale de l'architecture* 30 (1873), cols. 206–07.
36. Renate Goebl et al., "Die Wohnbauten der Hochgründerzeit (1865/70 bis 1880/85)," in Kunsthistorische Arbeitsgruppe "GeVAG," *Wiener Fassaden des 19. Jahrhunderts: Wohnhäuser in Mariahilf,* p. 56.
37. Ibid., pp. 54–55.
38. *Builder* 46 (1884): 939.
39. Blashill, "The Recent Development of Vienna," pp. 39–40.

Chapter 17. Architecture as Language: Representation and Instruction

1. Charles A. Jencks, *The Language of Post-Modern Architecture* (London: Academy Editions, 1978), p. 39.
2. Robert Venturi et al., *Learning from Las Vegas* (Cambridge, Mass.: MIT Press, 1980), p. 104.
3. *Allgemeine Bauzeitung* 27 (1862): 240–41.
4. A. Welby Pugin, *An Apology for the Revival of Christian Architecture in England* (Oxford: St. Barnabas Press, 1969), p. 4.
5. *Builder* 62 (1892): 100.
6. Pevsner, *A History of Building Types,* p. 293.
7. *Builder* 87 (1904): 487.
8. Stekl, in Baltzarek et al., *Wirtschaft und Gesellschaft,* pp. 261–65, 272–73.
9. Schorske, *Fin-de-Siècle Vienna,* pp. 39–45.
10. César Daly, in *Revue générale de l'architecture* 1 (1840), col. 204.
11. Ehalt, "Schloss- und Palastarchitektur im Absolutismus," p. 191.
12. Mayer, *The Persistence of the Old Regime,* p. 81.
13. Schorske, *Fin-de-Siècle Vienna,* p. 31.
14. Alfred Hoffmann, in Baltzarek et al., *Wirtschaft und Gesellschaft,* pp. 11–12.
15. Wagner-Rieger, Introduction, *Das Kunstwerk im Bild,* pp. 105–06; *Wiens Architektur im 19. Jahrhundert,* p. 212.
16. Haiko and Stekl, "Architektur in der industriellen Gesellschaft," p. 280.
17. Mayer, *The Persistence of the Old Regime,* pp. 112–13.
18. Wagner-Rieger, *Wiens Architektur im 19. Jahrhunderts,* p. 117.
19. César Daly, in *Revue générale de l'architecture* 1 (1840), col. 203; 20 (1862), col. 173.
20. César Daly, *L'architecture privée au dix-neuvième siècle,* 1:11–12.
21. *Builder* 15 (1857): 552.
22. For a critical appraisal of the value of the concept, see F. M. L. Thompson, "Social Control in Victorian Britain," *Economic History Review,* 2d ser., 33 (1981): 189–208.
23. *Building News* 18 (1870): 43.
24. Daly, Dedication to Baron Haussmann, *L'architecture privée au dix-neuvième siècle,* 1:6.
25. Greater London Council, *Survey of London,* vol. 38, *The Museums Area of South Kensington and Westminster,* pp. 74–81.
26. *Builder* 17 (1859): 6; see also 18 (1860): 129, 367.
27. Ibid. 77 (1899): 455–56.

Chapter 18. The City as the Embodiment of History

1. See the definition of climate of opinion in chapter 1 of Carl Becker, *The Heavenly City of the Eighteenth-Century Philosophers* (New Haven: Yale University Press, 1932), pp. 1–31.
2. Françoise Choay, "Pensées sur la ville, arts de la ville," in *La ville de l'âge industriel,* ed. Agulhon, pp. 159–62.
3. Schorske, *Fin-de-Siècle Vienna,* pp. xix–xxii.
4. Kerr, *The Gentleman's House,* p. 358.
5. *Builder* 44 (1883): 198.
6. Ibid. 52 (1887): 927–28.
7. Ibid. 62 (1892): 100–01.
8. *Allgemeine Bauzeitung* 1 (1836–): 259. George R. Burnell, "On the Present Tendencies of Architecture

and Architectural Education in France," in *Papers Read at the Royal Institute of British Architects, Session 1864–65,* p. 127.

9. John Stuart Mill, *The Spirit of the Age* (Cambridge, 1962), p. 58. I am indebted to Teresa Garcia, Vassar '83, for drawing my attention to this passage.

10. *Builder* 13 (1855): 389.

11. *Builder* 9 (1851): 428.

12. "Wenn aber irgend etwas charakteristisch für den Stil des Baues ist, so mag es der Geist der Neuzeit im eigentlichen Sinne des Wortes sein, der sich voll in ihm ausspricht!" Quoted in Haiko and Stekl, "Architektur in der Industriellen Gesellschaft," p. 265.

13. See in particular Walter Krause, "Historismus und Romantik," in *Historismus und Schlossbau,* ed. Renate Wagner-Rieger and Walter Krause (Munich: Prestel-Verlag, 1975), pp. 19–26.

14. Ann Lorenz Van Zanten, "Form and Society: César Daly and the Revue Générale de l'Architecture," *Oppositions* no. 8 (Spring 1977): 139–40.

15. César Daly, in *Revue générale de l'architecture* 32 (1875), col. 274; 27 (1869), cols. 60–61; 39 (1882), cols. 4–6.

16. Ibid. 39 (1882), col. 7.

17. Ibid. 1 (1840), cols. 201–02.

18. J. Barbey d'Aurevilly, in *Le Pays* (15 August 1861), reprinted in *Revue générale de l'architecture* 19 (1861), cols. 230–31.

19. Daly, *L'architecture privée au dix-neuvième siècle,* 1:10–11.

20. Cèsar Daly, in *Revue générale de l'architecture* 24 (1866), col. 8.

21. Ibid. 25 (1867), col. 6.

22. Ibid. 27 (1869), col. 52.

23. Ibid. 27 (1869), cols. 56–59.

24. Ibid. 1 (1840), col. 166.

25. "Citez, du moins, un ancien monument, digne d'intérêt, un édifice précieux pour l'art, curieux par ses souvenirs, que mon administration ait détruit, ou dont elle se soit occupée, sinon pour le dégager et le mettre en aussi grande valeur, en aussi belle perspective que possible!" *Mémoires du Baron Haussmann: Grands travaux de Paris* (Paris: Guy Durier, 1979), 1:28–29.

26. Ann Lorenz Van Zanten, "César Daly and the Revue Générale de l'Architecture" (Ph.D. diss., Harvard University Dept. of Fine Arts, January 1981), pp. 215–27.

27. Bédarida and Sutcliffe, "The Street in the Structure and Life of the City," pp. 26–27.

BIBLIOGRAPHY

Sources

Allgemeine Bauzeitung, mit Abbildungen, für Architekten, Ingenieurs. . . , nos. 1–83. Beilage, 1837–48. Vienna, 1836–1918.

———. *Literatur- und Anzeigeblatt für das Baufach. Beilage zur Allgemeinen Bauzeitung.* 3 vols. Vienna, 1842–49.

———. *Ephemeriden für das Baufach. Beilage zur Allgemeinen Bauzeitung.* Vol. 1, nos. 1–11, 1844–45. Vienna, 1845.

———. *Notizblatt der Allgemeinen Bauzeitung für die Tagesereignisse im Gebiete des Bauwesens. . . .* Vol. 1, nos. 1–14, 1848–50. Vienna, 1851.

The Architect. A journal of art, civil engineering and building. London, 1869–.

Bertillon, Jacques. *Essai de statistique comparée du surpeuplement des habitations à Paris et dans les grandes capitales européennes.* Paris: Chaix, 1894.

Blashill, Thomas. "The Recent Development of Vienna," Royal Institute of British Architects, *Transactions,* n.s. 4 (1888): 37–42.

Britton, J[ohn]. *The Original Picture of London, Enlarged and Improved.* 26th ed. London, [1826].

The Builder. An illustrated weekly magazine. Vols. 1–44 edited by G. Godwin. Vols. 45– edited by H. H. Statham. London, 1843–.

The Building News. London, 1857–. Vol. 3. Begun in 1854 as the *Freehold Land Times.*

Burnell, George R. "On the Present Tendencies of Architecture and Architectural Education in France." In *Papers Read at the Royal Institute of British Architects, Session 1864–65.*

[Byrne, Mrs. W. P.] *Realities of Paris Life.* London: Hurst and Blackett, 1859.

Camp, Maxime du. *Paris: Ses organes ses fonctions et sa vie dans la seconde moitié du XIXe siècle.* 6 vols. Paris: Hachette, 1875.

Cawston, Arthur. *A Comprehensive Scheme for Street Improvements in London.* London: Edward Stanford, 1893.

Cesena, Amédée de. *Le nouveau Paris.* Paris: Garnier Frères, 1864.

Cohen-Portheim, Paul. *The Spirit of Paris.* London: B. T. Batsford, 1937. First published in Germany, 1930.

Daly, César *L'architecture privée au dix-neuvième siècle.* Paris, 1870–72.

Dickens, Charles. *Dickens's Dictionary of London, 1879.* 1879. Reprint. London: Howard Baker, 1972.

Eigl, Kurt. *Wiener Bilder.* Vienna: Forum Verlag, 1975.

Eitelberger, R. von, and Heinrich Ferstel. *Das bürgerliche Wohnhaus und das Wiener Zinshaus.* Vienna: Carl Gerold's Sohn, 1860.

Elmes, James. *Metropolitan Improvements; or London in the Nineteenth Century.* 1827–31. Reprint. New York: Benjamin Blom, 1968.

Escholier, Raymond. *Le nouveau Paris: La vie artistique de la cité moderne.* Paris: Editions Nilsson, n.d. (c. 1913).

Falke, Jacob von. "Das englische Haus," in *Zur Cultur und Kunst.* Vienna, 1878.

Farrow, Frederick R. "The Recent Development of Vienna." Royal Institute of British Architects, *Transactions,* n.s. 4 (1888): 27–37.

Fellner, Ferdinand. *Wie soll Wien bauen.* Vienna, 1860.

Gissing, George. *In The Year of Jubilee.* London: Lawrence and Bullen, 1894.

Hamerton, Philip Gilbert. *Paris in Old and Present Times.* London: Seeley, 1892.

Hare, Augustus J. C. *Paris.* London: Smith, Elder, 1887.

Hayward, A. *The Art of Dining.* Based on 1853 ed. London: John Murray, 1883.

Head, Sir Francis. *A Faggot of French Sticks; or, Paris in 1851.* New York: George P. Putnam, 1852.

Huddleston, Sisley. *In and About Paris.* London: Methuen, 1927.

I'Anson, Edward. "On the Recent Improvements in Paris." In *Papers Read at the Royal Institute of British Architects, Session 1858–59,* pp. 41–51.

———. "On the Valuation of House Property in London." In *Papers Read at the Royal Institute of British Architects, Session 1872–73,* pp. 39–54.

———. "Some Notice of Office Buildings in the City of London." *Papers Read at the Royal Institute of British Architects, Session 1864–65,* pp. 25–36.

[Jarves, James Jackson.] *Parisian Sights and French Principles.* New York: Harper & Brothers, 1852.

Kerr, Robert. *The Gentleman's House.* London: John Murray, 1864.

Kerr, Robert. "Observations on the Plan of Dwelling-Houses in Towns." *Journal of the Royal Institute of British Architects.* 3d ser. (1894): 201–31.

Kerr, Robert, ed. *History of the Modern Styles of Architecture,* by James Fergusson. 2 vols. 3d ed. New York: Dodd, Mead, 1899.

Knight, Samuel. "The Influence of Business Requirements upon Street Architecture." *Sessional Papers Read at the Royal Institute of British Architects, 1876–77,* pp. 15–32.

Kortz, Paul, ed. *Wien am Anfang des XX. Jahrhunderts.* 2 vols. Vienna: Gerlach & Wiedling, 1905.

Leigh, Samuel. *Leigh's New Picture of London.* London, 1818.

Leonhard, F. "Städtische Miethäuser." In *Wien am Anfang des XX. Jahrhunderts,* edited by Paul Kortz. Vienna: Gerlach & Wiedling, 1905.

L'Illustration. Journal universel. Paris, 1843–1955.

Mercier, Louis-Sébastien. *Parallèle de Paris et de Londres.* Paris: Didier-Erudition, 1982.

———. *Tableau de Paris.* Amsterdam, 1782. Reprint. Geneva: Slatkine Reprints, 1979.

Mill, John Stuart. *The Spirit of the Age.* Cambridge, 1962.

Monin, H. *L'état de Paris en 1789.* Paris: D. Jouast, 1889.

Nash, John, and J[ohn] White. *Some Account of the Proposed Improvements of the Western Part of London.* 2d ed. London, 1815.

Noble, James. *The Professional Practice of Architects.* London, 1836.

Pichler, Karoline. *Zeitbilder.* Vienna: Österreichischer Schulbücherverlag, 1924. First published Vienna, 1839–41.

Pugin, A. Welby. *An Apology for the Revival of Christian Architecture in England.* Oxford: St. Barnabas Press, 1969.

Révue générale de l'architecture et des travaux publics. Paris, 1840–95, vols. 1–45.

Georges Riat. *Paris.* Paris: Librairie Renouard, 1904.

Richard, [N.] *Le véritable conducteur parisien.* Paris, 1828. Facsimile ed. Paris: les Yeux Ouverts, 1970.

Robert, Ulysse. *Voyage à Vienne.* Paris: Ernest Flammarion, 1899.

Robinson, W. *The Parks, Promenades & Gardens of Paris.* London: John Murray, 1869.

Sala, George Augustus. *Paris Herself Again in 1878–79.* 2d ed. London: Remington, 1879.

———. *Twice Round the Clock.* 1859. Reprint. Leicester: Leicester University Press, 1971.

Schlegel, Gert, et al. *Wien-Innere Stadt.* Vienna: Jugend & Volk, 1969.

Schutz, Carl, et al. *Die Wiener Ansichten: Die Wiener Strassenbilder des Rokoko.* Dortmund: Harenberg, 1981.

Steevens, G. W. *Glimpses of Three Nations.* New York: Dodd, Mead, 1900.

Strong, Rowland. *Where and How to Dine in Paris.* London: Alexander Moring, n.d. (c. 1900).

Texier, Edmond. *Tableau de Paris.* 2 vols. Paris: Paulin et le Chevalier, 1852–53.

[Tindall, Gillian.] "Expatriates' Paris." In *The Paris Spy,* edited by Raymond Rudorff. N.p.: Anthony Blond, 1969.

Tissot, Victor. *Vienne et la vie viennoise.* 19th ed. Paris: E. Dentu, 1878.

Trollope, Frances. *Paris and the Parisians in 1835.* 2d ed. New York: Harper & Brothers, 1836.

———. *Vienna and the Austrians.* London: Richard Bentley, 1838.

Tuckerman, Henry T. *Maga Papers about Paris.* New York: G. P. Putnam & Sons, 1867.

Vermont, Marquis de, and Sir Charles Darnley, Bart. [pseuds.]. *London and Paris; or Comparative Sketches.* London: Longman, Hurst, Rees, Orme, Brown, and Green, 1823.

Weber, Anton. "Familienhäuser und Villen." In *Wien am Anfang des XX. Jahrhunderts,* edited by Paul Kortz. Vienna: Gerlach & Wiedling, 1905.

White, William H. "On Middle-Class Houses in Paris and Central London." Royal Institute of British Architects, *Sessional Papers 1877–78,* pp. 21–65.

Secondary Works

Adburgham, Alison. *Shops and Shopping 1800–1914.* London: George Allen and Unwin, 1964.

Agulhon, Maurice, ed. *La ville de l'âge industriel: Le cycle haussmannien.* Vol. 4 of *Histoire de la France urbaine,* edited by Georges Duby. Paris: Seuil, 1983.

Babelon, Jean-Pierre. *Demeures parisiennes sous Henri IV et Louis XIII.* Paris: le Temps, 1977.

Baltzarek, Franz, et al. *Wirtschaft und Gesellschaft der Wiener Stadterweiterung.* Vol. 5 of *Die Wiener Ringstrasse: Bild einer Epoche,* edited by Renate Wagner-Rieger. Wiesbaden: Franz Steiner, 1975.

Banik-Schweitzer, Renate, et al. *Wien in der liberalen Ära.* Vienna: Verein für Geschichte der Stadt Wien, 1978.

Banks, J. A. "The Contagion of Numbers." In *The Victorian City,* edited by H. J. Dyos and Michael Wolff. London: Routledge & Kegan Paul, 1973.

Barker, T. C., and Michael Robbins. *History of London Transport.* Vol. 1. London: Allen & Unwin, 1963.

Bastié, Jean. *La croissance de la banlieue parisienne.* Paris: Presses Universitaires de France, 1964.

Becker, Carl. *The Heavenly City of the Eighteenth-Century Philosophers.* New Haven: Yale University Press, 1932.

Bédarida, François, and Anthony R. Sutcliffe. "The Street in the Structure and Life of the City: Reflections on Nineteenth-Century London and Paris." In *Modern Industrial Cities,* edited by Bruce M. Stave. Beverly Hills: Sage Publications, 1981.

Bertrand, Michel Jean. *Architecture de l'habitat urbain: La maison, le quartier, la ville.* Paris: Dunod, 1980.

Bobek, Hans, and Elisabeth Lichtenberger. *Wien: Bauliche Gestalt und Entwicklung seit der Mitte des 19. Jahrhunderts.* Graz: Hermann Böhlaus Nachf., 1966.

Briggs, Asa. *Victorian Cities.* London: Odhams Books, 1963.

Burnett, John. *A Social History of Housing 1850–1970.* London: Methuen, 1980.

Cannadine, David. *Lords and Landlords: The Aristocracy and the Towns 1774–1967.* Leicester: Leicester University Press, 1980.

Chalklin, C. W. *The Provincial Towns of Georgian England.* Montreal: McGill-Queen's University Press, 1974.

Choay, Françoise. "Pensées sur la ville, arts de la ville." In *La ville de l'âge industriel: Le cycle haussmannien,* edited by Maurice Agulhon. Paris: Seuil, 1983.

Chemetov, Paul, and Bernard Marrey. *Architectures à Paris, 1848–1914.* Paris: Dunod, 1984.

Chombart de Lauwe, Paul-Henry, et al. *Famille et habitation.* Vol. 1, *Sciences humaines et conceptions de l'habitation.* Paris: Centre National de la Recherche Scientifique, 1975.

Cobb, Richard. *The Streets of Paris.* London: Gerald Duckworth, 1980.

Costanzo, Dennis Paul. "Cityscape and the Transformation of Paris during the Second Empire." (Ph.D. diss., University of Michigan, history of art, 1981.)

Couperie, Pierre. *Paris through the Ages.* London: Barrie & Jackson, 1970.

Czeike, Felix. *Geschichte der Stadt Wien.* Vienna: Fritz Molden, 1981.

Daumard, Adeline. *Les bourgeois de Paris au XIXe siècle.* Paris: Flammarion, 1970.

———. *Maisons de Paris et propriétaires parisiens au XIXe siècle, 1809–1880.* Paris: Editions Cujas, 1965.

Daunton, M. J. *House and Home in the Victorian City.* London: Edward Arnold, 1983.

Davidoff, Leonore, and Catherine Hall. "The Architecture of Public and Private Life: English Middle-Class Society in a Provincial Town, 1780 to 1850." In *The Pursuit of Urban History,* edited by Derek Fraser and Anthony Sutcliffe. London: Edward Arnold, 1983.

Davis, Dorothy. *A History of Shopping.* London: Routledge & Kegan Paul, 1966.

Dixon, Roger, and Stefan Muthesius. *Victorian Architecture.* London: Thames and Hudson, 1978.

Dyos, H. J. *Exploring the Urban Past.* Edited by David Cannadine and David Reeder. Cambridge: Cambridge University Press, 1982.

———. *Victorian Suburb.* Leicester: Leicester University Press, 1961.

_____ ed. *The Study of Urban History.* London: Edward Arnold, 1968.

Dyos, H. J., and Michael Wolff, eds. *The Victorian City.* 2 vols. London: Routledge & Kegan Paul, 1973.

Eggert, Klaus. *Der Wohnbau der Wiener Ringstrasse im Historismus: 1855–1896.* Vol. 7 of *Die Wiener Ringstrasse: Bild einer Epoche,* edited by Renate Wagner-Rieger. Wiesbaden: Franz Steiner, 1976.

Ehalt, Hubert Ch. "Schloss- und Palastarchitektur im Absolutismus." In *Architektur und Gesellschaft von der Antike bis zur Gegenwart,* edited by Hannes Stekl. Salzburg: Wolfgang Neugebauer, 1980.

Evenson, Norma. *Paris: A Century of Change, 1878–1978.* New Haven and London: Yale University Press, 1979.

Feldbauer, Peter. *Stadtwachstum und Wohnungsnot: Determinanten unzureichender Wohnungsversorgung in Wien 1848 bis 1914.* Vienna: Verlag für Geschichte und Politik Wien, 1977.

_____ . "Wohnungsproduktion am Beispiel Wiens (1848–1934)." In *Wohnen im Wandel,* edited by Lutz Niethammer. Wuppertal: Peter Hammer, 1979.

Forster, E. M. *Marianne Thornton.* New York: Harcourt Brace Jovanovich, 1956.

Franklin, Jill. *The Gentleman's Country House and Its Plan, 1835–1914.* London: Routledge & Kegan Paul, 1981.

Fraser, Derek, and Anthony Sutcliffe, eds. *The Pursuit of Urban History.* London: Edward Arnold, 1983.

Friedländer, Otto. *Letzter Glanz der Märchenstadt: Das war Wien um 1900.* Vienna: Molden-Taschenbuch-Verlag, 1976.

Gaillard, Jeanne. *Paris, la ville 1852–1870.* Paris: Editions Honoré Champion, 1977.

Gallet, Michel. *Paris Domestic Architecture of the 18th Century.* London: Barrie & Jenkins, 1972.

Geist, Johann Friedrich. *Passagen: Ein Bautyp des 19. Jahrhunderts.* Munich: Prestel-Verlag, 1969.

Girouard, Mark. *Cities and People.* New Haven and London: Yale University Press, 1985.

_____ . *Sweetness and Light: The "Queen Anne" Movement 1860–1900.* New Haven and London: Yale University Press, 1984.

_____ . *The Victorian Country House.* New Haven and London: Yale University Press, 1979.

_____ . *Victorian Pubs.* London: Studio Vista, 1978.

Goebl, Renate, Elisabeth Klemm, and Hellmut Lorenz. "Die Wohnbauten der Hochgründerzeit (1865/70 bis 1880/85)." In *Wiener Fassaden des 19. Jahrhunderts: Wohnhäuser in Mariahilf,* Kunsthistorische Arbeitsgruppe "GeVAG." Vienna: Hermann Böhlaus Nachf., 1976.

Goebl, Renate, and Peter Parenzan. "Die Wohnbauten der Zeit von etwa 1770 bis 1840." In *Wiener Fassaden des 19. Jahrhunderts: Wohnhäuser in Mariahilf,* Kunsthistorische Arbeitsgruppe "GeVAG." Vienna: Hermann Böhlaus Nachf., 1976.

Gombrich, Sir Ernst. "In Search of Cultural History." In *Ideals and Idols.* Oxford: Phaidon, 1979.

Greater London Council. *Survey of London.* Vol. 36, *The Parish of St. Paul Covent Garden.* London: Athlone Press, 1970.

_____ . *Survey of London.* Vol. 38, *The Museums Area of South Kensington and Westminster.* London: Athlone Press, 1975.

_____ . *Survey of London.* Vol. 39, *The Grosvenor Estate in Mayfair,* Part 1, *General History.* London: Athlone Press, 1977.

_____ . *Survey of London.* Vol. 41, *Southern Kensington: Brompton.* London: Athlone Press, 1983.

Haiko, Peter, and Hannes Stekl. "Architektur in der industriellen Gesellschaft." In *Architektur und Gesellschaft von der Antike bis zur Gegenwart,* edited by Hannes Stekl. Salzburg: Wolfgang Neugebauer, 1980.

Hardy, Charles O. *The Housing Program of the City of Vienna.* Washington, D.C.: Brookings Institution, 1934.

Harrison, Frederic. *The Meaning of History.* London: Macmillan, 1930.

Haussmann, Baron. *Mémoires du Baron Haussmann: Grands travaux de Paris.* Guy Durier, 1979.

Herget, Elisabeth. Nachwort to *Das florierende Wien,* by Salomon Kleiner. Dortmund: Harenberg Kommunikation, 1979.

Hillairet, Jacques. *Dictionnaire historique des rues de Paris.* 2 vols. Paris: Editions de minuit, 1963.

Hitchcock, Henry-Russell. *Early Victorian Architecture in Britain.* 2 vols. New Haven: Yale University Press, 1954.

Hobhouse, Hermione. *A History of Regent Street*. London: Macdonald and Jane's, 1975.

_____. *Lost London*. London: Macmillan, 1971.

_____. *Thomas Cubitt, Master Builder*. London: Macmillan, 1971.

Hoskins, W. G. *Provincial England: Essays in Social and Economic History*. London: Macmillan, 1963.

Huizinga, Johan. *Homo Ludens*. London: Paladin, 1970.

Jackson, Alan A. *London's Local Railways*. Newton Abbot: David & Charles, 1983.

_____. *Semi-Detached London*. London: George Allen & Unwin, 1973.

Jacobs, Jane. *The Death and Life of Great American Cities*. New York: Random House, 1981.

_____. *The Economy of Cities*. London: Jonathan Cape, 1970.

Jencks, Charles A. *The Language of Post-Modern Architecture*. London: Academy Editions, 1978.

Joanne, Adolphe. *Paris illustré en 1870 et 1877*. Paris: Hachette, n.d.

Kellett, John R. *The Impact of Railways on Victorian Cities*. London: Routledge & Kegan Paul, 1969.

Krause, Walter. "Historismus und Romantik." In *Historismus und Schlossbau*, edited by Renate Wagner-Rieger and Walter Krause. Munich: Prestel-Verlag, 1975.

Krobot, Walter, et al. *Strassenbahn in Wien*. Vienna: Josef Otto Slezak, 1983.

Lanc, Elga, and Eckhart Vancsa. "Die Wohnbauten der Frühgründerzeit (1840 bis 1865)." In *Wiener Fassaden des 19. Jahrhunderts: Wohnhäuser in Mariahilf,* Kunsthistorische Arbeitsgruppe "GeVAG." Vienna: Herman Böhlaus Nachf., 1976.

Lane, Barbara Miller. "Changing Attitudes to Monumentality: An Interpretation of European Architecture and Urban Form 1880–1914." In *Growth and Transformation of the Modern City*. Stockholm: Swedish Council for Building Research, 1979.

_____. "Government Buildings in European Capitals 1870–1914." In *Urbanisierung im 19. und 20. Jahrhundert,* edited by Hans Jürgen Teuteberg. Cologne: Böhlau Verlag, 1983.

Lavedan, Pierre. *Histoire de l'urbanisme*. Vol. 3, *Epoque contemporaine*. Paris: Henri Laurens, 1952.

_____. *Histoire de l'urbanisme à Paris*. Paris: Hachette, 1975.

Lees, Andrew. "Perceptions of Cities in Britain and Germany, 1820–1914." In *The Pursuit of Urban History,* edited by Derek Fraser and Anthony Sutcliffe. London: Edward Arnold, 1983.

Lettmayer, Ferdinand, ed. *Wien um die Mitte des XX. Jahrhunderts*. Vienna: Jugend und Volk, 1958.

Lichtenberger, Elisabeth. *Die Wiener Altstadt: Von der mittelalterlichen Bürgerstadt zur City*. Vienna: Franz Deuticke, 1977.

_____. *Wirtschaftsfunktion una Sozialstruktur der Wiener Ringstrasse*. Vol. 6 of *Die Wiener Ringstrasse: Bild einer Epoche,* edited by Renate Wagner-Rieger. Vienna: Hermann Böhlaus Nachf., 1970.

Lipstadt, Hélène. "Housing the Bourgeoisie: César Daly and the Ideal Home." *Oppositions* no. 8 (Spring 1977): 34–47.

Mayer, Arno J. *The Persistence of the Old Regime*. London: Croom Helm, 1981.

Metcalf, Priscilla. *Victorian London*. New York: Praeger, 1972.

Middleton, Robin, ed. *The Beaux-Arts and Nineteenth-Century French Architecture*. Cambridge, Mass.: MIT Press, 1982.

Morris, A. E. J. *History of Urban Form: Before the Industrial Revolutions*. London: George Godwin, 1979.

Mumford, Lewis. *The City in History*. Harmondsworth: Penguin Books, 1961.

Muthesius, Hermann. *The English House*. New York: Rizzoli, 1979. Originally published as *Das Englische Haus*, 3 vols. (Berlin: Wasmuth, 1904, 1905).

Muthesius, Stefan. *The English Terraced House*. New Haven and London: Yale University Press, 1982.

Niethammer, Lutz, ed. *Wohnen im Wandel*. Wuppertal: Peter Hammer, 1979.

Olsen, Donald J. "The City as a Work of Art." In *The Pursuit of Urban History,* edited by Derek Fraser and Anthony Sutcliffe. London: Edward Arnold, 1983.

_____. *The Growth of Victorian London*. London: B. T. Batsford, 1976.

_____. "House Upon House." In *The Victorian City,* vol. 1, edited by H. J. Dyos and Michael Wolff. London: Routledge & Kegan Paul, 1973.

_____. *Town Planning in London: The Eighteenth and Nineteenth Centuries*. New Haven and London: Yale University Press, 1982.

Owen, David. *The Government of Victorian London, 1855–1889*. Edited by Roy MacLeod. Cambridge, Mass.: Harvard University Press, 1982.

Perrot, Marguerite. *La mode de vie des familles bourgeoises, 1873–1953*. Paris: Librairie Armand Colin, 1961.

Pevsner, Sir Nikolaus. *Pioneers of the Modern Movement*. London: Faber & Faber, 1936.

——. *Some Architectural Writers of the Nineteenth Century*. Oxford: Clarendon Press, 1972.

Pinkney, David H. *Napoleon III and the Rebuilding of Paris*. Princeton: Princeton University Press, 1972.

Rasmussen, Steen Eiler. *London: The Unique City*. Cambridge, Mass.: MIT Press, 1967.

——. *Towns and Buildings*. Liverpool: Liverpool University Press, 1951.

Richards, J. M. *The Castles on the Ground*. London: John Murray, 1973.

Robbins, Michael. *Middlesex*. London: Collins, 1953.

Robertson, Priscilla. *An Experience of Women*. Philadelphia: Temple University Press, 1982.

Roncayolo, Marcel. "La production de la ville" and "Le modèle haussmannien." In *La ville de l'âge industriel,* edited by Maurice Agulhon. Vol. 4 of *Histoire de la France urbaine*. Paris: Seuil, 1983.

Saalman, Howard. *Haussmann: Paris Transformed*. New York: George Braziller, 1971.

Saint, Andrew. *Richard Norman Shaw*. New Haven and London: Yale University Press, 1977.

Schorske, Carl E. *Fin-de-Siècle Vienna: Politics and Culture*. London: Weidenfeld and Nicolson, 1980.

Sennett, Richard. *The Fall of Public Man*. Cambridge: Cambridge University Press, 1977.

Service, Alastair. *The Architects of London*. London: Architectural Press, 1979.

——. *London 1900*. St. Albans: Granada Publishing Limited, 1979.

Sheppard, Francis. *London 1808–1870: The Infernal Wen*. London: Secker & Warburg, 1971.

Shorter, Edward. *The Making of the Modern Family*. New York: Basic Books, 1975.

Smith, Edward R. "Baron Haussmann and the Topographical Transformation of Paris under Napoleon III." *Architectural Record* 22 (1907): 121–33, 227–38, 369–85, 490–506.

Springer, Elisabeth. *Geschichte und Kulturleben der Wiener Ringstrasse*. Vol. 2 of *Die Wiener Ringstrasse: Bild einer Epoche,* edited by Renate Wagner-Rieger. Wiesbaden: Franz Steiner, 1979.

Stekl, Hannes. *Österreichs Aristokratie im Vormärz*. Vienna: Verlag für Geschichte und Politik, 1973.

Summerson, Sir John. *Georgian London*. Harmondsworth: Penguin Books, 1962.

——. *The Life and Works of John Nash, Architect*. Cambridge, Mass.: MIT Press, 1980.

Sutcliffe, Anthony. "Architecture and Civic Design in Nineteenth-Century Paris." In *Growth and Transformation of the Modern City*. Stockholm: Swedish Council for Building Research, 1979.

——. *The Autumn of Central Paris: The Defeat of Town Planning 1850–1970*. London: Edward Arnold, 1970.

——. *Towards the Planned City: Germany, Britain, the United States and France 1780–1914*. Oxford: Basil Blackwell, 1981.

Tarn, J. N. "French Flats for the English in Nineteenth-century London." In *Multi-Storey Living,* edited by Anthony Sutcliffe. London: Croom Helm, 1974.

Thompson, F. M. L. *Hampstead: Building a Borough, 1650–1964*. London: Routledge & Kegan Paul, 1974.

Thomson, Gladys Scott. *The Russells in Bloomsbury*. London: Jonathan Cape, 1940.

Tindall, Gillian. *City of Gold: The Biography of Bombay*. London: Temple Smith, 1982.

Van Zanten, Ann Lorenz. "César Daly and the Revue Générale de l'Architecture." Ph.D. diss., Harvard University, Dept. of Fine Arts, January 1981.

——. "Form and Society: César Daly and the Revue Générale de l'Architecture." *Oppositions* no. 8 (Spring 1977), pp. 136–45.

Venturi, Robert, et al. *Learning from Las Vegas*. Cambridge, Mass.: MIT Press, 1980.

Vergo, Peter. *Art in Vienna 1898–1918*. Ithaca: Cornell University Press, 1981.

Wagner-Rieger, Renate. *Das Kunstwerk im Bild*. Vol. 1 of *Die Wiener Ringstrasse: Bild einer Epoche,* edited by Renate Wagner-Rieger. Vienna: Hermann Böhlaus Nachf., 1969.

——. *Wiens Architektur im 19. Jahrhundert*. Vienna: Österreichischer Bundesverlag für Unterricht, Wissenschaft und Kunst, 1970.

Waller, P. J. *Town, City, and Nation: England, 1850–1914*. Oxford: Oxford University Press, 1983.

Warner, Sam Bass, Jr. "The Management of Multiple Urban Images." In *The Pursuit of Urban History*, edited by Derek Fraser and Anthony Sutcliffe. London: Edward Arnold, 1983.

Watkin, David. *Morality and Architecture*. Oxford: Clarendon Press, 1978.

————. *The Rise of Architectural History*. London: Architectural Press, 1980.

Weiss, Richard. *Häuser und Landschaften der Schweiz*. 2d. ed. Erlenbach-Zürich: Eugen Rentsch, 1973.

Westergaard, J. H. "The Structure of Greater London." In *London: Aspects of Change*, edited by Centre for Urban Studies. London: MacGibbon & Kee, 1964.

White, H. P. *Greater London*. Vol. 3 of *A Regional History of the Railways of Great Britain*. Newton Abbot: David & Charles, 1971.

Wibiral, Norbert, and Renata Mikula. *Heinrich von Ferstel*. Vol. 8, pt. 3 of *Die Wiener Ringstrasse: Bild einer Epoche*, edited by Renate Wagner-Rieger. Wiesbaden: Franz Steiner, 1974.

Wohl, Anthony S. *Endangered Lives: Public Health in Victorian Britain*. London: J. M. Dent & Sons, 1983.

Wohl, Anthony. *The Eternal Slum: Housing and Social Policy in Victorian London*. London: Edward Arnold, 1977.

Zeldin, Theodore. *France 1848–1945: Ambition and Love*. Oxford: Oxford University Press, 1979.

Zinn, Hermann. "Entstehen und Wandel bürgerlicher Wohngewohnheiten und Wohnstrukturen." In *Wohnen im Wandel*, edited by Lutz Niethammer. Wuppertal: Peter Hammer, 1979.

INDEX

Places (streets, districts, suburbs, buildings, railways) are listed under the appropriate city.

Absolutism, 4, 9–11 passim, 64
Aesthetic standards: eighteenth-century, 10–11, 13; nineteenth-century, 21, 24–26
Agulhon, Maurice, 253
Amero, J., 217
Arcades, shopping, 207, 225, 248
Architecture, styles of: Gothic Revival, 24, 26, 255, 259, 300; classicism, 25–26, 81, 260–61; Bauhaus, 26, 281, 308; "post-Modern," 26, 281, 308; London, 37, 257–60; Paris, 37–38, 260–69; Sezessionist, 81, 83, 172–77 passim (illustrations 173–75), 270, 276–80; English domestic, 112–13; "Queen Anne," 112, 164, 259–60, 283; *Heimatstil,* 172; art nouveau, 268; Vienna, 269–80; *Gründerzeit,* 270–76, 304–05; *Vormärz,* 270–71
Aristocracy: English, 13–15, 240; Austrian, 240–41, 287–89
Art: moral function of, 4, 5, 281–94 passim; as luxury, 5–6
Austen, Jane, 23, 110, 131, 199

Balzac, Honoré de, 108, 223, 225
Banking crisis of 1825, 21–23
Barbey d'Aurevilly, J., 301
"Baroque city," 285–86
"Baroque planning," 73–76
Basements, in London houses, 110–12, 162
Bastié, Jean, 150
Bateaux-mouches, 211
Bathrooms, 113, 131, 191
Baths, in Paris hotels, 212
Bedrooms: English, 108–10 passim; in Paris, 115–25 passim; in Vienna, 129–31
Belcher, John 283
Berlin, 131, 149, 172
Bertillon, Jacques, 178–79, 182
Betjeman, Sir John, 160
Birmingham, 160, 185
Blashill, Thomas, 64, 125, 181, 274–76
Bombay, 179–80
Bourgeoisie, in Vienna, 99–100, 126, 287–91
Bremen, 27, 92
Britton, John, 23
Budapest, 4, 172, 182, 282
Building acts (London), 13, 37
Building leases (London), 28–29, 184–85
Burckhardt, Jacob, vii, 296
Burnell, George R., 299–300
Byrne, Mrs. W. P., 214

Cabs: Vienna, 66, 235, 245; London, 192; Paris, 210
Cafés: Paris, 44, 213–15, 234; Vienna, 242–43
Central heating, 95, 131
Cesena, Amédée de, 44, 148–49, 212, 214, 217, 228–29
Children: in England, 102, 108–10; in Vienna, 131
Choay, Françoise, 296
Cholera epidemic, 21, 23, 37
Church of England, 15
Cities, attitudes toward, viii–ix, 3–4, 21–26
Clubs, London, 202–06, 259
Cobb, Richard, 150–51
Coffee shops, London, 199–200 (illustrations 196, 201)
Cohen-Portheim, Paul, 149, 150, 171, 229–30
Colie, Rosalie, 286
Commune, Paris, 54
Corridors, in Vienna flats, 126–29
Counter-Reformation, 4, 9, 64
Cousin, David, 122
Cubitt, Thomas, 16, 19–20, 21–22

Daly, César: on sanitation in London, 31–34; on luxury, 43–44; on Paris and London, 51; on exterior boulevards, 51–52; on rebuilding of Paris, 52; on Paris flats, 95, 114–22 passim; on London houses, 104, 109, 113; on social geography of Paris, 144, 146; on villa suburbia, 162, 166, 169–70; on London clubs, 202, 204–06; on parks in Paris, 233; on "representational" architecture, 286–87; on monumentality, 291; on art and education, 293; on history, 300–03; on Paris in 1840, 304
Daumard, Adeline, 148
Davioud, G., 207
Dickens, Charles, 23
Dining-rooms, 104–07, 115, 122, 124–25
Dinner parties, 112, 122
Domesticity. *See* Family life
Doors, intercommunicating: in Vienna, 100, 129–30 (illustrations), 131; in England, 103, 131; in Paris, 115–21 passim
Du Camp, Maxime, 54

Egalitarianism, French, 229, 234
Eitelberger, Rudolf von, 100
Electricity, Vienna, 131
Escholier, Raymond, 44, 96, 268
Eugene, Prince, 65

Falke, Jacob von, 104–07, 108, 125, 163
Family life, 89–90, 101–02, 189; in Paris, 90, 293–94; in London, 90–94, 189
Feldbauer, Peter, 253
Fellner, Ferdinand, 100, 126
Ferstel, Heinrich von, 78, 100, 127, 175, 176
Feyrnet, X., 48–51
Flats: in Vienna, 66–68, 96–100, 125–31; in London, 92–94, 113; in Paris, 94–96, 100, 114–25; in Berlin, 100
Fleming, Owen, 299
Förster, Ludwig von, 96, 98, 127, 236, 283
Franz Joseph, Emperor, 58, 69, 240
French working class, behavior of, 204–05, 218–19
French Revolution, 11, 35

Gaillard, Jeanne, 121, 142, 143, 148, 225
Gas lighting, 131, 222. *See also* Street lighting
Gautier, Théophile, 34, 199
Geist, Johann Friedrich, 248
"Gentrification," 133, 137, 150–51
George IV, 15–16
Gesamtkunstwerk, concept of, 283, 310
Gissing, George, 108, 113
Gombrich, Sir Ernst, 251
Grands ensembles, 150, 171
Ground landlords, 28–29, 184–85

Haedy, Christopher, 19–20
Hall, E. T., 93, 189, 200
Hamerton, Philip Gilbert, 56, 95- 96, 170, 231
Hansen, Theophil, 78, 176, 236
Hare, Augustus, 212, 217
Harvey, Lawrence, 263–66
Hasenauer, Karl von, 78–79
Haussmann, Georges-Eugène, Baron, 44–54 passim, 83–84, 146–48, 309
Hayward, A., 202
Hayward, C. F., 263
Head, Sir Francis, 166, 220–22
Head, George, 162
Hegel, Friedrich, 251–52, 296
History, 9, 289, 295–311
Hittorff, Jacques-Ignace, 202–04, 210
Hotels: London, 93, 190–91, 202; Paris, 211–13; Vienna, 127, 235, 236, 244
Hôtels particuliers, 95, 96, 245–46
Houses, single-family: London, 91–93, 257; advocated for Vienna, 100. *See also* Villa Suburbia